The Blood Contingent

The Blood Contingent

The Military and the Making of Modern Mexico, 1876–1911

Stephen B. Neufeld

University of New Mexico Press | Albuquerque

© 2017 by University of New Mexico Press
All rights reserved. Published 2017
Printed in the United States of America

22 21 20 19 18 17   1 2 3 4 5 6

Library of Congress Cataloging-in-Publication Data
Names: Neufeld, Stephen, author.
Title: The blood contingent : the military and the making of modern Mexico,
1876–1911 / Stephen B. Neufeld.
Description: First Edition. | Albuquerque : University of New Mexico Press, 2017. |
Includes bibliographical references and index.
Identifiers: LCCN 2016023753 (print) | LCCN 2016028897 (ebook) |
ISBN 9780826358042 (printed case : alk. paper) | ISBN 9780826358059
(pbk. : alk. paper) | ISBN 9780826358066 (electronic)
Subjects: LCSH: Mexico. Ejército—History—19th century. | Mexico.
Ejército—History—20th century. | Mexico. Ejército—Military life—History. |
Soldiers—Mexico—History. | Mexico—History, Military. | Mexico—Politics
and government—1867–1910. | Nation-building—Mexico—History. |
Nationalism—Mexico—History. | Political culture—Mexico—History. |
Social change—Mexico—History.
Classification: LCC UA603.N48 2017 (print) | LCC UA603 (ebook) |
DDC 355.00972/09034—dc23
LC record available at https://lccn.loc.gov/2016023753

Cover illustration: *Drum Corps* (oil on panel, 1889), Frederic Remington
Designed by Lila Sanchez
Composed in Minion Pro 10.25/13.5

Contents

Illustrations

TABLES

Acknowledgments

Writing *The Blood Contingent* has been a long and sometimes-arduous process that began in the earliest years of this century. This book simply could not have come into being without the assistance, guidance, and input that I have received along the way—as importantly to me, those thanked here have also been instrumental in teaching me how to be a scholar and have fostered my passion for Mexican history. My graduate advisors are due thanks for their generosity of time and intellectual support. Bill French has been an inspirational scholar for me and a good friend, always willing to listen and comment on my work. Kevin Gosner was unfailingly reliable and brought a degree of calm to the insanities of the PhD program. Bert Barickman's keen insight and intellectual fervor continue to make him a role model I can only hope to emulate; his brilliant and honest appraisals make this a better work. My major advisor, William Beezley, gave generously of his time and lent a sharp editorial eye, and he has shaped this work in significant ways. He had everything to do with my going to the University of Arizona, having invited me to the famed Oaxaca seminar in 2003 and convincing me to move to the desert thereafter.

While researching in Mexico City a number of individuals also made this work possible. At the Condumex/Carso archives, Josefina and the efficient staff went out of their way to find me the best documents and letters. The archivists at the Universidad Iberoamericana, Relaciones Exteriores, and the Biblioteca Lerdo all welcomed me and gave me invaluable assistance. At the Archivo General de la Nación (AGN), in the midst of a major move of my source materials, the archivists of Gallery Five (in particular Arturo) and the director of *acervos* were nearly always helpful and commiserated with me when they could not be. I am also grateful to the staff at the Secretariat of Defense (SEDENA) archives and, in particular, at the F. L. Urquizo Library for their willingness to help me along. Fellow academics also gave freely of their time, and I thank Jane-Dale Lloyd and Carmen Nava for their assistance and comments, as well as Isaac Campos and Linda Arnold for generously sharing important sources with me.

In undertaking research and writing, I also owe a debt of gratitude for financial support. Assistance from the Department of History at the University of Arizona largely made this work possible, and a four-year fellowship from the Social Science and Humanities Research Council (Canada) allowed me to live decently during my studies. Without either, I could not have done this. More recently, California State University, Fullerton, has supported additional research to finish this work, particularly at the college and department level, but also with a sabbatical in the fall of 2015.

In the process of revising this work, I'd also like to recognize the excellent advice and comments of my anonymous peer reviewers who have made this so much better, and also the thoughtful counsel of Timo Schaeffer, whose informal review was much appreciated. Clark Whitehorn has been an excellent editor to work with, and I am extremely grateful for his efforts. Conference comments from Peter Beattie and Hendrik Kraay have also improved my understandings of military life and recruitment issues. My colleagues in the CSUF History Department unfailingly offered great insights and support, and I couldn't ask for better folks to work with; especially useful commentary came from department "brown-bag" symposiums. My students, too, have shaped my thoughts on Mexico, the military, and history, and I owe them thanks for all that they have taught me.

Friends, compañeros, editors, and sounding boards—a number of good people gave me the emotional and intellectual support that this sort of task requires. Amanda Lopez, Maria Muñoz, Ryan Kashanipour, John Klingemann, and Amie Kiddle not only suffered through early drafts but also were fellow travelers in DF during the research. At U of A, professors David Ortiz and Jadwiga Pieper Mooney always treated me as a friend and colleague rather than as a mere student. Likewise, Robert Scott and Michael Matthews have not only improved my work but also kept things entertaining and provided me the encouragement to take risks with my writing. Thanks too to my bemused and patient family, and to my "brothers" Robert Fehr and Malcolm Day for their insights on everything from hydrologic sciences to military traditions to asking, "What's your point?"

Finally, deepest thanks to *mi amor*, Carrie Ann Lawson, for listening to my groaning and complaining and subjecting herself to the weirdness that is my life, both academic and otherwise.

We are what we pretend to be, so we must be careful what we pretend to be.

—KURT VONNEGUT, *MOTHER NIGHT*

The miserable soldiers fought blindly for concepts as lofty and incomprehensible as national tranquility, order, peace, progress, duty. What fault was it of the troops if they gave in to hunger, if they appropriated or snatched up whatever lay in their path? . . . He understood now that these troops could not be blamed for acting out of hunger. It's what city people did out of perverse ambition, wearing their white gloves and affecting the best manners.

—HERIBERTO FRÍAS, *THE BATTLE OF TOMOCHIC: MEMOIRS OF A SECOND LIEUTENANT*

Breaking Ranks

The Army's Place in Making Mexico

FROM THE HIGH SALONS OF CHAPULTEPEC CASTLE WEALTHY AND powerful men looked down on a country they perceived as fundamentally without order and dangerously without unity. They remembered the wars of their youth. They meditated on the polished spectacle of European armies. They imagined the rough peasant made literate and patriotic. And they dreamed, too, of a sovereign territory absent of conflicts with dissidents. In the vision they had of making a modern Mexican nation, the armed forces provided a skeleton upon which to incarnate peace. This fantasy prevailed during the years between 1876 and 1911 when Porfirio Díaz's governments held the reins of power.

Consider the deployed military as a symbolic performance with many meanings. Soldiers clothed in French woolen uniforms and gripping rifles of modern make presented to observers a dangerous and highly orchestrated display of ideas. Mechanical automatons embodied the ideal of obedient masculinity and modernist discipline. Or alternately, disheveled thugs with weapons threatened the national peace of mind. Or perhaps, victimized conscripts ineffectually sallied to enforce the delusions of a weak government. Or criminally underfunded patriots sought to preserve a woefully broke and undeveloped country. All could be true, all were true, and all were false. Had this military model successfully built real shared citizenship and effectively secured peaceful development, it would speak to the prowess of a certain type

1

of modernizing in the development of a postcolonial or neocolonial state. Instead, the modes and implications of failures drew my attention to how power relations entangled with the military experience. The army as an institution engaged nation formation from within a specific historical context.

An "army designed to fill its opponents with favorable opinions and bullets" does not arise from nothing.[1] Nor did it emerge without cause. Potent currents of international opinion and finance driven by ideologies of global capital, along with an ephemeral modernity, pushed the Mexican government to adopt a particular arrangement of powers. Consolidation of the modern regime called for developed industries, liberal democracy, and perhaps above all, visible proof of order in the nation. The evident power of the state apparatus to restrain internal opposition laid open the resources of the country to selective exploitation by capitalists—the armed forces created this illusion of potency in ways plausible, controllable, and seductive to elite actors. The *vida militar* (military life) constructed and reflected both the ideals and realities of this Mexican power. The military, as a metaphor for the nation more generally, described the limits and day-to-day experiences of entering into a condition of modernity typical of the late nineteenth century. It reflected the core contradictions of building nationhood at the fringes of the globalizing neocolonial system. It shaped men and women as subjects, objects, and aggregates in an emerging power structure but also offered them spaces as agents. The military entrenched traditions and assaulted naysayers. Yet it also embodied resistance to elite projects. These contradictions in the history of power teach the nature of flawed nation building and reveal the fissures in the imagining of Mexico.

In the pursuit of the modern, the armed forces served as instrument, model, and metaphor for national progress. I examine in this book how the military experience—as representative of the process—failed or fulfilled aspects of the broad national transition toward hegemony and sovereignty. This is the first work combining personnel records and military literature with cultural sources to address the setting of military life for soldiers and their families rather than politics or officers. In connection with nation formation and identity, this book moves away from studies of the army as an institution to broaden understandings of inculcations and the limits and fault lines of building Mexico as a nation.[2] More social and cultural in historical outlook, I examine the creation of political cultures rooted in or derived from the personal experiences of the lower ranks. In doing so, the book removes some of the privileged view that official narratives emphasize in order to explain the making of a bureaucratic institution from the bottom up and to more clearly describe how this process both encouraged the development of nationalism and limited it in important ways. In this fashion I build on the works of scholars whose focus has centered more on officers, education, and political conflicts.

The military experience in its variable forms demonstrated how and why power relations shaped national ideas like *mexicanidad* (Mexican-ness) in the late nineteenth century. This general experience, not restricted simply to Mexico, represented a global triumph of a particular vision of order and progress that facilitated the foundations of capitalist structures. My interest is in the experience in the army community and how it became an integral part of a new kind of national idea. The drive for modernist rule marked a change in social relations.[3] I seek to place the military experience within the context of these shifting frames of power relations in the ways that authorities dealt with a changing world, in particular those given shape by the abstract "nation."

As an ascendant idea, the nation was defined by the rise of a new order in Porfirian Mexico. Given the martial background of General Porfirio Díaz and the warfare that marked the times, military involvement in the modernizing society came as a matter of assumed necessity. Yet relative stability and technological advances enabled a much-reduced army to exert itself in unprecedented ways. While some excellent scholars have analyzed nationalism in their studies of peasant politics and popular militias, I attempt here to build on their efforts by examining institutional nationalism from the perspective of those enacting it federally at the bottom strata of society.[4] Military nationalism finds a basis in the massive and ubiquitous presence of the army as a displayed show of force and in modern meanings for citizenship, as well as in activities such as the intrusions of recruitment and the occupation of public spaces. All of these present us with a nationalism largely militarized by both participation and spectatorship. Moreover, the military developed in ways that eventually have led to legacies of political and criminal impunities and to a divorce from the trust of the larger public. The military contributed to an exclusion of its own members from civil citizenship and created a fissure in national unity, both of which continue to this day. The perspectives and experiences of the lower ranks and their families therefore demonstrate how a select group at the margins of society engaged with nation and identity and interacted with a process of development during a time of expanded global commercial interests.[5] They offer a new point of view for investigating a rapidly changing Mexico.

Far out of proportion to its size, the military influenced political life. The armed forces absorbed half the national budget and penetrated every area of society, with military officers becoming, among other things, many of the most important politicians, engineers, and writers. Tens of thousands of young men, often forcibly conscripted, entered a national army that extended the government into regions previously beyond centralized influence or authority. At the same time, the regime's ostentatious public rituals of parade stood in stark contrast to the army's violent eradication of highwaymen and indigenous rebels. The Mexicans' remembered hatred of Porfirian brutality, reified by Revolutionary rhetoric, has obscured the significant contributions the military made to national history.

By devising and enacting their particular visions of the nation, and embodying them through practices that ranged from drill and duels to parades and battle, the Porfirian military proved integral to the formation of nationalism and its constituent (and contingent) identities of gender, class, and ethnic organization. The histories of both the army's impact as an institution and the role of soldiers in civil society shed light on the historical roots of cultural and political forms that persisted into the twentieth century. The army rebuilt itself into a modern entity by revising regulations and laws, organizing its bureaucratic organs, and enhancing its violent capabilities with newer technology. It rationalized and justified its presence as a scientific and advanced institution. The military comprised both lens and example of how the process of becoming modern shaped the foundations of the nation.

This study first seeks to recover the experiences of the common soldiers and their families. Seen by many outsiders as marijuana-smoking brutes, troops struggled to assert themselves under the harsh discipline and in the poor conditions of an institution that had absorbed them, however unwillingly they had been dragooned. The vida militar demanded great sacrifices. The barracks community illustrated the fluidity of class and the geography of power within city and countryside. It revealed considerably stratified notions of masculinity in which the soldiers occupied disparate social roles as Catholics, husbands, sons, lovers, bureaucrats, and warriors.

Analyzing personnel files and less conventional historical sources, such as musical lyrics, photographs, interviews, and literature, made it possible to delineate the social experiences that defined the military men. My analysis also ventures into more intimate spheres of family, religion, and sexuality that allow a clearer understanding of Porfirian society and of power relations.

Those younger officers given command of this complex barracks community also shaped the military experience.

Middle-ranking and subaltern (junior) officers enacted conscription, warfare, jurisprudence, and civil engineering and became crucial agents of reform and development, bringing the nation and its projects into the wider countryside. The efforts they made represented a new domestic colonization, an invasion and occupation of the nation. In writings they described the nation, in cartography they set its bounds, and in practice they physically occupied public spaces with garrisons and fortresses, making, to the extent that they could, the nation dimly envisioned.

Methodologically, I seek to explain the soldier and his life through sources that range from bureaucratic paperwork to literary accounts to newspaper reportage to popular folk songs, to name but a few. I examined sources from both within and outside military circles that gave insight into state projects and daily life. As such, I attempted to find in the source materials cross-references that would strengthen the analysis and allow me to make broader claims. From official army sources I exhaustively read the yearly reports of the secretary of war, specialized manuals for officers, archival records of inspections and operations, the correspondences of officers in the field with higher command, the many military periodicals of the time, and most importantly, the thousands of personnel records gathered for troops and officers. For these latter, I primarily focused on troops in the Military Command of the Federal District, as it represented the largest body of soldiers and a clearinghouse through which all troops eventually funneled. I also made extensive use of military-related official records, such as those in the Foreign Relations archives, the Secretariats of Development and of the Interior, and the records in the City of Mexico archives and the Archive of Water. Since these largely present the top-down side of the story, I supplemented them with a variety of other perspectives. Newspaper accounts offer some of the views presented to, and for, the middle classes. The enormous archive of presidential correspondence from the Porfirio Díaz Collection features petitions and letters from all social groups. Foreign observers often offered a descriptive perspective, if one fraught with its own special biases, and proved valuable for showing how the army appeared to outsiders. Memoirs, both those autobiographic and those somewhat fictionalized, offered a particular literary insight into daily life, and one that could be compared or contrasted to the oral histories of soldiers as captured in the Instituto Nacional de Antropología e Historia (INAH) archives. In addition, cultural sources such as *corridos* (folk songs), poems, and images (photos, cartoons, sketches) gave significant insights into the world of the soldiers, who, being dead and illiterate, otherwise remain elusive. Given the wealth of these varied materials, I made the difficult decision to primarily limit the study to the years 1880–1905 (as the time of the most rapid changes). Ultimately, I sought to balance between official, cultural, and media accounts to describe the world of the soldier.

Nation formation, as a process, built from the combined military experiences. Miguel Angel Centeno argues that limited wars give rise to limited nations, and it follows that the limits of a military echo the limits of the society in which they take part.[6] What were the societal implications of thirty-six years of direction and formation by a military widely disdained as corrupt and ineffectual? Of a military, moreover, that set the terms and language for discussing and understanding what it meant to become "modern," and to become Mexican? The inception of the modern military ran parallel with the rise of the modern nation. The abyss between façade and reality that the army embodied also augmented clashes with new social classes. The unfulfilled promises and demands of social relationships in an age of accelerated technological advance and globalization ultimately set the stage for the military crises that led Mexico into the twentieth century and shaped the Revolution in 1910.

The Old Guard and Old Wars

The experiences of conquest, colonization, and independence set the military's prominent place in what would eventually become Mexico. The army historically made up one part of what scholars have called the baleful trinity, along with the church and hacendados (large landholders), and some blamed it for delays Mexico's economic, social, and political development (relative to that seen in Europe or the United States).[7] During the late colonial era, the Bourbon Reforms (1750–1810) set a centralized army against the interests of the *patria chica* (little fatherland), smaller regions that in governing themselves traditionally ran their own militias. As a corporate entity, the army had special rights and political influences that many in the early republic deemed antiliberal, antidemocratic, and antimodern. At Independence, the armed forces entailed widely scattered militias, remnants of presidios and colonial garrisons (largely *pardo*, or Afro-Mexican), a Spanish army of royalist regulars, and relatively improvised rebel forces. Infighting between these segments contributed to the length and destructiveness of the Independence

Wars. Once free from the Crown, the army still attempted to hold its power, and officers became politicians much reviled by merchant classes and common people alike. With the spectacular corruption and multiple failures of General Antonio López de Santa Anna, the army earned a lasting position in the baleful trinity.

As the republic staggered into being, endemic civil warfare raged between centralists and federalists and between Liberals and Conservatives. This continued to undermine national progress and confirmed the negative reputation of the army.[8] The possible (but unproven) connection between sympathetic soldiers and the rioting poor of Mexico City in 1828 led to an increasingly penalistic system of military service, with garrisons confined to barracks.[9] Ongoing financial crises drained the treasury and made the national army weaker and vulnerable to politicians' promises of funding; control over the armed forces became both ends and means for savage internecine struggles to control the national future.[10] Multiple foreign invasions (by Spain in 1829, the United States in 1846–1848, Great Britain in 1862, and France in 1838 and 1862–1867) did not create unity but rather widened the political divide inside the country and often threw the army into further ill repute.[11] As the Liberals gained the upper hand in the 1850s, they assaulted the church and its wealth in order to remove it from politics and to use its hoarded resources. This spurred their foes to an extreme resort of calling on the French to install Maximilian of Hapsburg upon the Mexican throne. It proved the last gasp of the early Conservatives, and with the defeat and departure of the French in 1867 the way opened for widespread reform initiatives as a Liberal nation.[12]

The army inherited few symbolic assets with which to convince citizens that it had played a heroic role in the founding of the nation. The Wars of Independence gained iconic currency through civic rituals that made the martyrdom of Miguel Hidalgo and José María Morelos touchstones of national pride, celebrated each September.[13] This tale, nevertheless, did not feature the army so much as it highlighted the indigenous, the clergy, and rebellious civilians. Important generals like the second president, the Afro-Mexican Vicente Guerrero, died young in ongoing feuds. Many Mexicans held Santa Anna, the caudillo extraordinaire, responsible for the loss of half of the national territory to the United States and for the discredited Conservative visions of nation.[14] When the army failed to prevent invasion, the image of the *niños heroicos* (child heroes, military cadets) and their last stand against the US Army at Chapultepec eventually became the nationalist icon, rather than the military more broadly. The battles against the French, especially at Puebla on the fifth of May 1862, became nationalist holidays, but they too celebrated the indigenous president Benito Juárez or the popular *poblano* militia, rather than the regular army. Thus a nineteenth-century pantheon featuring priests, "children," and the indigenous became associated with military nationalism and the foundations of mexicanidad—the regular army did not represent successes. The Revolution of 1910 would continue to build a nationality distant from the conventional army, and it was only with great efforts that regimes from the 1920s to 1940s managed to present the military as a positive part of the national project.[15] In fact, the army itself now dates its origin to 1914 and has recently celebrated its centennial. The nineteenth-century military, never a central piece of national pride or iconography, disappeared into legendary ill repute.

After 1867 the government faced numerous challenges to constructing a modern nation. Presidents Benito Júarez (1867–1872) and Sebastián Lerdo de Tejada (1872–1876) acted to reduce the swollen army roster, eliminate banditry, build railways, and resurrect foreign credit. Júarez expanded the institution of the *rurales* (the rural constabulary) and increased the forced retirement of officers.[16] Continuing financial weakness and lack of work for former soldiers meant that his efforts to contain crime or rural uprisings could not succeed, as opposition expanded more quickly than the forces slated to combat it. He also built a number of new military colonies, populated and led by semiretired officers who garrisoned previously hostile or barren areas. Both presidents of the Restoration era (1867–1876) relied heavily on local militias or National Guards to maintain order.[17] For Lerdo de Tejada, this dependence turned toxic, as the ambitious Porfirio Díaz seized power in 1876 through a coup with considerable support of the National Guards from his home state of Oaxaca.[18]

Díaz proclaimed a new era of progress to the nation and its army. He consolidated the Liberal project and harnessed it to the rapidly accelerating technologies and social changes of his time.[19] He and his advisors turned to the Compte-inspired philosophy of positivism, seeking through science and technology to resolve the persistent problems of the nation. From 1880 to 1884 Díaz's close friend Manuel González briefly ruled in a show of democratic lip service, and while doing so he initiated many unpopular new laws on Díaz's behalf. When Díaz returned to power he made himself the indispensable leader by balancing most of his opponents against one another and micromanaging the affairs of nation. The Porfirian style did not suit all. Serious internal opposition repeatedly emerged, including military rebellions and conspiracies in 1877, 1878, 1879, 1886, 1890, and 1893.[20] Scattered attacks by Apaches, Navajos, and Comanches and sporadic uprisings by Yaquis, Mayos, and Mayas continued through much of the era.[21] Army reform, a priority since colonial times, picked up speed. Officers drafted new ordinances and regulations, the General Staff became efficient and expanded in size, and they in turn updated education in the military college (Colegio Militar) and adopted new technologies in arms, tactics, and transport. Becoming modern, above all, required installing a façade to make the army appear to be a bureaucratically ruled and scientifically grounded organization with both a symbolic presence and a capability in keeping with other advanced armies.

The military also worked to make control over the countryside more rational. In an organizational shift from the decentralized regional armies and French-style departments that had come before, the Porfirian staff split administration into ten to twelve zones, three to five commands, and between nine and eighteen *jefaturas de las armas* (regional commands) across the nation. This varied somewhat over time and with different territorial demands. The reorganizing adjusted to perceived threats and accorded with military, rather than political, needs. It also broke from the French system as Mexico continued to recover its sovereignty.

With the army spread thin, it used rail and telegraph to respond to serious threats and allied with local subordinate forces to put out brush fires. The command staff would never allow any one officer to gain too much authority in one region. Making this more feasible, the federal government began to systematically dismantle the National Guard units and regularly transferred all officers to ensure that none gained personal loyalties from locals.

Reforms of this sort, according to some later critics, seem to have had little success. Yet efficiency, centralization, and anticorruption measures did not undermine the army nearly as badly as did the perpetual issues of meager funding and public disdain. Similarly, the army did not exist in a balance posed politically against the rurales (as some suggested after the Revolution), but rather the two shared many officers and some troops, they worked in tandem, and they typically operated against the same opponents. Indeed, the rurales had little choice; those not on publicity tours often lacked adequate gear or even horses.[22] The new Liberal nation thus became subject to a centralized and national army structure, without interference from regional strongmen, and through army service the elite attempted to instill patriotism in the reformed citizenry. The army with rurale auxiliaries counterpoised local governments and brought the federal nation into new prominence across the country.

This Porfirian Army and Life in the Ranks

With so many missions at hand the government desperately worked to fill the ranks of the army. The process of the *leva* (forced levy or conscription) brought the ordinary Mexican into the grasp of the state and its disciplinary mechanisms. Chapter 1 examines the reasons for mass recruitment, its processes, its effects, and the ways that conscripts sought to elude service at arms. Not all military men, by any means, entered service solely as victims or by force, but those who volunteered represented a minority of cases. Recruitment really was not the end of the world for most men; many eventually made a decent career out of military service, and some willingly reenlisted. It nonetheless represented for most an undesirable fate and a real conflict between communities, families, and the power of the government. It set the needs of an unconsolidated nation against moral economies and local autonomy. This ultimately undermined the military's intent of creating a positive image and framing service as honorable. The motives of the government meant little in the context of the anxiety and poor reputation that the leva instilled in the wider populace. Many civilians saw the process in the same light as kidnapping, or *rapto*, as inherently targeting the vulnerable and taking from them their integrity and honor.

The new soldiers and their families sought freedom from service in various ways. They evaded initial conscription by hiding the young men from detachments sent to collect them, which required on some level the collaboration of the broader community to keep silent or actively abet. For those taken, another option came in legal mechanisms such as the *amparo*, an injunction that could potentially free the conscript. This required knowledge, outside aid from family, and some good luck in circumventing the army's attempts to stymie this procedure. When all else failed, if community or family could not help, then the final resort came in the form of simple desertion from the imprisonment of high barracks walls guarded by armed sentries. Estimates of desertion ranged from 25 to 50 percent of the army's personnel, although this was complicated, as some left for only a short time, inadvertently missed role calls, and so on. With recruitment being so contentious, the regime found it a difficult task to fold peasants into barracks and soldiers into nation. With those whom they gathered and held, extensive training proved necessary.

Training and education in the Porfirian army generally appeared crude, brutal, and underfunded, yet it succeeded on some levels to instill patriotic sentiments and military exceptionalism. Chapter 2 examines the process of making the soldier through his daily experiences in barracks life. The recruit's day, marked and divided by horn calls, began with pay and with food. Soldiers earned little and scrabbled to find the funds for sufficient extra rations or little comforts. Budgetary issues and corruption drained the pay coffer and poor meals only heightened the sense of dishonorable service. The recruits' new lives echoed the poverty and subsistence lifestyles that lay outside the walls of the garrison.

The regime nevertheless sought to "create men" in this context. They worked toward an idealized standard that the elite deemed a national goal. The classroom might create this new soldier-citizen. Officers led them through new texts promoting literacy and patriotism and built valuable skills. They also struggled to train the men through drill and parade and in practical skills of war but often found budgets insufficient. The men learned regulations and how to march. They earned shoes, much to the great delight of many who felt footwear represented an integral part of civilized and modern status. At the same time, noncommissioned officers (NCOs) violently abused their charges physically, emotionally, and verbally in order to harden them and to shift their identities from civilian to military men. It did not endear the men to the sergeants and corporals, but it worked—many troops became inured to hardship and replicated the harsh treatments they had received against newer troops or outsiders. Complementing this brute training, the army also continued to use ritual as a means to create a sense of solidarity and militarism among the men. Frequent rituals built on group participation and repetition, with hints of religious confessional, to instill patriotic belonging and military subordination. Taking oaths before the flag, reading aloud regulations and their penalties (those too harsh for mere civilians), and taking part in ceremonial executions all separated the military experience from that of "normal" society. The regime made soldiers from these moments but never attained an ideal level of isolation between recruits and the communities around them.

One of the major exceptions to what the regime hoped to create as hypothetically homosocial spaces appeared in the presence of women and children in daily army life, examined in chapter 3. The women of the barracks played a much-occluded yet significant role in the function of the army while also adding elements of comfort that officers deemed dangerous to discipline. They represent a unique presence in a military at this time and in this state of development, and they present a fascinating aspect of the Mexican experience. The army relied on them for stability, for forage, and for morale. At the same time, the power of their gaze undermined the efforts of the officers to control the behaviors of their men, or at times, even to gain their attentions. *Soldaderas* have been little studied, and often only in the context of the Revolutionary armies, yet they certainly did not simply appear in 1910 or disappear in 1920.

Their presence exacerbated an edge of violence, testosterone, and hierarchy within the barracks, where both men and women fought for status and partners. The soldadera also became part of the institution itself in terms of using regulations and legal recourses and learning the military lore that sometimes eluded soldiers who did not share the women's often-lengthy time "in service." These women sold the troops food, contraband, and sometimes sex, but this rather limited vision of the camp follower does not suffice to describe normal affairs. With women came elements of family and sexuality unusual to armies at the turn of the century. Women decided and arranged marriages as they sorted out partners to their liking and with their own criteria. They thereby earned, and demanded, legal protections and eventual pensions. They transformed the barracks into a sexualized and heterosexual space where intense competition at times appeared as a small price for nightly comforts and intimacy. They also brought religion to an otherwise officially secular liberal institution. Soldaderas expressed their piety in churchgoing as outsiders unbound by army rules, and within the barracks they performed baptisms, weddings, and funerals. They presented an alternative order to that of the regime as they acted as women, as mothers, as priestesses, and as *mujeres de tropa*. They created genuine families within the fictive "army family" that officials intended to form.

Within this ideal Great Family, a particular brotherhood also emerged between the young officers graduating from the halls of the military college at Chapultepec Castle. Chapter 4 describes this experience. Junior officers received an excellent education and experience abroad and tempered this with traditional masculinity. They also learned firsthand of continued social inequality and of the nepotism that pervaded their society. Chapultepec by all accounts mirrored the curriculum and standards of its counterparts in Europe and the United States. Its products would theoretically emerge ready to bring the nation forward into a modern age.

The young officer or subaltern (those under major in rank) potentially provided the regime with a tool to demonstrate progress and develop as a country. The boys learned science and mathematics and practiced poetry and saber. They represented both the best of old traditions in dueling and the best of the new in technological mastery, despite the contradictions this may carry. For instance, both refusing a duel and fighting in one led to punishment, as the system prohibited cowardice and brawling alike. The subaltern also became one of the selling points for Mexico's image abroad as he traveled as attaché or staff with many foreign postings to military embassies and expositions. The government, through these contacts, sought to reconstruct its battered reputation and to reform the army into a modern force. It took selectively from what it encountered, implementing sweeping changes to military law, national reserves, standardized arms, and general staff and more aesthetic reforms concerning uniform designs or adopting marching song from various sources. That the new army the subaltern would eventually lead had no genuine mission in terms of foreign foes did not matter. The regime had other tasks for the junior officer and his charges.

The first half of the book seeks therefore to demonstrate how the army recruited and trained men, gained invaluable female support, and educated and presented its junior officers. The efforts to discipline and construct an idealized figure of "le militaire" theoretically could transform these young men, and perhaps the women as well, into viable citizen-soldiers fully enmeshed into the power structures of the nation-state. The high brass sought disciplinary power over the individual and his home community and then coerced transformation of these peasants brought in chains into barracks. Even in this most limited of arenas, the project faced resistance and obstacles. The regime never fully committed to the process and never supplied the resources required. The barracks spilled out into the streets, and the presence of soldaderas altered the dynamics of the patio. Subaltern officers straddled two worlds, the modern and the traditional. The mission of the army remained rather murky. In contrast to other countries, surveillance, punishment, and ritual led to incompletely convinced military subjects. This, to me, hints that elite efforts at instilling Mexican nationalism worked indifferently and that the people saw their nation in unique ways. Loyalties to family, the needs of the day, and a less Europeanized façade featured in their reactions to a changing society around them. The second half of the book addresses the continued failures, attempts, and successes of the army. This encompassed broader realms of the body, behaviors, and the practices of deployment beyond their initial training in barracks.

Concurrent and complementary to efforts at training, the ideal army imposed pseudoscientific programs intended to "cure" the national populace. This scaled downward to the barracks as a focal point. The medical systems of knowledge in the barracks community sought to ameliorate "horrid and amoral" sites at the cost of exposing the officials' limits and increasing resistance to their efforts. These systems are the subject of chapter 5.

The army initiated practices to reform military "bodies" wholesale as representatives of an elite vision of the ideal race, class, and gender composition that they aspired to see in the nation. The army doctors hoped that reform in the barracks might act as a metaphorical vaccine for the national body. With a clean, healthy army (and its followers), the entire country would somehow heal its broken morals, reject criminality, and cleanse its septic impoverishment. Medical officials began with vague proscriptions and prescriptions on hygienic practices. They imperiously demanded investments in water supplies, regulatory practices, mosquito nets, and facility renovations. They also started prodding and ogling the whole garrison to find sexual ailments and attempted to ban soldaderas from the barracks. Poor understanding of diseases, intrusive exams, and eventually, fatal treatments collided with an armed and skeptical audience who preferred their genitalia unexamined and uncauterized. Doctors nonetheless continued their efforts on the premise that the apparent "contagion" threatened the moral fiber of the nation. The army provided too few resources to alleviate even simple health issues; for instance, medics accomplished little toward improving the hygiene, air circulation, and heating in the old convents that the army used as barracks. Scientific reforms to the army diet likewise failed, as quartermasters provided simple and "backward" foods that they could afford, rather than the pricier Prussian meal plan the doctors preferred. The rations rarely tasted good, but at least the soldiers did not have much of them to choke down. Most sustenance still came from unofficial sources like the soldaderas. Ultimately the medical staff's overall plan tried to reform bodies through hygiene, environment, abstinence, and diet, and all connected back to their ideals regarding the disordered life of the soldier. The blame, they understood, did not fall on wise doctors but on the poor choices of a degenerate populace. Yet disorder to some was diversion to others.

The troops' leisure activities and politics of everyday life fell afoul of changing modern expectations regarding the orderly life and remained a point of serious class contention over broader cultural expressions. Chapter 6 examines how the barracks residents found their recreation. Although imprisoned by chances or circumstances within the high garrison walls, the community there made a life and sought entertainment. Perhaps more limited than civilians in terms of options, the soldiers enjoyed a range of improvised leisure activities, including gambling, card games, watching sports, strolling streets, and so forth. These allowed them to bond and relax, yet some activities clashed with regulations and expectations, especially when it came to drinking and smoking tobacco and marijuana. While tobacco featured as normal part of life, and even at times part of official rations, marijuana use became a high-profile issue due to press accounts and extreme cases. Either because it was laced with peyote or because it was different in its physiological effects from most cannabis today, it drove some soldiers into violent hallucinatory episodes. Given the ease of smuggling it into barracks and jails (compared to a whiskey jug), its high markup in price from market to patio, and its potent and relaxing effects, proscribing the drug had little chance of succeeding, and many recruits at least experimented. Drinking, also against regulations, nonetheless continued in all barracks, and some opened cantinas for the profit of officers. Less troubling to the army, music allowed the soldiers a seemingly harmless entertainment. Singers expressed popularly held ideas and narratives that at times challenged official versions of events. The soldiers adapted lyrics as they liked and criticized the army and the government in clever ways. Likewise, even in everyday speech a cant or slang developed in the barracks that allowed soldiers to communicate as a group without official control or knowledge. In this they expressed an unofficial sense of identity that the community embedded and made their own.

This context, a world of whispers and song and quiet comforts, remained alien and separate from officers' lives. Chapter 7 considers how the hard truths of living between two worlds confronted young officers with uncomfortable choices and compromises. Relatively unprepared subaltern officers deployed into service in an environment where many fell into bad habits, where bad policies continued by inertia, or where nepotism sent the crème de la crème to lucrative technical positions while the unconnected marched out to police the countryside.

Generally, the regime put too much responsibility on the shoulders of overly inexperienced young men. The subaltern officers compromised or adjusted in different ways. Some fraternized with soldiers while others exploited all those around them, whether troops or inferior officers. New officers and old soldiers alike learned to expect the hazing and corrupt demands from jaded career officers. The recently arrived subaltern socialized with those above and below and learned over time to bend rules, to allow malfeasance, and even to participate in the small-scale embezzlements called *las buscas*. Not all adjustments proved so relatively harmless, as in the case of applying the *ley fuga* (execution of prisoners). They learned soon enough that at times the unspoken expectations of their superiors included authorizing, or even carrying out, the shooting of unarmed captives who had been deemed bandits, rebels, or simply inconvenient. Some estimates claim as many as ten thousand people died in this fashion during Díaz's reign. The pressure on the subaltern to do this came as a result of a number of factors: overworked justice systems, simple inertial traditions, easily escaped prisons, and a degree of state theater intended to highlight ruthless order.

It nonetheless came as a choice, and with a responsibility for murder. On the whole, junior officers required flexibility to make a life with their soldiers. If the porous barracks and the presence of women within it eroded soldiers' adherence to ideal types, the everyday expectations of leading also undermined the construction of ideal officer-gentlemen. The true test of any army, nonetheless, came with war.

In the absence of foreign enemies, Díaz consolidated his territorial limits and internal hegemony. Chapter 8 seeks to explain the ways in which the army experienced the national effort to suppress indigenous resistance by the Yaquis in the north and by the Mayas in the south. By 1900 the self-colonizing impulse of the regime could, with new technology and discursive permission, finally annihilate indigenous "insurgency." Rather than chastise or accommodate, they needed, by the logic of modern capitalism, to eradicate challengers. Deployed to the edges of Mexico, the army represented the clash of the semimodernized majority with a remnant racial and cultural "Other" still rooted in the past. The government had no modern foreign opponents but it did have an ongoing ulcer in the highlands of the Sierras and another in the lowlands of the Yucatán. These fights continued antagonisms begun long before Díaz. Yaquis had fought for and against the federal state since the Independence era. The Mayan *bravos* had fought largely against it, and they nearly gained freedom in the middle of the century. Both groups used guerrilla tactics, relied on hostile terrain and climate, and maintained a deep sense of cultural coherence with religious foundations to oppose outside impositions. Both harnessed a deep folk Catholic piety as motivation and means to build solidarity, and both had run short of time.

By the late nineteenth century the national behemoth could deploy a massive force, rearmed and mindful of lessons learned at the fiasco of Tomochic in 1893. In addition to brute force, which had failed before, the government made diplomatic gains to seal the borders with Belize and the United States and thus cut off rebel support. The press, intellectuals, and governors applied new labels to stigmatize insurgents as savages, and the public accepted them. This encouraged the regime to adopt more extreme steps to quash rebellion. With new science and technology, the army could make prolonged and swift advances against indigenous foes, and radio, telegraphs, railways, and naval artillery eliminated the time and space necessary for indigenous resistors to find refuge. Lessons learned in the north, they applied to the south. With the end of armed resistance, the regime set in place bureaucratic fetters to make defeat indelible and perhaps permanent. Paperwork made for an articulation of power even as it rendered power invisible. The exquisite noose of acquiescing to a faceless system of regulation, of submission to permanent surveillance, the government offered as a sole alternative to the genocidal process of deportation and massacres. In a proclaimed crisis, a state of exception, the regime recognized no limits to taking extreme measures. The government and army sought ultimately to succeed at a self-colonization that left no embarrassing remnants outside the national polity and no corner of the country without developed modern usage. The indigenous could accept chains or die fighting; Díaz had little preference.

The regime directed its legitimate and violent authority into all corners of the nation and inscribed power upon bodies and minds, but this came with limits and soon created its own antithesis.[23] Through attempts to control the soldier's environment, food, and sexuality, the regime earned resentment and little gains. The troops found entertainment where they could and consistently ignored regulations; many deserted, and others actively mocked the government in lyrics and murmurs. The relations between junior officers and soldiers regularly broke the spirit and letter of regulations, a practice taken to the extreme when the orders came to execute prisoners. The stronger the "nation" grasped the barracks community, the more resistant it became to following the whims of rulers. The harder the army pressed the indigenous rebels, the more the national populace began to doubt its leadership and consider alternatives. The 1910 Revolution rose from these and other contradictions.

On Army, Nation, and Modernity

The role of the military institution in modern Latin American nations has received significant scholarly attention. Historians concerned with the roots of army intervention in national politics have seen this early phase (roughly 1870–1930) as crucial to the development of professional and political-military systems.[24] The common soldiers, their relationship with officers, and their direct interactions with the community around them, have for the most part been absent from these debates but nonetheless warrant a closer look.

The experiences and lives of everyday military members serve as the primary focus of what has been called the New Military History, best represented in Latin America for Brazil.[25] Through the study of soldiers' hopes, family lives, cultural expressions, historical memory, gender understandings, and collective identities, more recent scholarship (since around 1990) has begun reexamining the military life as a complex social relationship rather than a monolithic institutional bloc. This approach, as the editors of *Nova história militar brasileira* point out, is not new but a resurgence of the military history as written in the late nineteenth century, just prior to the so-called professionalizing of European-style militaries. An attempt to bridge the space between traditional military histories (whose interests are in battles, maneuvers, and politics) and social or cultural histories (bottom-up approaches discussing things like identity constructions and daily life), the New Military History sees the whole armed forces as an important facet of society without removing it from normal social understandings. It thus addresses the psychosocial gap in analyzing civil-military relationships, which some have proposed was missing.[26] This study attempts to situate the Porfirian army within this social and cultural historical frame as a way to understand nation formation and nationalism.[27]

The drive for nationalism resulted in the formation of a new collective community. Among insecure elite groups this drive often manifested instead as a taste for unchallenged power with the assumption that such power eventually would be approved by consensus. This identity ideally expressed and represented an imagined sense of belonging to a bounded group, within defined borders of territory.[28] The national imagination depended on smoothing away or homogenizing differences, for example, of language, ethnicity, and religion.[29] At the same time, becoming a nation required agreement on the requisites for citizenship, a simultaneous sense of separation from foreigners, and the development of a shared collective memory.[30] Some scholars have looked to literature, archeology, science, and entertainment to better illustrate the rise of the nation.[31] Others have seen the very idea of "nation" as an exercise in power (or a symptom thereof) manifested in institutions and in discourse, including systems of science and knowledge.[32] Many have agreed that the most pronounced movement toward nationhood correlated to the rise of a technologically advanced and socially coherent country, one that claimed the hallmarks of modernity. During the Porfiriato, the armed forces had a significant role in both the imagining and the governing of the nascent nation.

Nationality and citizenship have historically been tied to military service—the armed forces provided both school and forum for constructing what became the modern nation. Defining the nation as an imagined and limited collective identity, scholars have pointed to the military as an obvious central institution that prepares the citizen to understand and fulfill civic responsibilities.[33] The absence of persistent enemies can hinder this since few things work as well as a foreign enemy to inspire a nation into imagining its own virtues and solidarity.[34] Moreover, the functions and performances of the military in the public sphere have the potential to direct understandings of the nation, gender, class, and race. Military service connects these ideas to one another by re-creating an ideal citizen from the rough material of the conscript, giving him a new, nationalized identity replete with approved manliness and social status. They thereby construct a social fabric congruent with modern aspirations and capable of smoothing over political and economic conflicts. In other words, the Mexican army exposed lower classes to powerful transformative forces (drill, uniforms, ceremonies, and so on) that sought to build "Juan Soldado" into the perfect citizen.[35] His altered form would march in parades with thousands like him and infect spectators with a sense of nationalist pride—or so the regime hoped.

The demonstrative nature of ritual gave the military, and by association its government, a venue for performing the appearance of a legitimate presence.[36] The nation must seem natural, inevitable, and eternal in order to become "real."[37] Repetitively seeing the military on parade and taking part in civic rituals, with music, flags, uniforms, and standard arms, presented the populace with a spectacle of the nation as theater.[38] The performed military also constructs ideals of gender, class, and ethnicity. As has been argued for the United States, Brazil, and Germany, the soldier potentially embodies specific ideals of masculinity through bearing, posture, dress, and armament.[39] Lower-class "deficiencies" such as stooped posture and dishevelment could be attenuated in the soldier. Through drill and training a man worthy of the nation would become presentable to the public. In a similar fashion, soldiers in a national uniform could put off their ethnic, even racial, features, achieving homogeneity as they ceased being primarily *negro, pardo, indio,* or *mulato* and became simply soldiers.[40] Clothing makes the man, and in this instance, the epaulet makes the national citizen (as *le militaire*) in the relative anonymity of a military formation.

Implicated in this insight was the idea that the rights and obligations of military service, as well as the privileges, belonged exclusively to men. The civil republican link to the soldier gendered civic virtue and political participation as male.[41] Women had no recourse to genuine citizenship, as they could not fight or die for the country, and so they had, the logic goes, a lesser stake in the nation. The narrowness of this point of view ignores how women routinely played a significant role in the function and efficacy of the army and represents a patriarchal perspective much more than an accurate appraisal of military service. Nor was it guaranteed that all men would be enthusiastic about becoming soldiers.

An obstacle to using the military to create nationalism lay in the debate over recruitment. As Eugen Weber has persuasively shown for France and Peter Beattie for Brazil, the only way to instill liberal senses of nationalism through military service arrived via universal, or nearly universal, conscription of men. Obviously, this raised a number of serious difficulties for the military and the government, not to mention for the national population. First of all, it required tremendous central authority, and for much of the nineteenth century in Mexico this did not exist, so universal conscription was out of the question. Second, it required an economy robust enough not only to pay and supply this huge army but also to survive the loss of so much manpower from its workforce. Third, the process of circulation and mixing of populations of differing classes, ethnicities, and regions (which Weber identified as a crucial element of nationalism, albeit one developed gradually in the barracks) worried middle-class families, who opposed the army as a den of vice and immorality.[42] Beattie demonstrates that this element, in itself, retarded the development of Brazilian military nationalism for decades. Finally, the liberal ideal of egalitarianism proved difficult in practice, as the wealthy continued to find ways to avoid service and the poor continued to face arbitrarily enlistment (as they still do in so many places). Beyond fears of moral and sexual cross-class contamination, rich citizens claimed that their mandatory inclusion in military service would irreparably harm the economy they "alone" had built.

Debates over recruitment raged through the nineteenth century. Popular distaste for conscription led to unrest, and individuals attempted to avoid military service in any way possible. They hired replacements, deserted, bribed, and feigned illnesses to avoid honorable service to the nation. As a result, the calls of patriotism and the idea of nationalism had little purchase in the still less than prestigious armies broadly noted for poor living conditions and worse pay.

Porfirian elites continued efforts to innovate recruitment at the turn of the century. They debated general reforms in recruitment vigorously, with eight different schemes of recruitment considered.[43] Ultimately, although the Ordinances of 1900 specified volunteer service only, the army continued with the leva as it had since the eighteenth century—forcibly drafted criminals, vagrants, dissidents, transvestites, and prisoners of war entered the army in chains.[44] Officers locked them in barracks at night.[45] Predictably, soldiers suffered low morale. Desertions, by some estimates, reached epidemic levels of nearly 50 percent, and few considered the nation well served, or well represented, by its federal army.[46] By contrast, the rurales cultivated an image of disciplined masculine prowess and individuality, but one tainted with a presumed bandit heritage and a legendary brutality.[47] Few within or outside of the army considered the experiments a success.

Nationality and military service connected intimately, but making that coupling in nineteenth-century Mexico proved quite difficult. The great institutions of liberal nation building—factories, schools, and barracks—failed to convince popular classes of the viability and utility of the nation.[48] Elite writers and army reformers attempted to construct the iconic soldier as a representative of the ideal national man, one with the desired qualities in race, masculinity, and class, through public ceremony and historical celebration.[49] Yet the persistence of alternative visions of nation continued, in part due to the disparate experiences of warfare across the nineteenth century.[50] Enormous social divides of race and region, the perceived cultural gap between elites and subordinates, and the continued abuses within the army and its recruitment ultimately undermined the military as a foundation for a unified imagining of the Mexican nation. Despite these limits, the discursive and ritual presence of the military provided an understood visual language upon which a national culture would eventually build. While the initial claims of the elite fell short, the lower and middle classes of the twentieth century built their Mexico using the same cultural logic learned from these elite projects.[51]

The enormous crude strength of this new kind of national order appeared in its changing capacity to deal with ruptures in multiple ways, an apparent flexibility that nonetheless relied ultimately on brute force.[52] Two significant differences transformed the process's sheer efficiency at the dawn of the twentieth century: the injection of modern methods and tactics drawn from global sources, and elite access to the financial and technical resources of capitalism. In various points of disagreement the army acted to fuse differences in the meaning-making frameworks where hegemonic ideologies clashed and transformed.[53] In other words, it used updated organization and tools, along-side historical army traditions, in order to enact and to justify interventions against groups unconvinced by the government's claims. Where class and cultural conflicts rose, federal machine guns made arguments moot.

A persuasive argument about what it meant to become a nation hinged on reaching some sort of consensus on the modern trajectory—to define what it was to be Mexican required a sense of progress toward a goal. Moder-nity is a conceptual prerequisite to the national and a crucial self-description that determined the role of the military in the Porfiriato.[54] The modern emphasis premised an ideal worldview through public arguments over past and future and gave it shape in visible and articulable symbols and practices. No sense of the Porfirian nationalist project can be complete without some grappling with what modernity meant.

The regime's claim that Mexico had entered modernity relied on demon-strable practices and technologies and was thrown into stark relief by adhered-to customs and shared histories. The elite's proof of scientific and social progress came from collected statistics, they made this public in expositions and displays, and they made the modern real in the collapsing of space and time afforded through the technology of rails, telegraph, and telephones. At the same time, they cherished old styles of music, perpetuated dueling, and (at least in private) maintained close ties with the Catholic Church.

The military's responsibility for expressing and embodying modernity runs throughout this study. The army barracks, its personnel, and even the institution as a whole provided nation-building reformers a laboratory for enacting foreign ideas and social engineering. The soldier became a guinea pig in a nationalist experiment to find a modern façade. During the Porfiriato, education and science were proofs of modern progress but also represented the possibility of overcoming what some elites deemed the traditional prob-lems of race and class. The first chapters of this book all touch on this, exam-ining how officers applied scientifically justified regimens to destroy indigenous identities, to remove lower-class habits, and to erase traditional behaviors. At the same time, medical and hygienic reforms instilled "moral-ity," a concept deemed essential to the progress and modernity of the nation. The modern soldier, so reformed, would become the dutiful patriot. The mil-itary had to identify with tradition, as a first step toward refashioning the modern by contrast. Despite solid modern arguments against old practices the army maintained the traditional custom of dueling; it slowly replaced impractical uniforms that looked good on parade; and it reinvented festivals that glorified the military past. Modernity's inevitable encroachments often fell first upon the armed forces, as they took to new technologies and applied them with one eye on European advances. When all things solid melted into air, the army rebuilt its own vision of the modern nation out of the wisps.

The power of performance and ceremony to alter fundamental national understandings brings cultural history into this study. The often-incomplete successes in shaping participants and spectators applied to raw recruits in the drill square, to foreign embassies in the reviewing stand, and to subaltern officers in the dueling grounds. The first chapters here highlight the soldiers' experiences with nationalist ritual and official regimens and argue that with rare exceptions the performances did not overwrite old understandings (in the short term).[55] Yet even critiques, of which many appeared, eventually used the same terms and assumptions that military performances had displayed or embodied.[56] For instance, most critics accepted the need for leaving indigenous practices behind, but they argued over how best to make this happen. The army demonstrated the nation's trajectory toward modernity, whether through technological advances or patriotic sovereignty, and illuminated the only acceptable pathway—even if not all agreed as to the perfect pace to walk it. The shift between seeming modern and being modern came about through practiced repetitions. In this reiteration the military excelled.

The Voice in the Archives

Here I give voice to soldiers, families, and junior officers often left mute in studies that assume the military to represent a monolithic institutional force. They, and their stories, frame my understandings of power in an age of accelerating social changes. My position as historian, interpreter, interlocutor, and imaginer distorts the tale accordingly. Mexico's experiences came in fits and starts toward the modern era. In many ways, official histories failed to describe realities. So did the popular ones. I hope that my "stories," based on quite real people taken in composite, offer a useful counterpoint. Alone, though, no segment of this book tells the whole tale, and I urge readers to look deeply into the organization and conceits that frame my work to find the layers of meaning that I could not otherwise portray. My intention is to offer a challenge on the levels of narrative and question what we, as historians, construe as fictive speculations. As Simon Schama asserts, "The asking of questions and the relating of narratives need not . . . be mutually exclusive forms of historical representation."[57] Which parts of this work represent imaginative fiction and which historical reality I leave to each reader to interpret according to his or her own belief in authority and verification and accuracy versus precision.[58]

Relationships of power and gender, and the idea of family as a historical experience, impel the framing of this book with composite characters described in an unconventional mode. The tales of Diego, Melchora, and Salvador interspersed with the military history that I set out here and address some theoretical and source-based issues of my work. Each protagonist's story weaves individually into the chapters best suited to him or her, and they come together as a group in the final few, where their relationships hold more significance or influence. Their tales are speculative, untrue, fictional, and imaginative, despite reflecting tens of thousands of personnel records, a number of memoirs, newspaper accounts, and so forth. In other words, they are historical, real, and dubious at the same time. Their inclusion allows the construction of a clear narrative arc without feigned objectivity or the implied imposition of a narrative based on analytical fragments hidden in conventional text. They fulfill a function of the social historical approach by encouraging you to feel, to see, and to experience a history otherwise buried in the archive. The protagonists who became real to me as I sifted through mountains of sources, explained in simplified forms of convenience, are no more false than any other "true" accounting of the time.

The bases of their tales came from many different types of information, often incomplete and purpose-written. Prevalent punishment records, newspaper complaints, and vanity memoirs skewed the depiction of people who, on the whole, were likely less deviant and more remarkably ordinary than the archive suggested. I acknowledge a special debt to authors Heriberto Frías, Francisco Luis Urquizo, and Rafael Aponte, whose autobiographical accounts filled in many gaps.[59] Urquizo in particular offers insights, yet his sometimes-circumstantial accounts should not always be taken at face value. At age twenty he joined the Revolution as a *soldado raso* (simple soldier), fighting for Francisco Madero and Venustiano Carranza, and he served in the federal army for decades. He rose to the rank of general in 1941 and served as subsecretary of war during World War II and secretary afterward. His many books reflected his experiences as a soldier and officer and described life in the Revolution-era barracks with detail unmatched elsewhere. Fortunately, the army he served in remained largely the same on a day-to-day level until later in the 1920s. In the end, few knew army life, the leva, the barracks, and soldaderas like he did. That said, wherever possible I corroborated his accounts with Porfirian sources. The narrative conceit used here therefore attempts to get at the heart of the military experience and give a credible voice to a multi-vocal past. Discard some or all as you choose them, of course. In this sense I offer my work for historical dissection and a deeper inquiry into modes of historicity and narrative as they apply to what might otherwise become an oversimplified fairy tale of institutions and maneuvers.[60]

The story laid out here is the story of Mexico as it entered the twentieth century. The military serves as metaphor to demonstrate the changes to the national idea. If the army's project seems incomplete, if its methods and results seem crude or ill done, if the soldier's experience seems filled with contradiction and unfinished, then the same problems ran through the flawed façades of modernity and hesitant national hegemony of Porfirian Mexico. The power relations that limited and shaped society had particular clarity within barracks walls. From conscript to war, from drilling field to dueling green, and from cantina to battlefield, the many ephemeral shapes of mexicanidad took the shape of a soldier.

Among soldiers there are no friends or enemies of the government, all are servants.

—PORFIRIO DÍAZ TO COR. MIGUEL G. MARÍN, 1885

CHAPTER ONE

Recruiting the Servants of the Nation

Hushed whispers filled the market square on a normal Sunday morning in small-town Mexico. In a quiet, even quaint, place in the fertile lands some-where north of Mexico City at the end of the nineteenth century, young Diego strained to hear the rumors. Eighteen, unmarried, and from a terribly poor family, he sensed something ominous in the mannerisms of his neighbors. Perhaps, he mused, they still held his drunken uncle's weekly mishaps against him? Maybe his family's dismal efforts to support the parish and cofradía had finally fallen too short? The better-off villagers and farmers confiding with that outsider, the jefe político (town boss), went silent as he passed. Even with the rotten town jail filled from last night's celebrations, the streets seemed eerily quiet. Nowhere could he see any of his friends or young men his own age. Diego set his misgivings aside. On such a bright morning and with no work expected, he'd rather relax and enjoy the day than puzzle over the usual town gossiping. He went about his day, wandered aimlessly awhile before heading to his father's small house near the edge of the village. Diego had just finished a simple meal of his mother's beans and tortillas when the door of the house burst open.

"Cannon meat" was what they called Diego, as they took him at saber point from his home to become part of the so-called contingent of blood sent to serve the Porfirian government. His shocked mother prayed to the Virgen de Gua-dalupe and watched helplessly as six soldiers and a sergeant put him in

*shackles. Nearby, another man's mother wailed and pleaded on her knees to
no avail.*

This is a history of average soldiers.[1] Their views, the ways they came to see
themselves, their community, and their nation, resulted from interaction with
critical civilians, fellow soldiers, and unhappy officers.[2] The recruitment and
daytime regimen of ordinary soldiers provided experiences that speak to the
interactions between civilians and military officials as part of a human journey from peasant to warrior, perhaps to Mexican. Although this process had
its immediate effects on the individual conscript, it also had profound implications for families and communities. Similarly, the significance of military
service went beyond personal social networks and demonstrated a course
taken into modernity where class divisions, regional loyalties, and gendered
behaviors became fields of contention. President Díaz's call for "servants of
the nation" ultimately did not suit his purposes; the lower classes had their
own vision of the nation attached to local identities and served their nation
as they deemed best.

This incidental project of building a loyal or even fanatical body of soldiers represented a byproduct of the need to maintain a federal force capable
of reacting to all enemies. Yet I argue here that the cumulative effects of mass
conscription, even on rhetorical levels, demonstrated the application of biopower—a manifestation of state will to control populations en masse. Through
discipline and surveillance, ordinary people could be rearranged in their
behavior and outlook and become something closer to reformers' ideals. The
soldier-conscripts that officers pressed into service composed an experimen-
tal body of subjects that the army worked into its vision of ideal Mexicans. The
leva took the least powerful citizens and folded them into an institutionally
defined place in society.[3] Their point of entry, a fortified threshold they
crossed in chains, plays as metaphor for all the Porfirian projects that sought
similarly to drag the nation forward into a global capitalist system. It is telling
that Díaz called for servants of the nation, rather than allies or soldiers.

The military's historical context sets the stage as I examine how the leva
intersected with communities and the national state and how the public viewed
the army and demonstrate ways that prospective soldiers rejected service.
Taking men into the army persisted as a contention between the modernizing
state and the individual and his family, even as the Porfirian regime claimed
to leave old practices behind. Conscription demonstrated the profound power
and actual limits of the evolving nation to shape the citizen subject.

More abstractly, the governing elite worked at consolidating an ideal armed forces built on the ideal soldier figure of "le militaire." This elusive archetype formed from the conscript taken as object of the surveillance and vessel of new power relations. He, and the gendering was deliberate, became first and foremost a soldier-icon of the perfected citizen. Obedient and faceless masculinity dressed up doll-like and set to clockwork maneuvers held no threat to the regime, and offered much promise. This represented an orchestrated fantasy of the elite that clearly categorized national subjects as citizens, soldiers as objects, and all others as outsiders. As power passed through the fixed locality of the barracks it left upon the conscript the nation's indelible brand. New technologies of control also tied to new spaces and to power over now-modern bodies.[4] This conception underlies discussions of discipline and identity formation throughout the chapter.

The Background for Recruitment

The speed of the affair stunned Diego. Now it all seemed all too obvious, the town whispers, the filled jailhouse, and everyone's odd behavior that morning. At least broadly, he understood that the recruitment detachment (piquete) had swept him up with all of these other men. So it had always gone. His family, never lucky, had given brothers, husbands, and sons to the armies for generations. They had fought Spanish, American, and French invaders, they had fought for and against Liberals, but mostly they had fought simply because the levy had come for them and they had no choice. Few had returned, and Diego's family shared stories filled with glorious feats and horrible battles. The older men in town argued that those days had passed and today's soldiers had become mere thugs. "In truth," his abuela had once told him, "no one ever really knew what happened to those who disappeared." Rumors in town even said that the leva violated the law, but so what? None dared speak up, since after all, the recruiters happily devoured "complainers" too. "So it has always been," sighed Diego's mother.

The smoldering embers and smoking rubble left in the wake of nineteenth-century invasions by Spanish, American, and French armies began to fade into memory after 1867. President Benito Juárez (1858–1872) made attempts to reestablish Mexico as nation and as state. Creating order throughout the country became the central focus for the government, and the army was the primary tool in hand. In their own way, nonetheless, its officers became foremost among the president's obstacles. He could not afford to keep them, nor worse still, to demobilize them. From a height of seventy thousand men, Juárez worked to cut his forces down below forty thousand.[5] Critics lambasted the rising wave of banditry in the countryside and crime in the cities as unemployed soldiers found new means to survive.[6] Federal budgets fell short of even paying those troops still in service, let alone providing stability, and international creditors remained leery, especially after what they considered the barbaric execution of Emperor Maximilian.[7] The political power of the military as an institution exacerbated this dangerous situation.

The dangerously ambitious army and its officers did not appear out of nowhere. Since the colonial period (at least) the military had stood as one leg of what later Liberals termed the "baleful trinity" of power: the church, the hacienda, and the armed forces. Indeed, as the ultimate in power brokers, the military continued to provide generals to the presidency—with few notable exceptions, like Juárez, the leaders of the republic were high-ranking officers from Independence until the 1940s. In the vision of the national-era Conservatives this made sense, but it also did so to those of more Liberal bent.

Fear of the indigenous masses underlay a common agenda for both parties in the nineteenth century. To the Conservatives a strong military served as the basis for checking dangerously uncontrollable mobs like the ones that had sacked the granary of Guanajuato in 1810 or burned the Parián markets in 1828. The latter event also caused elite reformers to question the loyalty of the average soldiers whose *cuartelazo* (barracks uprising) had contributed to a lack of armed repression of popular unrest.[8] Officers therefore enacted a new sort of prison style in the barracks, envisioning a blandly nonracial army locked into barracks that cut them off from the streets. Politics happened outside insulated penal fortresses, or so they hoped. This army enabled the ruling class to quell unrest among the masses until such time as they became civilized under the aegis of the church and, possibly, a new monarch. Ultimately, men with guns empowered the guiding hand of the state.

The Liberals, in contrast, sought to accelerate the process of assimilation and civilizing through reform of land tenure, removal of church influence, and broader education of the poor—they nevertheless also opted to keep the military ready until the people matured into responsible modern citizens. At least rhetorically, a strand of populist Liberals did call for an alliance with lower classes based on suspicion of elites and patricians, yet in policy and practice this often fell short due to deep-seated prejudices.[9] Conservatives and most Liberals based their vision of the nation on a shared distrust of the lower classes. For both groups the perils of unchecked indigenous violence required containment, and only in their means of shaping new citizens did they differ. Until the late 1850s, the two visions of national inclusion manifested in civil wars and coup d'états, and with a final Liberal victory coming into sight the Conservatives played their last gambit by inviting a foreign invasion to install a European Hapsburg as monarch. Years of guerrilla warfare armed the much-feared masses and culminated with the execution of Emperor Maximilian in 1867. With the monarch's politically fraught death by firing squad came new challenges for the reinstalled Juárez regime.

Finally victorious against its Conservative and foreign enemies, the rather bloated and oversized Restoration-era (1867–1876) army asserted both moral and practical claims to the stewardship of the nation. Juárez could no more abandon his soldiers than they could betray him, the iconic symbol of their triumph. As he cut their ranks, he therefore needed to consider his policies carefully. The result echoed through the next half century as his regime resurrected the *depósito* (deposit), a compromise that allowed officers to remain in semi-active service on less pay rather than ignominious mass discharge.[10]

The depósito is a concept with intriguing connections to other realms of daily life. The term referred also to safe houses for abused women, to the shelving spaces in the mortuary, and, at least in Brazil, to the turntable used for anonymously abandoning babies at orphanages. It connoted the removal and storage of the unwanted and useless and helpless. The military depósito absorbed the old generations of unneeded officers, who kept their claims to honors and received partial payments of salary. The government saved money and also required the officers to maintain a known residence and present themselves regularly to the local garrison. In other words, the deposited veterans lost the freedom of mobility and anonymity that might tempt them into political interference, and for many, the struggle to receive their pensions from the intricacies of bureaucracy became consuming. With low rates of pay based on service records, many officers made grandiose claims of having participated in every battle and skirmish that had taken place in their lifetime, in hopes of earning bonuses. Had all of these deposited warriors fought at half of the conflicts they boasted about, outsiders would never have invaded Mexico successfully. For many old officers the deposit at least provided some means of living and keeping their dignity. By contrast, the petitions and pleas of ordinary troops to retain their occupations largely fell on deaf ears. Slowly the military corroded into an echelon of the highly aged and highly ranked.[11]

The army continued to decline in effective numbers through the end of the 1860s and the subsequent presidency of Sebastián Lerdo de Tejada (1872–1876).

The exigencies of control over an unruly countryside made armed forces a high priority as the army chased bandits, secured borders, and suppressed rebellions. Border issues related closely to banditry and spoke to the highly unfixed nature of the nation's edges. Direct communication and transportation between central Mexico and the north or southeast remained spotty at best. Northern towns and their militias operated within loosely construed bounds of law and quite outside the control of the federal government.[12] The Restoration did mark a turning point. Frightened by the near catastrophe of the Yucatecan Caste War (1846–1848), exasperated by the endemic banditry, and anticipating a US annexation of Baja California, the Lerdo administration worked hard to build border stability. It authorized and supported patriotic regional militias, including the National Guard, and expanded Juárez's corps of rurales (rural paramilitary police).[13] Yet in the aftermath of Maximilian's execution a lack of foreign trust and investment left the national coffers bare. Bandits flourished, US border troops pursued enemies into Mexico with impunity, arms from Belize flowed to Mayan discontents, and northern militarized communities in the Sierras showed no deference to the republic (see chapter 8). The arming and support of local militias built security but came at the cost of empowering the patrias chicas against the national regime. Military cuts only made this worse. As the Lerdo budgets and senior staff discharged more and more federal troops into unemployment, they also pushed many soldiers back into local employment with National Guard units.[14]

The dangers of this policy became obvious when one hero of the guard, Porfirio Díaz, used his connections to seize power in 1876 with his rebellion at Tuxtepec. The new president ironically had rebelled on the platform of "no reelections." He would subsequently serve from 1876 to 1910, aside from a brief presidential interregnum in 1880–1884 handled by his close friend Manuel González as a political sleight of hand. With Díaz's reascension to power in 1884 it seemed to observers that a new era of modernizing and progress could realistically arrive.

Expectations swelled among common soldiers as the energetic Oaxacan general took the reins. Many, especially fellow Oaxaqueños, felt a special bond with the charismatic warrior who had played a major role in defeating the French invaders.[15] Old enough for wisdom, young enough for dynamism, Díaz seemed to promise better days for the average soldier, whether rurale, reservist, or regular. High hopes notwithstanding, his vision for the armed forces proved markedly different. The federal army became the agent to impose order and progress, the antagonist of the patrias chicas, and a new secular priesthood of modernity. Officers' first steps streamlined the modernized national army in part by neglecting or disbanding the regional Guard forces. Díaz's own, more prudent, policies eviscerated the Guard units, as had been done to Juárez's federal forces, and that eventually fomented a recruitment crisis.[16] By the 1880s, new troops would be in high demand.

Díaz's government built a modern army. His forces, micromanaged from Mexico City, at times followed and at times inspired reforms that the US military enacted and borrowed selectively from the "advanced" armies of Europe. His priorities regarding the National Guard seemed clear as he federalized their forces (much as the United States had done). Díaz proclaimed his desire that the troops "be relieved of their current duties so that the men might go back to industry and to agriculture."[17] Regional militias and suspect National Guard units faced asphyxiation as the government slowly choked off supplies and funds at the end of an increasingly tight leash. This flew in the face of a tradition of local militias that flourished long before the Bourbon Reforms of the late colonial period in New Spain, before it became Mexico in 1821.

Overcoming regional military traditions posed a challenge to modern military doctrine that sought to instill the national regime with the sole claim to legitimate use of violence. Contrary to convention, recent studies have begun to reveal the importance of indigenous militias in maintaining the colony's security.[18] By the late 1700s these units had largely disbanded and municipally based militias and regular force garrisons took their place, many becoming the basis for the National Guard in the aftermath of the Independence Wars. Their existence proved problematic for a centralizing government, as local loyalty to the patria chica trumped national unity and as the militias offered too much power to caudillo strongmen whose agendas often clashed with the larger state. Quite aware of this, Díaz used neglect to undermine their power and build his own, even if some areas remained resistant long into his reign.

The regime also regularized its relationship with the troublesome US border in a surprisingly old-fashioned, even feudal, way. Leaders from each side visited the others' encampments with all the pomp and ceremony that protocol demanded; this ritual demonstrated a shared language and understanding of military lore that communicated equality.[19] By 1881 the connections between the two frontier militaries took a further stride closer as Mexican general Jerónimo Treviño married the daughter of US brigadier general Edward Ord.[20] Significantly, Ord had previously been a major proponent of annexing Mexico, a stance mitigated greatly by his new position as father-in-law to a tremendously wealthy and influential political officer who officially feted him during a tour of Mexico City.

Dissidents, bandits, and indigenous rebels by the 1890s had fewer sanctuaries when they could not cross international borders, and troops now pursued them to the finish. The new Mexican army, consolidated and modernizing, could focus on cleaning up banditry (often loosely defined) and tie the nation together as a coherent whole. This came in no small part through the practice of conscription.

Patrias chicas and local communities faced persistent onslaught as their men disappeared to distant barracks, strange soldiers occupied their towns, and their own militias faded through federal neglect. Porfirio Díaz's visions of a scientific, European-like modernity relied on this regulation of militarized manhood. Centralizing power and radiating it back through technologies of rail and telegraph, the modern regime rose. It organized its forces with new bureaucratic emphases, under formalized army echelons, and worked to make the army a mechanical tool for producing order. On the federal stage, this also depended on the dissolution of regional loyalties and capacities. Aggressive recruitment became a priority and facilitated nation building while enfeebling the strongmen and caudillos away from Mexico City. Critical to this achievement was that the peasants and criminals absorbed into the army would depart it radically transformed in loyalties and civilized in behavior.

The favored fantasy of the elite looked abroad for inspiration, largely to European models. In the most ideal terms they would build an army of dedicated volunteers steeped in patriotism and trained to effective violence, paid primarily with food and nationalism. The soldiers would surrender their ethnic and class loyalties. They would never again surrender to invading foes. As the embodiment of the nation, each citizen-soldier represented a piece of creating a modern and stable Mexico in the shape the elite determined. Deadly warriors, conditioned and trained in the use of cutting-edge weapons, the new troops would provide the means to guarantee the discipline and order the country needed.

The cultural and material obstacles the Porfirian regime faced in implementing this dream lay at the roots of the recruit's experience. The budgetary weakness of the government ran through several phases. Initially, the near bankruptcy of the government saw troops continue to decline in numbers and benefits, many lacking pay entirely, between 1876 and 1880.[21] With the restoration of credit and a balanced budget, after 1885 the army saw gradual improvements in conditions and more-regular pay. Troop numbers stabilized. From an official low of around twenty thousand men in 1881 to a brief peak at thirty thousand in 1886, they hovered near twenty-five thousand through the rest of the Porfiriato. Total figures are highly suspect, due to over-reporting for the sake of national security and prestige, shame over desertion rates, and officers skimming pay. But effective numbers aside, using the figures given by the secretary of war to Congress at least provides a somewhat reliable base figure with which to estimate change.[22]

Even with bigger budgets, change came slowly. With too many officers drawing pay in depósito and general indifference to soldiers' conditions, advances were matters of degree rather than profound reforms taking advantage of new funds. As budgets grew, so too did graft and corruption, and a soldier in 1910 was only marginally better off than his 1876 counterpart had been. Yet making a successful armed service did not depend solely on economic efforts. Creating a modern ideal soldier also required building public support for the military institution.

Witnesses to the poor conditions of soldiery, many civilians maintained disdainful and disgusted attitudes toward the military as a profession, and potential recruits generally shared their distaste. The cultural obstacle to creating the modern army emerged from the near complete failure of the regime to persuade average Mexicans that military service could be honorable and desirable. In lieu of volunteers, the regime felt compelled to levy troops, engendering resistance to official visions of nation—not least among the newest "servants of the nation." For the average young man, the prospect of becoming a soldier, particularly at sword point, had little appeal.

Loathing the Leva

They sat at the edge of the town square in front of the church, where the village whipping post had stood not so many years ago. Waiting in his chains, Diego finally stopped fidgeting and looked around at his fellow recruits. Pressed in next to him sat a stranger, an indigenous man who had come to town recently from the north looking for work. On the other side, old Domingo, who had lost most of a hand some years ago in an accident and now spent his days lounging near the cantina. Surely a sixty-year-old with one working hand and a drinking problem couldn't become a soldier? With relief, Diego did see one boy his own age also in the line. Pedro was odd, a bit simple really, and so seeing him taken for the army also seemed strange, but Diego assumed that the teenager's

always-drunk parents had struck some deal with town officials. They owed
everyone in town something, or maybe Pedro otherwise could have hidden from
the scarred and scowling sergeant who now loomed over them. The presence of
José María perhaps surprised Diego most. The guy always talked about joining
up voluntarily, but here he sat in chains. It made little sense, and Diego was not
sure he wanted him along—in town everyone knew José María's family as dan-
gerous people, and travelers nearing their farm did so at their own risk. The
villagers tolerated this, so long as they themselves felt safe, but no one really
trusted them. Diego waited for the soldiers to turn away and whispered a quick
question: "Why?" The shifty young man winked back and pointed to the nearest
soldier's shiny new Remington rifle. "You'll see," he hissed back with a smirk.

So much that Diego still couldn't understand, but his mind raced with the
thoughts of all the cities and places he might see. Perhaps José María's attitude
would not prove misplaced? Maybe army life would not be so bad. Maybe he
could go to the capital itself, with its palaces, cathedrals, and wonders! He
resolved to himself, though, that when he came back he would not become like
Tómas, the veteran soldier who bragged and drank every night in the town
square and bothered everyone. No, when he came home he'd have nice clothes,
real shoes, and maybe even money to take care of his family. He'd take care of his
mother. Lost in his daydreams, he almost missed it when the sergeant ordered
them to their feet. The time had come.

The leva had plagued poor Mexicans since the Bourbon Reforms of the eighteenth century.[23] It continued to do so during the Porfiriato despite official
claims of the implementation of a new policy of volunteers and *sorteo* (a lottery system). While in theory a *reemplazo* (replacement) or substitute recruit
could be purchased by anyone for a mere forty pesos, this represented a pro-
hibitively high figure for many. As a strange coincidence, this figure matched
the cost of a first-class burial—a commentary perhaps on the assigned value
of a life in Porfirian Mexico.[24] This option also required finding a willing
substitute from a community already (presumably) combed over for recruits.
The petitioners also had to have knowledge of the procedures and paperwork
the military required to process the request. This made the leva much more
difficult to evade.

Moreover, examining the troops taken, it becomes evident that the leva
acted also as an instrument of class discipline and eventually as a means to
blunt the rise of politically active—and threatening—industrial, middle, and
urban classes.[25] From a near-standing start, the country experienced a

significant development of industry that accelerated between the 1890s and 1910. While class struggle did not emerge as a real threat early on, by the turn of the century new worker classes began to clash with the entrenched wealthy capitalists, to the horror of a nascent and insecure middle class. The military had little to do with urban or factory unrest in the early Porfiriato, but it was not coincidental that the drive toward a modernized and professional military rose alongside the growth of new social tensions.[26]

With urbanization and industrialization, the army and its recruitment policies produced four major effects that worked to counter new forms of unrest. First, military service absorbed a body of young men that otherwise might have become part of the new industrial classes, particularly as these men came from the poorest of families in both rural and urban settings— prime worker material.[27] Despite the need for workers, the army continued to siphon away, for a time, the impressionable youth of the country. Military service reduced the sheer numbers of unemployed or underemployed men in their late teens to midtwenties. Rather than joining in with transient rural labor (the *población flotante*) or moving into cities with uncertain job prospects, these men instead spent years under the close supervision of officers. They did not become radical miners or anarcho-syndicalist manufacturers as they otherwise might have. Much as in punitive penitentiaries, the barracks removed potential troublemakers from the temptations of dissent. Rarely did soldiers side with strikers when conflict arose.

Second, officers noted that teaching these men discipline filled the prescription for eventually providing new industries with ideal workers. After five years of drill in arms, the former soldier could become the ordered factory worker without sympathies for anarchist unions and replace the disruptive elements. The ideas and challenges of factory discipline mimicked in many ways the life of regimen that the soldier, or former soldier, presumably internalized. Many armies still use this logic in recruitment advertisements today. Some among the elite assumed the obedient and unquestioning subject of military discipline would stand opposite the unruly and dangerously political shop-floor anarchist. Once he finished his honorable term in military service, the soldier would become the perfected worker in the nation's expanding industrial sectors.

Third, the expansion of working classes had created rising tensions that soldiers met with arms and bloodshed with increasing frequency as industry built in importance. The use of armed force against protesters reached a climax in 1906 and 1907, as soldiers massacred strikers at Cananea and Rio

Blanco.[28] Military service thus not only absorbed young men away from industrial work but also provided the means to suppress unrest. Politicians called on the troops to fire upon their own people and expected that they would do so without hesitation. The presumption came from a new understanding of the army as solely the tool of the state. It was not only in Mexico that modernizing military organization along nationalist (as opposed to regional) lines and inculcating a sense of absolute duty to the republic appeared as an objective.

Armed forces throughout the industrializing world underwent similar reforms in terms of new technologies, new regulations, and new recruitment schemes from the late nineteenth century into the early twentieth. This was not mere coincidence. By the turn of the century similar social pressures worked against the continuation of liberal oligarchic capitalism, at least in the form it had taken, with widespread disenfranchisement of the emerging working class. The period of readjustment occasioned by industrial unrest proved likewise similar in its symptoms, as a reformed and modernized military violently repressed worker unrest. A few examples of American strikes thus broken include the following: in Chile at Valparaiso (1903); at the Pullman strike in Illinois, United States (1894); in Chile again at Antofagasta (1906) and Iquique (1907); and with "la semana tragica" in Buenos Aires, Argentina (1912). In all of these cases, as with the Mexican examples above, the military followed orders with exemplary obedience to the national dictate in the interest of the bourgeois classes. The use of the leva to create a military apparatus that fulfilled the needs of the industrial order first, rather than those of local powers, worked to consolidate the new political economic system.

Fourth and finally, the use of the army as a supplemental labor force for building roads and public building allowed the direct replacement of hostile corvée workers with a presumably more controllable lot. Previous local arrangements for public works had often made use of the same vagrants who now fulfilled the leva quota. They typically angered communities and proved unreliable and unmotivated, particularly as municipalities or town elites used their labor without offering much (or anything) in payment. In contrast, the federal military garrisons that sprouted up in many Porfirian villages became a common workforce under the orders of officers who many times abused the privilege to enrich themselves. Soldiers did the work, if grudgingly, and had limited recourse beyond grumbling. This did win accolades on occasion, particularly when troops came in to help with disaster relief. In theory at least, this arrangement could also smooth relations between the populace and the federal government, but in practice it often highlighted the abuse of authority enjoyed by some corrupt officers.

None of these measures, however convenient for the capitalist elite, made military service popular among the poor. In the end, the leva continued to push young, poor men into a life not of their choice. The system disproportionately victimized the least powerful in society.

The impoverished knew their vulnerability to any opportunistic public official, but so too did dissidents, migrants, cripples, and those deemed deviant. The short path from vagrant to soldier haunted those down on their luck and afflicted those who did not fit in with other townsfolk. While the vast majority of recruits came from rural communities, cities and towns also gathered what officials termed "contingents of blood" for the army. The new recruits overwhelmingly represented the central areas of the Bajío and the Valley of Mexico, while southern and northern states tended to have fewer contingents, even in proportional measures of population. Sources show a predominance of recruiting from Mexico (state and city), Hidalgo, Jalisco, Guanajuato, Queretaro, Tlaxcala, Colima, Michoacán, San Luis Potosí, Zacatecas, Puebla, and Veracruz. While the army recruited soldiers elsewhere, it did so less frequently and officers generally exempted areas with active uprisings as providing less-trusted troops.[29]

Mexicans hated the leva for its method of implementation, its implications for family, and the harsh conditions that soldiers were likely to face.[30] In contrast to attitudes toward European systems of compulsory military service, responses to the leva went well beyond mere distaste; it was one of the most despised institutions of the Porfirian era. Even policies of forced deportation, such as those faced by Yaquis, did not create the nationwide sense of fear and disgust that the leva built.[31] Indeed, the leva represented a forced deportation in its own right, as it seized men from their homes and sent them to faraway garrisons. The institution offended most citizens' senses of liberty, eroded trust in the government, highlighted the lowliness of their status, and ultimately framed the army as the bane, the nemesis, of the people whom it purportedly served.

The selection process engendered a sense of deep injustice and vulnerability among the most likely candidates for the leva. In contrast to service in more prestigious local militias or National Guard units, people generally saw recruitment to federal forces as shameful. The politics of the leva saw its victims selected as a means to exercise power over a community, disciplining, commanding, and punishing those whom authorities picked and, by extension, their families or supporters. Meeting the quota set by the secretary of war, state governors and the *jefes de reemplazos* (chief recruiting officers) sent orders to regional jefes políticos, who either delegated the task to municipal officials or personally worked to gather the needed men. Generally there was one jefe de reemplazo in each of the twenty-eight states and territories, usually a lieutenant colonel or colonel, who worked closely with the governor.

Local officials, and particularly the jefes políticos, used this power to control constituents though the threat or practice of adding men to the list for recruitment. Ironically, the jefe's only official duty connected to the military was to prevent any attempts to take recruits by force. Although occasionally the jefes políticos acted as intermediaries between local civil and larger military commands, more generally the army acted as an apparently objective balance against embedded jefes seen by locals as corrupt and discriminatory.[32]

Under pressure from above to secure replacements for troops discharged, dead, or deserted, many officials looked first to empty their jails or to discard weak or lazy workers and in the last resort offered impoverished men from the community least able to resist. Among them came many with serious health issues, but officially doctors often overlooked ailments in the interest of meeting quotas. For example, in 1889 medics detailed the health of incoming recruits, noting about a 9.8 percent rate of rejection based on health, mostly for hernias, bad constitutions, weak legs, heart defects, high obesity, and obvious syphilis. Only nineteen of seven thousand were rejected for alcoholism.[33] At times they even sent men with missing limbs, congenitally ill, or obviously diseased, despite the likelihood that medical staff would eventually reject them. The quota had to be met. A blood contingent of dissatisfied, angry, criminal, crippled, or undernourished illiterates became a near inevitability. The young recruit saw this firsthand.

Yet numerous accounts reflect the tenuous position of the jefe político. In Tulancingo Puebla, for example, a jefe named Silva raised the ire of residents by refusing to hear their complaints. This resulted in an armed uprising and the arrest of both Silva and the local military detachment.[34] In point of fact, the jefes políticos frequently overstepped their authority in the leva process. They legally had no jurisdiction to incarcerate recruits, to work with or command army units, or to order compliance with the leva. Occasional charges of abusing authority resulted from the frequent failures of the jefes to follow these strictures.

They nevertheless stood to profit from well-planned recruiting, removing political enemies and even, in one case, conscripting a sixty-year-old man in order to steal his land.[35] Additionally, when jefes circumvented local authorities, particularly the municipal presidents, they stripped communities of the power to police their own population. While perspectives on those who deserved consignment sometimes aligned, for example in the case of criminals, the political or economic abuses of the leva by an outsider infuriated many communities.[36] At times the jefe overstepped community norms.

The patria chica had long operated with a set of expectations that included relative autonomy and acceptance of federal commands on their own terms. Practices including law enforcement and taxation customarily followed the lead of local traditions. Expectations became semisacred. In even the poorest towns some families, luckier or wealthier than others, attained a protected status against outside interventions. When this or similar presumptions fell afoul of ignorant or indifferent authorities it sparked crises of moral economy. Jefes need not trespass against the law to incur rebellions based on failed expectations. Townsfolk chose which injustices required stoic acceptance and which they would resist, violently if necessary. Their anger echoed in the opposition of the "better classes" to conscription.

The seemingly arbitrary selection of recruits dismayed even the most stalwart defenders of the military, yet calls for reform fell afoul of the Porfirian elites' class prejudices. Further, in a nation only beginning to regain its economic strength, removing the best and brightest of the elite classes from the active economy might deliver a crippling blow to business and development. If *gente decente* were to serve under universal service alongside the usual dregs, would this not corrupt the best youth of society?[37] In the words of one writer, it was impossible to have good and well-educated youths "share a barracks, let alone a room, with the promiscuity and moral dangers of the drunk, the petty thief, and the criminal," as it would "extinguish [his] not very well cemented habits of work and morality."[38] Other writers added that truly universal service would create an enormous and expensive army that really had no threatening enemy and worried about what foe it would manufacture domestically.[39] New foreign invasions seemed far from likely. Surely, they argued, money could be better spent on education and building commerce, in order that these men with an education in nationalism since primary school could ply trades to improve the country. Men like Porfirio Díaz agreed. Middle- and upper-class women could, as mothers and teachers, become the primary inculcators of the new nationalism without risking good sons to the hardships and vices of the barracks.[40] The better classes persuaded themselves that becoming modern in barracks, however necessary to the nation's progress, introduced a corruptive element best borne by the poor.

As such, the gente decente expected that the lower class should surrender their sons willingly to the army despite this being a fate too morally questionable for their own kin. The vulnerable classes knew from experience that they faced the loss of good lads, having seen the return of men turned vicious and vice ridden, or not returning at all. As one witness explained, "Then they took them, took them to other parts far from here, to the central states, there were some who returned again, others never came back."[41] When a recruit departed with the chain gang, the community mourned and prayed for his return and feared that the man who came home would not be the same one who left. To ask that the family simply trust the army to take care of their child's immortal soul and bodily health must have seemed extreme when the boys disappeared down the road under guard and in shackles. The distrust and disdain of gente decente for ordinary soldiers differed little from that of the poor. This negative opinion the underclasses shared, especially those who had not aspired to become soldiers in the first place.

To be chosen, taken, and corrupted, as they saw it, seemed nothing less than a masculine form of government-machinated *rapto y estupro* (kidnap and deflowering). The practice of stealing women from their homes, deflowering them, and eventually marrying them was long-standing and legally recognized during the Porfiriato.[42] Honor as a concept shaped gender roles and built on dichotomies in which shame, weakness, and femininity opposed courage, strength, and manliness. To be helpless before male watchers and subjected to their whims marked one as discursively feminine. Conscripts chosen specifically for their vulnerability and bound to public service lost the pretense of owning their own honor.

The meanings of the practice of rapto applied loosely to the experiences of conscripts. Often bound up in previous relations and correspondences, sometimes also a means to circumvent family desires, and occasionally a simple act of criminal violence, rapto functioned as a tradition of courtship. As a patriarchal form of power relations, it performed gender on intimate levels, yet also quite publicly. As a semilegal form of captivity narrative entrenched in the popular consciousness, it bears a strong resemblance to the processes of forced recruitment, and one that reversed the usual gendered expectations for men. This metaphor should not be stretched too far, of

FIGURE 1.1 Barracks of Tlatelolco, 2010. Photo by author.

course, as conscription was hardly on par with rape. Recruits nonetheless experienced forms of vulnerability that they had never faced previously. Forcibly carried off, physically overpowered and bereft of family, and publicly shamed by sergeants and officers, the newly dishonored soldier understood his profound powerlessness against the violation of the leva.

A military career set one at odds with "his people." The taking, public and violent, represented only the first stage of a process that fundamentally changed the man. Stripped of his "manly" agency, the recruit supposedly became an automaton of his officers through brutalization and isolation from ordinary society. The new soldier feared this transformation and resented being taken, even if he might not have seen the irony in the many cases in which he himself might face rapto charges later (see chapter 4). In the fictional cave hideout of the bandit El Zarco a rapto victim named Manuela famously realized her plight as she found her romantic sanctuary descending into a dark and hellish purgatory.[43] In similar fashion, the towering barracks walls of Tlatelolco trapped many new soldiers. There they encountered a site of rough living and harsh treatments that stripped away the innocence of village life, if such a thing existed. In both sites tough men remade their kidnapped inferiors through force and habit. Captives learned to surrender their will and to give up their pretense of personal choice.

The rapto metaphor might also have another application here. Women occasionally used or orchestrated the traditional rapto y estupro to their own advantage, pressuring their chosen into marriage. In cases where fathers objected to the courtship the rapto provided a means to legitimize the relationship. That is, some planned and chose to be taken away. Some new recruits chose likewise. A few saw a romantic element in the idea of returning home as a hard man, as a competent warrior, and perhaps even as a war hero. Others chose to accept military service for their own ends, whether financial or in search of adventure.[44]

Indeed, for all that the leva stirred hatred it undeniably also provided a few men a welcome escape. Although some men did volunteer, contrary to popular perceptions, their numbers represent an extremely limited number of the total forces. Nevertheless, their choice affords an interesting contrast to their more reluctant comrades in arms. The military offered certain advantages, allowing an already marginalized man to leave his community and perhaps make a living elsewhere. For sons of the poorest families an army life might become the best possible way to care for dependents. Numerous letters to Díaz indicate that this circumstance allowed some an opportunity that simply did not exist in their hometowns. Pleading with the president, León Martínez claimed he had never known any life other than soldiering and that after thirty years he had been discharged because of his age and now found himself in misery. He asked for new work, or at least for the government to review his service records and grant him a pension.[45] Pedro Ehlera wrote the president requesting reinstatement, since his discharge was unfair, and claimed he had no other means by which to provide for his family.[46] A twenty-two-year-old soldier from Puebla likewise asked to retain his position without further charges for a broken window, as his prison pay was scant (only twenty-five centavos daily) and his regular army pay provided the only support for his widowed mother and grandmother.[47] Low-ranked soldiers were not alone in their complaints. Sergeant Miguel Jiménez argued that his captain had suspended him for complaining and then discharged him for his further complaints.[48]

Volunteers committed to Mexican security also appeared from time to time. A few begged for positions in order to take part in what they saw as an inevitable war with Guatemala. The concern in 1885 that a war was brewing, which received considerable attention in the army and press, inspired men like Ignacio Gómez Cárdenas to volunteer to fight despite having no experience. Military service did appeal to a few, out of patriotic fervor for some, for others as a way out of prison or poverty.[49] From records and accounts it is difficult to construct the degree to which some soldiers truly took to the army life and how many simply made the best of a bad situation. Some did come to accept nationalist messages, especially as they developed a military identity through ritualized practices (see chapters 2 and 6). It is not unreasonable to assume that some did sign up to answer a call to duty. Family traditions, among all classes, also impelled army service. Yet on the whole, most recruits arrived in chains and fervor alone never filled the barracks.

Others seem to have taken to the army for more nefarious reasons. Troopers could, and did, take advantage of army service to steal rifles, clothes, and even horses on their way to joining or rejoining bandit gangs or rebel forces. If they got away, a successful "raid" of this sort could be worth as much as 300 pesos, close to a year's decent wages. Some recruits with similar motives in mind signed up under false names, a tactic that backfired horribly for one recruit who called himself Porfirio Caballero ("Porfirio the gentleman," perhaps a quip at the expense of the president). After being caught deserting, he completed his three-year term of service, at which time officers reentered him on the rolls for additional years of army life when they discovered his real name, Arcadio Ramírez.[50] In 1894 a soldier of the Second Regiment was likewise charged, among other things, with "change of name" before a formal council of war.[51] For others, there was a short step between desertions en masse and the formation of a bandit gang, as in the case of the Sixth Battalion in 1888. Most of its soldiers had originally been "enlisted" straight out of the Guadalajara prison, and General Pedro Galván reported that upon their desertion they had become the terror of Tepic.[52] Perhaps for a good many soldiers, the difference between banditry and army service lay in the relatively steady pay the former earned.

Still another reason one might be volunteered into service was the misfortune of having the wrong family. For some guardians of incorrigible young men, army service seemed a possible solution to reform their ways. One uncle, despairing of his nephew as obstinate, impassive, and lazy, wrote to Díaz asking that the boy be sent to the navy to become a man of worth.[53] He asked that this enlistment happen soon, before the boy became lost and fell to even greater depths, but it was apparently too late; in a letter the next month he reported his nephew had since been jailed for robbery.[54] Mothers wrote the president or senior officers to ask for positions for their sons for the financial or moral sake of the family. In these cases, the sons rarely made their own pleas, and it might be assumed that many had no idea what their mothers tried to do for (or to) them. Yet for all these exceptions, the army largely remained a destination both feared and loathed, and the usual situation victimized the unlucky.

Of Rumors and Anticipation

With a shout, they moved out. Leaving Diego's mother behind, soldiers chivvied the raw recruits down the road with slaps, kicks, and curses until finally the village fell out of sight. Ear ringing from the yelling and blows, Diego did his best to keep pace. He could feel the pitying eyes of the townsfolk on him and his chain mates. He could still hear his mother as they marched along; her sobbing added to his feelings of doom and fear. In the shadowed windows of the "better" families' houses he spied other young men his age watching from hiding. He hoped they felt some shame, as he angrily spat in the dust. The town disappeared behind the dust they kicked up from the narrow road and soon fell out of sight entirely. Mile after mile they trudged. Mounted troopers kept pace alongside and ignored them save for the occasional curse or kick to those who slowed. When evening fell, the soldiers and sergeant ate and laid out thin sleeping blankets. Those in the cuerda watched without shelter, and Diego finally slept despite his damp shivering and grumbling stomach. For days they marched on; only a few times did they get some bread and a bit of water from the guards. Other groups joined theirs as they went, troopers escorting similar chains of sad-looking men. A particularly well-dressed soldier in a sharply pressed blue uniform joined them after a week or so, and the cuerda's food improved suddenly and markedly. Diego belatedly realized that this must be their officer. When they finally came to a great city with dozens of buildings, he gasped through his exhaustion and wondered aloud if they could see the Cathedral Basilica of the Virgin from here. The soldiers all laughed, and the sergeant (with another cuff) informed him that this "little dung heap" was not, in fact, Mexico City.

The cuerda marched on, loaded onto a train car, and set off. To Diego and most of the others the ride came as a first, exhilarating for its velocity and noise and stench but also terrifying—everyone had heard of how the gringos who drove these things frequently sent them off cliffs to show their hatred of good Catholics. With some relief, they finally rolled into the city amid a bewildering chaos of cattle, pilgrims, and crowds. Great ornate buildings rose on all sides, the noise and clatter of carts on cobblestones echoing among them. The sounds of music, animals, children, and commerce filled the busy streets. The cuerda split then. Diego never again saw old Domingo or shifty José María, and simple Pedro not for some years. They formed up and again marched through the streets. Now the shame returned, too. Filthy, smelling, and ragged from days on the road, Diego and his fellow half-starved conscripts shuffled in rusting chains through avenues filled with onlookers. He, all of them, became a blushing spectacle for bystanders predisposed to think the worst of soldiers. The chains informed the average civilian that the military ranks contained all of the evilest criminals in the nation—Diego overheard a mother telling her child that "these scum would not wear shackles if they did not deserve it." Bleerily, and maybe through a few tired tears, the high stone walls of some ancient church or nunnery came into sight. Its twelve-foot doorways opened as a dark and gaping mouth to swallow Diego and his fellows. Who knew what horrors awaited within?

Popular rumors, press criticisms, deserters' tales, and public sightings reinforced the negative, and mostly accurate, preconceptions of the vida militar. However much recruits hated the selection process, the daily grind and poor conditions of army life represented the greater dread for any soldier. Even the rare volunteers must have suspected that they faced a bleak life, poor pay, bad sanitation, surly officers, dangerous fights, and frequent punishment. Even though he was a teenager at the time, Trinidad Vega remembered in a later interview how they viewed the military in his small town. He recalled that some, having only failed to pay a debt, would be sent to the army to face extreme mistreatment. He remembered that this punishment represented the greatest terror of the people, a truly horrible threat, and went on to describe how poorly the men were treated, how inadequately they were paid, and how degenerate they all appeared to civilians.[55] Another eyewitness to the era, Ignacio Súarez, recalled seeing a cuerda being marched down the streets in downtown Mexico City. He saw what they called an army contingent and described them as drained and heartbroken peasants marching under the guns of vigilant guards. Traumatized by the sight, he asked his mother about them, and some sixty years later he felt that the elimination of the leva alone might have prevented the Revolution.[56]

The popular view of the military emerged from a combination of scandalous media coverage and common sights such as the chain gang of the blood contingent. The fetters and slave-like connotations contributed to the sense of shame that the military spectacle could bring. The recruits, seemingly criminals, arrived at their destinations in filthy and often-half-starved conditions, having marched for days or weeks. Many, as the previous section indicated, did not begin their journey in a state of robust health. The public scenario did not occur by chance but rather constituted part of the process of breaking recruits prior to beginning their training regime. Nonetheless, the image presented to bystanders did nothing to dispel common perceptions of the army as a shameful and lowly institution. Military parades and other positive portrayals ultimately failed to bring the same visceral response that the cuerda engendered among ordinary people in the garrisoned cities.

Similarly, the mainly middle-class press made no secret of its opinions on military life and the brutal conditions of the common soldier. Newspapers pointed to the savage fighting and alcohol abuse that marked barracks as spaces of ill repute and gleefully commented on the lowly soldaderas (see chapter 3).[57] *La Patria* described the horrible state of the Twenty-Fourth Battalion, on service at the National Palace with threadbare, dirty uniforms unsuited to the season.[58] The vociferously critical *Regeneración* frequently printed articles sarcastically titled "Military Gallantry" in which the authors attacked the abuses of officers toward soldiers, and soldiers toward civilians.[59] These represent but a few examples of the hundreds of stories depicting the unsavory nature of military service that the Porfirian press presented to its middle- and upper-class readership.[60] Every drunken brawl and every lovers' quarrel received scurrilous detailing in papers that reinforced the preconceptions of the readers. The uncontrolled soldier became the antithesis of the good citizen, and the wild barracks the opposite of the honorable home.

Press critiques emphasized the distance between the gente decente, with their presumed civility, and the bestial nature of the lower-class soldier. The imagining of a threatening underclass reinforced by contrast the rhetoric of progress and order, but it also created an image of the army that clashed with its official representations as the embodiment of the modern (see chapter 7).[61] The apparent gap between modern army and savage soldier nonetheless suggested the possibility of civilizing the indigenous and poor through the application of proper military discipline. This impulse to perfect subjects through institutions of control, as described by Michel Foucault, constructed quintessential modernity.[62] Surveillance, bureaucracy, and regulation promised to perfect the new, obedient subject. Without public support few would choose such a life. But once again, newspaper portrayals themselves did nothing to enhance the prestige of the vida militar.

The role of the army in securing a sense of peace or order in the cities rarely played a prominent part in newspaper accounts. Assurances by officials that they safely incarcerated new recruits in their barracks had little credibility. Residents encountered soldiers in neighborhoods around the barracks on a daily basis, although by regulation they should not have. The unsanctioned escapes from the boredom and discipline of the barracks increased local prejudices against the soldiers; after all, the thinking went, they would not have been taken in the leva without some reason. The press took up this complaint about the troops, denigrating their lack of civility, as part of solidifying the respectability of the new middle classes by contrast. The Black Chronicles, a common periodical column, gleefully told of the malfeasances of lower-class public criminality and often remarked on soldiers and their women. While most recruits would not have read these columns, every misstep they took would become part of the literate community's perception of the soldier class.

Beyond chance meetings with troops in the street, ordinary Mexicans learned of the soldier's life through the most popular media of their day. Folk songs and other popular verses provided an oral tradition, with occasional printed lyrics and broadsheets, which worked as political pamphlets on issues of the day. In verses sung or recited in public venues the military life and its various injustices became well known to the broader public.[63] Public spectacles of the recruit cuerda, the military parade, and the firing squad further developed a complex vision. The army appeared to take unsavory types and polish them into exemplars of modern manhood, and at the same time crime and executions belied the success of this process. To the lower classes, soldiers seemed robust, proud, well fed, and well shod—they also seemed violent, vice ridden, and imprisoned. The discursive gap between the ideal modern warrior and the typical ill-treated recruit could not be easily bridged.

The army did itself no favors in reinforcing these popular impressions by using military service itself as a means of punishment. Soldiers accused of bad conduct regularly saw time added to their five-year term, *pour encourager les autres* (for the encouragement of witnesses). Officers rarely justified this addition as intended to "repair" behaviors; they clearly stated it as the punishment that the troops felt it represented. Units already infamous for poorly disciplined troops or terrible conditions, rather than becoming the object for reforms, became the destination for wrongdoers dropped from better battalions and regiments. For example, everyone knew that the Ninth Cavalry Regiment and the Sixth Battalion of Infantry were dumping grounds for the incorrigible.[64] The circle thus became complete: the leva swept up citizens deemed potentially criminal, placed them in circumstances and associations likely to lead them into breaking regulations, tried them on assumptions and arbitrary rulings, and assigned them back to the military as punishment for their misdeeds. A hierarchy of units appeared in the military's common lore, and some postings clearly held more prestige than others. The disease-ridden battalions of the Yucatán and coastal areas became the ultimate garbage heap for the worst cases, drawing everything from suspected murderers to rebellious officers, incorrigible slackers, political dissidents, and public transvestites.

The Yucatán saw the frequent arrival of what the military command considered worst cases, and troops popularly, if inaccurately, considered it a one-way voyage due to tropical diseases. In a nation that did not normally allow a death sentence for crimes, how could the recruit and his comrades understand this kind of sentence? Any officers who failed in rebellion, or succeeded in dissent, also faced the prospect of transfer to the "pestiferous" southeast.[65] Nonetheless, officers did not universally despise these positions, and active service there boosted the careers of such men as Brigadier Generals Mariano Ruiz and Victoriano Huerta. Mariano Ruiz left a successful stint as a congressman to command in the Yucatán, for which he received several decorations, while Huerta's time in the Yucatán, with daily letters to Secretary of War Bernardo Reyes, proved crucial to his later political aspirations.[66]

Service in the southeast also became the experience of ordinary men caught breaking social mores in an increasingly homophobic society.[67] One sublieutenant, Manuel Cantaneo, received a mere discharge in 1879 after conviction by the *junta de honor* (honor board) for practicing, with a well-known member of society, "actos opuesto al sexo" (acts opposite to his sex).[68] By contrast, in 1901 when police raided the Famous 41 dance, they marched twenty-three civilian men through the streets in dresses and sent them to an unknown end in the Yucatán—merely for wearing women's clothing (and even that was done only by half of those apprehended).[69] The military acted in this way as a barometer for social mores more generally. Changing notions of acceptable masculinity over time became apparent in the increasingly harsh reprimands within the military, although these largely vanished into vague charges of bad conduct or the like.

Nor were homophobic reactions the only charges to spur such exile. For Second Captain Antonio Navarro a charge of adultery, with a year and a half in prison, preluded a tour in the Yucatán, where he died several years later.[70] This case raises many questions, especially in a nation where sexual infidelity by men usually did not occasion disapproval. Although the vague details in the file do not say, it seems likely that Navarro's error came in choosing a woman that his superiors saw as fit for protection. In other words, the harsh reaction did not reflect respect for marriage as an institution, or for women in their own right, but rather reinforced patriarchal ownership over the mystery woman's honor. Quite possibly Navarro cheated either on a well-connected wife or with one. In no way did this ruling improve military effectiveness, nor did it honor the civilian penal code (since male adultery did not count as a crime). The military justice system prosecuted in this case based on its own version of ideal sexual behaviors, setting the bar for officers as gentlemen much higher than their civilian counterparts. At least in terms of this unfortunate officer the sexual regulation within barracks life encompassed a new, secular form of monastic service and indicated a modern impulse toward the social correction of deviance. Exceptional cases of this kind nonetheless did little to assure the general public of the moral soundness of the army as a whole. Again it is telling that Navarro's eventual punishment for his sexual escapade came in the form of deployment to a dangerous war zone, and proved fatal. When even the army saw soldiering as a punishment, the notion of honorable service in arms seemed a distant possibility.

Flight or Fight—Resisting the Leva

As reality set in, Diego realized that he had a lot of company in his growing distaste for army life. The sense that soldiering represented a prison sentence strengthened as he watched so many scheming of ways to escape. He recalled how the children of the better-off villagers had simply disappeared that Sunday morning; probably many had slunk off the night before to camp in the old mines of the hills until the all-clear came. No outsider could have found them there, but only those with good connections received the warning. Around him he saw less fortunate recruits seeking desperately for ways out. Some literate few wrote to their mothers for help, or even to lawyers, and the recruits soon gathered together to watch as the letter writers were marched off to other units or to disappear into prisons. Messages from the outside arrived at times, promising soldiers that a legal case had begun on their behalf; Diego listened to the mail call in vain and heard mainly the names of men long since moved on to different places. The officers laughed and ordered the letters returned to sender without adding explanations. It seemed that outside help could not come. Many men, for a night or a week of freedom, scaled the high walls or sprinted through an open gate into the city beyond. That most returned under guard so quickly amazed Diego. Apparently the army could catch you anywhere! With no contact

from his family, who likely had no resources to help anyway, and with no oppor-
tunity to make a run for it, Diego instead began to find a place for himself.

Many recruits went to extreme lengths either to avoid recruitment or to
return to a civilian life before their five-year tour ended. Four options might
offer them this chance: flight before the piquete arrived, obtaining an amparo
releasing them from service, obtaining *licencia absoluta* (an early discharge),
or deserting their unit. No measure was certain, and notably, all required a
degree of resourcefulness and usually support from family or their immediate
community. The process thereby set ordinary Mexicans of the vulnerable
classes into direct conflict with the officers and institution of the army.
Extended and immediate families provided the means of resistance to the best
degree they could. They proffered simple conspiracies of silence, abetted fugitives, paid bribes, found replacements, fed prisoners, and actively petitioned
the courts. The recruit's outside help often determined whether he could
escape from unwanted conscription. For many, indeed most, these networks
fell short, since the army had its own strategies to maintain their forces.

Fleeing before the leva was a likely response for many men, as the piquete
rarely arrived as a surprise. In smaller towns the impending leva would be
an ill-concealed secret and taking to the hills was a seductive possibility.
With family or community support, a fugitive might easily stay out of reach
and outwait the small detachment sent to escort replacements. Evidence of
this comes from the fact that jefes políticos routinely over-reported the number of potential recruits, some of whom certainly disappeared and left the
jefe with only excuses once the army unit arrived for pickup.[71] The rather
tenuous power of local constabularies proved insufficient at times to enforce
their will in the case of well-connected locals, and they often neglected local
jails to the point of their becoming merely symbolic.[72] As a result, detachments sent out by jefes de reemplazos consistently failed to meet quotas and
often obtained only a few jailed men.

Far from representing simply resistance to recruitment, this community
action to regulate its own terms of conscription might better demonstrate
how consensus on the local level engaged with state power. Influential families and village-level officials could legitimize their own status by selectively
protecting or offering up men to the piquete. If the whole town refused to
cooperate then the jefe político had few options. This intransigence embodied
a potent example of "weapons of the weak" that permitted some groups in the
towns to resist powerful outsiders.[73]

Jailers could look the other way, eyewitnesses could grow mute, gates could mysteriously unlock, and family members could "forget" they had sons or brothers. In other words, those who eventually ended up in the cuerda were not simply selected for this fate by a faceless jefe de reemplazo a hundred miles away—their neighbors and coworkers often elected to sacrifice them.

In areas where the army had higher quotas pressure undoubtedly fell on town officers to provide manpower, and a sense of duty to the community would encourage locals to offer men up as their *cargo* (charge). In the choice of who went local communities had a degree of power to hide or protect their own and to push forward outsiders or troublemakers as volunteers. Yet even these unfortunates had recourse to the law.

The amparo, a legal injunction often based on constitutional law, represented one of the most controversial and intriguing facets of the whole leva experience.[74] Constitutionally, the national government absolutely could not force army service on any Mexican. Military law backed this, proclaiming since 1824 that all federal soldiers were to be volunteers or selected by lottery. This often contrasted with state laws that mandated militia recruitment in different ways, but for the federals, volunteer-only service became law in 1848.[75] Although the military authorities continued to use the leva regardless of its legality, victims increasingly challenged it in the courts with some success, much to the chagrin of an elite enamored of both modern jurisprudence and large armies. The usage of the amparo became one of the most vexing constitutional issues of the Porfiriato. Enshrined as a fundamental legal right in the 1857 Constitution (Articles 101–2), reformers altered its terms in 1882, 1889, and 1897 to reduce its abuse, primarily by impressed soldiers.

The amparo ideally provided a check on executive powers by allowing citizens access to the courts. The legal framers of 1857 never intended it to allow all citizens to challenge government. To make a claim required legal expertise and literacy, which few of the lower classes enjoyed. Yet by the late nineteenth century practical knowledge of the process became widespread as families sought to challenge the conscription of their children. Their applications showed not trust or faith in the legal system but rather a high level of frustration and desperation in the face of injustice. In keeping with the Constitution, normal families could at least essay to obtain the release of loved ones from the barracks.

The use of this process highlighted the contradiction between military agendas and civil rights. In 1889 a reform to Article 779 rejected any applications for amparo after ninety days' time, which assisted the cause of recruitment.[76] While further reform in 1897 (Article 809) worked to discourage overuse, Article 746 then permitted women and minors to petition for amparo without legal representation, provided they could persuade the court it affected a matter of their personal integrity.[77] They routinely argued that the recruit played a vital role in providing both sustenance and moral guidance to their family. By depicting the potential effects on the welfare of domestic harmony, they evoked the discourse of the *hogar* (hearth) that the elite associated with class progress and social development.[78] In part set forward as a means to discourage women from joining the workforce and in part a reification of ideal modern gender behaviors, the critical importance of the mother as guardian of national honor could be invoked against the government. It also emphasized the importance of the breadwinning man in creating the home and ensuring family morality and well-being. Officials could not genuinely oppose the idea that family hardship trumped the induction of yet another reluctant trooper. In this manner, families, and especially mothers and wives, put increasing pressures on the military recruitment system by pointing to loss of their man as a direct affront to their family's well-being and integrity.

The injunction case thus presented a critical point of resistance to military service from the perspective of officers, judges, soldiers, and families alike. Most often, mothers initiated the petition of amparo. With or without legal counsel, they pursued this course first by contacting officers in the unit that had taken their son. Once officers identified the soldier, his case went forward to the judge, who determined whether a legal right existed for amparo. If he discovered that the conscript was a criminal or a deserter or was serving under false name, he dropped the case. Meanwhile, officers held the recruit under lock and key in a military prison or isolated within the barracks, at minimal pay. Assuming they would not grant the release, officers minimized the chances that the soldier would desert or, worse, spread knowledge of his case to others in the barracks. Even once a judge conceded the amparo it did not absolutely guarantee freedom. Eduardo F. Marín languished in the jail at San Juan de Dios in Puebla, charged with desertion, for four painful months after the granting of his discharge.[79] Nonetheless, records show that amparo petitions did release some two thousand men each year from their five-year military term.[80] Significantly, this amounted to nearly 10 percent of the usual army strength and does not include the thousands more held in jails awaiting an amparo ruling. The constitutional abuse of the leva, and the reaction to it, led to direct sapping of Porfirian military strength.

Problems did arise that required these soldiers. Banditry continued to plague the nation, indigenous groups rose up in the north and south, political groups rebelled, and on occasion, military units mutinied. The amparo meant that the army lacked the manpower it needed, no matter how many young men might be swept up.

As the high rate of amparo discharges seemed far too generous for their purposes, army commanders used various means to prevent what they felt was an abuse of the system. For some officers, constitutional reform appeared to be the ideal solution to the problem, and so they pushed Díaz to rewrite the law.[81] This he would not do; having invested himself in a liberal image and depending to some degree on popular affection, he discarded this option as politically untenable. Strict adherence to the law, at least in appearance, represented one of the most sacrosanct of liberal ideals, a legal fetish that emulated other modern nations.[82] He could, and did, tinker somewhat, but he avoided wholesale reform.

Other officers pressed for universal service, seeing the problem in terms of basic injustice rather than constitutional violation. Rather than mess with the laws of the land, they envisioned a better system than mass levy. Manuel Mondragón insisted that not only would brief universal service help everyone but it would also be a source of education and regeneration for the lower classes, who would naturally be proud to serve with their social betters.[83] Bernardo Reyes's "Essay on Recruitment" argued that solely recruiting from the indigenous classes represented the great shame of the nation and that only truly fair recruitment might provide the material for building the honor and discipline the army so needed.[84] His Second Reserve, an experiment in voluntary service between 1901 and 1903, offered another possible alternative to large conscript armies but ultimately proved politically impossible.[85]

More conservative and angry officers posed a serious challenge to amparos by interfering directly with local judicial officials, a measure of the deep political problems within a militarizing society. Don Porfirio himself wrote to Judge Bernardo Ruiz Sandoval in Zacatecas, asking him to concede fewer amparos and thus save the government the time and work that went into consigning these men. He admitted that in this matter perhaps there existed disagreements between the executive and judiciary, but he believed these could be overlooked if the judge acted "with some tact."[86] General Carlos Fuero, as governor of Chihuahua, instructed the judges in his state to make amparo trials less easy, in order to make it possible to meet the reemplazo quota.[87] Others followed suit, including General Julio Cervantes, fighting the Yaquis in Sonora, who found that with men disabled or deserting, his command had shriveled to about half strength and requested that Díaz suspend the amparo to allow him to gain his needed replacements.[88] The military-focused politics of the regime repeatedly allowed pressures such as these to overcome judiciaries and further alienated civilians from the armed forces. Again, military service became a punishment, a sentence, beyond even the Constitution's power to prevent.

More devious and pragmatic still, some officers avoided loss through amparos by applying sabotage designed to make the petitions far less likely to succeed. If judges acted "untrustworthy" and constitutional reforms were unlikely, then the army would simply find some other way to fill ranks without interference. Their greatest advantages in subverting the amparo lay in the legal ignorance of petitioners, the recruits' (and their families') lack of resources, the sheer bureaucratic inertia of the military institution, and the ninety-day limitation on injunctions instituted in 1882. The three-month probation period also likely allowed a recruit's superiors to evaluate his worthiness and decide whether to oppose a petition. Officers routinely misinformed families as to the destination of their son, his unit, and its location in order to prevent timely intercessions. They also moved recruits quickly to new areas and battalions, and army clerks "lost" or "misspelled" any documentation.[89] Of course, the army and courts could not accept an amparo application that lacked accurate data of this kind. Families or lawyers had to scramble to get the process started in the face of this resistance and sent numerous letters to clarify the facts. The officers then pled ignorance to families' inquiries—for at least ninety days, at which time the amparo came too late.

Making the procedure more uncertain, some officers used the families' fear and desperation as an opportunity for graft, as in the case of José de los Angeles. In 1899 his sister Rafaela Hernández wrote to the military commandant of the Federal District. She had offered to buy a replacement for her brother for forty pesos and had sent the money to an officer named Pisquinto Millón at the Third Battalion. The authorities looked into it and initially could find no such officer. Eventually they tracked down an off-duty colonel who had taken the money, but he claimed that in the interim the proffered replacement had deserted with the girl's money in hand.[90] The case, and the cash, disappeared and the recruit served his term.

The family proved essential to successful cases of amparo or replacement, and few soldiers could initiate the process themselves. Orphans, those estranged from family, and those successfully hidden in far-off barracks had little luck in opposing the army's will. Certainly some soldiers knew how the process worked, and it became a topic of conversation among troops. But locked away in the garrison and bereft of finances or outside contacts, soldiers had no opportunity to pursue a court case. Indeed, officers treated those identified as enabling amparos, or as a barracks lawyer, as serious offenders. Along with troublemakers, transvestites, and adulterers, one soldier who acted as a barracks lawyer, giving advice to his comrades, found himself sent to the Yucatán in 1886 to fight Mayas and mosquitoes.[91] Although it offered the best chance, however, the amparo did not represent the only legal option for release from service.

The petition for discharge allowed a third option for resisting the leva. Given the military's need ad for new recruits, it is not surprising that few discharges (licencia absoluta) appear for soldiers prior to the completion of their five-year term. Even for officers, commanders rarely permitted a release from service. Nonetheless, mothers wrote to officers and to the president asking for the discharge of their sons. They frequently cited special circumstances to justify their request. As one of many examples, the señora and widow Clementina de Calapis wrote plaintively to the president. She had five children, four still at home, and they desperately needed their brother to come home from service. At least, she bargained, bring him to a unit in Mexico City, from where he could still care for the family.[92] She clearly believed that even locked in barracks and with minimal pay, her son could somehow maintain the family and its well-being. Perhaps this simply demonstrated her psychological need for the boy, or perhaps it suggests that she saw other locally deployed soldiers making a difference in her neighbors' lives. Other mothers were less eloquent: Antonia García de Bueno simply asked that her son be returned to her home from his detachment in the Yucatán.[93] Nonetheless, and in many more examples, the answer almost always came back a respectful no from the president or his functionaries. National needs trumped those of simple families, and not even the angel of the hearth, the mother, could override military order. Once denied legal redress, the captured recruit had one last resort.

Desertion was the most commonly used option for the reluctant soldier to return to civilian life. When other means failed, some 25–50 percent of soldiers decided to flee their units.[94] Officers guarded the new recruits day and night, denied them any access to the streets for the first few years of service, and held roll calls numerous times each day.[95] Regulations distinguished between simple desertion, missing roll for three days, and aggravated desertion in combat zones, which incurred the death penalty. The American journalist Thomas Janvier reported that in central Mexico no desertions succeeded and the government executed all transgressors, although military records clearly show this to be a false impression on his part.[96] Although officially denied any rights to leave barracks without guard for three years' time, until officers deemed the soldier to be trusted (a *soldado de confianza*), troops routinely appeared on the streets and around town. In part this reflects a norm within the army of allowing some freedoms to keep soldiers happy, as officers could collude with troops to *dar franco* (grant leave). If recruits abused this privilege, and they often did, then both soldier and officer could face punishment. Despite this outlet and these precautions, desertion remained a serious challenge that drained army resources.

The resourceful found opportunities for escape in sometimes-ingenious ways. In the most common method of escape soldiers scaled the walls of the barracks late at night, often waiting for the changing of guards to facilitate evasion.[97] For the most part, these men would not be missed until early morning. This was not always feasible. Barracks buildings typically were surrounded by forty-foot walls. Some soldiers waited for orders to march or to go on patrol to make a break for it, risking gunshots from their compatriots and officers.[98] On the other hand, given serious accuracy problems in the army (see chapter 2), perhaps this did not seem so risky. Still others took advantage of relatively lax security at military hospitals. They faked illness, a common problem for medical staff, and counted on the drunkenness of guards to make a getaway. In at least one case, a soldier disguised himself as a doctor and simply walked out.[99] One improvised escape plan involved local pigeons. Having convinced the lieutenant of the guard that he had seen a wounded pigeon, a soldier sprinted after the bird in chase, rounded the corner of the barracks, and ran on into the city. Unfortunately, he stopped short of the refuge or anonymity of the countryside, and a troop recaptured him in a nearby cantina some hours later. The officer received the punishment for this infraction, perhaps for his gullibility.[100] Ordinary soldiers nonetheless had good reasons to attempt escape, if little hope of achieving liberty.

Trial records offer insights into the deserter's world. The testimony hints at oppressive conditions, although witnesses routinely reported that the deserter had faced absolutely no mistreatment from officers. Rather, they would claim the decision to desert was baseless, *sin razón* (without reason). More likely, the witnesses standing in front of a council of war had good reason to withhold honesty. Complaints of mistreatment could lead to dishonorable discharge or worse.[101] Those who fled often had their own reasons. One deserter appealed to the court's mercy, claiming that he had a young family and the army pay was simply too little to provide for their needs.[102]

Other documents demonstrate the relative foolishness of the pursued. For example, getting on a train headed for Mexico City proved to be the downfall of the deserting sailor Luis Airaldi in 1885. To no one's surprise but his, guards awaited him at a station down the line.[103] The combination of telegraphs and railways enabled officers to capture the least savvy of would-be civilians quickly. Catching deserters had long been a favorite sport for bored officers. "The Mexican Armies and Generals" by A. Conquest Clarke portrays an army in 1867 that sounds unhappily similar to the one that Díaz's regime tried to hide from foreign view in later years.[104] Clarke's highly critical account derides the ragged conscripts as a rabble of imminent deserters, and he offers an entertaining description of the sport of rounding up deserters from horseback. Cooperating with local gendarmes, experience taught the pursuers some sure methods for hunting down soldiers on the run. They generally began with known haunts near to barracks areas, in particular the favored cantinas and *pulquerías* (bars selling cheap, unrefined agave drinks).[105] The next-surest method of recapture was searching the deserters' homes if they came from nearby. Troops immediately invaded and ransacked the homes of a deserter's nearest family members and neighbors.[106] This tactic often succeeded, but at the same time it did nothing at all for the popularity of the army, as private citizens vehemently denied that soldiers had the right to search their homes. In a sketch, Frederic Remington shows how the arrival of an armed search party occasioned what appears to be angry resistance and immediate gossip among neighbors.[107]

In the image, soldiers surround a peasant while his wife looks on from the background, and the apparent arrogance of the officer appears in his posture and aggressive stance. By contrast, the soldiers slump as they loom threateningly over their target. Much as with the flight from the leva discussed earlier, this interaction suggests an engagement with local communities and their moral economic vision of military service. Hiding deserters also could lend some measure of power back to the locals, but it did not often hinder the military police. As much as the leva did not engender devotion, the notion of duty and the idea that recruits arrived in barracks for good reasons made local populations quite open to turning in deserters. If the community had not sheltered the man from the piquete, then why would they risk angering search parties to protect him after desertion, when he became clearly in the wrong? Gossip and rumors about such men called into question their virtue and reinforced local justifications for having surrendered the man to begin with. For many deserters there was no going home.

The total number of successful deserters cannot be accurately assessed. Many false rosters in units confuse totals, and the reenlistment of troops, sometimes under false names, makes estimation difficult. That said, the rates of desertion did not reflect absolute losses to the army. Although the población flotante and bandit gangs certainly absorbed some fugitives, a larger number eventually were returned to service, with extra years in the army as punishment for their recapture.[108] Temporary abandonment of the barracks aside, the reluctant army recruit likely could not permanently avoid his military fate.

One implication that stems from this rather fluid service was that the Porfirian military absorbed, vomited, and reingested a far greater proportion of the population than has been previously suggested. Given that the army officially consisted of only twenty to thirty thousand soldiers in a given year, many historians have underestimated its significance. But the wrench thrown in these logical gears lies in turnover. A number of soldiers in any roster were fictional names added to pad the payroll. A number of soldiers also remained in service for long stretches, up to thirty years in arms. Yet a majority only saw service for less than their five-year terms. At a natural attrition rate, plus desertions, units regenerated most of their numbers every three years, meaning that during the Porfiriato some two hundred thousand men experienced armed service in the federal army alone. This is borne up by figures showing recruitment of nearly 6,000 men in 1902, which, if considered average, would indicate 216,000 new federal soldiers over thirty-six years' time.[109] As a significant portion of the eligible population of males in a country of only ten million, this created an enormous shared experience—and one that created a shared and implacable hatred for the effects of don Porfirio's leva and its impact on their lives, their comrades, and their families.

Conclusion

Building a modern army from the castaways and rejects of society did not prove an easy task. The Porfirians' need for a rejuvenated military rose in part from the demands faced by a modernizing and industrializing society. The garrisons removed potential troublemakers and turned them into a repressive mechanism against the rising working class. The manner in which the state claimed its "contingent of blood" continued to enrage ordinary Mexicans. The apparent arbitrary nature of the leva proclaimed the vulnerability of marginal men. The leva caught up hundreds of thousands and became representative of the especially derogatory public view of military service. Yet the system would not have functioned at all without the engagement of the communities.

Every community and every family became a part of the military apparatus. Although the leva appeared to the elite as an absolute necessity in order to create the modern military that the nation needed, ordinary people learned through press reports, songs, and rumors that army service embodied a horrible fate for their sons. With local communities and families, recruits attempted to resist and avoid recruitment. When outright hiding and legal suits failed, many recruits attempted instead to desert their units. Officers caught most and sentenced them to further service at arms. Once selected, most soldiers would encounter an intractable institution that did not readily allow them to escape. Once chosen, the army would do its level best to re-create them as servants of the nation.

The often-controversial practice of forced recruitment tied to basic ideas of identity and power on fundamental levels. The leva had tremendous consequences for the recruits, as did the ways that they resisted its grasp. Their experiences of the leva affected their communities and families and reflected how federal power clashed with local expectations. In these ways military service also acted as a metaphor for broader social and class divisions, as the process of stocking and training a national army occurred at the expense of the patria chica.

Diego made the best of his situation. He learned how to get by and also how he might, in subtle ways, bend the rules. For months, the young conscript would learn the life of the barracks, the rules of the army, and the vices of his comrades in arms. Despite homesickness, abuse, and deprivation, the new soldiers tried as best they could to make a new life and, in doing their duty, perhaps to become modern men, if maybe by accident. Seen as vice-ridden marihuaneros by many, young and reluctant servants of the nation like Diego nevertheless played a significant role in constructing the progress and order the republic so desperately needed. Whether he agreed or not, the army began branding him with the mark of the vida militar from the moment he entered the dark barracks gate.

In a way it was slavery. . . . The soldiers weren't free, the army wasn't free.

—TRINIDAD VEGA, INTERVIEW WITH XIMENA SEPÚLVEDA,
1873

CHAPTER TWO

Sculpting a Modern Soldier through Drill and Ritual

Poor Diego remembered how, having marched in a chain gang for days, he had staggered through the gate in the imposing walls of the barracks. Shaking and sweating, his imagination raced and, exhausted from his ordeal, he had queued up to a desk. He was now a soldier, as the sergeant forced him to make his mark on a five-year contract. Around him some other recruits with better literacy signed their names. The veterans stripped Diego of what little he owned. As one soldier remarked, "They'll take even your memories of any other life." A simple set of worn, tan uniform gear replaced his formerly white cotton clothes. They gave him shoes but made him put them away and wear sandals instead. A belt with a baffling number of compartments held it all together, and an odd, short-rimmed cap replaced his practical straw hat. Handed a blanket and mat, he looked with longing toward the area where snoring rows of soldiers lay. But before he could sleep Diego needed to make yet another change—shears appeared and they made him a soldado raso (shaven soldier) on the spot. As each tuft of hair hit the floor, he felt reduced and changed, less like himself. The sergeant next told him his place. They assigned him, and defined him, with numbers: as part of a squad of 10, a platoon of 30, a section of 60, a company of 180, and so on up to a battalion of 900. He had arrived in the late evening, as was often the case for recruits, and he and his compatriots finally trudged to sleeping mats for their night's repose. Exhausted as he was, Diego tossed and turned while the sentinels cried alerts and alarums every twenty minutes, a special treat for new arrivals. Nothing could be less restful for a boy from a small, quiet village, especially one worried sick about the next day's ordeal. Though drained and sore from the long road, Diego managed but a few fitful hours of slumber. And with the rising sun, his new life began.

A world of sounds greeted new soldiers and would soon regulate and determine the rhythms of their days in the vida militar. The introduction to a strict regimen of time in an isolated barracks, although an old tradition, bears much similarity to the installation of clocks in town squares.[1] Ritualizing daily activity around a new pattern helped break new soldiers of old habits, prevent desertion, and train obedience. In the usual hubbub of the barracks they heard shouting sergeants, barking dogs, sentries' challenges, crying children, mournful corridos, drill orders, and even singing parakeets. This rich soundscape intruded day and night, but most important were the clarion calls of the bugle that ordered life between dawn and nine in the evening. Throughout this musically ordered day, the soldier learned his new profession and much more.

The officer corps had distinct aspirations for what the new recruit would become as a servant of a modern and unified nation. They looked to a heroic past, to personal experience, and abroad to the best military nations of West and East. Porfirian elites framed these desires in ways connected to masculinity (make them men), liberalism (make them citizens), modernism (make them efficient with science), and pragmatism (make them useful). The conscript ideally would become a hard, disciplined killer with manageable gender behaviors and a deep loyalty to the official vision of Mexico. Further, this would ideally see him uprooted from his upbringing, his patria chica, his racial identity—leaving behind all but his new devotion.[2]

Positivist elites sought to define the nation as it transformed economically and technologically, modeling their ideal on European patterns.[3] In this milieu, the ideal citizens would lose indigenous and lower-class traits and homogenize in line with a new rhetoric of modernity and nationality. The soldier became the exemplar of this ideal—but the recruit forced into the service of arms did not, would not, fulfill elite aspirations. From their initial capture and resistance, we move into barracks to see the daytime regimen, where instruction and conditioning clashed with the soldier's agency and the government's poverty.

Communities across Mexico provided the raw materials to construct an ideal figure, "le militaire," who represented a fetishistic ideal of modern order.[4]

In the most straightforward sense he embodied the monopolistic use of violence that legitimate governments enshrined within themselves. At more abstract levels the soldier exhibited the results of power in his modified and disciplined body. He became a symptom of state building called forth when conflicts reached extremes that could not be otherwise managed. The everyday practices that agents enacted during the construction of this ideal figure nonetheless warped the template and gave birth to a subject who often defied elite hopes. Ordinary limits, budgetary and otherwise, made the social engineering project unstable.

Here we examine the training of the recruit as he became a soldier. Following the army's regimen this chapter delves into the quotidian activities of the barracks: pay muster, mealtime, drill practice, classroom lessons, formal inspections, and military rituals. Ultimately I evaluate the process and relative successes of the Porfirian efforts to build an ideal, in le militaire.

From "Dawn" To "Silence": Formal Instruction of the Recruit

Officers had a sharp vision of what the soldier could mean to the modernizing nation. How to accomplish this lofty task of remaking the peasant into a soldier? Traditions established long before Independence relied on the power of tough and committed NCOs (noncommissioned officers, sergeants and corporals) to instill discipline with iron fists. For the Porfirian upper crust, this still seemed the best solution, perhaps the only one. Training would instill the virtues of the soldier: élan, self-abnegation, obedience; the civic goals of patriotism, literacy, and mexicanidad; the practical skills of marching, drill, and shooting.[5] Through a daily regimen of rituals and classroom work, they attempted a transformation process to sculpt the raw material of the leva.

The idea that training soldiers could somehow make Mexico a modern success story depended on numerous assumptions. Before he deeply internalized patriotic self-abnegation, a recruit had to forgive the army for the manner in which it recruited him. He had to believe, on some level, that he deserved the abuses of training and that good motivations lay behind them. He had to insulate his life in the army from his prior civilian self and reject prevailing civilian opinions on the soldiers' inferiorities. At least to a degree, he would also need to accept the army's lessons on nonlocal patriotism and appropriate manliness. Implements of disciplinary biopower could overcome only so much. The project's significance lies in the process and what it tells us about identity construction and its possibly surprising results—many soldiers did actually become something recognizably similar to the ideal citizen. Among many soldiers a loyalty to the regime took root and their discipline set in deeply. This conception underlies discussions of discipline and identity formation throughout the chapter.[6]

Soldiers had their own ideas, and a different vision. Ultimately the young men experienced transformation—in circumstances, conditions, and understandings—as they went through a process to become soldiers that included recruitment, orientation, and daily instruction. The oppressive discipline nonetheless often worked to affirm the conscripts' previous conceptions of indigenous and regional identification. Under pressure, many took comfort in assumed ties and old loyalties. Furthermore, the disciplinary program to instill nationalism and foster order and progress took on new meanings for the enlisted men, who may have been servants of a nation but whose agendas often remained far removed from the aspirations of their civilian and military commanders.

The experiences of daily life shaped identities of gender, race, and class and connected also to nation and place. Many of them indigenous illiterates and mostly impoverished, the recruits the army threw together bonded with one another under pressures to conform to a new institutional life.[7] A new army, a new soldier, which instructors hoped to construct, required the erasure or overwriting of lifelong habits of thought and behavior. They remedied posture, taught hygiene, and insisted on respectful shows of obedience. Officers forbade the settling of personal disputes with "manly" violence or with vulgarity, broadly defined. Expressing such proscriptions proved far easier than enforcing them.

The military as an institution also sought a clean slate and rejuvenation through selective renaming and bureaucratic reorganization. The highest ranks sought to distance the federal military forces from older regional battalions, especially since the army had fared unevenly or poorly in the wars since Independence. The units personally raised by regional caudillos or wealthy oligarchs did not fit with a nationally directed army and needed to be folded into existing or newly christened units. The process began with nomenclature. Colorful and storied specialist units became numbered segments of the whole. They lost names like Cazadores ("hunters," similar to *chasseurs* or Jägers elsewhere), Tiradores (sharpshooters), or Fieles ("loyals" of a certain place). Their history, their origins, and their character would likewise fade into forgetting. The fetish of renaming also applied to military cartography. Hundreds of towns with the same name—for example, Santa

María—complicated deployment of troops by telegraph and railway.[8] The army assigned new, unique names as it rationalized mapping of the nation, adding landmarks to place-names (e.g. Santa María de Altos) or simply altering them entirely. The military operated, then, with a sense of place that literally did not match local communities' ideas of themselves.[9] It should not surprise that many soldiers similarly received new names, being given nicknames to simplify a roster with too many Juans, Josés, and Pedros. This also occurred with some soldiers whose indigenous names seemed too strange or hard to pronounce, and of course, the immediate renaming allowed officers an opportunity to hide recruits from the amparo or to reenlist them under a new name.

In an era of clean slates, the ideological drive of positivism met neatly with technological tools and pseudoscientific conceptions in the barracks. Positivists believed that society progressed in definable stages along a trajectory from the superstitious to the modern, and the Porfirian government (both military and civilian elements) strongly held to this vision. Racial sciences of early eugenicists informed these policy makers on how to apply "progress" with the lower orders. Maintaining the civilized façade required constant attention, and it went only skin deep, but they hoped that, with time, it might sink in completely. Through discipline of diet, habit, clothing, language, and sexuality the "native" would become the modern Mexican. The building in 1901 of a grand Panopticon-style prison named Lecumberri exemplified the faith of the elite in applying scientific surveillance to troublesome populations. Progress on race and class conflated with, permitted, progress in the nation. Disciplining these values into the army ranks called for a calculated effort.

Toque de Diana/Call of Diana—0600

Dazed and still half-asleep, Diego quickly stepped into line when the others formed up, hoping to avoid yet another blow from the surly sergeant. Instead he found himself shoved and cursed back toward the rear of the queue by scowling soldiers. He and the two newest soldiers lined up at the end, unaware even of what purpose the line served. One of the officers (Diego had started to realize who they were) sat at a table with paper and quill and ink, with a small metal box to either side of him. Each man came forward, said his name, and waited while the officer fished a small stack of coins from one case. Diego's eyes went wide. Back home even that small pile would feed his family for weeks! The

soldier stood quietly as the officer then reached out and retrieved most of the
coins, placing them in the second box. He scratched something out on his papers
and gave a dismissive wave. The soldier quickly pocketed the remaining money.
As the line went on, Diego noted that some men handed off a portion of their
coins to the NCOs or to other soldiers as soon as they got them. Some soldiers
received smaller portions to begin with, or larger, and it all seemed to depend
on whatever it was that the officer scribbled out in front of him. With four
recruits still ahead of him in line, everything stopped. The box had emptied. The
officer shrugged unapologetically, took up his boxes and papers, and disap-
peared into the office areas at the edge of the patio. From the soldiers ahead of
him in line, Diego and the other new soldiers learned a few new words that day
that would not be suitable for proper company. Instruction had begun.

First nights in barracks were rarely peaceful experiences, but the new constant of life was the early morning call of "Diana." A poetic touch, this
referred to the dawn, and the call might vary greatly depending on time of
year and on particular barracks' or units' traditions. Depending on the taste
of the band, the horn rang out for as little as a minute or as long as a half hour
and signaled the official day to begin. In the dawn's light, the bleary-eyed
soldiers wearily sorted themselves from covers and sleeping mats, disentan-
gled from women, stepped over dogs and children, and shuffled into the
parade square.[10] They lined up in their files and companies as the surly sergeants called out *lista* (roll call) and answered to their names with "Presente,"
while the missing were noted for punishment or pursuit. The sergeant of the
day would then offer each man his daily pay, which provided for many men
the best reason to wake up.

In theory, soldiers received between twenty-five and thirty-eight centavos each morning, a figure set by the Secretariat of War and Navy to ensure
a "basic quality of life," which was not necessarily forthcoming. A number of
factors mitigated this desired outcome: the availability of funds, the expense
of daily life, and the cost of vice. Soldiers' complaints of nonpayment may
have been the most venerable tradition in this army. Perhaps the chief complaint in any army, accounts from Julius Caesar's Legionnaires or Sun Tzu's
pengs reflected late or short pay as an ordinary feature of military life and
clearly one that continued well into modern times. Far-flung garrisons, particularly those in active and mobile campaigns, at times outmarched pay
trains for weeks on end. Some officers, but by no means most, continued
providing pay out of their own pockets and wrote to Díaz or the secretary of

war for reimbursement.[11] More commonly, soldiers simply went without pay or had to seek other income by theft, extortion, or pimping.

Officers also extorted monies from troops in a number of ways, making lack of funds more common. A favorite graft was to draw from paychests to pay for forage for nonexistent animals or at inflated prices, leaving soldiers without centavos.[12] Still other officers demanded *obsequios* (gifts), from subordinates and freely took this for themselves from pay coffers. Endemic lack of government money for payroll also afforded Díaz an excuse to deny permission to local authorities who wished to raise their own forces, and instead he pled poverty and used federal soldiers' plight to prove his point. It is worth noting that as Oaxaca's governor he supported underfunding the state's public security forces.[13] In other words, the lack of proper pay for troops in general became a justification for a fully federal army, implicitly better funded, in place of regional forces. This ongoing pay crisis was yet another cancer on army morale and another source of civilian hatred of the leva.

Assuming the men received their pittance, daily expenses leeched most of it away quickly. Less mobile or inactive units with decent officers met for their pay after Diana, and the amount depended on service, year, and location. Pay varied: in 1890 the army set daily pay for the infantry at thirty-one centavos, for cavalry and artillery at thirty-eight centavos, for sappers (combat engineers) at fifty centavos. Writers suggested averaging all to forty-four centavos. Troops in expensive areas (like the big cities) were to be compensated better as well.[14] By contrast, an officer's servant's wage (*mozo*) averaged around a peso (one hundred centavos) per day, skilled workers doubled that, and members of the Presidential Guards received about 1.5 pesos plus expenses. In comparison to standard costs of living, while marijuana seemed extremely cheap (fifty centavos per kilogram), rice went for twenty-four centavos per kilogram, corn for four centavos per kilogram, and milk for twelve centavos per liter.[15] The common soldier's pay, if used in street markets, therefore might barely meet his own needs, and certainly would not support a family—but that assumed he kept the whole amount. It also did not adjust adequately for inflation or compensate for institutional fees.

Sergeants immediately deducted between twelve and fifteen centavos to pay for official rations. Most soldiers supplemented these simple and insubstantial three meals with other food purchased from the soldaderas.[16] The extra food that the women supplied, plus laundry service, small sundries, simple medicines, various contraband, and sexual services, quickly drained the remainder of the soldiers' thirteen to twenty-five centavos.[17] The soldaderas assured some quality of life for a relatively low price but left troops with empty pockets in the process. Between services, support, and feeding, the soldier absolutely required this new "family" member. Most prerecruitment wives stayed in the village, and so most married soldiers added a new "wife" (also called a *mujer de tropa*, *amasia*, or *vieja*) to fulfill their needs whatever the monetary or eventual emotional costs. The last financial drain came from the numerous and expensive vices also made possible by the presence of soldaderas, practices that had tremendous consequences (see chapters 3 and 6). The informal costs of barracks life rose due to inflation at its gates. Officers required bribes at times to allow goods to come in, and at other times the soldaderas took advantage of the opportunity to hike the prices of their "imports." Soldiers paid or did without.

Pay officers fully understood the situation and made use of it to further control troops and instruct them on their place in the army. Soldiers incurred debts when payroll came late. They sought advances and they trod carefully around those who controlled the unit's purse strings. Standing in the pay line itself instructed humility, as the recruits waited for their pittance in a manner not so unlike begging for charity. The narrow edge between well fed and indebted hunger could further tie soldiers to their battalion. Just as surely as with an unwise mortgage today, those who owed future pay to officers, soldaderas, or other soldiers could not so easily flee their situation, or at least could not hope for cooperation. Lack of funds also, in theory, discouraged misbehavior, since prison time came at the malfeasant's own expense for food, and no rations came his way. The call to receive pay thus represented a generally welcome but not always positive event.

Toque de Rancho/Call to Rations—0630, 1200, 1800

At 6:30 the Toque de Rancho sounded for the first of three daily meals, the next at 12:00, and the last at 6:00 p.m., where official and unofficial rations met hungry young men. A rotating order of squads moved through the long lines to be fed by a skeletal cooking staff and then settled on the ground to eat over the next half hour. The horn call of Atención (attention) announced the arrival or emergence of soldaderas with baskets of various foods for the men with whom they had a relationship or with coin to pay. As with the men, these ladies followed the regimen of the trumpet, and upon the call of Media Vuelta (about turn) at the end of mealtimes the officers forced them out of the barracks and into the streets. The more punctilious units also demanded that men wash up before meals, but usually hygiene fell short of even basic measures.[18] In any case, the contents of these rations represented an important point of contention as well as interest in the fashioning of a modern soldier and in the maintenance of morale (see chapter 5).

Instrucción/Call to Instruction—0800, 1500

Having eaten, Diego lined up again with his comrades in the parade square. The intriguing and mysterious women had filed out and he resisted the urge to steal another glimpse at them as they passed. A file mate, not so cautious, took a hard slap on the ear from a passing cabo (corporal). For the next few hours, and every day thereafter, Diego learned soldiering in this square. Countless hours of marching, turning, front facing, all made easier when he learned left from right, became reflex. The horns spoke directly to his spine, it seemed at times. Occasionally the troops would head out to the edge of the city and shoot rifles. Diego knew he was not particularly good at this, and his few practice rounds rarely came near the target, but he still felt an excitement with the gun kicking against his shoulder. He could actually imagine himself a soldier! Other instructions sat less well with him. Every day it seemed like the interminable classroom read-alongs never ended. He listened to the officers read patriotic stories, recited his memorized responses, and struggled to learn his letters. He memorized tedious lists of regulations and suffered from the all-too-frequent beatings delivered by the NCOs. Some days he felt unsure which he hated worse. Everything in the barracks seemed full of threats. Even many of the songs they sang for fun were about executions! But, and in this he did take pride, he finally had shoes! His mother would be overjoyed.

At 8:00 a.m., with the night guards relieved, the soldiers reassembled for instruction in the main patio, and again later in the afternoon, at three. Instruction entailed a wide range of activities intended to instill skills, virtues, and discipline. Live exercises, marches, target practice, bayonet fencing, and parade drills taught practical skills. Classroom work on theory, care of equipment, and literacy furthered this objective. Rituals and selected texts complemented the practical with the psychological effort of inculcating nationalism and élan. Results lagged behind rhetoric in all areas. Popular wisdom suggested that expertise requires ten thousand hours of practice. Repeated work to build muscle memory and reflexes requires constant commitment. Porfirian soldiers and their superiors met significant issues in training for even basic skills. With the training regime underfunded and its objectives too ambitious, ideal soldiers did not easily materialize.

Frustrated officers met numerous obstacles in the practical training, and recruits quickly became disgruntled, bored, and resistant. A major problem, as in any military, was lack of resources and funds. Poorly fed, often unpaid, the soldiers predictably lacked much desire or energy to make efforts to please their officers and NCOs. Because the budding arms industries produced relatively few shells, the crucial skills of marksmanship depended on pricey imports and soldiers went undertrained.[19] Target practice often could not be entertained because it undermined readiness by depleting the ammunition magazine. Further, officers restricted issuance of live rounds even in combat zones, as they feared it led to desertions and hence banditry. A generation of older officers also turned to French élan building rather than German and English firepower as an underlying training philosophy.[20] Bayonet charges proved cheap to teach compared to live-fire practice. Moreover, some officers resisted the building of a truly effective army, preferring a paper tiger, and at times they prevailed. A less trained force that presented itself well and had well-ingrained patriotism might prove less dangerous to government and yet maintain order through intimidation. To give these officers the benefit of the doubt, some also realized that in actual combat the recruits inevitably faced a steep learning curve that training did not simulate, and so further instruction did not justify the cost.

As a result, combat efficacy fell short. The figures given for the live-fire practice indicate that solid marksmanship would reflect coincidence rather than training. Soldiers' somewhat dismal shooting records should not be surprising, since few managed to fire more than five shots a time, about once a month. The few opportunities to shoot only ensured that the rifles worked, and soldiers could not even sight them in properly. Hardware did not explain the problem. Infantry units by this time had switched to reliable Remington and Mauser rifles and carbines. Some drop in accuracy between infantry rifle and cavalry carbine due to barrel lengths they expected, but lack of practice for either service best explains the troubling skill levels demonstrated.

Despite offers of significant cash bonuses for good shooting, up to two pesos for each bulls-eye, few soldiers seem to have mastered the skill. In comparison with their European counterparts, Mexicans' lack of practice and poor quality of ammunition greatly reduced their battlefield efficacy (see table 2.1). For instance, an infantry rifleman, on average, hit a target roughly the size of six men standing shoulder to shoulder only half the time from only a hundred paces away. By contrast, the British soldier of the same era was trained to high accuracy from up to six hundred meters away and was expected to hit a two-foot circle at three hundred yards with fourteen of fifteen shots in under a minute. The Mexican rates in 1903, with a rifle similar to those of the British, more resembled the expected accuracy of the Prussian soldiers firing enormously inaccurate muskets a full century earlier, who achieved 25 percent at 225 m, 40 percent at 150, and 60 percent at 75, albeit with a two-by-thirty-meter target.[21] Because units in active combat zones and units practicing in garrisons show little to no difference in accuracy, the effects of normal training fall into further doubt. Soldiers with mortal incentives to improve fared no better on the range than did comfortable garrison soldiers in downtown Mexico City. This evaluation also reflected a shift in doctrine, as targets began more closely to represent individual enemies rather than a company or platoon of soldiers. The inadequacy of the training nonetheless should have become grossly obvious as early as the 1893 fiasco in attacking the village of Tomochic.[22]

Still, some things the army did quite well. On the march, few nations could match the Mexican soldier. Foreign observers commented on the astounding pace and endurance of troops, each of whom carried his regulation pack of 21.25 kg (47 lbs.), They bore a considerably lighter load than the European average of 28.67 kg (7.42 kg or 16 lbs. lighter), a fact approved by Porfirian doctors for medical reasons. The old stereotypic notion of the lower-class Mexican as beast of burden may reach back as far as the *tameme* (Nahuatl porter). It had changed little by the late nineteenth century. Writers and thinkers of the time routinely praised this facet of lower-class endurance and strength, even as they implied its bestial nature.[23] This may, happily for the Porfirian soldier, have also influenced officers' choice not to overload them with gear for fear of reinforcing this negative mule-like appearance. In any case, on the actual campaign trail a great deal of the soldiers' gear continued to rest on the shoulders of their soldadera companions.

TABLE 2.1 Average shooting percentages, 6×2m target

	At 100 m	At 200 m	At 300 m	At 500 m
28 battalions of infantry (range)	52.6 (30–71)	31.1 (19–31)	30.6 (11–56)	18 (7–31)
14 regiments of cavalry (range)	26.6 (18–43)	N/A	18.9 (11–38)	5 (2–10)

Source: AGN Gobernación, sin sección, Caja 745, Gobernación, Expediente 11, May 24, 1900.

One assumes that the doctors came to this recommendation due to the smaller average size of recruits. Oddly, the soldiers nevertheless carried about the same forty-five-pound load as did larger US troops of the era.[24] They practiced this skill frequently, both to satisfy the tactical needs of the army and to maintain a reasonable fitness level. If not in a fixed garrison, all units had to go on prolonged marches at least three to six times each month, taking one third of the garrison for up to twenty-four kilometers over varied terrain. For three months they would go on four-day marches of twenty, twenty-two, twenty-five, and twenty-six kilometers with a full load of equipment and attempt different maneuvers and situations.[25] Perhaps more impressive to observers, soldaderas in the field not only kept up but also outcarried and outdistanced their male counterparts.[26] At marching the army excelled. One wonders if officers did not fear the application of this facility in desertion and retreat. Despite having a shorter gait than foreign soldiers, "the Mexicans could be counted on to achieve thirty km a day over virtually any terrain."[27] From this constant wear and training rose further issues, nonetheless, over the supply and type of footwear.

Responsible for maintaining their own kit and replacing worn-out gear, troops complained about shoes if they had them, or about the shoes they did not have. While traditional *huaraches* (rough sandals) remained standard issue in many units, proper modern shoes (Western style) became required for dress reviews, honor guards, and military parades. Nonetheless, many units outside Mexico City never received shoes and keenly felt their lack when parading with better-equipped rurale or police units. Envy of these better-shod counterparts undermined pride in their battalion, and soldiers who returned home after five years without shoes reported a sense of betrayal.[28]

Shoes mattered. Officers pressed for universal supply of leather shoes, despite utility problems in places like jungles, because they saw the huarache as a visible marker of backward, uncivilized, Indian identity. Given soldiers' vehement demands for uncomfortable footwear, it seems they too sought distance from their patria chica in a simple matter of dress. Vega remarked with admiration about the boots he saw Revolutionary forces wearing. He also felt angered that federal soldiers had to carry shoes in their packs in case of a formal parade while wearing their huaraches normally.[29] To him, having shoes represented an improvement in class status that should not be reserved only for show. In an image of the drum corps from 1899, indigenous troops paraded for artist Frederick Remington in their huaraches and white cotton clothes.[30] By contrast with other troops presented him, these unusually retained the markers of race or class that the government usually covered up and that many soldiers resented.[31] For example, he captured in his painting the darker skin tones common to average soldiers and matched their modern caps (*kepis*) with more normal cotton outfits rather than the French-style uniform of most units. With their faces indistinct as they march down a dusty, unpaved road, they depict a typical detachment without much individualization. For most units the issue of shoes nevertheless represented a fundamental agreement between soldier and state, and one that offended moral economies when old huaraches continued in use. The decrepit sandals made the man.

Most days, and for new recruits quarantined to barracks, practical instruction consisted of drill on the patio. Considered by military theory to be the best possible means to instill discipline, drill focused on practiced repetition to create social cohesion and solidarity. The act of moving and working together built "muscular bonding," the kind of unconscious collectivity that organized and choreographed movement evokes, whether in dance, ritual, or parade-square motions.[32]

However important this routine seemed to theorists, NCOs and troops alike found the practice tedious, pointless, and contentious. Complicating matters, poorly trained sergeants and corporals could only emulate their own training, and some recruits actually had never learned the difference between left and right.[33] Troops may also, at times, have been exacerbating the difficulties on purpose, resistance through acting stupid, as protest. An unhappy soldier in the Second Reserve recalled how he and his comrades had acted, in his words, like monkeys and deliberately fouled all attempts at proper drill maneuvers.[34] Forced into seemingly pointless and boring routines, some troops chose subversion, employing the "weapons of the weak."[35] They dragged their feet, they played dumb, and they made their officers suffer through drill with them. Perhaps the result of soldiers' ineptitude, perhaps the cause of it, the NCOs enforced drill order harshly, with brutal beatings and obscene insults.

Punishments and Pain

Nursing new bruises and muttering complaints under his breath, Diego settled in for another night. Every small error earned him kicks and slaps from the always-watchful sergeants. They swore at him and punished him for no reason at all! Flinching as he rolled onto a bruised rib, Diego whispered to his file mate, "I'd like to catch that sergeant in a dark alley some night." His friend replied,

"He'd like that too, the big bastard." They fell silent as the cabos made one last pass through the patio.

Days wore on to weeks, and weeks to months, and the routine ground onward. Perhaps despite himself, he became competent as a modern soldier. Constant lining up and responding to snapped orders or tinny horn blasts made the poor villager into something new. His shame of the first night's stumble though the city in chains transformed into a uniformed swagger. On parade Diego knew he represented a grand sight in the ordered ranks of troops moving together through streets. He winked at girls they passed when he thought the officers could not see him. But back in barracks, drill instructors rode the recruits without respite. When the sergeants cursed, Diego jumped to attention. He despised the constant cruelties inflicted on soldiers but was amazed when, a year later, new conscripts arrived and acted like clumsy monkeys! When one fresh idiot tried to push past him in the meal line, Diego never thought twice and laid the recruit out on the patio with a black eye. To his relief, Diego's sergeant just laughed at this along with the rest of the veterans.

One cannot set this practice of corporal punishments within our norms of behavior. For many recruits a substantial yet reasonable beating for mild insubordinations, while never popular, at least fell quite within anticipated bounds of normal response. The thrashings and nasty treatment of troops did serve another purpose by providing the inoculation of hatred.[36] NCOs had the responsibility to expose new soldiers to the psychological stress of personal animosity, through dehumanizing, in order to prevent them from having to process the idea on a battlefield. Through vicious treatment, the theory asserts, the NCOs would better prepare their charges for the inhuman task of killing other men without hesitation. In ordinary circumstances most humans avoid deadly response to other people. Soldiers, for instance, more readily slash at opponents than stab at them, despite the latter having more likely fatal effects. Indoctrinating face-to-face and reflexive killing into normal men requires instilling some degree of antisocial outlook or even a mild psychotic break. Some exhibit sociopathic symptoms, and these soldiers in particular became valued and courted as truly useful on the battlefield, if not so welcome in barracks. The character of the hardened soldier would be created, or revealed, through violent beatings. The best of them the army would groom to become the next generation of sergeants. In the Porfirian officer corps, this method had many adherents, although a small minority argued that "sweetness" might better instill civilized decorum to balance their natural savagery.[37]

I have no doubt that recruits' negative experiences with verbal abuses constituted a form of symbolic violence. Physically painful or damaging acts complemented this. The profane assaults on the troops' psyches worked to undermine how they saw themselves, how they built self-esteem, and how they chose to present themselves to others. In the long term soldiers adapted to the presumed truths of the abuses, if not literally than in their sense of deserved subordinate status. As in so much of the training, this idea of breaking old habits of self through harsh infantilization offered the subsequent opportunity to reconstruct what officers deemed an appropriate modern military identity. While every salute ingrains an unthinking gesture of submission, all routine also becomes solidarity. Repeatedly performed symbolic violence directed at vulnerable subjects removed their choices and dissolved their subjectivity. They became objects, sometimes even in their own minds. Even those recruits who openly despised the treatment, moreover, eventually came to abuse newer conscripts and subordinates using the same lingo formerly used against them. They became hard.

Soldiers rarely complained officially of ill treatment for fear of reprisals, but private memoirs recall that the prevailing means of drill instruction involved vicious blows, kicks, and foul verbal attacks. The government had officially banned corporal punishment in 1824 as a break from colonial habits but also to court the support of soldiers and militias across the nation more broadly. It did not fully end in practice, and the army reinstated it temporarily during the 1860s French Intervention. Juárez rescinded the ruling once he regained power, likely for reasons similar to those of the framers of the 1824 Constitution. Nonetheless, it continued as the de facto means of ensuring obedience and order in army units, normally just out of sight of officers. Managing so-called brutes through force seemed normal given the racial and eugenic assumptions that framed barracks life. The lower orders, the common soldiers, had to learn obedience immediately, and perhaps in time this would bring them to virtuous service.

The recruit would learn to listen and instantly obey by means of fear and intimidation. Broken like an animal, officers hoped he would become a beast without will of his own. In the words of Francisco Urquizo's autobiographical protagonist, the corporal as a superior could demand that he endure and obey, that he would become submissive, docile, crushed. Urquizo uses the phrase *agorzomado*, which connotes completely broken and hints at a moral and mental decay.[38] Sergeants and cabos—generally larger, violent, and fully adults— regularly struck troops. Officers chose NCOs in part due their capacity to

encourage discipline and enforce unwritten rules of subordination. These
came from traditions or customs and set limits on unruliness in the ranks, or
at least minimized the degree of subversion possible. They established through
violence a crude pecking order that roughly acceded to the official hierarchy of
power. The intimidation regime complemented formal regulations. The troops,
through selected overseers, policed their own behaviors. Career NCOs facilitated this coercive disciplining through basic, yet unsanctioned, violence. The
denigration that accompanied it went beyond crude force.

Obscene language reinforced the NCO's masculine status over the emasculated recruits, as the latter could not reply. Obscenities tended to insult the
recruit's manliness, his sexuality, and his family. Called *chingada, pendejo,
maricón, hijo de puta,* and *cabrón,* regardless of any offense taken, the new
soldier could do nothing.[39] The blasphemies and curses highlighted power
relations and intensified a recruit's feeling of vulnerability before his new
superiors. The verbal abuses feminized, emasculated, or infantilized him. The
hapless recruit had little recourse but to accept a tirade that mocked his status
and questioned his manliness. The possibility of simply brushing aside such
a tirade in a jocular way diminished with the real chance that an NCO would
follow it with a physical beating. Troops, sometimes referred to as *los razos* or
los pelonas due to their haircuts, also faced sexualized humiliations. A veteran
recalled that the recruits stripped naked for their officer, and he remarked that
it was only with this figurative castration that one became a true soldier.[40] As
the young trooper took the verbal attacks over and over, superior officers
worked to break his original gender identity and independence, at least in
theory.

The simple practical application of intimidation and demeaning came
naturally to most NCOs, who would also have had their own experiences as
a recruit as source material. It did not represent a part of concerted planning
but rather a cycle of abuses. Still, the discipline created worked to exacerbate
a power differential that also at times took on symbolically embodied
meanings.

Following ritualized sermons, soldiers were set to the repetitive tasks of
sweeping the parade square or, for those under punishment, the intentionally
emasculating tasks of *limpieza* (cleaning). Beyond ensuring basic hygiene, the
tasks held a deep cultural significance that threatened their masculinity and
shamed them publicly. For all soldiers, the call of Orden at 11:00 a.m. signaled
an hour of repairing and cleaning arms and equipment. But in between morning instruction and noon rations, sergeants also used domestic chores as a

special means to discipline their charges. Frustration with minor infractions could yield a beating. When these failed, cleaning duties came as the next-harshest resort. To outsiders this perhaps seems an odd thing to consider as escalation, but with troops' gendered expectations of the time the NCOs knew they had a potent tool.

Cleaning represented one of the most shameful possible punishments available. Soldiers whose masculinity already faced attack bitterly resented being put to menial tasks, which made them into servants for their comrades. Their chores included close scrubbing of sleeping areas and latrines, preparing food, and doing laundry—all, as far as they were concerned, women's work.[41] Some in the working class feared that barracks life would create effeminate men. While this did not appear to entail as serious an anxiety as seen in Brazil, it nonetheless made many uncomfortable. Soldiers' complaints in their personnel files support their view that this labor was not manly. Not near as onerous as road labor nor as tedious as drill, limpieza nonetheless instilled dread due to its shameful nature.[42] If soldiers viewed themselves as manly, then clearly those engaged in women's work were neither macho nor real soldiers. Troops so detested this chastising that some petitioned to be sent to military prison rather than be lowered to maidservant for lengthy periods.[43] Outsiders too derided these duties and the men who did them, and El Imparcial referred to all soldiers as mere "monkeys with brooms."[44]

While using a broom sounds relatively benign, sweeping had had an association with women's work since precolonial times and thus reference to a broom represented a serious insult.[45] In Nahuat homes the ordering of the universe depended on the women's sweeping of the domestic sphere, which mimicked and created harmony. Among the Mayas, two harmful deities of the Xibalba underworld haunted the untidy home and hid in unswept corners waiting to stab the residents. Ancient mythic notions of appropriate gendered behavior, in particular sweeping, continued in new forms into the twentieth century as custom and tradition.

Sweeping appears in numerous cartoons and images in Porfirian newspapers as a marker of male shame. Depictions of indigenous men wielding brooms in El Hijo de Ahuizote emphasized their lack of couth and their inherent lack of proper masculinity. A famous Posada image of the Famous 41 transvestites showed mustachioed men in gowns sweeping the street on their procession to the ship that would transport them to Progreso.[46] Officers clearly chose in this case to highlight exactly which crime the men had committed,

FIGURE 2.1 José Guadalupe Posada, *Calavera de los patinadores*. Hoja suelta, pub. por A. Vanegas Arroyo.

choosing to have the men dress in drag (all of them, not only those captured in dresses) and indicating their deviance with the brooms. They framed the whole experience as a threat to masculinity. In this context, servicio de limpieza reinforced gendered expectations and added public shame to the officers' and sergeants' tools for training. If the soldier lacked honor, shown by insubordination, then they would publicly shame him. They reinforced the hierarchy of the army ranks within a cultural façade of expectations, making relative social status manifest with the seemingly innocuous task of sweeping. Of course, this also produced a clean barracks, so everybody (else) won.

While one side of the experience thus made soldiers through reduction, another agenda sought to build citizens through scholarly instruction. Formal education became an evolving priority, particularly the goal of returning men to the countryside after five years as full literates. Díaz's famous 1908 interview with US reporter James Creelman revealed his belief in the essentially childlike nature of his indigenous subjects. The president claimed they had potential, as did the nation, which only a proper and firm education might release. The interview relates Díaz's vision of an immature nation in need of a strong, patronizing leader, who, given time, might eventually make modern citizens from primitive peoples through education.[47] Likewise, many officers believed that illiteracy prevented the inclusion of the uncultured peasant into civilized politics and society.

Orden—11:00

The army, alongside the schoolhouse and factory floor, could elevate the illiterate and backward to modernity. In the new liberal, secular society, proper civil behavior, or *civilismo*, might entail little more at this initial stage than literacy. Of course, this proved a loaded term; there exist many variations on the literacies that applied to ordinary Mexicans.[48] The assumptions of the elite prescribed that the modern citizen evolved into one who shared particular values of anticlericalism (in politics), consumerism, patriotism, and so forth. To bring that vision to fruition, some saw the barracks as an ideal space. Díaz's military embraced this idea, and the impetus to teach soldiers more than simple, rote skills would see increasing efforts and sophistication in the educational programs taught in the Troop Schools between 1876 and 1911.

The liberal project since 1821 had called for the creation of an educated yeoman class.[49] The turmoil of the nineteenth century and the lack of state finances had left this aspiration largely unfulfilled, and land redistribution had long since failed to build a critical mass of small farmers.[50] With a new stability and a proper treasury, the regime made concerted efforts to improve education.[51] Undertaken with an eye to foreign sciences, education became a fetish for the positivists building a nationalist society. Literacy programs in the barracks, one facet of this, seemed an obvious and cost-effective place to start, costing a mere 20,000 pesos a year in 1900, going up to nearly 50,000 pesos by 1906.[52] The long-term gains from developing a more civilized populace of readers justified an investment in the barracks. Society would benefit and progress along positivist stages if only the poor caught up. In Troop Schools the officers had the perfect opportunity to address this target audience. Males, poor and young, with no concrete stakes in their old community and with their attention guaranteed by the heavy fists of NCOs, could be successfully inculcated with modern knowledge. These young men represented the counterparts to those put to work on potentially radical factory floors, to recalcitrant indigenous "savages," and to traditionally religious farmers. Properly taught, they would oppose these dangerous elements at bayonet point. The right education fixed all.

Assuming recruits did not act out too badly, a sharp contrast lay between drill square and classroom. Hard physical practice of marching and bayonet charges, punctuated with beatings by NCOs, left the trainees bruised and sore. Of course, the classroom had its own discomforts, with poor ventilation, hard seats, and, often, droning, monotonous instruction where losing your focus sent you back to the mercy of waiting sergeants. Even more, the ordeal of learning to read and write presented a true mental torture for many recruits, some of whom barely spoke Spanish. The classroom presented a less arduous physical challenge, but much like the drill square it did involve a degree of symbolic violence. Recruits learned, for example, a version of their own history and society considerably foreign to that expressed in their homes and families. They learned to parrot it under threat of physical harm. Forced education also broke identities.

The evolution of the education program reveals changing conceptions of the soldier's role.[53] In the earliest years of the Porfiriato, the only instruction troops might receive in classrooms was rote readings of regulations and ordinances. This remained the case for over twenty years, until, in 1898, Secretary of War Felipe Berriozábal initiated new Troop Schools within the barracks and gave them a fourfold curriculum. They were to study the national language (reading and writing), basic arithmetic, basic geometry, and civic instruction. The last combined national geography with historical lessons to teach basic patriotic knowledge; the nationalist lessons of Independence received special focus.[54] Upon the turn of the century, nonetheless, these basic lessons were transformed into a course package both more sophisticated and more patronizing.

Beneath the fervent and obvious lessons of official history, some powerful currents eddied. Antiforeign sentiments built a rhetorical style that privileged a conception of Mexico as a coherent natural whole recovering from predatory invaders. In this depiction individual states or towns become parochial segments of the all-important nation. The patria chica receded, submerged into the narrative of the country as a whole. If the institution succeeded in teaching this mode of thought, then soldiers' childhood tales of local heroes and state prominence would be supplanted by loyalty to president and nation.

As secretary of war from 1900 to 1902, General Bernardo Reyes added to the instructions a degree of modern concern and realistic pragmatism. He identified problems in method, materials, and texts that he felt created difficulties for the students. Although training was a priority, he did not see the point in overburdening soldiers and mandated that schooling could not exceed one and a half hours per day, taught by subaltern officers, and that the curriculum should be both practical and convenient. To this end, his office would let the barracks know which texts to use, and they would reflect the needs of a modern military man, presumably adding a scientific or positivist slant.[55] The texts added, for example, more instruction on math, geometry, and physics while reducing tales of old battles, although some of these still appeared. The practical side of Reyes did not suit the idealistic secretaries who followed him, perhaps indicating his faith in the Second Reserve project of developing citizen-soldiers that he set up between 1900 and 1903. After the reserve's cancellation a renewed emphasis on broad barracks instruction emerged.

While the soldier of 1902 to 1905 received more variety in course topics, instructors also subjected him to an enigmatic class called Thing Lessons (Lecciones de Cosas). These peculiar classes, orally instructed, consisted of an enumeration of objects and places, whether they were natural or industrial in their formation, and their correct pronunciation. After three years of such study, soldiers would also be capable of saying whether the thing in question was solid, liquid, or gas.[56] While it is difficult to ascertain why such a class seemed necessary, it may have entailed a combination of basic physics, Spanish language, and military lore. Nevertheless, more ordinary topics prevailed as Secretary Francisco Mena again reformed the schooling regulations in 1906. Further changes, including an increase to six subjects and an increase in classroom hours, emerged under the secretaries of war who followed Reyes.

The new Troop Schools seem to have made tremendous efforts to bring a real elementary education to a tier of society long deprived of it. The soldiers received a minimum of one to two hours of this classroom instruction each day, excepting only weekends, one week in December, and two weeks in June. Discounting units on campaign, nearly twelve thousand men received instruction in 1905 alone. Milada Bazant de Saldaña reports the official claim by the military that 50 percent of soldiers became literate, including an additional twelve thousand in 1907, but given critiques of the training I believe this literacy claim is perhaps exaggerated.[57] Teaching officers forced a common national language and common national history onto disparate and regionally distinct men of mostly indigenous background, if only in the barracks. Soldiers nonetheless had their own common language, only partially mitigated by official indoctrinations of "proper" Spanish (see chapter 6).

The hours of instruction went beyond mere practicality or literacy by delivering a specific patriotic message in texts. Officers eventually selected two works in particular at the height of the educational drive: Jorge Súarez Pichardo's *Hechos ilustres de la clase de tropa del Ejército Mexicano* and Ernesto Fuentes's *Historia patria*.[58] Nearly identical in form and message, both lauded the soldier as a patriotic heroic figure and urged him to adopt the self-abnegating and obedient martial ideal.

Fuentes claimed that he would use simple language in order to promote "a virile gymnastics" of patriotism, whatever that might have entailed.[59] Notably, the level of his writing was considerably higher than an early reader could manage after limited hours of classroom literacy instruction. Given the relative difficulties of the texts, it is reasonable to speculate that in most cases the officers read the books aloud and troops followed along. Fuentes's text reinforced values through rote memorization, which both authors urged, and helpfully included the definition of such useful terms as *feminine spirit* and *doña Marina*: respectively, the timid spirit of women that is unlike that of soldiers and a loyal, tender, submissive, and always-useful helper to Cortés.[60] Here the readings emphasized through contrast the nature of ideal masculinity and subordinate indigeneity.

The author also lauded the modern politician, especially the one who, coincidentally, ultimately approved and paid for the text. He described Díaz in predictably glowing terms as a great statesman whose understanding of the need for bayonets had made the national army a great institution.[61] His praise sounded extremely similar to the hero worship published in the infamous Creelman interview for *Pearson's Magazine* a year earlier. When asked whether the greater force for progress came from schools, factories, or the army, Díaz asserted, "Education and industry have carried on the task begun by the army" but then allowed, "and yet there are times when cannon smoke is not such a bad thing."[62] The rhetorical eloquence and flattery that marked both the textbook and this interview were intended to instruct an audience in the same truth—all of the nation's progress came due to the greatness of the president and, of course, his army. Fuentes thus hoped to instill in the student-soldier a sense of proprietary pride and hence loyalty. Through lurid high prose he tapped the imagination and attempted to make readers a part of the epic trajectory of the whole nation. For newly, or barely, literate young men the power of the written word meant something. Most would see few written documents in ordinary life, but those ones would be crucial: love letters and legal titles. As intermediaries also would have read these aloud, the pattern of the barracks read-along would have seemed quite familiar to any recruit—and he would have taken it seriously.

Súarez Pichardo, on the other hand, offered a book that he felt suited the terribly limited intellect of the Mexican recruit.[63] He provided a series of historical tales from the nineteenth-century's wars and used heroic examples to inspire. He encouraged teachers using his text to follow each day's reading with a memorization exercise for the soldiers that reinforced his explanation of definitions for honor, or military brotherhood.[64] Throughout his text he lionized Mexico's war heroes as representatives of true manhood. In one chapter he did speak of the heroic women who raided a French camp, killed the sentries, and captured the detachment. Nonetheless, he made a particular point to show that the real reason they were heroes was because they had sacrificed their sons for love of the patria—the commando attack by itself did not impress him.[65] Both books employed overblown, melodramatic, and overly complex prose. This suggests that reading never became a practical skill for the majority of recruits. The demands to produce national sentiments simply proved more powerful than the efforts to establish functional literacy.

The task of homogenizing populations toward a national standard, as described for France, did not entirely happen in the barracks or classroom.[66] Weber argues that by the late nineteenth century peasants from many regions became Frenchmen, united in a sense of nationalism and as secular citizens with a common tongue. These notions they learned from holidays, schools, and army service. This movement toward a cohesive hegemony fell somewhat short in Mexico. Nonetheless, the army's efforts did spread something akin to a national culture among some thousands of men, half of whom identified as purely Indian, and must be regarded as a limited success.[67] Nationalism on the popular level built narratives about history and society onto shared practices.[68] The shared miseries of the barracks aside, soldiers left the service with a repertoire of historical tales and ceremonial experiences—for some the instruction would provide a basis for imagining mexicanidad as natural, inevitable, and sacred.[69] Recruits, as with the protagonist in Urquizo's work, did experience a feeling of solidarity and respect for the ideals of nation.[70] And where mere rote learning led to dubious results, active physical involvement more clearly built deeper identifications.

Building on this rote instruction was the ritual performance of nationalism in drill square and street.[71] Part of the daily regimen saw the soldiers gathered for the reading of regulations. As each ordinance was read aloud, the punishment for infraction followed—a dismal recitation of years in prison up through execution. Standing at attention, the soldiers heard the constant recitation of legal infractions, from desertion to murmuring to murder. The ritual reinforced the semisacred nature of army service, for each sin a penance, with the sergeant filling in as inquisitor or priest. The repetition and participation recalls the Catholic call and answer, making the rite familiar and adding echoes of mass that evoked a lifetime of practiced response.[72] It added authority to regulations. Officers often spoke of the soldier's "sacred duty"; now they made that phrase seem true. The macabre nature of the price for each "sin" even engendered in the participants an odd sense of macho pride. After each charge was read, the tone changed for the penalty. As Urquizo tells it, officers read the punishments loudly and lovingly, proudly exclaiming death penalty after death penalty in a litany of threats for the recruits to absorb.[73]

The effect of such ceremony trained the social body, although subjects inherently resisted change.[74] The process of training the soldier conformed to the idea of inscribing power on the social body. It took from the recruit as it added to the soldier. It scorched the man as it forged the Mexican. The everyday, mundane reiterations of training inculcated the habits that officers sought, yet at the same time, they became normal practices loaded with hidden resistance.[75] Recruits did not try to become bad fighters or even (mostly) to remain illiterate or inept at drill. They did constantly struggle to maintain their class and cultural ideals of rugged masculinity, of solidarity, and of individuality. The social body resisted inscription because homes and communities already had profoundly marked these adult men with contrary cultural assumptions. The degree to which army training actually did manage to alter the recruits and gain their loyalties represented a remarkable and impressive feat of social engineering.

A practiced habit intoned with solemnity, even in an absurd context, becomes over time serious work at inscribing the body with power. In other words, a disciplined subject obedient to authorities and responsive to newly given norms emerges slowly from participating in the rite and seems natural. So long as the trappings and ritual pretend to hold genuine meaning, the actual message matters little and may even contain obvious contradictions. The long recital of helplessness in the face of inevitable punishments, seemingly emasculating, oddly reinforced masculine pride as the participants displayed their stoic fatalism. Fear and tragedy celebrated in ritual created awed acceptance. Executions brought death, discipline, and ritual together in one.

Fear anchored this repetitive ceremony when soldiers took part in executing their comrades, as either witnesses or shooters. The military periodical *Vanguardia* gave considerable space to descriptions of the executions of soldiers. It told the sad story of Sergeant Zuñiga, cursed with alcoholism, who tried to shoot an officer in a drunken rage in 1891. Troops from several units witnessed his execution, conveniently carried out in the cemetery, where he was shot to death as an example.[76] Another execution notice reads like an obituary, listing family members and hometown, and suggests official

FIGURE 2.2 José Guadalupe Posada, *Fusilamiento de Capitán Clodo Cotomiro*. Hoja suelta, pub. por A. Vanegas Arroyo.

remorse, as the prisoner's general purchased him a good lunch out of his own pocket.[77] Nonetheless, witnessing these ultimate sanctions played a role in reinforcing soldiers' fearful behavior and obedience, while it engendered even more hatred of the army's harsh discipline.

Many soldiers came to grips with the trauma of the executions through shared cultural expressions, especially in music. Corridos sung by soldiers built on shared sentiments by elaborating on execution cases that received considerable press, such as the death of the soldier Bruno Labastida, a coronet player shot in 1890.[78] The tale likely inspired "De Bruno Apresa," in 1902, another tragic execution song about the Second Regiment of Morelia.[79] An article reprints the reportage of an unnamed daily newspaper, telling of the sentencing, the defense, the arrival of the soldier's mother, his last dinner, his last good-byes, his procession to the execution site, the execution itself, and the autopsy after. It reports that the man was executed to fulfill the demands of rigid laws, a tragedy over which even the president "struggled against his sentiments." Labastida may well have been the protagonist of a famous corrido, with Apresa (synonymous with "arrested") used as a pseudonym to make the song more broadly applicable to later execution stories. In the song, Bruno and his sergeant both had relations with the same lady, but one night she brought a plate of food to the noncommissioned officer rather than the soldier. While on sentry duty, the enraged soldier shot his rival in the back but accidentally also wounded his corporal. The song suggests that the accidental wound led to Bruno's sentence, implying that murder of a rival would not suffice. While the military court might not agree, the common culture of the corrido audience likely felt this constituted a crime of passion and honor, equivalent in some respects to the elite practice of dueling.[80]

In hardly a speedy process, Bruno spent a hard two years in jail (where his family would have had to pay to feed him) before finally being taken to the firing squad. He waved his fellow soldiers a jaunty informal good-bye, alleviated their worried guilt, and calmly addressed a wider public. That crowds came, if indeed this was Labastida, was confirmed by newspaper

EL FUSILAMIENTO

Del SOLDADO BRUNO APRESA

En el Llano de la Vaquita, el día 29 de Abril de 1904 á las 6 de la mañana.

FIGURE 2.3 José Guadalupe Posada, *El fusilamiento del soldado Bruno Apresa*. Hoja suelta, pub. por A. Vanegas Arroyo, 1904.

reports of great mobs of lower-class spectators lining the procession route for the execution. Once in place, Bruno proved his manliness yet again by refusing a blindfold:

Muy güenos días, mis amigos—,	Very good day, my friends—,
a todos les saludó.	I salute you all.
—¡Adiós, muchachos!—les dijo	—Good-bye, lads!—he told them
cuando el kepí se quitó;	when he took off his hat;
Bruno, con mucho valor,	Bruno, with much bravery,
del público se despidió.	bid the public farewell.
Llegó el capitán Guerrero,	Captain Guerrero arrived,
se arrimó para venderlo,	he tried to blindfold him,
Bruno Apresa respondió:	Bruno Apresa responded:
—Déjeme mirar el cuadro.	—Let me see the square.

An odd thing happened when they finally shot. The squad fired eight bullets but could not kill him because he carried a holy talisman in his mouth. In counterpoint to his interaction with the gloating priest, Bruno had his own folk religious practices that ultimately proved to make him bulletproof:

Ocho balazos le dieron,	Eight shots they gave him,
pero morir no podia	but he could not die,
y era por una medulla	and it was because of a medallion
que en la boca la traía.	that he held in his mouth.

He was not so fortunate, nonetheless, when his captain fired the final shots into his head at close range. The song thus demonstrates who was to blame, truly, for the soldier's tragedy. He ultimately fell at the hands of an officer, not a soldier, having been initially protected by folk religion, not by a priest's benediction. Army and church shared guilt with the "bad" woman who started it all. Adding to the critique, for some reason his execution was witnessed by a foreigner, although the press reports of Labastida's death make no such mention. The strong anti-US feelings of many Mexicans, still raw after 1848, continued to inform the public even in corridos absolutely unrelated to economics or politics in a formal sense. The corrido ended by repeatedly proclaiming Bruno's manliness. Tough, masculine, and not for sale to foreigners, the tragic figure of the soldier struck a chord and represented how the singers envisioned their own military ideal:

que hombre como Bruno Apresa	such a man like Bruno Apresa
en el mundo no le ha habido.	the world has never had.

For the audience, the tale ended with a reassurance of a kind of immortality, and the lessons within the song transcended gossip to inform how they should feel about the army life.

Informal folk songs and regulation reading reinforced obedience and order in their own way, but the most affective rituals came with the less frequent military ceremonies for funerals, anniversaries, and changes of command.[81] More profound rites also accompanied events commemorated on April 2, May 5, and September 15, which generally demanded that entire battalions and regiments gather formally to declare allegiance to the flag. In a lengthy ceremony, soldiers and officers performed a mass dialogue that built solidarity and demonstrated a martial brand of patriotism and nationalism. According to Urquizo, this ceremony had particular power, and he found it extremely moving. An officer addressed the massed soldiers in the name of the republic and commended their discipline, bravery, and patriotism. He went on to associate the flag with their great honor and asked them to swear that they would follow the flag with loyalty and constancy, defending it in combat until victory or death. To this they would all shout as one, "Yes, I swear."[82] The flag ceremony, perhaps because of its rarity, seemed to hold an especially emotional power.

Final Roll Call—1800—and Calls of Retreat and Silence— 2000 and 2100

The official routine also ended with a certain degree of ritual. Each day at 6:00 p.m., with the end of instruction, the whole unit from trooper to colonel assembled on the patio of the barracks. In this moment of solidarity, and prior to the last meal, soldiers listened to a final roll call and the names of those slated for punishments. This fulfilled the practical task of ensuring no one had deserted and determining who needed to be especially watched or locked away at night. At the same time, gathering the unit together helped reinforce their identity and sense of difference from civilians. The parade highlighted an "us versus them" mentality. This exclusivity from the outside framed the basis for the vida militar.

As the official day drew toward a close the final message for troops reminded them of their vulnerability to army whims. With the last call for rations, soldiers queued in the parade patio. They then stood, forced to wait patiently for their last mealtime—like mere animals. The troops "seemed like animals trained to the commander's voice."[83] From the point of view of the instructing officers, much depended on such as successful training. Were troops the obedient beasts of the nation? Of the officers? Could the recruit master his so-called base or vulgar nature? Could he rise above "animal" and embody the modern nation? Much depended on this. For all of their efforts, the successful education of the soldier remained in doubt.

After two hours of free time that followed the last meal, soldiers gathered for one last quick head count in the main patio, a redundancy with an ulterior motive. With soldiers safely gathered in files a distance away, the last call of Atención brought the women back into the barracks for the final time. Officers and NCOs assigned to the gates screened women for contraband, mistreated some, and took bribes from others. More than just letting in women, this last call saw the barracks invaded by children, animals, and goods, all flooding inward with the somewhat ironic call of Retreat. With the even more ironic call of Silence, the barracks erupted with the noisy and noisome throng. The long day had set soldiers under the continuous surveillance of authorities, under active discipline. But with the arrival of night military officials retreated into a profound silence.

Between the calls of Diana and Silence, horns rang out to set the rhythm of the soldier's day. Careful planning orchestrated each moment and introduced the recruit to the expectations of his military and political superiors. Reflexive and uniform obedience set the soldiers apart from ordinary civilians. Yet simply building an effective army represented only part of the daily agenda.

Conclusion

Officers worked to create a modern, national, nonindigenous soldier—descriptors that they came to believe were synonymous. He would, ideally, be literate, patriotic, and disciplined through constant instruction, painful beatings, and grueling drill. The soldier's nationalism, officers hoped, could rise out of hyperpatriotic textbooks, ritualized recitations, and participatory ceremonies. Rhetoric could become reality if they but reiterated it and performed it with enough frequency. The mainly indigenous recruits would become purely Mexican, without racial or regional identities, by giving them Spanish language and elementary education, new clothes and shoes, and new hygiene and cuisine. With their limited resources, it was perhaps predictable that these methods did not persuade their subjects.

The new servants of the nation came to the army reluctantly and resisted its grip constantly. This struggle to survive underlay their understanding of their place in a modern Mexico. While officers and intellectuals attempted to civilize the lower-class body and mind, recruits instead retained most of their old habits and loyalties and even would develop new vices in urban garrisons. Men forced into a service they knew to fear and loathe faced five years of boredom, humiliation, and deprivation. Inadequate facilities and resources hindered proper training. NCOs attempted to break them, and no time or energy remained to rebuild them. Poor pay and rations made life uncomfortable, and the recruits' dependence on soldaderas led to conflicts and a sense of vulnerability. Superiors made this pressure on a soldier's masculinity worse through their means of instilling discipline. Ceremonies and rituals affirmed loyalty to the ideal nation, but their comrades and conditions continually reminded them that the Porfirian nation still felt alien.

The ideal army experience that officers envisioned broke and rebuilt the man through routines that conditioned behavior at a less-than-conscious level. The daily training of the soldier aimed to make discipline the normal state. Elements of aural signaling, not unlike Pavlov's bell, resonated through this structure as horn calls broke the day into discrete sections some ten times between dawn and dusk. The routine became inescapable, as the sounding of the bugle reached every corner of the garrison and into the community around it. Each day thus became orderly and predictable, and the recruits' activities at each soundpost worked toward reflexive obedience. Training thus moved far past merely marching in tandem. Discipline wrought the ideal soldier-citizen and his mexicanidad. The army experience became metaphor for the nation.

The disciplinary impulse set upon soldiers was intended to instill an eventual self-surveilling self-control, just as ideally ruled "le militaire."[84] This powerful idea made a reality out of sheer efforts of will. It applied equally to the national transformations that the Porfirian regime attempted. A sense of modern propriety and conscientious shame could drive individuals to better the society around them as they used technologies and gave up traditional vices. Elite reform projects targeted many sites, including railways, pulquerías, department stores, paved streets, urban parks, schools, and firehouses.[85] It was a modernist social contract. The modern Mexican could enjoy the fruits of new scientific advances and institutional improvements in exchange for personal discipline as a worker, mother, merchant, consumer, and so on. This applied especially strongly to those under the constant gaze of the state, such as prisoners and, of course, soldiers. The troops' experiences of disciplinary forces make them another useful metaphor for the nation as a whole.

Ex-soldiers speak of the deep stirring they feel, many years later, when they hear the provocative call of a military trumpet. Training methods have resulted from deliberate and prolonged experimentation whose goal has always been to make men willing to break a profound taboo hardwired into our species: thou shall not kill. As difficult was training reluctant soldiers to follow reflexively the orders likely to cause their own, or their friends', deaths. The army had few resources with which to make this ideal outcome real. It had, often, less than promising material to work with, and perhaps due to this, or simply the cycles of tradition, officers resorted frequently to violent methods of teaching. Tragically, this turn to the extreme also marked many other elements of Porfirian nation building.

From peasant to recruit to soldier, the youth would complete his transformation by night and in between regimented hours. In the gathering gloom between jacale *(barracks) walls, another side of life, the unofficial education of a levied recruit, helped fashion a new Diego immersed in crime, disease, and vice. Here too he would find love, and even a family.*

It's a disaster . . . to facilitate the means for the troops to satisfy their physiological necessities that nature has imposed on them. This evil is the women's access to the barracks during the night for them to accompany the men. It is degrading, immoral, and unhygienic and . . . causes an infinity of conflicts.

—MANUEL MONDRAGÓN, *PROYECTO DE ORGANIZACIÓN*, 1910

CHAPTER THREE

Women of the Troop

Religion, Sex, and Family on the Rough Barracks Patio

Just a small-town girl, or maybe not even that sophisticated in truth, Melchora grew up in a largely indigenous area in the south of Mexico. Blessed or cursed with an outspoken nature, she grew tired of everyone in town demanding that she dutifully find a husband of their liking. "She's nearly sixteen and she's almost run out of time," gossiped the market square. Melchora dismissed them, since she had replied often enough that her skills as a farmer, cook, and market woman did just fine. Her boasts, the man would later claim, enflamed him beyond his control; one night a neighbor dishonored Melchora without love notes or possible witnesses. Her family could not offer any proof or pressure him into marriage. Her elderly father ominously began sharpening his machete. Always sensible, Melchora packed her small bag with clothes and left town that night to prevent the fight that likely would kill her beloved but feeble father. She found her way north, sleeping in ditches or churches and begging meals along the way with so many others similarly attracted to the promise of Mexico City. Weeks later, barefoot, ragged, and scarcely aware of the great city around her, she shuffled into the chaos of the market areas. Since her options proved limited she sought work, or free food, among the vendors. A few rather frightening men noticed her. They began drawing nearer, seeing only a young woman alone and vulnerable. She fearfully looked around for a haven, perhaps a church or the like, when a woman brazenly pushed her way through the crowd and put her hand on Melchora's arm. Her other hand rested on the

handle of a rather large knife. The approaching men suddenly found other
errands to concern them and moved away.
   "Come, niña," said the older woman, "we will find you a place."

Women and family experienced Porfirian military life just as did the male
troops. The soldadera mattered as much as the soldier. She had a central place
in the daily practices of the army. She reflected a broader community of
norms and expectations and embodied gendered relations of power.

   Inside the imposing military buildings, most of them former convents
or monasteries, a confluence of influences affected conscripts and those
around them. Contrasting with the formal regimens that sought to obtain
and shape subjects as national citizens—stripped of old habits and identities—at night and in between times the agent asserted his or her own personality. This informal element of transformation built on a number of related
sets of practice and custom, each containing its own direction and consequence. The social experience of military life with its rough leisure, sexuality,
drugs, and hygiene had a profound impact on civilians' perceptions, soldiers'
welfare, and community relations.[1] The interior world of the army mirrored,
in its own ways, the manner in which the nation embarked on a gendered
modernizing campaign.[2]

   The Porfirian regime often targeted the vulnerable of society in efforts
to present a modern façade. Women attached to the troops, found in a place
of institutional surveillance and control, often fell afoul of this impulse. This
had much in common with how the elite discursively approached womanhood and family more generally through the period. Although mere over-
simplifications of virgin-mother and whore binaries have little purchase on
reality, the regime made much of the "angel of the hearth" as a model for
class proprieties.[3] The patriarchal modes of power relations came to hold the
family as not just the exemplar of population management, of biopolitics, but
also as its implement.[4] Patriarchy in the home is patriarchy in the nation, as
Chilean feminists pointed out in the 1980s. The Porfirian elite would have
enthusiastically agreed. They consistently worked to establish their gendered
ideals of power as appropriate and natural in, among other places, the barracks. This became yet another model for families nationwide. If it failed
there, under the watchful eyes of the agents of state, it might undermine the
entire ideological project of official manliness.

   For women, no less than men, this experience built identity. In this
chapter I examine the roles of military women, their issues of sexuality, and

their interpretations of religion. I conclude with reflections on how the experience of the gendered military demonstrated the distinctive peculiarity of the nineteenth-century Mexican army and the nation that it built. Women became soldaderas for many reasons and with many differences of experience. Their influence transcended the women's mere functional place in the army, and the cultural insertions of these not quite civilians, not quite soldiers provides a new and fascinating visage of the barracks as a community rife with all the dramas of sexuality, violence, piety, and life.

The Soldadera in la Gran Familia

To Melchora, so unlike Diego, the great walls of the barracks seemed more sanctuary than dungeon. Her new friend Josefina explained it all as they walked from the marketplace. The decision to become a soldadera, a mujer de tropa, was not lightly made. She faced a hard life, nothing easy about it, but the army, Josefina explained, needed them and they did have options. Worried, Melchora asked the obvious: did this all just mean becoming a prostitute? Josefina laughed. "Don't believe all of the gossip and tall tales," she said. "Here women can be women," she proudly asserted. "We are not like other women." She admitted that some soldaderas sold sex but insisted that none needed do so. In the ranks of the women of the troops, Melchora would learn army duties better than most soldiers and find a place in a community that valued her toughness and intelligence.

The infiltration of women and children into barracks life represented a unique feature of the Porfirian military compared to its international counterparts. The presence of families, lovers, and offspring created a community separate from, yet connected with, broader urban and civilian communities. Conflicts, sexuality, religion, and relationships complete any attempt to demonstrate a vision of Mexican society and the military.

The ambiguous status of the soldadera and her role in the garrison set her apart from society; as one asserted, "Soldaderas were simply not like other women."[5] Not civilian, not military, they embodied a liminal identity. Merely by being there, they brought a feminine element into army life. One conception of the military institution envisioned it as a family in structure and purpose, a framework that highlights the distinctively sexual nature of this army.[6] The unusual presence of soldaderas and of family played in counterpoint to the conception of the army as a "second family." Uneasy with soldaderas' sexuality, some officers worried that they threatened the idea of a martial fraternity. The presence of women and children oddly made the possibility of having a family more difficult. Patriarchy under Porfirio Díaz complemented what some officer-writers termed the Great Family, a military that would obey the president as a father and love the *patria* (fatherland) like a mother. Again, this emphasizes the second-family conceit, even as some officers like Mondragón realized that the new soldiers needed first to mourn the loss of their "old" family back in the village.[7] The military fraternity as substitute family also appeared, for instance, in officers' poetry.[8]

Bonds of brotherhood aside, for most soldiers, feminine figures intervened in their patriarchal understanding. Mothers still had a presence, for example, as seen in the profound effect of a letter from his mother on the protagonist of Urquizo's army memoirs.[9] The soldadera more directly brought a feminine touch into the army. She represented an individual common to army practices and integral to the barracks life. The presence of women and families within the military quotidian played an essential role in shaping how soldiers saw themselves, how they exercised their masculinity, and how local communities envisioned the barracks. Civilian outsiders picked up on the negative imagery of the women, dirty and wild, who contrasted with commonly held ideas of military masculinity. Perhaps they were right. The women facilitated the development, or better, the affirmation, of troops' habits, vices, entertainments, conflicts, and sexualities.[10] Reinforcing some practices, introducing others, the soldadera became one shared point of reference in armed forces across the country.

Given this ubiquitous presence, no study of the army can leave the soldadera and her *compañeras* out. The women added nuance that helps explain the army life, and their omission reflects officers' dreams rather than troops' realities. Ultimately, the women's experiences also merit historical attention for their own sake.

The soldaderas had tremendous influence on the average soldier's life. They potentially undermined discipline, facilitated leisure, instigated crime, damaged reputations, and tainted hygiene. All the same, the soldaderas also enhanced the army's efficacy and life quality.[11] They, and the roles they played, had direct influence on the process of civilizing the lower-class men. In so doing, the soldaderas represented a way in which gender constructions emerged in the barracks and a significant divergence from the modernizing militaries in Europe, the United States, and Latin America.[12] Gender as a concept entails the social understanding of behavior, norms, and presence as a power relation based on perceived sexual (biological) differences. The persistent inclusion of women and children did not occur in other military groups by this era in history. Mexican elites therefore found themselves in an unhappy compromise. They needed the women. Yet having them made the Mexican army different from others, and perhaps unmodern. They chose instead to ignore the family and female presence as best they could, accepting its benefits and harms, and surreptitiously sought to manage women. The soldaderas did not always cooperate.

Prior to 1850, female camp followers appeared in armies the world over.[13] Undertaking similar duties, they facilitated the subsistence of armed forces in the field and in garrisons and formed what has been called the campaign community.[14] This rear echelon composed of women, children, vagabonds, and other opportunists followed "their" army units in the field or gathered near their garrisons and maintained basic needs of maintenance and forage. The long civilian "tail" of older-style militaries functioned to provide for the "head." The female presence, nonetheless, always added an unsavory moral element to military life, and in the eyes of theorists and officers, women presented a significant challenge to maintaining discipline. Men acted out differently under the gaze of family, and sexual rivalries encouraged violence and, at times, desertions. European armies set increasingly rigid restrictions on the presence of women in the army as military ability to handle logistics improved. With the advent of railways, armies could leave the camp followers behind and provide food and materiel at the same time.[15] The carrying capacity of steam engines preempted the female hauler-forager on the new battlefields of Europe. Most militaries around the world looked to emulate Europe as the most modern and advanced example, and by the middle of the nineteenth century camp followers began to disappear while barracks became idealized as male-only—homosocial—spaces.

The garrison represented by the mid-nineteenth century a special meaning in the gendered loci of new nations. It ideally meant a place for men, of men. This surpasses a mere designation of male-only—the importance of the homosocial environment comes from the stress on sameness and uniformity that comes as result of exclusions of women (or any other gender). Male-only loses the nuance that sets the ideal barracks as a place of solidarity comparative to, not the opposite of, a convent of nuns. This, officials accorded, could be a place where gender differences had no place and where the institution could shape its own version of manliness based on science, and on middle- or upper-class norms. Sometimes the split hair matters. Although the Mexican

army usually looked to Europe as inspiration for modernizing reforms, soldaderas continued to have their place.

Soldaderas had, in some ways, barely reached their apogee in Mexico.
While European artists like Delacroix portrayed the camp follower as a traditional historic artifact, soldaderas remained active well into twentieth-
century Mexico, even as rail networks improved. During the early republic,
Santa Anna's ill-supplied and exhausted troops at San Jacinto could have
attested to the desperate need for soldaderas, who in that case had not made
it to the battlefield in faraway Texas. Poor sentry work and deficient ammunition left his forces at a grave disadvantage, and arguably, both would have
been somewhat mitigated had the soldaderas been present. The soldadera
defied official distaste through the whole century and became an iconic figure in the armed phases of the Revolution (1910–1920), even though some
forces under Pancho Villa reportedly attempted to rid themselves of the
ladies.[16] According to one of his veterans interviewed many years later, Villa
increasingly disparaged and avoided female troops, whom he regarded as
inherently uncontrollable. This notion also appeared in stories about Villa's
army that stressed the violent, wild nature of his female troops. One notices,
nonetheless, that Villa still maintained these forces in arms when he needed
them and that men began their bad-mouthing years after these ladies disarmed, or from safety across the border. Given that these accounts came long
after the soldadera had been officially dismissed from national life and her
services reimagined, they must be considered suspect.[17] Soldaderas would
also overstay their official ban from barracks in 1925 and with appearances
on Cristero War battlegrounds into the early 1930s.[18]

Richness of life in the Porfirian army derived in large part from the presence of soldaderas. The women came from a wide range of places and backgrounds and stayed with soldiers and garrisons for different durations and
motives. Some came as sutlers, servants, wives, lovers, or prostitutes; others
became such.[19] They presented the range of legal and customary definitions
of women's gendered roles. Moreover, their tasks in barracks and on campaign varied, including combinations of cooking, laundering, feeding, selling,
hauling, smuggling, fornicating, and offering invaluable emotional support.[20]
Their roles encompassed a great range of tasks. While soldiers could not del-
egate certain duties, for example cleaning of barracks, almost everything else
fell on feminine shoulders. In a sense Mexico thus represented a highly modern army, in a twenty-first-century manner—not by choice, but the Porfirians
made use of an integrated-sex armed force outside of combat duties. Women

made it work, they did not fall into some sort of "kept" status as weaker partners, and whether smuggling or snuggling they played an essential role. For many, the difficulties of army life came as a last-resort option.

Both urban and rural garrisons attracted women who had followed husbands or lovers during recruitment, but most came to the barracks due to unemployment, underemployment, or homelessness. The waves of urban migration that so worried the gente decente brought girls and women from rural backgrounds without family supports or a community of their own—many found a living and a community in the army.[21] In a period of accelerating urbanization with relatively low industrial-sector opportunities, women had few good options in the city. Much like their male army counterparts, many among the soldaderas came from a segment of the population low on employable skills, family supports, usable educations, or community networks. A soldadera took the work she could get.

Despite largely middle-class press opinions, relatively few became prostitutes, and indeed many became soldaderas precisely to avoid this fate.[22] In the old European context some have proposed that the women fit a triad of camp-follower possibilities of prostitute, whore, and wife that seems rather limited even there.[23] More commonly they entered into relationships and marriages they deemed appropriate, and some simply worked as domestics and *vivanderas* (sutlers, or sellers of small sundries) without sexual duties. For the most part, women did not prepare official rations.[24] They cooked and sold supplemental food to the soldiers and junior officers, either on street corners or at nearby kitchens (see chapter 5). Laundry service, sometimes done in tandem with poorer soldiers, also brought them small incomes.[25] In exchange for their services, the women earned a living, received a degree of recognition from the army, obtained some protection in their often-dangerous neighborhoods, and got a solid, if unhygienic, shelter for sleeping.

The press agenda of the self-proclaimed better classes made much of the presence of these women in bad areas of town, mistaking cause for effect. They did not become soldaderas because they came from a slum; they moved to the rough places where the government preferred to house garrisons. Lacking their own homes, they made do with ramshackle daytime shelters and did their cooking and laundering wherever they could set up a small grill or find water sources. That this proved unhygienic goes almost without saying. Cleaning and washing water proved scarce. The possibilities provided by working with the army nonetheless ameliorated some of the worst drawbacks. Women gained limited rights to barracks' spaces, occasionally transport when the garrison deployed, and often the protection of a jealous man of their choosing. Genuine friendships, love, and community cemented the ties between them as well.

Garrisons had both a stable and a fluid population of women that represented some of the most enduring personnel of the military. Women could come and go and had the option to find other employment or attach themselves to other barracks.[26] Far from the dreams of the common trooper, then, women had a sort of agency. Nonetheless, in the urban barracks many stayed beyond the average term of a soldier; because officers frequently faced transfers to new regions, the soldaderas and NCOs often had years of on-site seniority.[27] In truth, even NCOs fell short in comparison. Women who had lived the military life for years, even decades, understood the unwritten codes and official regulations of the army, and even the basics of drill and march, far better than most relatively recently arrived troops.

Military accounts mostly, and not surprisingly, fail to mention this, but many of the women simply had more years of exposure to the army life and, without a doubt, as much or more aptitude to learn. Many men deserted or escaped the army within a few years, while many soldaderas stayed for life. On campaign, Frías's memoirs suggest that the women not only kept up with the deployed soldiers but also actually anticipated orders well in advance, and even set up camps ahead of the marching troops. It was also the women who judged which men would succeed as soldiers, and they selected their mates from those men.

Regardless of their education, they knew how to load a train, how much food a march required, and where to find resupply quietly and off the record. They might not always take up arms, but the women nonetheless held a body of knowledge that made the military function despite, and contrary to, popular accounts in the civilian press. The army thus always had a hard core of local veterans—a few thousand half-trained sergeants and corporals and thousands comparatively more experienced women—that did not conform to the administration's ideal of a European-like military. From their somewhat ambiguous place in the military system and the urban community rose a need to categorize them socially, to ascribe to them labels that would make sense of their class and gender position.[28]

The Soldadera's Violent and Disruptive Presence

First impressions stamp deep. Melchora entered alongside dozens of women, many with children, and she alone came with her hands empty of baskets, blankets, and packages. She puzzled over how these tough, proud women apparently submitted meekly to officers' surreptitious gropes and overt intrusions into belongings. She saw, too, how some slipped the men a few coins. Yet the guards turned none aside, and when some became a little too "interested," the women did not hesitate to slap hands with a scowl. Blushing young lieutenants stammered apologies and passed them on into the fortress. The guards could only go so far, it seemed, and clearly everyone in line knew the limits. Melchora, smirking a little, and not paying attention, bumped heavily into a woman some ten years older and somewhat larger than herself. Whirling, the soldadera punched her in the stomach. "Welcome to the barracks," whispered Josefina as she passed the stunned girl and they shuffled on past the laughing guards. "Don't mess with the veterans," she advised belatedly. Through a haze of tears, Melchora entered the patio for the first time, stars appearing overhead and lines of strange men waiting ahead. However alien to the place, she felt immediately that she had come home. Here she would make a life. And one day that damned soldadera would get punched back, too.

The soldaderas, in finding their place, challenged the military authorities. Defined by some as a "woman belonging to soldiers," *mujer de tropa* also had a significant double meaning as "trooper woman." On the one hand, as property, the responsibility for their actions rested on the shoulders of their male counterparts. The army demanded that the women respect military ordinances and barracks rules, and officers expected soldiers to maintain a degree of control over the women or face punishment detail.[29] This most likely indicated the inability or unwillingness of the officers to personally enforce rules on the half-civilian women in their garrison. They needed to operate within certain limits to make the situation work at all. On the other hand, as troopers of a sort the officers also had a personal responsibility to police soldaderas' behavior. They had the authority to restrict access to the barracks. Officers could, and sometimes did, proclaim a woman a *mujer de mala vida* (woman of the bad life) rather than a mujer de tropa and ban her entrance. Generally this meant that the woman had been identified as a prostitute without a specific regular partner and one whose presence caused disruptions through alcohol abuse, fighting, and so forth. Officers who routinely allowed indiscreet women, therefore, faced up to fifteen days' arrest in the Flag Room (Sala de Banderas) for "receiving women of the bad life that distract [men] from their obligations."[30]

This regulation theoretically protected soldiers from the life of disorder that a prostitute caused, but in practice, military officials rarely invoked this option, choosing instead to accept bribes and favors for garrison access. Extortion regulated entrances into the facilities, and even known "bad women" could find their way inside. This also applied while on campaign, and even in the field, officers attempted to keep an accurate registration of the women attached to their force and to regulate their interactions with soldiers.[31] While the unit marched women could face harsh disciplinary measures, or even outright abandonment, but only when they acted individually. When they acted en masse the officers could not easily challenge their behavior without demonstrating to the troops exactly how limited their authority truly was. Even with complete redeployments by rail, the women at times convinced the army to acquiesce to their needs. One officer went to great lengths, for example, to provide railcar space for women and children and their belongings when his unit relocated from Chiapas to Central Mexico.[32] He, at least, saw them as integral parts of his battalion, perhaps as family. In many other cases women faced much less consideration, and the army subjected them to the same casual indifference and indignities that men faced.

Rafael Aponte offered a vision of what the women experienced daily.[33] When the bugle called Atención each evening around six, lines of women filed up at the portal to the barracks. They brought with them their children, their pets, their *petates* (sleeping mats), and their baskets filled with food and trifles. The officers at the gate might leer at their bodies, steal some of their victuals, and prod through their belongings with a bayonet. Eventually they allowed women to enter the patios and seek a place to sleep or to set up a *tiangui* (storefront) in which to sell their now-abused goods for a few hours' time.

Despite the unsettling chore of passing through this guard post, women continued to come and officers continued to allow their presence.[34] Notably, even with disruptions that invariably arose when women and children inhabited the barracks, no guards ever excluded them for more than a short while, including even those at the National Palace.[35] While the gate inspection seems at first glance to suggest the soldaderas' impotence against officers' whims and gaze, it may have been only an incidental harassment of little weight. Control of women's access entailed more compromise than officers liked to admit. In some cases, officers had specific orders to establish an understanding with the soldaderas regarding conditions for entrance, implying a measure of agency on the part of the women. Their instructions called on the junior officers to negotiate, not to dictate, which women had access.[36]

These young men with little real power typically made whatever arrangement the more experienced soldaderas proposed to them. Indeed, women even seem at times to have given orders, or at least to have hinted with assurances, and to personally have taken responsibility within the garrison. Attempting to dodge blame, one sergeant allowed women into a restricted area against orders simply because one woman claimed it would be permissible.[37] He obviously presumed that these orders from a normal soldadera trumped his own. Unfortunately for the sergeant, his immediate superior beat him for the transgression. At least in this one case the junior officer had the weight of regulations on his side and still chose immediate (and illegal) corporal punishment rather than bring the matter to his superiors. He also may have felt some confusion over the standing of the woman's orders. The ability of the soldaderas to offer insolence to officers in other venues makes this interpretation of their agency that much more likely.

Women had ways of exercising their own influence, disrupting military order and decorum with tremendous insouciance, and officers could do little to counter them. One of the most powerful displays of Díaz's army as modern, organized, and cosmopolitan, a performance that legitimated the nation itself, was the military parade. Yet officers complained that women frequently fouled this spectacle of order, especially during the larger parades on May 5 (Battle of Cinco de Mayo), April 2 (Battle of Puebla), and September 16 (Independence Day), by running alongside the streets where their men paraded. In one description, the soldaderas trampled everyone in their way, even knocking over other spectators in order to stay close to their units. The author went on to complain that although officers had made superhuman efforts to keep the women away from the men, they had failed. With the least slip of caution, the women made contact and the soldiers committed "excesses" they regretted later. These transgressions often led to the soldiers' hospitalization—what precisely these excesses might be remained mysterious. Rather than blaming the soldaderas, this officer concluded that the men had gotten soft, not like in the old days, and were not accustomed to hardships.[38] The connection he made played into the normative discourses on gender. Women, according to many, made men softer and weaker through their sentimental influences. This reflected a fault in men's character and something inherent to the nature of women. Given the tenderness this attributed to women, their choice to disrupt the parade and face official censure seemed unusual.

Why would the women do such a thing, facing the jeers of the crowd and the ire of the officers (and maybe of the soldiers, too) later? They might have

seen the parade as an opportunity to gain recognition of their role in the
military, and they took part in the only way they could. Possibly they saw the
spectacle as a celebration and participated in a carnivalesque fashion, adding
their own inverted statement of parading, masculinity, and theater to the
occasion. Their actions could also demonstrate fear of separation from their
men, however temporary and however orchestrated. Regardless of their
motives, they shattered an important military fantasy by becoming visible to
the watching audiences, by compelling viewers to acknowledge the presence
of the soldaderas in the midst of the apparently modernized military. For a
modern regime set on a clear separation of streets, homes, and barracks this
marring of the ceremonial occupation of the city offended at a basic level.
March in parades entailed a claim by the regime over the public sphere. The
unruly soldaderas, inadvertently or not, had defied this. By claiming a space
in the streets, the homemaking women of the barracks shattered the ideal
separation of spheres, and they did so in the face of officials and civilians.

Nor did officers punish soldaderas once back inside the barracks walls.
Generals and colonels could order subordinates to discipline them, but fear of
soldiers' reactions put limits on superiors directly interfering with "their"
women. Soldiers stood at attention some distance away during the gate queue
and so permitted harassment to some degree. Yet officers knew that to enter
the main patios at night proved dangerous at the best of times, and to mistreat
the women while there would be inciting violence.[39] Beyond physical perils,
interfering with the women also correlated with high desertion rates, and
since officers on night duty could not leave their posts, the ill will of the
women might lead to many hungry evenings. For example, a sublieutenant in
a Mexico City barracks faced charges of deserting his post while serving as
officer of the week. Having angered his troops and their women, he could not
procure his dinner nor command a soldier to fetch it, and so he left the gate
to buy his meal himself and was later punished.[40] Aponte remembered his fear
of the rough and scarred soldiers he encountered in the barracks, as did
Manuel Mondragón.[41] This is not to call the toughness of the junior officers
into question. Recruits and veterans in the barracks typically had years of
brawling experience and considerable muscle in comparison to the somewhat
more pampered late-teenaged subalterns. Soldiers also demonstrated a frequent lack of basic judgment when it came to protecting their women's honor.

Therefore, this anxiety did have a basis. A Major Herrera complained to
his commander about drunken civilians in the Twenty-Fourth Battalion barracks who stabbed him while his soldiers watched. Not only could he not count

on the assistance of his martial brothers, they did not apparently care if he survived. This becomes clear since after the knifing a corporal not only robbed him of every centavo but then also ate Herrera's dinner and laughed at him. In terms of respect, in terms of basic safety, not even the major's food survived. Yet as in many trial cases, the aggrieved man left out some important details.

The stabbed man had violated important elements of the barracks' unwritten code. Herrera's immediate superior clarified the actual events, asserting that the major had hit and cursed at an amasia in the barracks and was roughed up for his troubles. In other words, his beating and stabbing, possibly at the hands of the soldadera herself, rose from his own actions. Not only did his superior fail to support his claim for justice, but he clearly felt that the major had brought it on his own head and deserved at least that much violent repercussion. That it came from someone who was technically a civilian, and a woman, did not matter. The social expectations of the barracks, its local moral economy, dictated that interfering with the women warranted a violent reaction, and officers, just the same as troops, did not enjoy any impunity from this. The major's abuses demonstrated limits to control in the garrison. As a further note, the questionable Herrera may not have been the most scrupulous of men; at his funeral two years later *both* of his wives attended.[42] The barracks had its own limitations and rules.

Even on campaign, the soldaderas did not follow officers' orders or give them the respect they demanded.[43] During the expedition against Tomochic in 1893, Heriberto Frías described several incidents that highlight the relative autonomy of the camp followers. Attempting to keep close order on the march, officers ineffectually shouted at women bringing water to their men in columns, and the women only responded with laughter.[44] As men rose in the morning, Frías complained about the insolent looks that he received from the women, who lolled about until it was time to march. In the actual fighting, the women defied orders, and perhaps good sense, in order to run ahead of the siege lines to collect water under fire. Understanding both the troops' dire thirst and the likely hesitation of villagers to fire on women, they simply acted—much as good soldiers should. At the same time, Frías also exhibited some ambivalence toward these women that he and his comrades, clearly, could not control. Unruly, immoral, and pitiable on the one hand, he also saw them as angels and heroines worthy of his respect.[45] He often found this dual nature of gender in Mexican military life fascinating, and it appears not only in his 1893 account but also in a number of his later poems and publications.[46]

The frequent failure of officers to exert control over soldaderas more accurately reflected the reality of gender relations in the barracks then did the letter of the regulations. Officers' interference with women had limits. Soldiers and NCOs frequently, and with good reason, also surrendered claims to power over women upon whom they depended. And the mujeres de tropa at times mobilized resources to protect against violations of their personal sense of propriety.

The women maintained the order of their own ranks, occasionally with violence, but largely avoided criminal prosecution if not press censure. Soldaderas made their own code and enforced their own rules. Poaching customers or lovers, interference with children, or simply establishing a pecking order or seniority could lead to vicious fighting with fists or knives. These fights did not, as Buffington has shown, preclude fatalities nor did they seem to the combatants a great divergence from the upper-class ritual of dueling. To the middle-class press, nonetheless, the fights that often spilled out into more public spaces and bars simply confirmed their suspicions of the women's animalistic depravity.[47] Such a depiction, highly biased, oversimplified the way that the conflicts settled barracks into an order for both sexes.

Soldaderas also did not always tolerate male abuses that crossed a certain threshold, and they used legal recourses at times to ensure their safety.[48] The women understood the military regulations almost as well as any of the officers and could call out men who had violated the ordinances too grievously. Other times they would either leave the unit or ostracize the offender. In rare cases they might embargo all of his companions too—an entire battalion of hungry, sex-deprived men would likely succeed in adjusting even the most hardened misogynist's demeanor. Their behaviors and the reactions of those around them further revealed a moral economy understood by the military system.

Yet one should not get the impression that violence against women occurred infrequently or that it was generally punished. Domestic abuse did lead to charges on occasion, as women or officers pressed a complaint, although more often it likely remained unpunished. In one example, a junior cavalry officer received reprimand after being reported by his mother for beating his sister. While his mother later recanted and claimed he had since stopped, his justification for his actions was that as the head of the house he had simply fulfilled his duty to defend the family's honor, discouraging his sister from shameful relations.[49] Given his status as an officer, albeit a lowly one, his explanation sufficed and he received only a minor punishment. In contrast, the army charged a soldier for lightly wounding his amasia. Unusually, he did so in her home rather than in the barracks, and it may be that his charge stemmed more from his state of drunkenness.[50] Antonio Martínez in Puebla also received charges for wounding "his woman," one Bibiana Medel, another charge aggravated by alcohol.[51] In these as in many other examples, formal legal processes deliberated on the extenuating circumstances—location, rank, severity, and most common, alcohol use. The cases of women beaten in non-public (nonbarracks) locales, or by a drunken officer, did not often make it to trial. This potential for violence did not define women's roles.

Conscripts depended on the women's willing assistance for their quality of life, and despite certain limits, women had a degree of mobility and choice that outstripped those of the usually restricted troops. Without a woman, the soldier faced poor food, cold nights, and the loss of contraband, a situation made worse if he was imprisoned. Once jailed a soldier became especially dependent on the soldaderas and their mercy. Prison pay did not meet market prices, and jailers did not provide rations. One had best be on good terms with the local women. On occasion the health of prisoners suffered in this system. For example, medical officers wrote that in prisons of the Seventh Regiment the rations given by women to individuals did not always arrive, or proved insufficient.[52]

Women also provided another underestimated service by caching contraband. At times men could get out and get their own food, alcohol, and so forth, but keeping these once they returned to barracks could prove problematic. With few hiding spaces and no personal gear, the men would lose their ill-gotten gains to thieves, bullies, or simple expectations of sharing. The soldaderas came and went with closed baskets, flowing skirts, and grubby kids—all of which could become caches for small items and holding spots for personal belongings. The women also had regular access to allow for restocking these goods, and regularity of supply also came with its own premium of value.

Of Intimacy and Privacy in the *Vida Militar*

Melchora acclimated to the routine. She felt grateful in evenings that she had a safe shelter and made close friends among the other women. As the months passed, she had begun to make her living selling enchiladas to soldiers; she purchased them herself from a pulquería, so she had an excuse for charging troops so much. Dominga, the woman who had hit her on that first evening so long ago, she had since repaid in kind. They might never be friends, but they shared a degree of wary respect at least. Oddly, then, it was Dominga and not her close friends who first noticed where Melchora's gaze lingered when they gathered with the soldiers. "That boy," she grinned, "he's new. You must wait. But when he's ready, we'll get him for you." Awkward and oblivious, Diego had no idea he had been targeted, and he wouldn't know for months. When the soldaderas finally felt the soldier met their approval, they quietly let Melchora know. She contrived to stray near him and waited for his stuttering and halting advances. They drank together, and she shared her sleeping mat with him that evening. This became a regular arrangement, she began bringing him food (at cost), and she even pulled her knife on a soldadera who batted her eyes at him once too often. The battalion understood that she and Diego were husband and wife, even if they had never stepped inside a church together or appeared before a priest. Half a year later, her belly swelled. She resolved to be a proper mother, even in this unusual lifestyle she had chosen.

Having a regular female partner therefore made life better. The acquisition of what the men sometimes disparagingly termed viejas ("old ladies") could prove challenging.[53] Finding potential mates seems to have entailed a rite of institution. Men new to the barracks often had simple expectations of what they might need in order to attract a woman. For instance, one mourned that his inability to obtain a soldadera stemmed from his lack of *fierros* (irons). This loaded term had three possible interpretations: he lacked metal coins to buy love, he lacked a knife to fight for it, or he lacked an erection to make love to her.[54] The protagonist of *Tropa vieja* moved through various stages in his search for a woman. At first he was content to pay for sexual services, managing to bargain with a woman whose regular partner fell asleep early. From this temporary, and dangerous, circumstance, one of the more experienced soldaderas approached him next. She made it clear that he had passed some threshold to become an acceptable partner, perhaps by his behavior in the barracks or simply by time in service. With his agreement, she searched for a suitable partner and presented her a short while later.[55] His new compañera fulfilled his wishes exactly: she was experienced in the army life, relatively attractive, and safely available. Presumably he fit her tastes, as the two wed on the spot.[56]

Choice of partner demonstrated a normative set of gendered assumptions and behaviors. It was assumed that one should marry. The appropriate partner had put in enough time and proven that he or she could thrive or at least survive the barracks life. These men had proven they could work within the system, at least sufficiently to avoid either overly frequent imprisonment or banishment to another unit. The men could not be too much younger or older. The women selected from their best prospects, and for at least some of them romance also played a part of the calculus.

The nature of the chosen relationships greatly influenced gender behaviors. While some women sold goods to all, emotional and sexual relations often had an exclusive nature. The relatively open sexuality nevertheless had a strangely egalitarian effect on the garrison, which worried some officers. The power of the NCOs to maintain boundaries between their charges and themselves, essential to keeping order through coercion, eroded when women put them all on a relatively equal footing for sexual access. Aponte noted that this even competition made all the men equal and undercut military authority. Likewise, another soldier argued with his corporal that "since we are all in barracks and the women here *rolan* [have sex] with everybody, we are all equal."[57] Nevertheless, this sort of arrangement did not represent a normal state of affairs, and prostitution came at a high price, indicating its relative rarity.

Sex for one night was often far beyond the meager pay of a recruit, costing as much as two pesos, an amount equal to a careful month of saving and sacrificing.[58] Moreover, purchasing sex did not, by any means, necessarily lead to the sort of reliable relationship where a soldier had a partner who would continue to assist him in prison or on campaign.[59] By regulation, women and families were always to have access to soldiers jailed or hospitalized. Some soldaderas thus traded on their scarcity and mobility to demand a degree of autonomy and respect in exchange for stability.[60] This is not to imply a purely cold or calculating functionality, and couples could and did form romantic and loving relationships as well.[61] Indeed, some new soldiers observed the couples in barracks with a poignant sense of loneliness and exclusion, while foreign observers during the Revolution also noted the apparent happiness of many couples they witnessed.[62] Nonetheless, the nature of most relationships set unusual limits to male power and influenced soldiers toward increased macho displays.[63]

The blame for machismo did not lie with women alone, of course, but the presence of women often led to posturing, competition, and frustration as soldiers interacted with peers, civilians, and officers. The archive shows bias on this issue, as cases that make it to the historical record reflect excessive and criminal exceptions to gendered relations. Far more often relationships developed as they did everywhere else. The couples loved, respected, honored,

FIGURE 3.1 José Guadalupe Posada, *La soldadera maderista*. Hoja suelta, ca. 1911.

nurtured, and tolerated one another. Macho or macha displays demonstrated deep feelings and profound betrayals that simply went beyond the limits of the norm. Still, between Mexican couples in general power tended to fall more into male hands.

Machismo, a hypermasculinity based on norms of misogyny and violence, and often binge drinking, emerged from the sexual and gendered relationships between soldaderas and recruits. Sex represented an important commodity and power for soldaderas, in addition to being an end of its own. Given men's virtual imprisonment, withholding sex or changing partners afforded some women a degree of power over relations with soldiers. Barracks sexuality, nonetheless, also contributed to the construction of masculine behaviors that mitigated this power difference. Other factors, such as training stresses and officers' abuses, certainly also played a part—nevertheless, the exacerbating factor remained the presence of the mujeres de tropa.[64] Officers rarely intervened in their troops' efforts to control their rivals or their women unless the violence spilled into public view or escalated into serious injury.[65]

Soldiers and NCOs in barracks violently competed over women, often encouraged both by onlookers and by the alcohol women supplied. In part, establishing hierarchies and hazing newcomers drove men to violence in the garrisons, with precedence for contraband, comforts, and respect going to the strongest or meanest.[66] The ubiquitous fighting over soldaderas was part of common military and popular folklore, appearing, for example, in the corrido "De Bruno Apresa," where a soldier kills his sergeant over a woman's affections, and a plate of her food. The song makes special note of how this proved poor Bruno was truly a man among men.[67] His tale particularly emphasizes the notion of masculine pride and, in the first stanza, pins the blame for his actions on a woman (often the culprit)[68] who caused his execution:

Día veintinueve de abril,	The 29th of April,
señores aconteció	gentlemen account
que fusilaron a Apresa	that they shot Apresa
y una mujer lo causó.	and a woman caused it.
En mil novecientos dos	In nineteen hundred and two
fue por los diablos tentado	he was tempted by the devil
y un crimen cometió.	and he committed a crime.

Bruno and his sergeant both had relations with the same lady, but one night she brought a plate of food to the noncommissioned officer rather than the soldier.

This was quite in keeping with the barracks culture of soldaderas. Bruno's femme fatale, the army audience would understand, took the blame for the troubles because a mere man could not be expected to resist temptation and a soldera should know better than to provoke such envy:

el enojo comenzó	the rage began
por un plato de comida	over a plate of food
	[but the real cause beneath was that]
—que ambos tenían relaciones	—both men had amorous
de amor con una mujer.	relations with one woman.

El señor don Bruno Apresa	Mister Bruno Apresa
se encontraba haciendo guardia,	found himself on guard duty,

| cuando el sargento pasó | and when the sergeant passed |
| le dió un balazo en la espalda. | he shot him in the back. |

His execution reaffirmed the limits on military men to protect their access to women.

Brutal clashes over women went beyond folk-song heroes. An extraordinary fight over a woman occurred in Mexico City in 1896 between two sergeants from neighboring battalions.[69] When Pio Gutiérrez and Candelario Carrillo discovered that they both were living *en amasiado* (as lovers) with Candelaria Montes, one challenged the other. They met outside city limits with pistols for a duel of honor. NCOs being lower than gentlemen, the authorities stopped the proceedings—it became a mere fight rather than a permissible duel because of their class status. In the trial Montes defended herself and Gutiérrez, saying that Carrillo had propositioned her repeatedly and been rejected, as she was not an available woman. Carrillo then allegedly sent her various letters that dishonored her, which she shared with the court. The letters referred to her as too stubborn to give him sex and as a disgraced woman and insulted her parentage. One obscene missive, barely literate, read in part, "Ques mull mulota y mull hijo de chingada y mull desgraciado . . . si uste no le da chigadasos mandermela para darselos yo uste es mull muela," followed with a number of "su madres" and "su padres."[70] Carrillo defended himself to the judge, pointing out that since he was illiterate, the letters could not possibly have been his. Despite his entreaty, both sergeants received punishment for the unsanctioned fight, and presumably, Gutiérrez and Montes lived happily ever after. Sexual relationships, the reward for and the cause of fierce competition, had an important place in the army's daily life.

The barracks' reputation for promiscuity, as reported in the press, emerged in part from class differences about appropriate sexual modesty and prurient modern prescriptions.[71] Soldiers' and soldaderas' unsanctioned appearances in pulquerías, for example, in La Noche Buena, occasioned the army to react with charges of "misdemeanors committed as pairs in public." One soldadera who frequented another pulquería they denigrated as depraved because "she does not even need a petate to *chingar* [fuck] her soldier." The implication suggested that she would have sex anywhere and was poor enough, vulgar enough, to do so. Other inhabitants of the barracks fell afoul of the "new" need to be dressed in public that came with modern regulation of city spaces and a prurient sense of late nineteenth-century morality that tied into hygienic standards.[72] Despite mounting disapproval from the press and the higher classes, ordinary lust would not be denied.

Couples in the barracks made do without privacy and, often, without much modesty. Sleeping areas normally comprised large open areas covered with individual petates and *cobijas* (covers). Soldiers, amasias, children, and pets slept together with little room and no real separation; indeed, officers allotted each soldier a mere one meter by two meters of space, the same as a grave.[73] At times officers also ended up sleeping among troops, reducing space further. One was charged for slumbering there when he was supposed to be on watch in the hour of "greatest danger," possibly at the hour when most desertions took place.[74] Gente decente commented negatively on this dangerously sexual environment that they deemed barbaric and animal. The perceived perils of the growing modern city in an era where scientists began to understand communicative diseases as hygienic issues led the public to take an extreme stance on the imagined wildness of the barracks. A new middle class formed around consumerism and fed periodicals' hysterical reporting, while they distanced themselves from their dark reflection in the lower classes.[75] If the bourgeoisie held the moral high ground, the soldier displayed the savage other, and the idea of crowded patios of fornication bred moral panic.

Unlike accounts from Brazil, homosexuality did not present a major public concern in regard to barracks.[76] A degree of silence on the topic combined with a widespread, and not entirely mistaken, conception that the army was populated by overly heterosexual and macho soldiers.[77] This certainly did not mean that homosexual encounters and relationships did not happen, only that they did not manifest in press or military accounts, or popular memory, as they had in other countries.[78] If anything, the overt sexuality of the soldadera (whether real or imagined) acted as antidote to public fears of sodomy in the army, despite the rise of homophobia in other spheres of Porfirian life.[79] While the press thus vilified the barracks as filthy and immoral, as a sexual space created in contrast to home purity, the troops at least engaged in the "right kind" of sex. In comparison with the truly homosocial spaces of the Brazilian barracks that many feared promoted all types of male depravity, the Mexican public at least felt reassured of their soldiers' relative heterosexuality.

The soldiers and their women were indifferent to interpretations of army sexuality and accepted both the lack of privacy and the censure of publicity.[80] This both reflected lower-class norms regarding intimacy and conferred religious authorization. Sexual intimacy among the poor traditionally had an openness enforced by small living spaces and lack of separated bedrooms.[81]

Only the rich could afford rooms designated simply for sleeping, let alone different rooms for couples or children. Cultural norms varied, and in some indigenous areas Catholic or mainstream taboos on sex simply never applied.[82] Above all, in the barracks patio the only option for modesty was a combination of covers and the polite evasion of gaze by one's comrades. One soldier remarked on his initial uneasiness with this, recalling that at night he could hear the kissing and see the forms of couples *entrepiernadas*, entangled at the crotch, and he felt ashamed.[83] Still, within months he himself had paid for sex in the barracks and had married a soldadera, hence joining in with the sexual spectacle of the army patio. Religious approval provided a further degree of comfort and acceptability for a couple's semiprivate sexuality.

Norms are one thing, but hormones have their own persuasive powers. Propriety among youths in their late teens and early twenties represented a disposable asset. In any barracks historically, even today, a degree of discretion rules behaviors. Masturbation causes blindness, at least among those a bunk or two to either side of the perpetrator. Not so different, the Porfirian patio occasioned little acknowledgment of ongoing sex.

Widespread uneasiness over unsanctioned sexual liaisons and unusual family structures left the women of the barracks in a position of ambiguity. One officer reflected that soldaderas were neither loving wives nor grasping prostitutes but possibly both at the same time. Social anxiety about the diverse functions of soldaderas contributed to the various terms used to describe them: *galletas* (hens), *viejas* (old ladies), *mujeres de tropa* or *de soldado* (women of troops or of soldiers), *vivanderas* (sutlers), Juanas, *coronelas* (lady coronels), *amasias* (lovers), *esposas de tropa* (troop wives), *mujeres legitimos* (legitimate women), *curanderas* (healers), and *chusma* (scum).[84] The women personified functions, possession, endearments, and legal status as different types of wives and purveyors. The women's defining labels came from numerous sources, including the press, officers, NCOs, conscripts, and most importantly, themselves. *Mujer de tropa* was the most generic of these terms, and it emerged from official regulations and popular conceptions. In practice, nonetheless, this included a variety of legal and social statuses.

Perhaps least common of these were the women legally recognized and church endorsed as proper wives, sometimes referred to as a *mujer legitimo*. The army forced most soldiers into service against their will, marched them far from home, and hid them from family inquiries. Accordingly, few wives of married recruits had the ability to follow or find their husbands, and many lacked the resources to try. Impressing the poor and the criminal also limited the numbers of previously married men, and recruiters made some attempt to avoid taking those with families to support.[85] The recruiting piquete especially targeted marginal men; prospective wives and their fathers typically did not. Some men also sought a clean marital slate by joining the army. The majority of troops listed themselves as "soltero" (single) in their personnel files, even if for some this may not have been true. It also depended on how they defined "marriage" as a concept.

Marriage itself proved a somewhat ambiguous status that did not, for the poor, rely on church endorsements or legal formalities. Many in society's lower classes recognized the existence of marital rights (similar to common law) that, although disputed by some authorities, nonetheless received acknowledgement and respect from the military institution. Officers accorded weight to customary claims of union. Even higher societal circles could not always agree on civil versus religious primacy in regard to registration of life events. For the army, de facto status claims sufficed and helped officers maintain morale. As such, officers employed the term *mujer de tropa* and even the less formal *amasia* as accepted and regulated categories. Officers certainly afforded formal marriage more weight for themselves, and officers were held to high marital standards. For example, Cipriano Andrade faced six years in prison and a 500-peso fine for his bigamy.[86] For mere soldiers the standards differed and less official marriage had benefits. A mujer de tropa could appeal for rights to pension, access to soldiers, and protection against abuse, regardless of civil registration.[87] Widows, orphans, and children received small pensions if their soldier should die, about fifteen centavos a day in assistance. To make their claims legitimate and bolster their family status, soldaderas brought religion into the barracks.

The Priestess within la Gran Familia

Melchora understood that outsiders talked about the sinful and shameful barracks. She could not have avoided this talk; each day in the streets imprecations and slander by civilians reached the soldaderas. Their disapproval hurt. The ladies of the barracks still tried to go to church, and they tried to be good women. They, unlike these ordinary people, sacrificed every day for don Porfirio and his army. Even the president had bent on his secular ways to have a grand Catholic wedding, and all agreed that his young wife, Carmelita, had civilized the presidential palace. How then could Melchora and her cohort do any less? Their presence tempered the barracks. They, not officers, brought culture to rough recruits in their own way. Melchora and the soldaderas sought to refute civilian slanders, maintain their traditions, and re-create their piety on their own terms. When she came to full term with her son, for instance, Melchora did not seek out army medics. Parteras (midwives) still worked in the neighborhood, despite official legal efforts to exclude them. Hers, an old professional well known to the soldaderas, delivered little Rodrigo without issue. Squalling baby in her arms, she entered the barracks that night, and with a tearful Diego they drank in celebration. But the next morning, as a respectable woman, she roused him up and in the soldadera tradition they baptized the child. The entire unit of soldiers and soldaderas stepped forward to confirm their role as godparents and protectors to Rodrigo. His soul and fate lay in the hands of the whole community. In contrast to the murmurs of civilian detractors, Melchora had secured her child's spiritual well-being without even a priest on hand—clearly the army did have a moral center. After all, everyone sins, but not all took such care of their souls.

Officially, the Liberal army and the nation had left their religious, superstitious past behind. The church represented to Liberals a reversion to colonial backwardness and an institution whose hoarding of wealth and questionable influence over peasants threatened Republican progress. The many civil wars of the first half of the nineteenth century theoretically settled the question in 1857 by applying strict controls over the church in the Constitution and related laws. The new liberal regimes from that time forward excluded the church from politics, annexed its properties, and eliminated *fueros* (special rights). This created a vacuum of authority. The army took over as a secular priesthood, a harbinger of modernity, much of it housed in the seized convents of the old colony.[88] Soldiers did not have access to priests, could not attend mass, and generally did not receive sacraments. US and European armies provided a chaplain or padre to all units at all times, while Mexican soldiers, in contrast, saw a priest only on the day of their execution. Only in such cases did the army concede to provide for the souls of its victims. More generally, the soldiers themselves replaced the priesthood in public spaces by enacting solemn rites of nationalism, with regulations as their bible and while enjoying the poverty of monks. In theory, recruits abandoned the church along with their indigenous roots or regional identities. In practice, the soldaderas acted as a spiritual bridge by bringing folk Catholic rites into the heart of the ideally secular military.

The soldaderas manifested religious understandings through ceremonies, particularly marriages and baptisms, that they themselves performed. In early modern Britain, the rite of marriage in the campaign community proved quite simple: participants set a sword or two on the ground and leaped over them, declaring, "Rogue follow, whore follow."[89] The Mexican rite simplified this further as couples (approved by their comrades) simply clasped hands, and both partners verbally agreed, "Arreglados" (arranged).[90] The customary practices of marriage among lower classes depended on community acceptance of meanings: in this case the observed bond meant more than norms that favored public courtships and church sanctions.[91] Since priests could at times be scarce, and sacraments pricy, ordinary people often made do with less formal but equally valued custom.

The marriage agreements, acknowledged by soldiers and other women, gained a quasi-legal status when recognized by officers as sufficient for pensions or petitions. Similarly, these understood marital bonds conferred a degree of regularity and respectability for sexual relations. In contrast, women deemed amasias represented a higher degree of uncertainty or social anxiety than mujeres de tropa, and they occasioned greater conflicts between rival males and denigration from married soldaderas.[92] Not only did these marriages and relationships create a hierarchy among the women and cement their relations to men, but they also helped to legitimate children. Offspring of the barracks could obtain rights and papers as *hijos naturales* (natural children)—but only with the father's acknowledgement.[93] While this implies patriarchal power, I suspect soldiers faced considerable pressures from peers, women, and officers to accede. With such obvious presence of family responsibilities, the immediate community responded. Most officers considered informal garrison marriage as a sufficient recognition, and this represented a likely motive for some women to press for wedding. It seems that women understood the official benefits of a barracks marriage, especially in terms of access to facilities, receiving pensions, and demanding legal protections. Moreover, they also valued the intangible recognitions of community and moral standing.

Children appear to have been ubiquitous. For example, in an image by Posada (fig. 3.2), a simple depiction of the barracks required inclusion of child and soldadera as he illustrated a corrido songbook titled *La gorra de cuartel*. His intent seems to dwell on the rather chaotic scene just within the barracks gates. The soldiers slump somewhat and do not stand in a sharp line, and their hats (the title subject of the accompanying corrido) sit askew. An officer appears to attempt to gain the men's attention, yet he must do so over the racket of wagons, a soldadera with a basket of goods, passing cavalry, and a child almost literally underfoot. The artist presents a normal or usual situation of the barracks as a site of confusion and noise. Children fit right in.

Furthermore, this sanctioning of a number of "legitimate" children opened the barracks to all children, because gate officials did not typically ask for documentation. Nevertheless, some soldiers and soldaderas deemed the barracks unfit for raising kids. One remarked that no child should sleep in such lousy, dirty conditions or see, once old enough, how his father was beaten or how other soldiers groped and used his mother.[94] In their own darkly humorous way, the soldiers even mimicked the daily punishment of ritual reading in the context of punishing couples who had children. In solemn ritual they intoned, "Here there is a child that has the misfortune of coming into the world; the soldier Juan Carmona and the soldadera Juana Torres confessed to this crime and are convicted as guilty; nobody can punish them [enough] for that which they have done, giving life to a being doomed to suffering."[95]

Not surprisingly, those who had children often took steps to ensure their welfare through the religious and social bonds of baptism and *compadrazgo* (godparentage). Baptisms had even greater formality and ceremonial detail

Cuento "LA GORRA DEL CUARTEL"

FIGURE 3.2 José Guadalupe Posada, *La gorra de cuartel*. Hoja suelta, pub. por A. Vanegas Arroyo.

than did weddings. In one such example, the whole battalion gathered together on a Sunday and gathered the necessary candles, blanket, and water.[96] One soldier presided and, lacking a true priest, called on the spirit of Miguel Hidalgo and invoked the patria to witness the ceremony. According to the account, the women gathered together, crying, and the men took the rite with all seriousness, and the bugler played the Toque de Diana. When the father called for a compadre, the whole battalion and its women accepted the charge—the child became godson to the entire unit. No mere satire, when father and child died in battle, his comrades took on the burial as the appropriate duty of comadres and compadres.[97] The godparents shouldered the responsibility to care for the family's well-being, whether physical or spiritual. Soldaderas accepted as part of their duties that they would offer prayers for the dead and arrange masses after battle.[98] Thus religion continued to play a role in soldiers' lives, even if the official church itself faded from view.

Beyond motivating kin structures of folk religion, children also raised troubling issues in the barracks relating to health and hygiene. Parents and teachers could attest to how well youngsters communicated every illness they encountered. Witnesses routinely mentioned the swarm of children that entered some barracks by night and, tellingly, always made reference to their lack of cleanliness.[99] Given that most of these military families had no other home and the lack of water supply that plagued many garrisons, filthy children represented an inescapable norm. Some who grew up there eventually became full members of the army, soldiers or soldaderas, as teenagers. Many more simply disappeared into the communities around the garrisons.

Along with up to three children, women likewise brought dogs, cats, and even parakeets into the barracks, which further annoyed officers. Doctors had grave concerns over the medical implications of these nightly intrusions. They reported outbreaks of cholera and typhoid and pointed to the women and children as both unfortunate victims and likely culprits. This led some experts to demand reforms and inoculations. More sought to lay blame on the apparently perilous body of the soldadera.[100]

Conclusion

The unique presence of women and families in the Mexican garrisons shaped gender relations and encouraged religious infiltration. Family centered the soldiers' and soldaderas' experiences as part of a meaningful community that took precedence over the army. Military officials challenged the presence of women as they attempted to restrict the mujeres de tropa's access to men or exposed them to hygienists. The women reacted, on occasion successfully cowing officers. Until driven from the barracks in the late 1920s, they gave conscripts access to drugs, alcohol, and tobacco. These vices further degraded the soldier's image in public forums.

Women of the troop added a vibrant and anachronistic element to the military project to fix power relations within the nation. They embodied modern contradictions. By this I simply mean that they embraced a life on the fringe of official limits or discourses, and as active agents they created the social fabric around them. They maintained, to a degree, a religiosity "lost" to official agents of the state. They built a community, but not one sanctioned by government. Soldaderas interrupted the discipline of the barracks even as they made its function possible. They asserted an alternate family that competed with the military's self-conception as la Gran Familia. The limits of governmental influence, even within a totalizing institution, took on the form of the soldadera.

The barracks and the bodies within them reflected the successes, failures, and assumptions of the government in its efforts to bring about a positivist and scientific modernity as it built the nation. The national imagined community writ large began with smaller imaginings, in the engineering of institutional power within the walls of schools, penitentiaries, and barracks.[101] Far from controlling the urban garrison's environment and behavior, the regime officials could not even achieve their ideal separation of the military space from the community that surrounded it. Streets, homes, and barracks bled into one another as soldiers and their families interacted with the city and outside civilians.[102] The true isolation of domestic from public spheres, and of either from the military, could not occur. Elite dreams of ordering lower classes included no space for women and family in the army.

The discipline and education of the daily military regime gave way to the darkness of night. In the barracks' after-hours lifestyles the successes of drill, ceremony, and classroom largely reversed. The practices there, especially those associated with vice and promiscuity, the elite labeled as lower-class behavior that did not suit an institution intended to impose and represent the new scientific and moral nation.[103] Officers employed what they deemed the appropriate modern tools, especially discourses of hygiene, to assert authority over the actions and meanings of behaviors.[104] The identities forged in the process of acting out in the face of discipline thus created a counterpoint to the official versions of mexicanidad.

Women of the barracks lived an experience where notions of gender, honor, power, and historical change concentrated within a specific visible space full of government interventions. Men taken as recruits underwent often-brutal processes of identity construction, but they did so under the gaze of women. This changed much. The women themselves fought the institutional impositions of control over their own ways, and often with greater success. Power, oddly enough, fell more lightly on the women than it did on their men. They established their own hierarchies, administered to their own souls, found their own husbands, and cured their own ailments. They, not the army or their husbands, chose where they lived and largely how they lived. For this alone they would be deserving of study as unusual agents in a time of patriarchy. They also demonstrated marvelously some of the limits of the Porfirian elite's capacity to shape power relations in the ways framed by this book.

Love and sexuality built character on levels deeper than any national programs. The Porfirian soldier moved beyond the attempts to force him into the modern project as his interaction with women and his everyday practices engendered a man of a different sort.[105] A recruit's self-identity as a man, as indigenous, as moral, lay at stake. He and his comrades wanted to enter the modern world on their own terms, resisting scientific prescriptions and moral regulations that conflicted with their convenience. Yet to focus only on the men misses a critical part of the whole. Women and children had always been present in Mexican army life. Many, as we shall see, enjoyed a more thorough knowledge of institutional ways than did the men, and they completely understood as women where they fit into daily life. They challenged popular ascriptions of rough or vulgar class behavior. They confronted reformers and they harried officers. They disrupted state theater. And the experiences of soldaderas, equally to conscripts', demonstrated the effects and the meanings of military life in the late nineteenth century.

Military discipline presented a narrative shaped by various forces, but all built on conflicts that centered on embodied behaviors. Sexual activity and gender relations forged alternate ways to see family, and even religion, and created conflagrations that fed the troops' rough masculinity. Conflicts rising from the circumstances of military life came under scrutiny from all sides and often came from breeches in the theoretically isolating walls of the garrison. Agency, environment, and community acted in concert to shape the barracks dwellers in ways that contrasted sharply with the disciplinary efforts of the army.[106]

Far from the elite agenda, troops and families found entertainment and bonded and reinforced their sense of community and an awareness of their difference from civilians. They expressed resistance and discontent together in song, while building common or customary understandings. Ultimately, the community of the ranks represented a counterpoint to the civilized soldier sought by the modern scientific nation. Custom, family, and leisure of the barracks subverted the discipline in pursuit of the national citizen.

The mujeres de tropa represented a unique and significant barometer of a changing political culture. They maintained some ideas and practices while embodying a femininity outside of the usual discourses. They challenged the regime in fundamental ways. If they could not be barred from the barracks practically and if officers could not quarantine their soldiers away from the "nefarious contagion" of womanhood—then perhaps it fell to the medical staff to find scientific means to do so.

Not long after little Rodrigo came, Melchora felt drained and tired. The other women said that it was normal. But next came itching, scratching, and a bit of pain, and all of it in uncomfortable areas. Obviously something was wrong. The barracks, never a clean place, had infected yet another victim.

A bad gentleman cannot be a good soldier.

—ANTONIO TOVAR, *CÓDIGO DEL DUELO*, 1891

Mexico counts on an instructed army united in its ideas and aspirations and nobly educated; and it [Mexico] no longer will have motive to fear for its independence, for its decorum, and for its tranquility . . . when the army will know how to complete its duties patriotically and scientifically.

—*PERIÓDICO MILITAR*, 1881

CHAPTER FOUR

The Traditional Education of a Modern Gentleman-Officer

The Next Generation of Sword and Pen

Salvador woke in a soft, clean bed to the sounds of birds and distant clamor of cooking. In his early teens, his world narrowed to the battle between hunger and staying in a comfortable doze. Today he had extra reason to get up. His father, a moderately wealthy man in this small city, had called for him to come speak about his future. Salvador had his eye on going abroad to engineering school, or perhaps a seminary education, although he had no particular calling to the church. He, and his father, agreed that the boy showed little aptitude for business. He went to the study with some trepidation and excitement. He left it in shock. The old man had pulled strings and gained him acceptance to the military college at Chapultepec. Didn't all the best officers study abroad? He began packing his bags; there was no arguing with father, and it seemed he was off to the vida militar.

Building a modern Mexico fell on the shoulders of young military men. The literature of nation building abounds in *whys* but relatively little attention has been paid to the *hows*—to the daily mechanisms of penetrating and managing the peripheral regions far from a central regime.[1]

In the smoke-filled salons where governors and senior officers sipped French brandy, they mulled over the best means to enact their ambitious plans. The brass believed that the new generation of technical officers, especially the subalterns (those below the rank of major), combined youthful energy with a scientific education. These young men could possibly carry a new order into the countryside. Junior officers took on the responsibility for enacting and enforcing a modernistic transformation of Mexico. They, the products of Chapultepec's military college, became a chosen instrument of power.

Unlike more reluctant cadets, young Fausto Becerril's formative years had inclined him to the military life—he had always wanted to become one of the officers whom Porfirio Díaz set to building the modern nation.[2] Years later he remembered the center of Mexico City as a clean place without beggars, trash, or disorder. As a child he had enjoyed listening to the military bands practicing in the barracks at San Yldefonso, across from his home, and had idolized his father, who was an impoverished but proud lieutenant of artillery. When his time came, he eagerly enrolled in the military college at Chapultepec Castle. He attended balls and danced with generals' daughters, even strolling with the young ladies of the Carranza family in the Alameda. His time at the college ended during the early Revolution when the victorious insurgent president Francisco Madero sent the young man into exile on a secret mission in Japan. His degree of loyalty to the regime proved so robust that he still refused to divulge any details of that assignment some sixty-five years later. Upon his return, Becerril directed the national arms factories and advised Joaquin Amaro on reforms to the army.[3] Hardly typical of the junior Porfirian officers, Becerril nonetheless represented the ideal scientific and loyal gentleman whom the regime hoped would usher the nation into modernity, perhaps in contrast to less-well-connected junior officers.

The education of officers in the military college developed a corps with both specialized skills and social talents. The staff of the college explicitly intended to form not simply good soldiers but honorable gentlemen. Indeed, no division between the two existed in the eyes of senior officers.[4]

The subaltern officer classes comprised a group of young men from all the good families, and a few besides. The military educated the youths to become the hope for a nation rebuilt in keeping with a peculiar vision. The country would reflect positivist ideals, gain international prestige, and obtain a stability and order never previously enjoyed. The training of men capable of bringing this to fruition thus became a significant priority. The nuances of their education system mirrored the mind-set of the elite, and its priorities were their priorities. Exploring the training regimen inside and outside of the classroom proffers an opportunity to imagine the Porfirian's ideal world. The gentleman-officer, scientific, decorous, and honorable, embodied a militarized dream. This chapter seeks to analyze how the education shaped the man and his nation.

The castle of Chapultepec took in boys from privilege and transformed them into serious young officers to lead the country forward. Here I examine the subaltern officers in their forming. From the official education and day-to-day training experience of the military college the men learned a scientific and rational approach to modern warfare and a shared military lore that ran deeper still and molded their worldview. They built a habitus specific to their class position. This identity faced challenge and, paradoxically, reinforcement in the informal educations of sociability and traditions. The rawest of officer cadets also found themselves enmeshed in an international capitalist military system. Many gained extra education at foreign military schools or as military representatives working with attachés and embassies abroad. This experience confirmed to some of them that they had a special destiny in directing Mexico away from tradition and toward the progress they saw in London or Paris. The army's experiences interacting with political and economic cosmopolitan elites influenced how officers came to see, and deal with, their own peoples at home. Their worldview became a basis for power relations between civilians and government.

The Crucible of Chapultepec

The first sight of the grand old castle startled Salvador, but he tried not to show it. Rising out of the green-mossed stone above a vast forested terrain, the fortification dominated the cityscape with a seemingly timeless power. Like most young Mexicans, he immediately recognized the tower from which Juan Escutia had thrown himself, wrapped in the flag to prevent US invaders from taking it, a half century earlier. He could only hope he would prove so brave, if the occasion came. They installed him in a tiny and uncomfortable room without a view, but at least he lived in the same building as the president himself. At times over the next years they would cross paths often enough that this lost its thrill. With little time to prepare and having just met his classmates, Salvador began a new and intense regimen of languages, mathematics, artillery, tactics, and inevitably, more mathematics. He spent far more time doing calculations than he ever dreamed possible, but he also learned practical skills of managing logistics and military law. In exercises each year, publicized by journalists, he and his classmates gained experience in maneuvers and imagined themselves winning glory for Mexico. Although he might not know it,

Salvador absorbed a curriculum quite comparable to that offered at the best
military schools abroad. Not all of his lessons came from the classroom.

The directors of the school, serious men all, gave the institution impressive
consistency, gravitas, and prestige. One of the great strengths of the college
came from the remarkable continuity of leadership during what some called
the institution's golden age. Sóstenes Rocha (1880–1887), Juan Villegas (1887–
1900, 1903–1906), and Joaquin Beltrán (1900–1903, 1906–1912) headed the
school for over thirty years and often remained involved in the college when
not actually in charge.[5] Sons of military men themselves, Rocha and Villegas
had the greatest impact, moving the academy back into Chapultepec Castle
(1883), reforming its curriculum, heightening the prestige of French doctrine
and engineering, and energizing students with their charismatic leadership.[6]
Rocha, who had served under Santa Anna and Juárez, as well as against Díaz,
brought with him firsthand knowledge from Prussia and Paris. Students
greatly respected Villegas, nicknaming him "Juanote" for his positive attri-
butes.[7] Beltrán, for his part, oversaw the school in years of change and
upheaval during the reforms of Secretary of War General Bernardo Reyes
(1900–1903) and with the rise of rival institutions (Escuela de Aspirantes, for
example). The leadership of all three, in many ways, cushioned the college
from censures of the military and regime even after the fall of Díaz.[8]

Cadets came to the college to become proper men with modern habits
and traditional values. Military authorities envisioned these youths as a valuable resource, if only their potential were unlocked. They recognized that the
scions of the emergent middle classes and nouveau riche would, in the cruci-
ble of Chapultepec, meld with the sons of the best families. This potent combination of social classes, military sciences, and martial comradeship
constructed what some termed either a caste or a guild.[9] The authorities hoped
this group would be capable of delivering the country into modernity.

The prospective officer cadets faced several obstacles to enrollment at the
military college. Limitations of resources and space kept class sizes small,
usually numbering less than 150, which improved instruction but restricted
entrance. Sixteen-year-old boys (or fifteen, if from army families) needed to
prove a basic level of education in mathematics, French, and Spanish in
application. Letters of reference and petitions from family, especially from
mothers, flooded the desk of the president every fall seeking positions and
scholarships in the next January-to-November term.[10] More often than not,
the administration denied these pleas to bend regulations. For example,

when a Señora L. Zafra wrote to Díaz in 1880, she asked a place for her son Pepe Sánchez, who lacked baptismal records. The president replied that he could not help, the regulations at the college were simply too severe for him to override the generals in charge, and he apologized for his inability.[11] Petitions of this type in the case of poverty, youth, or missing documentation came by the hundreds. The college had extremely firm rules; even Díaz's nephew Félix had to scramble to provide his paperwork.[12] Similarly, high status could not always facilitate admission, as General Jerónimo Treviño found in trying to gain positions for family friends in 1884. The directors even denied General Albino Zertuche's son the next year, perhaps showing a measure of distrust for a rival to Díaz's popularity in Oaxaca.[13] Five years later the *Revista Militar Mexicano* ran an obituary for Zertuche, which highlighted his great popularity and humble origins, and so it is possible that Díaz felt some animosity toward the family. Superficially, the refusal does seem politically motivated. Of course, the son may have had undisclosed issues of criminality or other complications that insiders already knew about. Beyond politics, other selection requisites weeded out the "wrong" types.

Restrictions to entrance went beyond the simple letter of the regulations. Motivations other than pedagogy limited the success of applicants who did not fit with the social-class requirements set by the college. The pre-education standards went beyond the means of most poor families, as their children could not attain proficiencies without the assistance of private tutoring or church seminary. For example, when Manuel García Vigil became a cadet he gave up on his religious education at the bidding of his family, who deemed the military better for his future.[14] His futile dismay at the change of course, ignored by his family, did not motivate him to excel as a student, and he limped through his college years with many scandals. Ironically, perhaps, this derailment from the clerical life later motivated him to fight as a Revolutionary, attaining the rank of general in an army that worked hard to purge clerical elements from the nation. Given the language requirements alone, the officer classes tended to draw men from somewhat larger urban centers rather than small towns, where fewer opportunities to learn French existed. Finding appropriate teachers outside the church also limited cadet opportunities, and some 40 percent failed to pass entry exams.[15] A typology of the usual cadet began to take shape from these limits.

Students did not always arrive at the college with social polish, but they came with some money. The vast majority of cadets came from quite similar backgrounds, often from military families, from the upper-middle or upper classes, from the nonindigenous castes, and from larger cities. The bond of sixteen pesos a month, plus the cost of uniforms, and the need for stipends set the price of schooling well beyond the reach of many families.[16] Even for the middle classes this could be a burden, as their average incomes ranged around eighty pesos monthly. Some families managed to raise the money through loans, and their sons thus became an investment, for whom the pressure to succeed rose accordingly.[17] Observers noted few cadets with indigenous or nonwhite features, a function largely of incomes.[18] Similarly, only a handful of foreign students attended the college. Among personnel records one finds only a few from Spain, the United States, and Germany, and one from Japan.

Once accepted, the students shared in a daily regimen instantly recognizable to their counterparts in Europe or the United States.[19] Their daily routine of classes and work changed little during the decades of the Porfiriato, running from January 8 to October 25, when field exercises began. Cadets woke at 5:00 a.m., bathed in the large pool, and after breakfast and inspection, did gymnastics, fencing, and drill until 9:00 a.m. This they followed with eight hours of study, a brief free period and supper, and finally an extra hour of study before the 9:00 p.m. call of Silencia marked the end of the day. Especially around examination time, students often studied in a guarded room until after midnight in lieu of sleep.[20] Meals were, by all reports, excellent, although diners had to do without proper napkins, a fact that horrified some overly proper observers.[21] Their reading materials were, by regulation, strictly censored and selected for moral content. Despite a rigorous schedule, students also found spare time for musical entertainment, particularly on Thursday nights, and by 1900 they played occasional baseball games.[22] In preparation for their eventual duties, the cadets acted as guards in barracks in eight-hour shifts. In keeping with upper-class expectations, the janitorial staff spared them from actually cleaning the school.

Their courses of study reflected a mixture of traditional and novel military skills. Cadets learned updated regulations for maneuvers, for field service, and for military jurisprudence. They trained in the use of new technologies: telephone, telegraph, railway, and photography. They studied topography and military geography and specialized in mathematics and sciences. French-, Spanish-, and English-language courses, along with a basic run of world history and geography, composed a scant education in the humanities. Students enjoyed a more traditional curriculum as they honed their swimming, fencing, marksmanship, and equestrian skills.[23] These courses did not vary greatly from those offered at West Point, Berlin, Sandhurst, or Vienna.[24] The basic skills taught reveal some of the common assumptions and preoccupations of military leaders at the end of the nineteenth century.

Estudios sobre la ciencia de la guerra (Studies upon the science of war), published by Sóstenes Rocha in 1878, illuminated many of the goals for the college that he ably directed.[25] He asserted that instructors had to present history and geography in purely uncritical formats in order to instill patriotism in a standard, shared way. The cadets learned by rote material that focused on knowledge of their potential enemies, in classes that did not encourage political questioning or revisionist analyses. The goals of nationalism and literacy trumped analytical development. One reason for this, which Rocha makes clear, came from the need to create a sense of the nation as homogenous and as lacking in regional disparities that would distract from wholehearted service to the central government. Rather than a default curriculum chosen out of laziness, his essays on military education indicate a rather deliberate pedagogical undermining of any lingering loyalties to the patria chica among his cadets.

Rocha's book went on to stress a unique blend of the modern and traditional. Innovations of technology, including optics, railways, telegraphs, cartography, or armaments, ideally would be harnessed to an officer class committed to the venerable traditions Rocha revered.[26] He intended to mold cadets to match his public image. The perfect cadet would be brave in battle and polished in salons, ready to face opponents with pen or sword, and able (like Rocha, who had fought against Díaz) to serve even a sworn enemy for the good of Mexico. His work went on to discuss the importance of adapting different foreign systems into teaching and into warfare.[27] One Spanish reader of the work concluded that Rocha's career and thoughts clearly demonstrated how he had brought science and wisdom to the military college.[28]

Some historical descriptions of the Porfirian era have presented a simplistic division between political factions seen as scientists versus soldiers, a depiction that fails in light of the cadets' training and subsequent careers.[29] Even those who became line officers with only four years' training attained a considerable degree of education, better than most in civilian occupations. US journalist Thomas Janvier reported that the college had become a prestigious institution and impressive far beyond its military education alone.[30] The cadets demonstrated that the divide between *científico* factions and the military rested on a weak premise of political leanings rather than actual learning.

With training in several languages, considerable study of mathematics, and a solid grasp of military lore (laws, tactics, and procedures), the graduates superseded the unlettered brutes whom critics of the regime derided. The military journals bear this out, as all branches of officer ranks contributed articles that ranged from complex mathematics to editorial letters and even, on occasion, patriotic poetry. One officer, Heriberto Frías, went on to great success as an author of books such as *Tomochic*, following in the footsteps of great military authors like Ignacio Altimirano.[31] He and other authors also published a great volume of other works, including poetry.[32] The technical officers with an additional three years of specialized education break the political dichotomy further, as they clearly represent a scientific (modern) soldier. Graduates of the college achieved the intentions of Rocha, Beltrán, and Villegas, becoming men of both the plume and the sword.

Gentleman Officers

Staring down the cold edge of a frightfully sharp-looking sword, Salvador had a moment of clarity and the past months flashed before him. It had started so innocently. The girl had such amazing eyes, you just couldn't help but stare, and she even smiled at him, not anyone else! Her hair smelled so nice, her laugh haunted Salvador when he tried to sleep, and she even came from a wealthy family! Maybe Salvador would normally have been more careful, but wasn't a woman like this worth some risk? Probably that she came from such a good family prompted all that came next. The other cadet, Bonafilo, had no patience for this sort of rivalry. Before Salvador knew what had gone wrong, he had received a calling card from the other man's second, and everyone expected them to meet out on the fringe of Chapultepec Park at dawn. The officers and instructors all knew, but no one interceded. Salvador focused. The first slash came at him with startling speed. Yet, did his enemy hesitate? He slashed back with all form and lessons forgotten in the moment, probably screaming, and with blurred eyes. In moments, both teenagers bled from shallow cuts and panted with exhaustion. At the same instant, they decided that honor had been satisfied and stepped apart. Salvador prayed that he'd never have to face this again, or against a more earnest opponent, but at the same time his ego swelled. He had upheld his own as a gentleman. He returned to his bunk to face his punishment, sore but secure in his prestige.

The education of the cadet did not end in the classroom. Mealtimes provided students with social training, as they chatted and socialized with one another and interacted with servants under the eyes of their instructors. Only with proper deportment at meals as well as in classes would cadets earn approbation and hence liberty on Saturday evening and Sunday. For those with family or connections in Mexico City, this weekend respite did not escape supervision.[33] For others, it seems to have been an opportunity for mischief and bad company. Cadets strutted through streets and parks in their off time, outfitted with flashy uniforms, shining sabers, and all the restraint of any testosterone-filled teenager. As one recalled, all the students quickly found girlfriends in town, and he retained fond memories of his cadet years for this reason, even fifty years later.[34]

Chastisement from the staff covered a great range of cadet misbehavior. Faults in classes, fighting, contraband, lateness, or a myriad of other infractions would mean a Sunday spent without seeing one's girl—a week of teenage misery. The worst offenders they physically locked in, as Victoriano Huerta found on numerous occasions as a young student. The future dictator apparently had a running tab at a cantina near Peravillo named Reforma del Niágara, where he drank heavily, and his behavior led to numerous punishments.[35] Similarly, Manual García Vigil's troublesome behavior earned him frequent detentions and eventually expulsion for knife fighting.[36] The roughness of behavior represented a genuine need to earn respect. For instance, the military brother of Felipe Ángeles instructed him to take all violent measures necessary to overcome the bullies who bothered him, and in order to obtain the respect of his peers.[37]

Some precocious students fell afoul of the military justice system as if they were adults, with serious charges, including deserting their units, drinking in barracks, and causing scandals in public. Eduardo Nieto and Enrique María Rabago rode around downtown Mexico City in a carriage, loudly drunk and accompanied by a known prostitute. Charged with generally disturbing the peace, they then insulted the arresting officer. Other such incidents received lurid press attention and immediate punishments that might include expulsion. At times the school kept the misdeeds relatively quiet. For example, the directors dishonorably discharged two cadets for staining the honor and decorum of the military college (with no further explanation published). Those smuggling alcohol into Chapultepec likewise faced discipline.[38]

Cadets who roamed the city presented an image that foreign observers often noted. Their European-styled uniforms and proud comportment presented a picture of military vigor as they occupied public areas in parks and squares, young men of means and army connections with class pretensions. The government celebrated this image as proof of the national progress, lauding the cadets as a new generation of scientific, learned, and professional leaders. Their "cockeyness," as one American asserted, demonstrated the cadets' pride in their honorable profession and in their gallant traditions. He mused that this certainly would manifest in officers who would not disgrace their service or nation.[39]

The social and political process of winnowing "technical" from "practical" officers surpassed purely academic evaluations. All cadets at least occasionally met the president in the course of living in Chapultepec, but real access to the halls of power came from family connections. Socialite parents brought their sons to balls and to dine with other elite families, reinforcing and extending the social networks of the wealthy and influential. Thursday evenings at the college featured dance lessons set to military band performances, where the cadets perfected their steps with one another.[40] One graduate recalled an evening gathering where his father introduced him to various important personages and he found himself dancing and conversing with the beautiful daughter of a general. Perhaps a symptom of the aging military or perhaps an indictment of the festivities, during the dinner the elderly Coronel Tornel quietly died at the table.[41] The US consul general David Hunter Strother wrote in his diaries of his own occasional encounters with cadets, whose deportment he found quite acceptable.[42] As the diplomat's son intended to attend West Point for his career, Strother's attention to the youths had a personal motivation. An education at the military college provided social capital and a career path, much as it would in the United States. For the highest of families, the officer cadet sons had meteoric rises though the ranks and enjoyed considerable special treatment.

The president's son and his nephew, once through the requirements of the college, received swift promotions and comfortable postings. Porfirio Díaz Jr., for example, in 1894 became a military attaché to the United States and in 1895 received his commission in both the special general staff and the military college, thus earning double the usual income, all paid in US dollars.[43] Porfirio's nephew Félix Díaz rose from sublieutenant to lieutenant colonel only fourteen years after graduating, also holding positions as inspector general of the police, congressman, and consul to Chile.[44] Cadets soon learned that grades alone did not separate line officers in training from the specialists of the professional staff (Plana Mayor Facultativo, or PMF) or engineering (see chapter 7). Merit counted, but patronage undermined the high standards that the college tried to maintain. In one example of this, Garza, the tutor to Porfirito, wrote despairingly that he could not help the cadet any further with his personal instruction and that the young man's position in the elite engineers hung in the balance.[45] Despite little scholastic improvement, the student continued on without hindrance and soared through his career.

The difference in social prestige continued after graduation, as line officers faced a far shallower career arc and worse conditions than did their counterparts. On average, an officer of the technical branch could expect regular promotions out of subaltern levels in about ten years. By contrast, for line officers it often took at least double this time. Some of these men went decades without promotions.[46] Without luck or patronage, many officers both young and old ended in the deposit, a holding pool for officers at half pay awaiting deployment.[47] The higher ranks could expect lengthy or even permanent placement; for lowly subalterns this limbo condition generally lasted only a few months.

The social element of Chapultepec life had a dark undersurface. Cadets' social lives did not entirely improve through promenades and womanizing, as this on occasion led to duels with swords or pistols over slights to their own or to a lady's honor. One notorious duelist, José Sáenz Botella, also known as "el Milord," fought several high-profile duels.[48] The first pitted him against a fellow cadet, Antonio Portillo, over a girl they both fancied. Director Villegas opposed the fight due to their youth, but General Pacheco petitioned successfully to Díaz to allow it, arguing that if it were the president's son then the issue would be clear. Having exchanged a number of pistol shots fewer than the agreed-upon ten, Portillo had an arm injury and the two boys forgave one another fully.[49] El Milord went on a year later to duel successfully against two brothers over insults given at a ball, wounding Santos Ruiz with a sword and deliberately missing his brother Ramón with pistol shots.[50] The duelist, one should remember, sought not simply to kill (although that might happen) but rather to resolve a conflict. Forcing the perpetrator of an insult to appear and face the prospect of vengeance at times sufficed on its own. A superior duelist might choose to await his opponent's shot, counting on a miss, and then have his options open: he could shoot for a kill (if truly enraged); give a wound of varying severity (to make the point clearly); or fire obviously wide, into the ground or the air (if he already felt satisfied). The bravado of the latter choice spoke volumes. Cadet Rafael Saavedra had less luck or skill and took a serious pistol wound from his duel against Eulogia Magaña in 1892, once again in a rivalry over a woman. Upset, the cadet's brother Captain Ángel María Saavedra avenged the family by killing Magaña in a subsequent duel.[51]

Duels struck to the heart of martial traditions of masculinity. By the time a cadet graduated he knew the means and motives of the duel at a deep level—a "man" understood the stakes of honor and eagerly defended it. In practice, sixteen-year-old boys hacked at one another or fired guns at ever-decreasing distances.

Specialized training helped, as cadets and officers benefited from many hours of practice in shooting, fighting, and fencing. The army established high-quality schools of the sword and sponsored foreign teachers and champions to assist. Prizes for swordplay came from the War Secretariat, and regimental instructors gained considerable status for their skills. For a few years students may even have received training in jujitsu from the enigmatic Count Coma, who went on to Brazilian fame as an early progenitor of Gracie family martial arts. As a result, a number of military men became exceptionally able in the deadly arts. Nevertheless, the reported dueling injuries indicate a general unwillingness to commit murder, and even in this most traditional of practices deliberate misses or slight wounds often prevailed. This pattern correlates closely to what historians claim for European military schools and societies.

The army as an institution demonstrated ambivalence toward dueling. The custom had become quite rare in France, Britain, and the United States and was on the decline in Germany and Latin America. Conflicted over modernizing versus conserving traditions, the army had Colonel Antonio Tovar formulate a new code of dueling that would bring Mexico up to date.[52] Tovar, at the time also a congressman, wrote the president in 1891 to apprise him of the new rules.[53] His primary concern revolved around managing duels between officers of great difference in rank. The code forbade duels on the eve of battle but otherwise affirmed that refusal to fight meant the man lost his gentlemanly standing and fell outside the laws of honor (Article V). The reasons for the duel also fell under scrutiny, and in order to maintain military order the only acceptable motives reflected those purely personal in nature. Díaz thanked Tovar warmly, and after consulting with General Rocha, the army soon implemented the code.

While some officers worked on writing a code and setting aside a building for duelers, others wrote prohibitions of the duel into military law that
forbade its practice altogether. The ordinances gave a range of penalties, and
perpetrators faced from two months in prison for a no-injury duel to two years
in the case of a fatality. This applied only to a proper duel, and the code clarified that some deadly fights counted as murder—if done for money or
immoral reasons, if the fighter cheated, or if the duelists had no seconds present.[54] A double standard extended to the vague regulations enforced by juntas
de honor that would cashier any officer too timid to fight a duel. Military men
thus faced a difficult situation in defending their honor. For most, the decision came easily to fight and spend time in military prison or locked in barracks, instead of ending a career and reputation with an apparent show of
cowardice.

Taking State Theater Abroad

*Long hours of classes finally coming to an end, Salvador had some notion
(theoretically) of his job as an officer. A proper career did not rest solely on the
academic record, of course, and so he petitioned his superiors for a posting that
might make his career. He knew that nepotism counted when he saw classmates with less academic success move on to promotions and honors. His bit-
terness concealed, he simply kept trying. Having become good friends with his
old dueling foe, he prompted Bonafilo to pull strings for him with his better
social connections. Bonafilo set Salvador's name forward and, despite some
weak grades, a message came down. Salvador opened the orders with trembling hands and gave a shout—his deployment had him representing Mexico
as an officer cadet with a commission heading to Europe. Proud and grateful,
Salvador packed his things and prepared to take ship to France as an attendant
for a more senior officer. He didn't realize it then, or ever, but his demeanor
instantly changed. During the rest of his career, he rarely failed to mention, at
length, how prestigious this posting had been, to anyone who listened. When
other officers seemed uninterested in Parisian tales Salvador chalked it up to
jealousy.*

*His initial impression of Europe underwhelmed the young officer. After mis-
erable weeks at sea, they arrived but no pomp or ceremony greeted them.
Salvador felt disappointed but kept his chin up.*

*Through months in Germany and France, he strutted through the streets
secure in his uniform and unaware how little he impressed bystanders. He*

attended meetings and toured arms factories, and he sat in the stands at military parades. He wrote appraisals, assured of his expert perspective on modern technologies of the army. His superiors reported on his work as functional but not particularly useful and spared no criticisms in his file. In the short term, the commission made Salvador a representative of the Porfirian regime abroad, for good or ill, and he counted on this to save his career. For some reason he never managed to find a reliable patron.

For cadets who survived Chapultepec and absorbed the proper written lore, a number of assignments abroad with commissions or diplomatic service beckoned. Missions outside of Mexico carried officer representatives and contingents of troops to its neighbors north and south, to Europe, and even to Japan. At considerable expense, the secretaries of war and of foreign relations selected and deployed envoys: some traveled for temporary commissions or expositions; others, as attachés, spent years abroad.[55] Over the years, Díaz sent many of his senior military staff on missions to Europe, although sometimes he also used this as an expedient and face-saving means to exile his political adversaries. Nevertheless, most went to fulfill one or more of three main tasks: to facilitate the business of the arms trade, to gather information from foreign military sources, and to represent an image of modern Mexico.

Diplomatic army officers learned a common military culture and language that looked outside Mexico for much of its new identity. As such, the self-perception of these officers formed relative to foreign militaries in the arms trade, the venue of reviews, parades, and the military journal.[56] Soldiers sent to the United States and to Europe as part of the conversation of nations accomplished a number of practical tasks, including the negotiation of arms deals, resolution of diplomatic issues, and observing foreign modernization efforts. One important motive rose from the need for acceptance and membership in international military circles. Displaying an impressive modernizing army to the military attachés and arms merchants of these foreign nations gave Mexico a credibility that denied the actual, rather poor, state of its military. Evaluating and being evaluated constituted a form of cosmopolitan inclusion into the modern world and an increasingly important part of the Porfirian projection of the nation abroad. It is significant that Mexico did not simply absorb or mimic other nations' militaries and their cultures but that they interacted in a reciprocated relationship.

The assignment of military attachés also held political ramifications that dictated possibilities and opportunities. The skilled Captain Carlos de Gagern

FIGURE 4.1 "Salón de clases del 1er. Regimiento de Artillería Montada," México. "Parte expositiva," *Memoria de secretario de guerra y marina*, 1906.

spent years in the German legation, at times fighting to receive even his expense money, and his Prussian ties made him ineligible when he wished to transfer to France. Instead, the secretary of foreign relations suggested that he should move on to Italy, Belgium, or Spain. Others among the attaché pool had close relations with Díaz and his general staff. For example, Francisco García became attaché in Great Britain (1892–1897), Fortino Davila served in Washington (1906–1911), Gustavo Salas in France (1908), and of course, Porfirio Díaz Jr. went to Washington (1893).[57] While Díaz's son was perfectly capable, his appointment to the important Washington, DC, attaché position upon his graduation at age eighteen still clearly demonstrated nepotism.[58]

In an interesting aside, an attaché to Mexico also needed to meet the cultural standards of the host nation, as demonstrated by US ambassador Clayton Powell's son. Appointed as attaché in Mexico City (where his father resided), the young man reneged on a debt in the Jockey Club, refused to accept a proffered duel, and departed Mexico in shame shortly after.[59] Porfirio Jr., who had turned down an alternative commission to Great Britain in the Royal Artillery or Horse Guards, spawned a similar dueling scandal as attaché to the United States.[60] Falsely identified as Díaz, Lieutenant Francisco Márquez attended a theater performance two years after Porfirito had left New York.

During the show, he talked loudly and incurred dirty looks from a British spectator. Márquez gave the man his card, a precursor to challenging him in a duel, but the man tore up the card and beat the attaché with his fists. A German baron advised the Mexican to ask for a duel formally, but since the Englishman's refusal might lead to more fisticuffs, Márquez timidly declined to do so. Diplomatic staff quickly corrected the erroneous newspaper accounts of the affair by pointing out that the younger Díaz was not in fact in the United States and sent the shamed attaché home.[61]

The attachés abroad, for the most part, behaved admirably, and hosts received them graciously. Captain Pablo Escandón, for example, moved to France with his whole family and convinced the newspapers there that the army included only the uppermost classes, unlike in colonial times.[62] Fortino Davila earned fulsome praise from his hosts, and the ubiquitous Samuel García Cuellar became a favorite at almost every exposition held in the United States. As good role models these envoys seem also to have instilled proper decorum in their staff, particularly among the younger officers who accompanied them.

Recent graduates and cadets became part of the transnational military world. The opportunity to attend and participate in the rash of world's fairs, expositions, exhibitions, student exchanges, and international conferences entailed a crucial part of foreign relations to the modernizing and investment-hungry Porfirian regime. Military delegations attended all the large events, and many smaller ones, even if at times this simply meant sending an attaché and a band. To list only a few destinations they visited: 1882–1883, Paris; 1884, Cuba and New Orleans; 1892, Madrid; 1893, Chicago and Washington; 1895, United States and Paris; 1897, Russia; 1898, Paris; 1900, Paris; 1885 and 1901, Buffalo; 1904, St. Louis; 1906, San Antonio; and 1907, Jamestown. Young medical officers had the chance to study surgery in Paris and attended medical conferences in Washington, Chicago, and Russia. Military college students represented their nation at the Paris Universal Exposition and also attended some world's fairs as observers and displays alike.[63] Additionally, students went on exchanges from the military college to Sandhurst or West Point and from the navy school to France or Spain.[64] In these events and in daily diplomacy, the arms trade primed Porfirian pretensions in a way that other displays did not.

The European arms trade had a profound impact on the development of military knowledge in the Americas.[65] Given Mexico's long reliance on foreign-made weapons and ammunition, army attachés sought to enhance the ability to manufacture arms at home in order to reduce vulnerability and gain

FIGURE 4.2 "Sala de estudio en el Batallón de Zapadores," México. "Parte expositiva," *Memoria de secretario de guerra y marina*, 1906.

prestige. In the meantime, they would also facilitate favorable terms of trade for weapons that Mexicans could not yet produce, or could produce only in limited amounts at great expense. Foremost among the nations they turned to was France, where envoys dealt with the manufactories of Schneider-Canet (Creusot) and Banges, the St. Chamond foundry, and the shipyards of Le Havre.

A large part of the attachés' task required them to evaluate weapons that foreigners had offered for sale. As early as 1879, it became evident to experts that the Banges cannon system had become outdated, and Eduardo Paz helped the government to arrange a purchase from St. Chamond of new artillery pieces. His deal revealed the expense of the undertaking. Despite near insolvency in that year, the government agreed to pay 400,000 pesos in ten bimonthly payments for the updated guns.[66] Commissions to Germany in 1890 and 1896 lauded the weapons produced by Krupp, and yet by the turn of the century attachés still turned to the French pieces after undertaking comparisons. Manuel Mondragón, who had patents with St. Chamond and had attended St. Cyr, observed demonstrations alongside Japanese and Rumanian diplomats. These tests convinced him of the French guns' rapidity of fire and reliability.[67] Further studies bore him out, despite his conflicts of interest, as the British found the steel used at St. Chamond superior to any other in Europe.[68] Attachés sent by Reyes, like Gilberto Luna, continued to support French manufacturing in 1901 and also sang the praises of the Mondragón 75 mm artillery they produced.[69] A letter from the director general of the Societé Anonyme Capital supported this view and urged then secretary of war Reyes to move ahead with production of the Mexican-designed pieces.

Commissions to Germany, predictably, disagreed with this assessment, and attachés there generally found the Krupp artillery to be better quality but more expensive. To a point, these divisions between pro-French and pro-German factions reflected political rifts within the army echelons back home.[70] Further commissions examined factories in Hamburg and Westphalia, including one by General Rocha, who found artillery pieces with an exceptional twenty-four-kilometer range and a price tag of 500,000 francs.[71] The competition between the European rivals in the aftermath of the Franco-Prussian War encouraged Mexican commissions to play the two countries against one another as they sought a trading advantage. Unlike other Latin American nations such as Chile or Argentina, Díaz's regime stiffly resisted becoming a client to either of the Europeans and maintained a relatively healthy distance from military-industrial neocolonialism.

Attachés managed to sell some of their own arms to foreigners, thus proving, if to a limited degree, the viability of their national arms industry (see chapter 7). At times optimism and flattery trumped reality, as when Sergeant Francisco Ramírez wrote to Díaz with hopes that by taking the Porfirio Díaz rifle samples to the Universal Exposition in New Orleans he would be able to sell some fifty thousand of them.[72] Sadly for the sergeant's dreams, the rifle had no patent and so the government declined permission to display them. Mexicans also sought to sell arms directly to foreign armies. In another example, the German military attaché was favorably inclined to purchase at least the designs for a particular grenade and felt that with this weapon in hand no foreign power would dare invade Mexico again.[73] The best arms, nonetheless, remained Mondragón's artillery pieces, especially the 75 mm, and his automatic carbine that represented a substantial advance in technological innovation. Ahead of its time, the latter had fatal delicacies that made it unreliable in the field, and European armies only used it in World War I out of some degree of desperation. The commodity that most often caught the foreign eye was the junior officer himself. He represented a new type of modern officer, and his experience abroad helped to shape an image of Mexico even as he brought home ideas for reform and change.

The Officer Abroad: Cadets and International Military Borrowings

Junior officers became part of an odd, informal set of international comparisons. Foreign militaries defined their own identities against the counterpart presented to them, and competing in fashions, borrowing ideas, and purchase of technologies were certainly mutual interactions. Military diplomacy revolved in great part around the science of armaments, especially in reporting on the modern and the novel. The semipermanent staff of embassies abroad routinely undertook reviews of foreign military troops and also attended unveiling ceremonies for new technologies, which they then might recommend to their government.

The missions and attachés contributed to an artificial template of comparison to countries whose only actual interaction with Mexico found expression in the pages of the military journals. The comparative base came through clearly, for example, in US colonel William Wade's article about the Mexican army. He evaluated on internationalist standards, placing Mexicans as equivalent infantry to Prussians, better cavalrymen than the English, and better at artillery than Americans. He concluded that an alliance of US naval ability and Mexican land forces would make an invincible combination.[74] In comparisons at foreign expositions, the army and artillery won extravagant praise and numerous prizes, which despite their ceremonial nature revealed a degree of respect. At the Parisian Universal Exposition of 1900, for instance, the list of gold, silver, and grand prizes awarded the Mexican contingent filled pages.[75]

Comparison and chest buffing did not preclude missions from learning about the best tactics and materiel used by foreign armies, and the legations routinely sent reports back to their secretariats. The training and gear of the Prussian army, especially after 1870, became a particular object of study for possible emulation. In 1881 Joaquin Gómez Vergara sent a full catalog and pictures of military uniforms to Porfirio Díaz (then secretary of development) from Berlin.[76] Attaché Gagern followed up on these reports with lengthy studies on German barracks and a report on the military college system that focused on Lichterfeld. He stressed points he felt Mexico had improved already, including scientific training, full literacy, and modernized facilities. These elements all became priorities for the military college under Rocha, Villegas, and Beltrán.[77] Attention to Europe continued in later years, as Reyes sent a number of military missions abroad to study telegraph systems in Spain and to take part in training in Germany.[78] He also sent a commission under

Lieutenant Colonel Pablo Escandón to study the function of European General Staffs in February 1900.[79]

Successful officer-gentlemen helped to sell the nation. The social network and image building that came from these interactions among military circles demanded that contingents attend ceremonial events and exhibits that otherwise had no martial application in arms sales or education. An article in *El Universal* reporting on the commission sent to France in 1890 detailed the banquets treating the cadets and officers, a young Felipe Ángeles among them, and it commented primarily on their bearing and toast making. As something of an afterthought, it also mentioned that they would be visiting an arms factory to acquaint themselves with the latest development of military arts and to meet with the French war minister.[80] Some officers making social and diplomatic trips abroad also received foreign decorations as part of the ceremony. General Joaquín Beltrán, founder of the General Staff, received both the Légion d'Honneur from France and the Order of the Sacred Treasure from Japan.[81] In 1910 Díaz Jr. was granted the Orden Militar de San Benito de Avis from King Manuel of Portugal, and governments festooned Díaz senior with military decorations from all of Europe.[82] These relatively low-profile affairs built social prestige on one level, but participation in international expositions had a central place in cementing an image of the army in foreign eyes and within the nation too.

The Porfirian Departments of War, Development, and Foreign Affairs went to considerable effort to send army contingents to major expositions. The frenzied involvement at the world's fairs provides one set of examples and has garnered significant historical study.[83] At the Buffalo Exposition in 1901, Mexican soldiers, musicians, and rurales combined to provide an impressive spectacle at the express invitation of the US secretary of state. He loved their performance, as did the officers who accompanied him, and the press reported hearing loud cries of "Viva Mexico" from the audience.[84] The soldiers enjoyed what they described as modern and hygienic lodgings, while the rurales walked the fairgrounds in pairs on display. The soldiers and musicians later gave a ten-minute review for five thousand viewers that, according to General Miles, proved Mexico's progress and standing as one of the great nations of the world.[85]

The young officer abroad still dealt with some of the same complications that troubled barracks back home. From underneath the shiny exterior, some old disciplinary problems bubbled to the surface of the contingents. Free time may have encouraged gambling and contributed to the lack of spending money for contraband. Sergeant Macano Avila, who attended the 1900 Buffalo Exposition as part of the honor guard, claimed to have lost his pistol. The suspicion of Captain García Cuellar, and probably a well-founded one, was that the sergeant had gambled away his expensive Colt pistol and should pay for a new one himself.[86] Similarly, other soldiers on tour sold or gambled away raincoats, weapons, or other expensive kit, presumably also to obtain spending money. The great composer Juventino Rosas even sold the rights to some of his music in San Antonio to pay for more alcohol.[87] Officers accused two soldiers at another exposition of stabbing an American sailor but later exonerated them. Investigation showed that they had rushed to a victim's aid and fell afoul of language barriers as misunderstood Samaritans.[88] It seems the two soldiers had gone to help a mugging victim, but with their poor English skills and with tempers running high, the responding officers mistook the two confused heroes for thieves. Once calmer heads and an interpreter intervened, the two received a commendation for their efforts.

These experiences of course assumed that the soldiers managed to arrive at all. In 1909 a massive military parade in New York City featured troops from a dozen nations and reported millions of cheering spectators. Unfortunately, the Mexican contingent had become lost and never arrived, although the *New York Times* later proclaimed them found, albeit tardy and confused.[89] Keeping up appearances had begun to falter as military budgets weakened.

The 1907 International Military Exposition at Jamestown, Hampton Roads, could have been a prime spectacle for demonstrating Mexican military progress but fell short for a number of reasons. Financial crises at home and a cooling relationship with the United States discouraged a full effort to shine, despite considerable efforts made by the attaché Fortino Davila. The Mexican embassy rejected the initial invitations to attend, despite Jamestown organizers' impassioned pleas and compliments on past performances, like that at St. Louis.[90] Eventually, and with seeming reluctance, the army authorized participation only after the publication of a list of other participating nations showed some eighteen Latin American countries had committed to come.[91] Davila commissioned a 2,200-square-foot building for Mexico to stand alongside the 110 buildings of other nations and some US states, but it would not be ready in time for the actual opening of the exposition.[92] Despite the primarily naval nature of the fair, unrest in Quintana Roo required Mexico's ships, so none could attend the event. The diplomatic guests coming from New York even had to charter their own transport.[93] Instead, the attaché arranged for the General Staff's band and a display of materiel from the National Powder Factory to represent the nation, even as the big show involved over fifty naval vessels from across the globe. In stark contrast to the full company sent to the San Antonio Exposition only a year previous, the army sent only a tiny group to Jamestown.[94] Ultimately, the press reported the event as a great success and reprinted the speeches given by President Theodore Roosevelt as well as a full description of the opening day's schedule and highlights.[95] In contrast, back in Mexico City the government simply received a technical report from Davila on electric lighting for warships and showed little excitement. It appeared that the heyday of military spectacle abroad had passed, at least for the time being.

Young officers and cadets grew up in this context. Having sent contingents abroad and accepted attachés at home for years, the military brass had to make choices regarding the knowledge gained in the conversation with these other armies. Foreign influences on the army aroused heated debates within military circles. There were three schools of thought supporting French, German, or Mexican doctrines. The latter, primarily favored by Victoriano Huerta and Félix Díaz, stressed guerrilla tactics and small-unit mobility (see chapter 8). The curriculum of the college generally followed a French model, using French texts, uniforms, and fortifications.[96] The tactics taught modeled those of the French, stressing artillery dominance and the importance of the bayonet charge when leading conscripted (low-quality) troops.[97] The French system favored the aggression and élan that Napoleon embodied, whereas the German favored the more calculated precision of the Prussian General Staff. In emulation of European states, the pro-German General Reyes encouraged the adoption of German tactics, marching songs, and spiked Prussian helmets. While the German doctrine never caught on fully in Mexico, the *pikelhaube* helmet remained part of some units' dress uniforms until the Revolution.

In truth, it seemed the German advisors made a poor case for introducing their arms or training, or as likely, Porfirian officers saw relatively little they wanted or that they could afford. Certain units adopted, to some degree, a Prussian ascetic with spiked helmets or bushy Bismark moustaches, and some did try to teach German-language marching songs to their befuddled troops. At the same time, the big guns (where the money mattered) the Mexicans still designed for themselves, and they commissioned their building to French factories. The army bought German rifles but also US arms and French uniforms. What the Mexican army lacked in standardization, it at least made up for in creating a unique mixed look.

Since either French or German militaries represented an equally optimal (if unlikely) model for the Mexican elite to emulate, choosing between the two models eventually became merely a matter of taste.[98] Whether the French or German systems truly could prove effective for fighting a war within Mexico mattered less than the need for the military to enact cosmopolitan ideals. The editors of the *Boletín Militar* argued that there could be only one science of war and unabashedly urged imitating the Europeans as the only way to advance. International expositions thus served to highlight the similarities of armies, and although Mexico lacked money to construct Prussian-quality soldiers, the attempt mattered more than concentrating on differences in outcome.[99] This perspective ignored the real transformations of the army, as well as the means by which it was happening. The reformers' transnational borrowings struck to the heart of the military's mission. The notion of reforming the army à la Europe made less persuasive sense when papers and politicians asked, who did the army intend to fight? French reforms, after all, made sense in the context of their losses to Prussia in 1870; they sought primarily to prevent any future Germanic incursion. Mexico, on the other hand, did not require the same measures in order to invade Guatemala and had little chance of devising a strategy capable of stopping the US Army. Felix Díaz proposed a mass guerrilla army to harass invaders over a long-drawn-out conflict. But this type of new army had little appeal to his uncle Porfirio, as it seemed too wild, too dangerous, and not terribly modern looking. The regime's final answer on how and why to reform did not address any foreign foe or seek truly to capitalize on European experience but rather sought to devise a good-looking army capable of repressing dissidents inside the country. The enemy waited within the republic. This ominous note to a professionalizing rationale played a significant role in the great tragedies perpetrated across Latin America in the twentieth century.

Reforms on a large scale characterized both the United States' and Mexico's military organizations in the late nineteenth century. The two nations coevolved in a manner that suggests mutual recognition of professional goals rather than a catering to European efforts to influence. By choosing between models, and adapting them, Americans and Mexicans created their own modernity, all the while watching each other's progress. Porfirian officers looked to reform their military through adaptation of tactics, legal codes, and regulations from Europe.

Chapultepec graduates working abroad brought home ideas from all over, but the military elite carefully selected which to use and ultimately coevolved as an institution alongside their US counterparts. In many Latin American nations, foreign missions and military trainers spread their knowledge as part of a "civilizing mission" with the implication that favored status and diplomatic influence would surely follow. These foreign missions, mostly from France and Germany, penetrated with great success into the social fabric and military life in Brazil, Argentina, Chile, and Peru. In Chile the inculcation succeeded so well, in fact, that Prussianized Chilean officers began their own military missions to countries like El Salvador, Nicaragua, and Paraguay. Mexico, in contrast, never systematically invited foreign advisors and instructors to educate their military in the nineteenth century. A much-cited article implied that strong pro-French elements in Mexico prevented the success of Prussian agents.[100] Yet the French did not send advisors either, and Mexico constantly moved away from French systems until the turn of the century, despite the French education of some important Porfirian officers. It has remained a largely unexamined question exactly what foreign influence meant to the military and what this influence entailed. Compared to the military colonialism that took place in other Latin American regions, Mexico resisted becoming the subject of any single European power.

In place of the establishment of foreign military systems and standardization, the professional Porfirian officers selected between a number of alternative models and sciences of war. Moreover, they did so in tandem with their American neighbor, each undertaking similar reforms and drawing on European experiences in similar ways, although with quite different results. This should not be too surprising, as these two military establishments in many ways presented a closer and more persistent contact zone, each army continually seeing the other as rival and neighbor. In a critical difference from other Latin American nations, Mexico had immediate ties to the United States. A shared history of warfare and conflict, a high degree of trade and societal connections, and active diplomacy marked a unique relationship that encouraged Mexican development without Europe's direct interference. Whereas nations like Peru and Chile created a new Europeanized military class, Mexico professionalized in a context informed by cosmopolitan ideals and close relations to the United States.

In 1881 the administration of Manuel González ordered its attaches abroad to provide a complete set of French regulations and ordinances and two years later produced a completely overhauled general ordinance for the military.[101] This new code differed considerably in language and contents from the 1857 regulations it replaced. High rhetoric largely disappeared, and new ordinances appeared establishing a medical corps and a General Staff and standardizing the use of railways and telegraphs. Quite different from the French originals, these ordinances described an explicit plan for guerrilla warfare and the use of bandits and smugglers as scouts, perhaps drawing on successful experiences of the nineteenth century. The document also provided the means to professionalize the army further by stressing accounting practices that diminished graft and beginning the process of federalizing all military installations and materials. These sweeping reforms, bolstered by provisions in the 1900 military "Organic Law," reshaped basic structures and functions in the military.

Contrasting sharply with its Latin American counterparts, Mexico engaged the international military community on almost even terms. Its selective modernization, technical prowess, and performative aptitudes offered hints at the army's potential as a national and stable institution. This possibility never truly came to fruition. Ultimately, revolution would shatter the Mexican image abroad, vilify its leadership, and annihilate the federal army.

In the meantime, the junior officer-gentleman schooled in sciences and manners afforded the regime a symbolic figure and a versatile agent who could build the nation. Steeped in a military lore from college and from international exposure, the subaltern promised success for shaping an army of modern soldiers from mere peasants and for advancing the schedule to self-colonize the republic's dark corners. This young officer, an ideal type, embodied all the honors of the soldier's tradition along with all the tricks of technological advances, and to the regime, he carried on his shoulders the Mexican future.

Conclusion

Given guidance and specialized education by select veterans, the military academy graduates became the gentlemen warriors and literate myrmidons that the regime required of them. They exhibited and exemplified what they had absorbed in college about class and caste. They feared neither dueling saber nor arithmetical proof. They understood law, tactics, engineering, and leadership. They danced waltzes and ordered servants, built bridges or destroyed forts, ate like the French and drank like the Germans. Perhaps, as some hoped, they could even embody the bridge between the modern and the traditional.

By the end of their four or seven years, cadets became officers and gentlemen of a particular sort. Selected for, and instructed in, class differences, they left the academy with rote instruction in their duties and practical experience in masculine behavior. Expected to become *espadachines*, swordsmen and womanizers, the college led them to believe they were destined for great things. Most of the approximately 2,500 Porfirian graduates discovered their army life to be harsher than expected. As they deployed to factories, barracks, camps, and embassies, all were challenged and many disillusioned.

The subaltern officer incarnated the hopes and aspirations of the middle classes, and much of the elite, as they shaped him into le militaire. He differed from the common soldiers and surpassed them, potentially, in his motivation, his breeding, and his stakes. The inscriptions of power sculpted more deeply upon the officer than upon common recruits. If the officer class proved more completely trainable, thought some, then these men absolutely would model appropriate civilismo for troops. Chapultepec as a totalizing institution fell somewhat short of the hypothetical biopower of asylums and prisons, whose transformative discourses made societies modern. Contradictions within the culture of the institution, such as the forbidden-yet-required policy on dueling, undermined morale and consensus. A sense of injustice was built into the military habitus and consequently eroded faith in the institution. This limited Porfirian governmentality, the capacity and modes to affect management of entire populations, since the most-relied-upon agents simply failed to work with government wholeheartedly. Worse still, broken subalterns trained the rest of the army. The officer did become a role model of sorts to his troops, but perhaps more as a demonstration of cynicism and opportunism

In final analysis, the subaltern officers of each branch represented the best and worst of the Porfirian system. Educated to internationally recognized standards, they also represented a limited echelon of class and ethnic backgrounds that further set them apart from average Mexicans. They built a network of communications and modern improvements for the nation but did so in ways that alienated them from locals and, if necessary, did so in order to crush regional dissent. Opportunities to show this capacity abroad allowed young officers to sell foreigners on an idea of Mexican modernity.

Where training left him ill prepared and his forces underwhelmed expectations, the officer claimed the legitimate right to own violence (or at least to borrow it from his government). Brutality became a traceable symptom of power relations as they passed through the sites of military presence.

The training of the subaltern officers came almost incidentally from within the walls of the military college. The men learned from one another as they socialized and built (or reinforced) family networks. They read the same specialized literature, hated the same teachers, dreaded the same exams, and plotted the same careers. Inequalities of access to elite supporters undid some dreams, while poor aptitude or misfortunes cut the legs out from under others. The subaltern officers that the college issued thus shared much of a fraternal subculture that took on tones of historic tradition and modernist pretensions. They shared adolescent experiences in a demanding and harsh institutional environment. Regardless of differences in family or patronage, many remained friendly throughout their lives. Yet the castle had a rotten core. The continued nepotism and near-feudal arrangements of military appointment and promotion spoiled the prospects of many otherwise-qualified cadets. The European-styled expectations of teachers, and those learned by students who traveled, did not prepare the graduates for the realities of their new career. Their experience, in other words, illustrated how the increasing inequalities and social gaps in Porfirian Mexican society could poison even the sheltered young officers in Chapultepec. Class and social injustices sabotaged the project of preparing a professional officer corps for the republic.

Subaltern military officers led this charge in Mexico during the late nineteenth century.[102] As a corporate body and as individuals, these young officers worked to create a nation along the lines intended by the centralizing and modernizing elites out of the numerous patrias chicas of the country. Their education guided their efforts in ways particular to a social context of class and expectations. Once deployed, they represented national interests with varying degrees of success and in disparate manners.

The young officers emerged from their college experience with a considerable degree of shared culture and with a narrowed social network that forever set them apart from their civilian counterparts. Many traveled abroad, and as they studied sciences and engineering and foreign tongues they looked at Mexico's progress from without, as cosmopolitan men. At the same time, they ran into parochial expectations and archaic traditions that included fighting duels and writing obsequious poetic elegies to their superiors. This reflected the deep ambivalence of their increasingly geriatric higher officers, who attempted to embrace barely understood technological advances while still clutching the withered laurels of past glories. The subalterns had limited options in choosing their own path. They sought to use the newest engineering and weaponry in the field, but this proficiency gained them little. They remained dependent on family connections to make a career, as traditionally had been the case. Nonetheless, as the dynamic agents of the Porfirian projects to build a nation, their bipolar worldview came to matter a great deal.

Officers embodied both venal corruption and impressive self-abnegation. Some even managed to model both simultaneously, as in the case of Victoriano Huerta, who combined vicious self-interest with patriotic professionalism. The noteworthy accomplishments and successes of the officer classes included a relative peace, enormous growth (economic and technological), and progress in health care and hygiene. They also brought out the regime's worst. Mexicans continued to remember the army for its pogroms against indigenous tribes like the Yaquis and Mayas, its support for land-seizing hacendados and exploitative foreigners, and its role as the hand wielding modernity's whip.

Salvador could not believe his change in fortunes. After less-than-stellar reviews from officers, young Salvador returned to Mexico with no further possibility of traveling abroad. Still, this was what he had trained for all this time. He had under his belt a number of prestigious commissions, a full education from the military college, and experience operating in the field during practice maneuvers. How much more prepared could he be for taking command of an actual army unit? Orders came. Given his record, Salvador's superiors sent him as a subteniente to an ill-reputed barracks in the capital. He would shape them up into proper soldiers, he thought, or die trying.

CHAPTER FIVE

The Touch of Venus

Gendered Bodies and Hygienic Barracks

The coarse conditions of the city, with its mucky, wet streets, garbage-filled alleys, and dank, odorous corners, had shocked Diego when he first debarked from the troop train. When he met Melchora, months later, she had for her part already adapted to the environment. Lack of proper "facilities" no longer bothered her too much, if they ever had. Diego soon grew inured too. The city, for all of its splendors, wallowed in the kind of filth that only a true metropolis can create or tolerate. The couple rarely saw the nicer suburbs and basically forgot how relatively clean their old villages had been. They did not visit the broad green boulevards that marked the better parts of town. Salvador, for his part, missed the high clean air of Chapultepec and the modest luxury of his childhood home. He loathed the rank air in the barracks. As a man of the higher classes, he saw this entire miasma as unnecessary. Diego's and Melchora's basic acceptance of their surrounds reinforced Salvador's suspicions that their poorer neighborhood's dirt and bugs and smells had a basis in simple ignorance and vulgarity. He remembered Paris as a city almost pristine, at least compared to the eastern parts of Mexico City that now he frequented. As the three scratched at fleas or lice and sweated in the musty old convent barracks, they all dreamed of a better home. Porfirian científicos would agree. The matriz, a term that meant both "headquarters" and "womb," embodied military aspirations for hygiene and control over the army to which it gave birth.

Much changed in the late nineteenth century. New technological advances and the emergence of new social classes changed how people lived and who they were on basic levels. Efforts to using science to shape citizens came to the forefront among elite power brokers. Porfirians particularly focused on the military as a site where modern knowledge and scientific discourses could directly alter subjects. This process helped give rise to government hygienic initiatives that sustained medical professionals as they gained powers over policy. Medical advances dovetailed neatly with positivist schemes. Science inscribed power on bodies as medical professionals justified interventions into health and environments based on eugenic thinking.

In seeking to overcome the visibly evident failings of healthy bodies, experts intervened and conflated ideas of morality and ethics with good breeding as determined by specialized knowledge. Hygiene, taken very broadly, had a positivist and pseudoscientifically based capacity to "fix" the Mexican. Oftentimes, those whom experts deemed most in need slipped past their reach. The barracks, in contrast, brought a captive and theoretically malleable population into the interested hands of state medical agents. Little could be accomplished in molding racial procreation (in eugenic style), but doctors could, and did, intervene with an expert body of scientific knowledge—a system of connaissance—permitting them to shape diet, treat disease, and alter environments.[1] Continual tampering with these elements of life, along with ongoing publication of unchallenged scientific rationales for them, inexorably changed shared public ideas of health and morality. This demonstrated the inscription of power upon bodies, if in a quite simplified form.

For example, elite designations defined the female body as the source of diseases related to the disordered life. Women then had to live within legal bounds, as structures of knowledge offered the only options for the choices they could make. The scientific guild made decisions on their behalf. They had been written so, within the discourses of male medical prowess, and the doctors explained women's place in myriad symbols, beliefs, images, and literatures. Taken as common knowledge, this became a reality of lived experience and of power relations. Likewise, this extended into general conditions for the lower class (of any gender), who became categories related to hygienic ideals, as defined by classes interested primarily in distancing themselves from "inferiors."

Here we explore the operation of scientific-medical systems of knowledge as they encountered day-to-day realities of army life. I examine the emergence of a military medical professional and the ways that such men worked to shape garrisons and improve their patients. In this, I build on the works of Claudia Agostini, Heather McRae, and others who have asserted the political nature of the medical sphere and examined its intimate connections to power, knowledge, and sexuality.[2] In the army, this relationship was concentrated due to the controlled confines of barracks and with the subjected status of soldiers under medical officers. My findings, therefore, add depth to this significant body of literature within a narrow field of subjects.

I question how these procedures differently affected men and women, the decent and the lowly classes, within the context of the barracks. The chapter seeks to demonstrate ways that doctors faced limitations to power and confronted alternative ideas of sexual (and gender) norms that they twisted as a discourse into proof of lower-class immorality. The images and belief systems that they framed as hygiene ultimately set the scientific modern state as the final authority over bodies—but this did not come free of resistance. Changing concepts of health therefore revealed greater truths in national hegemony and the creation of mexicanidad premised on a specific version of being modern. The army provided an exceptional petri dish for elite knowledge work.

As hygiene became an integral element of military life, soldiers and soldaderas dealt with sometimes-invasive scientific prescriptions that sought to enhance public health at the cost of personal liberty. These programs, as in the case of syphilis regulation, challenged army sexual and leisure practices and ignited conflicts with military officials.

Evolutions of Military Medicine

Sublieutenant Salvador grumbled angrily as he scraped what he hoped was mud from the bottom of his shoe against the barracks steps. He ignored the scowls of the soldier nearby tasked with mopping things up. Salvador's friend Francisco laughed, his uniform and shoes fastidiously neat and clean as usual. "You know," he mused, "that's exactly what I've been telling you—a clean barracks will solve your problems." Salvador had long since grown weary of this sanctimony from the medical officers; even Francisco seemed tiresome sometimes. "The barracks, well, así es," Salvador demurred. It didn't help that the doctor had it so easy. Like all of the medical staff, he had received considerable education and then flown through the ranks, he had been sent abroad to learn from the best, and when he chose, he could retire to a lucrative private practice! Or so, at least, it seemed to Salvador. The medics didn't even have to sleep here in the barracks they so freely criticized. Francisco poured a healthy dollop of "purely medicinal" tequila into each of two cups of coffee and handed one to his friend. "It takes the chill off," he smiled. "Besides, if I must go poke and prod that lot," he waved toward the troops lounging on the patio, "I deserve a little fortification." Undoubtedly uncomfortable for a young man from a good family, the exams for lesions, sores, and rashes constituted a weekly ordeal for Francisco. Salvador waved off his friend's complaint. He'd happily do the poking if it afforded him a chance to jump up the ranks and get the social status the doctor took for granted. Not that he would want to try any of the weird remedies and alchemical concoctions that the army medics took on faith, but he could pretend to believe. All doctors, to Salvador, were the same theatrical charlatans with butcher knives that they always had been. Diego and Melchora would have quite agreed with this assessment.

The doctors who served the army had profound influence on the military as an agent of change.[3] The medical corps formally took shape in 1880 under President Manuel González, with a formal structure for training, rank, promotion, and hierarchy, twenty years after its inception. Prior medical staff had no rank but *médico* (medic) and worked as a form of auxiliary or parallel service. This service had worked tolerably well in the crises of nineteenth-century warfare and with the limited medical knowledge of the time. With the advent of more peaceful times, direct trauma interventions became less important than maintaining general health and well-being. The expansions of medical knowledge by the end of the century also shaped the corps and its close ties to the modernizing government under Díaz. The better-trained and -organized doctors now expanded their roles, adding pharmacies, veterinarians, and ambulances to the army, but also took responsibility for engineering hygiene programs and eugenic planning for the nation more generally.[4] Before the top medical officers could entertain these reforms, changes to the education system would be necessary.

The training of army doctors, quite separate from the education of other officer branches, revealed underlying philosophies driving the medical corps and the nation as a whole. Before 1860, medical staffing generally fell to unit commanders, and they did relatively little to vet civilian educated doctors. Indeed, as with many armies in the nineteenth century, a great number of these men were little better than butchers or barbers, with similar tools and anatomical knowledge. Far more often, army units relied on the folkloric remedies and Catholic magic of the curanderas among the soldaderas.[5] A good commander would sensibly seek the best doctor he could find for his troops—not an easy task, since considerations of expense, expertise, and willingness to live in the field primarily left the worst, cheapest, and most desperate doctors to the army. Further complicating matters, evaluating the skill of a doctor could be fraught with difficulty; the line between primitive medicine and outright charlatanism confounded even contemporary experts.

In a comedic early nineteenth-century example, the protagonist of *The Mangy Parrot*, by José Joaquín Fernández de Lizardi, managed to pass himself off as a medical doctor simply through pretension and a touch of Latin learned in seminary.[6] His masquerade aroused suspicion but not outright rejection from a self-important physician whom the author selected as his object of ridicule. Pompous and dangerous to his own patients, the doctor could as easily have fit into some of the satirical cartoons published by *México Gráfico* at the end of the century. Not underestimating the comic intent, this uneasiness with early medicine was hardly exceptional. During the Porfiriato, despite great advances in training and medical knowledge, patients continued to find themselves at equal risk in the hands of a doctor as in the care of the soldadera with her folk cures.[7]

Aspirants faced stiff competition for entrance to the medical school, a condition that suggested the social acknowledgement and prestige associated with this training. As with other specialty education, admission often involved nepotism. Family connections served multiple functions by restricting the quality of applicants to some degree but most of all by creating relationships within elite medical, military, and political networks. Generally this insider system worked well, but in one case, Beatriz Álvarez had to write to the president to ask that her son not be admitted to the army's medical corps. She preferred instead that he be sent to study in Paris. While this seems a bit unreasonable, the president acquiesced because the young doctor had trained only in gynecology.[8]

With the inception of regularized medical training in 1880 new degrees of expertise did, nevertheless, become the standard. European advances became the de rigueur measure for medical corps staff, and participation in international medical conferences or training seminars brought new abilities into the military hospitals. Coursework at the prestigious Pasteur Institute in Paris, for example, allowed Medic Major Daniel Vélez to study modern abdominal surgery for one year.[9] The Military Instructional Hospital in Mexico City taught the latest in diagnosis and treatment, using expensive foreign-made equipment. As concerns shifted, so too did the curriculum. For example, new courses in hygiene and in syphilis appeared in 1890 and 1891.[10]

Only about half of the aspirants managed to pass the strenuous training, and it was difficult enough even to enroll.

Families with long military traditions, such as the Montes de Ocas, featured prominently among the top medical officials. Best remembered for contributing a niño heroico to the resistance against the United States in 1848, the Montes de Oca family later boasted a number of officers in various services. The highest ranking of them directed the medical corps for years.[11] With political capital stemming from an exclusive entrance policy, the corps managed to attract accomplished physicians to teach despite relatively poor pay. Alternative possibilities for revenue, as in other services, somewhat compensated for this, as corruption, embezzlement, and bribes afforded a reasonable standard of living.

Furthermore, medical officers had by far the easiest time resigning their commissions and returning to a civil practice, as indeed the majority did after only three years on average. The government chose to give preference to semipermanent and permanent postings to the larger hospitals as one means to retain more staff. Since there were only eleven military hospitals, this measure did not make a great difference. Most young medics continued to deploy with troops for at least a time.

The medical corps also stands out from other services in the usual career arcs of its personnel. With fewer ranks in the hierarchy, graduates attained higher responsibility and pay grades fairly quickly. Graduates moved from aspirant lieutenant to medic major immediately, and within a short time those rose to the ranks to lieutenant colonel or colonel. The corps became top-heavy, with seventy-eight higher officers (jefes) to only fifty-eight regular officers in 1902. The promotion scale depended on available posts, the higher grades generally taking over hospitals, military zones, or branches such as the pharmacies. The relatively swift promotion arc certainly appealed to some, even if field service did not.

Yet field service locales provided their own possibilities for study by an inquisitive doctor. Manuel Balbás's memoirs on the Yaqui campaigns combine natural history with partisan perspective.[12] He notes the state of "savagery" of the Indians, but also makes comment on their traditional dances, songs, and family life. A strange combination of patriotic militarism and humanist pity led him to produce a tract that valorizes indigenous culture and Mexican nationalism. As he published this in his later years, he argues along with Manuel Gamio and José Vasconcelos that the ultimate solution for civilizing indigenous peoples would be education: in his words, "school,

school, and more school."[13] Although Balbás did not see his efforts as anthropology per se, a field still undeveloped at that time, he provided a picture of rare precision of the peoples he encountered. His work and that of other specialists in the countryside helped to produce a body of knowledge about health and customs that embedded the medical service into projects to shape mexicanidad and nation formation. The potency of medical expertise in new and transnational circles afforded to Porfirian doctors the indomitable position of final word on matters of hygiene, breeding, and class; this status the regime reinforced with its positivist rhetoric and, in the breech, with armed police and soldiers. Connaissance then encompassed other elements of power, which reaffirmed its own "natural" superiority.

Professionalizing a modern military echoed broader efforts to professionalize a pseudoscientific medical profession. Anthropology was one facet of this new set of sciences. The barracks became a laboratory for exploring eugenic and racially based ideas of progress.

Eating like a Modern Mexican

The dining call rang out through the barracks and the ladies waiting outside began to prepare their meals as well. Queued again into a long line, Diego shoved his way past the newer recruits and waited his turn. His morning coffee had long ago worn off, and his stomach grumbled noisily, in chorus with all those around him. A whole morning of drill, marching, and sitting in classes took its toll. He looked forward to the meal, even if they weirdly ate at a noontime break instead of the proper late afternoon dinner time. The cook, if that term really applied, splashed corn gruel and beans into Diego's wide-brimmed bowl and then tossed him a hard lump of gritty bread. What the meal lacked in quantity, it also lacked in flavor. As he inhaled the bland portion, he had to smile. Across the patio, the teniente grimaced and poked at his meal. Diego didn't actually mind his food so much since he still remembered the dire poverty and hunger he had suffered growing up. He did complain, of course, that much was expected, and he felt no need to break with an old army tradition. Diego also knew with a bit of smugness that Melchora even now would be preparing a proper meal with decent tortillas and beans and so on that she would bring in shortly. Poor Salvador, he thought, would have to try to buy some of them, and the soldaderas always overcharged the idiot. Once again, food provided another moment of unity. One thing Diego, Melchora, and Salvador all agreed on, army rations had little in common with real food.

Medical and logistics officers looked for ways to properly feed troops in ways that could be affordable, healthy, and modern.[14] Above all, they equated modern progress with the emulation of Europe, and nutritionally this meant a deliberate distancing from normal Mexicans' usual diets. Soldiers' tastes, on the other hand, would create demand for supplementary food and a hatred for official rations. One of the many hardships of military life, food sat very near to a soldier's heart and critics of the regime emphasized the poor quality of rations. Francisco Madero cunningly appealed to the poor conditions and worse food in his 1911 pamphlet sent to federal barracks calling for Revolutionary support.[15] Perhaps tragically, had the prescribed diet actually been allotted, the troops would have been close to content, at least in regard to the quantity they could eat. Even so, they would have grumbled and complained about the food, a practice that represents a sacred right for soldiers in all places and eras.

The official scientific ration sufficed in a number of ways. Medical staff evaluated each item in minutia and detailed fat levels, cooking shrinkage, various nutrients, gluten amounts, and potential digestibility. They recommended specific meats and vegetables based on the expertise and experience of French and German army dieticians.[16] They had great faith in wheat and European cereals. The meats should be cooked until they lost half their quantity to shrinkage. Drinks should not be served at extremely cold temperatures, for fear of causing pleurisy (lung inflammation). Wine was far better than mezcal. While the doctors did give attention to native foods and drinks, their anecdotal scientific evaluations continued to look abroad for validation.

Their conclusions supported eugenic thinking as worked out through comparative studies. They gauged progress by comparing biometric data on soldiers' strides, heights, and weights. Despite this apparent sophistication, the doctors claimed that fish and shrimp had no value for a healthy diet, but reptiles such as tortoise they considered quite appropriate.[17] Nutritious common dishes such as *atole* (corn gruel) they deemed unsuitable save as a last resort, due to their association with indigenous identity. As with drinks such as *pulque* or food like *huitlacoche* (corn fungus), certain consumables remained closely linked to pre-Hispanic, and hence backward, populations. Health scientists presumed that deficiencies in the lower class's character and morality could be rectified with an appropriately modern diet. Atole they dismissed out of hand. They extolled instead the virtues of coffee with sugar as a morning substitute.[18] Similarly, after a lengthy discourse on the dangers of alcohol, Dr. Alberto Escobar continued to sanction a shot of *aguardiente* (hard alcohol) with troops' morning meal in order to help them ward off the chill.[19] He also discouraged tobacco use unless soldiers had coffee, which he believed would mitigate its harmful effects.

The faulty assumptions of army doctors closely mimicked those current with European medical sciences. Medical research continued to rely largely on anecdote and probabilistic speculation, and so since alcohol felt warm going down (and this they long knew to be true), they deemed it an acceptable cool-morning beverage. These ways of thinking about substances with physiological effects likewise imbued many with practically supernatural healing properties. This framework applied to cuisine and its connections to race through eugenic thinking about observed populations.[20] Physically changing subjects through their diet altered essential and unseen bodily differences that lay at the heart of racial categorizations. Social constructions made this process selective, for instance, in excluding the venison eaten by upper classes as traditional while denigrating the same meat on an indigenous table as holding back national (and racial) progress. The menu made the man.

The goal of creating modern, nonindigenous men informed much of what these doctors recommended. They saw Europeans as having the height of science and culture and felt, by the same logic, that consuming European food would mold the soldier into a modern figure. As such, the traditional meals of maize, chilies, and lime they replaced with wheat breads and coffee. This "tortilla discourse" reified authentic or national Mexican foods within elite cookbooks and restaurants while excluding the common varieties as dubious nutritionally.[21] For the positivists, Mexicans had to cease eating corn staples if they hoped to "catch up" to the wheat- and rice-eating developed nations.

Their beliefs, justified by the best pseudoscience of the day, led them to portray food as the measure of a dichotomy between the modern Mexican and the "backward Indian." To build the new national man, they needed a new cuisine. Still, even Escobar could not bring himself to suggest banning beans; perhaps he had a weakness for them. Atole and other common Mexican dishes with indigenous antecedents continued to feed many barracks despite medical advice. They were cheap and the medical staff's arguments over the nature of modern versus primitive did not matter all that much to quartermasters on tight budgets.

In an army short on funds pragmatism ruled the day. It could not have escaped hard-pressed supply officers that the doctors who made the regulations were the same men whose patients did not often survive. If nothing else, prescriptions of electroshock, mercury, and strychnine may have warned off some sensible officers from totally believing the dietary prescriptions they heard. Many officers also had grown up on atole and beans and saw the traditional diet as entirely appropriate for mainly indigenous recruits. A new menu did not persuade all officers, nor did the numbers compiled on caloric needs and inputs compel changes.

Medical recommendations fell short of reality given an uneven and underfunded supply system. Quite aware that rationing had not been standardized, Escobar pointed to the improvements made in quality and quantity between 1882 and 1885 but reiterated the importance of following the official diet as set out in ordinances (see table 5.1). While these figures highlight the differences in nutrition and variety, it is in sheer amounts that the official diet puts the actual rations to shame: a total of 400 g meat, 500 g bread, 100 g rice, and 242 g sugared coffee—well in line with European standards. The German army, for example, gave soldiers 250 g biscuit, 270 g preserved meat, 150 g preserved vegetables, salt, and coffee as an iron field ration; their regular rations typically doubled these amounts.[22] Also of note, the partaking of a main meal at noon (almuerzo), uncommon in France or Germany, where they ate later, did not raise concerns.[23] Even among modern doctors, complete emulation did not present an absolute goal. Cultural factors, including Spanish traditions, could still preclude wholesale reform.

In contrast to official requirements, rations continued to vary depending on location and availability of supplies.[24] Soldiers in the Yucatán complained to their commander of insufficient rations, which in their general's words "were unfit to maintain basic health." Worse still, cattle sent there for the purposes of providing pox vaccinations ended up in the stew pot for a rare treat rather than helping to inoculate the men.[25] Especially in active field operations, the chance for an actual rich meal easily trumped the mysterious mumbo jumbo of the doctors. Rather than blaming this on the lack of discipline among hungry troops, the governor of the Yucatán (himself former military) claimed that the fault fell on the shoulders of the científico faction in his local government.

Issues of food supply plagued even better situated units. Soldiers in garrison at San Juan de Ulua, despite the proximity of supplies in Vera Cruz, complained that they had to beg in the streets even to get bread. Replacement recruits on the march notoriously lacked any rations until arriving at a barracks. Díaz specifically had to order one officer not to allow them to die of hunger.[26] In a somewhat more stable locale along the northern border, replete with ranches, the common meal of the Ninth Battalion included white atole, beans, some bread, and tortillas. Unlike the official prescriptions, they rarely

TABLE 5.1 Rations for troops

	Official recommendation, 1887	Battalion 3, 1882	Battalion 15, 1882	Battalion 26, 1883	Battalion 20, 1884
Morning meal	141 g coffee; sugar; liquor; 160 g bread	None given	78 g bread; 286 g coffee	24 g bread; 140 g coffee	30 g bread; 280 g coffee
Noon meal	400 g meat; garbanzos; greens; butter; 100 g rice; salt; potatoes; beans; 160 g bread	160 g rice; 82 g meat; 215 g broth; 462 g beans; 152 g bread	170 g bread; 110 g broth; 105 g meat; 140 g beans; 128 g rice	450 g broth; 120 g meat; 140 g bread	303 g rice; 178 g meat; 200 g broth; 360 g bread
Late after- noon meal	141 g coffee; sugar; 160 g bread; beans	92 g bread; 239 g arvejón (peas)	75 g bread; 282 g coffee	30 g bread 320 g beans	30 g bread; 280 g coffee

Source: Escobar, Manual de higiene militar, 95, 120, 125.

saw meat, perhaps once a month and on special occasions.[27] Sources remain silent on the type of meat, perhaps ominously so. It seems ironic that in this modern, secular institution troops and officers would have such compelling reason to anticipate religious holidays. When Urquizo wrote his novelized memoirs many years later, he still remembered with gratitude the days of festival, when he and his comrades enjoyed oranges and a somewhat meatier gruel than usual. Religious events benefited men hungry for some comfort foods. Since this represented an uncommon circumstance, where did men find sustenance when the quartermasters failed them? Many young recruits missed home cooking and depended on soldaderas to supply it.

Relatively active lifestyles and stingy rations left troops hungry, dissatisfied, and dependent on outside sources for proper nutrition. Particularly on exercises, the men burned through up to 3,000 calories each day, but their approved diets scarcely provided around 1,500. Troops did not die of starvation, so clearly sufficient additional food came into barracks. Soldaderas had a thriving market for food that included canastas (baskets) with enchiladas, tamales, and fresh bread. It is not clear where they prepared these dishes. During barracks reforms in the early 1920s, additions to kitchen space, deliberately intended to replace soldaderas' efforts with a stable cooking staff, indicate that no facilities previously existed for these women, at least in the Mexico City buildings.[28] Likely, given the relative lack of civilian complaints, soldaderas were able to do their cooking in out-of-the-way corners, local cantinas, and pulquerías, or they simply purchased their wares from locals who had kitchens. An unusual exception, the amasia of Agapito Maldonado had her own house, and presumably she did her cooking there.[29] Wherever the food came from, the inability of the military to feed itself properly shaped the soldier's daily life and gravely undermined the men's dedication to their profession or gratitude toward their units.

The soldier's feeling of dependence undermined the goals of military solidarity and masculine independence, leaving men in a state of need that only the mercy of their women could fulfill. The informal nature of the arrangement also encouraged contraband and other lapses in discipline; for example, women often smuggled marijuana into barracks inside of bread loaves or in enchiladas. The soldier, for his part, would feel no debt of gratitude to the army for providing his three square meals each day, nor did he change his diet from the cheap and often-traditional dishes he obtained. As the army failed to live up to its presumed obligation of feeding them, men's loyalty likewise waned and hunger cut the legs out from under a sense of duty. The precarious nature of service, where food (and to a degree, shelter and clothing) did not always suffice, became obvious to recruits. Men, especially young men, think from their stomachs, and as Napoleon said, an army marches on its belly. Pseudoscientific experiments in redesigning the lower orders through their palate could not overshadow the primal fact of a grumbling stomach. Grueling activity sought to shape up the recruits. Gruel itself was part of the prescription; medical staff reformed rations to meet the newest scientific and European nutritional standards and discarded traditionally Mexican foods as backward and unhealthy. Cuisine represented only one element in the remaking of social classes.

Body, Hygiene, and Polluted Milieus

Out in the streets ordinary people pulled their children in close and frowned at Melchora as she passed. It was as if she had leprosy, she thought. For her entire first year it made her blush with anger and shame when people assumed the worst of her and the other soldaderas. "They are no cleaner than me," she fumed. In truth, the women and children of the barracks had little choice in the matter. Melchora and the others spent long hours every day gathering water, finding little for drinking let alone bathing. During the day, while they waited outside the ex-convento, they had no particular place to, well, go. All they had were local alleyways, and for obvious reasons this angered the neighbors. Inside the walls they tried to wash up, but water continued to be in short supply. One learned to make do. People got sick. All around the patio people lay coughing or flushed with fevers. Many tried to hide the sores and pustules that the doctors said came from syphilis. Melchora, no prude, still couldn't hide her blush when the new battalion medic insisted that he needed to look under her skirts. He accused them all, the whole lot of soldaderas, of carrying diseases. He demanded their cooperation and told them it was for the good of their men. Melchora did not think Diego would appreciate her exposing herself for his "good," and she worried that if her husband heard of this the doctor would fall victim to his temper and jealousy. She knew that Diego also had no chance to avoid his own examination, and she and her friends had giggled about the spectacle of all the men lining up with pants around their ankles. But for the medic to demand this of her! That could not happen. The soldaderas around her agreed. Some tapped fingers on knife hilts, others muttered and glared, and the doctor, realizing his peril, declared the exam postponed. As he left he turned to them: "This isn't over," he threatened.

Becoming modern Mexicans proved most difficult with an unhygienic, uncivilized lower class that some found far from becoming. The regime sought, as had governments since the Bourbon Era, to apply education and hygienic measures to civilize the poor through politicized sciences, turning science to political ends.[30] Improved public works, clean, paved streets, and foreign-trained doctors were to usher in a modern age, reducing mortality and instilling morality.[31] Among the reformative projects they undertook, the bodies and barracks of the Porfirian army received special attentions. One of their first targets was the soldaderas.

Clashes between military aspirations, public images, and soldaderas' rights grew into a power struggle over hygiene and the female body. Control over the public sphere included managing elements of gendered "deviance." Negative public impressions regarding women who spoiled military parades, fought in the streets, and flaunted sexuality in the barracks put pressure on military staff to enforce order and control. Medical advances and new sanitation laws envisioned the soldadera as the locus for diseases and the primary obstacle to military health, and hence to national progress. Despite these pressures, soldaderas continued to exercise their own moral economy on the army, in at least one case with riot and forgery.

FIGURE 5.1 "Primer patio del Cuartel del Batallón num. 13, en la Piedad (D.F.)."
México Militar, 1901, 400.

As Porfirians examined their policy on syphilis and conscripts, Dr. Ángel
Rodríguez recounted an earlier failure to curtail soldaderas and their pox.[32]
In 1876 the Second Division in Puebla, under General Ignacio Alatorre, had
ordered a weekly exam for all women belonging to the corps, and those who
passed received tickets to enter barracks. An exception was made for those
that jefes deemed to be *realmente* (truly) married. Presumably a church-
sanctioned wedding trumped venereal diseases.

The soldaderas answered with violent mass protests, threatened medical
staff with death, and frightened the officers. The women of the troops brought
ordinary garrison functions to a halt. They ceased bringing food. They undermined officers' authority. They threatened to instigate mutinies. And they
themselves apparently terrified some of the officers standing against them.

The discontent of soldaderas led directly to a tremendous rise in soldiers'
desertions. Despite this, the general persevered, and finally the women submitted to the regulation of showing a health ticket that gave such information as
nationality, age, name, and physical features, as well as the results of an

every-eighth-day physical examination. Still defiant, the women next made a mockery of the sanitary vigilance by ingeniously forging their own tickets. The division's officers eventually discarded the practice, and although it reappeared in ordinances in 1881, by 1893 almost no garrison followed the procedure.[33] The ordinance proved too costly to administer in terms of the medical staff's time, but more significantly, it created too much disruption of garrison order and morale. Officers largely chose to skip the process in self-defense and for the sake of order, regardless of any doctor's recommendations.

The high incidence of venereal diseases represented a failure for military hygienists who considered themselves at the forefront of modernizing reforms, and they attempted to redress this in various ways. The usually short term of service meant that sexual ailments had little immediate dangers for soldiers, but doctors continued to seek measures they could enact for their own reasons. Syphilis and gonorrhea, they believed, could be controlled only through the carriers, whom they identified as the soldaderas. Unfortunately, the ambiguous position of these women, as both wives and possible prostitutes, rendered this an improbable proposition.[34] Some doctors came to recognize, especially in light of the Puebla experience, that they could more reasonably expect to treat the men captive in barracks. They nevertheless persisted with pressures on women, in part since cultural assumptions they worked from suggested that men only followed their natural impulses. Men's frailty of willpower could not be overcome, so the carriers of disease (women) remained the physicians' main concern for countering the "Touch of Venus."

Their attempts reflected the limited scientific knowledge of the day, although they drew from the best medical studies available, particularly those of Philippe Ricord and Etienne Lancereaux from France.[35] European doctors also viewed their military forces as potential foci for venereal diseases, but they made special note of how the ravages of syphilis applied especially to Mexico and Central America.[36] Ricord and his students had considerable influence on Mexico's hygienists, and their model of syphilis became the basis for Porfirian understandings of the disease. The French believed that environmental conditions had considerable influence on the spread of the disease, particularly those such as hot climates, alcohol use, racial mixture, and urban crowding.[37] They concluded that the best prophylaxis required supervision of prostitutes.[38]

Their careful scholarship did not make this immediately practicable. European scientists had identified syphilis as separate from gonorrhea in

1767 and as a three-stage disease early in the nineteenth century.[39] The first stage was chiefly diagnosed by the presence of chancres on the penis, which might not appear until after a period of incubation that could last as long as one month. Notably, women resisted easy diagnosis because their sores appeared internally, and there was widespread reluctance by women and distaste among doctors for use of a speculum to inspect within their privates.[40] Such an invasive penetration seemed much too intimate for most, and especially so in the context of the military's mandated (coerced) examination. Doctors had more luck discovering the second stage, whose symptoms included pallor, spots, and rashes. If untreated, with time this exacerbated into stage-three syphilis, where organs and tissues began to decay and dissolve, potentially resulting in hemorrhage, organ failure, insanity, and death. In theory, they could properly diagnose this and distinguish it from allergies, rashes, or other ailments. Issues of public good did not convince their prospective patients to cooperate when their modesty felt compromised, and the medical profession in general did not enjoy much popular confidence.

Ricord and his followers showed, for example, much less certainty about the transmission of and treatments for syphilis. They believed that contagion certainly occurred through vaccinations and on occasions spontaneously, the latter being proven by the infection of respectable women. Since these presumed-to-be-chaste women could not possibly have cheated on their partners and yet still caught sexual diseases, the doctors assumed that other causes must clearly exist. Occupations such as cooking, laundering, and glass blowing seemed to be related to the disease. The researchers could not with certainty say that syphilis did not spread through kissing, but they did not believe semen had any transmissive properties.[41] Hence, they believed that the best means to prevent epidemics of syphilis in soldiers would be accomplished by the strict regulation and inspection of the women they had contact with—the location of the disease.[42] The question of how to control venereal diseases among the soldiers raised a number of practical issues.

Diagnostic methods fell short of the primitive, relying primarily on visual and olfactory inspections. In Great Britain, the military's weekly genital inspections of soldiers gained the charming moniker of the "dangle parade."[43] The French government mandated tests every other day, while in Mexico, from 1872 on, physicians considered checks every eighth day sufficient, or at least practical and affordable.[44] True diagnostic proof of syphilitic infection was not possible until the perfection of serum testing in 1949, so the once-over truly represented the height of medical sciences.[45] Nonetheless, this entailed special difficulties when doctors deemed women to be the carriers of the disease, as medical tests for women proved even less reliable than those for men. Given the possibly lengthy incubation stages of syphilis, the lack of external symptoms in women, and the existence of asymptomatic carriers, demanding invasive checks of females in contact with men engendered great resistance. In Mexico as in Europe, officials could force only known prostitutes into regular surveillance programs, and even that policy often failed.[46]

Failure also marked the attempted treatments for syphilis. In Europe and the United States, doctors and researchers had experimented with numerous possible cures, from exotic woods to pure opium, and returned again and again to using mercury.[47] The alchemical mysticism surrounding mercury as a substance encouraged scientists to imbue it with mysterious properties. After all, it looked strange, it acted unusually, and so it must have some sort of effect on people. The French school under Ricord and Lancereaux, while warning of overdosing with mercury, continued to prescribe it as the best possible treatment, with the addition of potassium chloride to mitigate its harmful effects. While this seemed, from anecdotal evidence, to reduce symptoms of syphilis, the treatment had no real effect on the disease and led to the slow, painful death of many patients from heavy-metal poisoning. Mexican hygienists followed suit and prescribed mercury and calomel cures in the modern fashion. Influenced by positivist ideology and by the recent rise of neo-colonialist tropical medicine, physicians worked assiduously to prove themselves on the world stage.

The new Porfirian military medical staff undertook to diagnose and treat recruits as best they knew how. They saw the army as a particular concern, even though the apparent prevalence of syphilis among soldiers fell below that of civilian populations.[48] Moreover, this was low even for soldiers. In 1892 only 1,785 soldiers were diagnosed as syphilitic, a mere 7 percent, which compares extremely favorably with rates close to 30 percent reported by many armies in World War I.[49] But the barracks was supposed to be far better, and far more controllable, and so the soldier would need the full efforts of hygienists. Regulations for medical inspections insisted that each battalion, regiment, and garrison have a *médico-cirujano* (surgeon-medic) on staff and that they would hold an inspection of the genitals each week. The medical corps also worked to improve the training of military doctors.[50] These men saw regular evidence of syphilis in the army and feared its effects on local communities. In the case of Díonicio Silva in 1877, they worried that his syphilitic issues would "aggravate the disorders he could commit on the street," which suggests they feared possible madness or further infections.[51] The corps published a number of studies on the subject of diseases and attributed causes based on moralist, not scientific, sources. For instance, in 1888 they laid blame on the soldiers' bad lifestyles and complained that this represented a waste of time in training troops.[52] In 1891 the Military Hospital for Instruction began offering its doctors a clinical class on venereal and syphilitic diseases to remedy their lack of knowledge.[53] Physicians produced knowledge about sexuality and bodies, issued professional recommendations, and executed official policies to police unhealthy behavior.

Their efforts to survey and discipline subjects within gendered assumptions perfectly exemplifies the theoretical conceptions of Foucault. The power of knowledge systems depended in no small part on the ability of authorities to transmit ideas, to repeat them, and to provide degrees of surveillance where those who felt watched automatically fulfilled these notions. People consented, by acquiescing, to the authority of those suggesting courses of action that fit an imposed sense of rightness. Once it became conventional wisdom, few struggled against it. Women of the barracks had a difficult fight to avoid the measures "rationally" taken to limit the perils lurking in their genitalia. Through published scholarship the medical corps changed basic power relations by establishing authority over discourses of lower-class sexuality.

Ángel Rodríguez's study suggested a number of new and old ways to deal with syphilis in 1893.[54] He argued that the "entrenched enemy" of syphilis could be beaten only if the army followed his suggestions. He thus presented disease in stark and combative terms and enlisted soldiers and their lovers to his cause. He argued the need to ban soldaderas from barracks, to quarantine the ill, to inspect soldiers' genitals, regularly and thoroughly, with punishment for anyone hiding his symptoms, and to force soldiers to clean their genitals rigorously. He added that if they did not find it repugnant to do so, all soldiers should be circumcised, and he emphasized the need for education. That this might seem foreign to their Christian religious sensibilities he never admitted, but also he seemed unaware of the pain that his proposals implied. A study by Major Zurado y Gama echoed Rodríguez the next year, stressing that with education and read-aloud regulations, soldiers would understand the damage syphilis would do their health and to their family.[55] His appeal to a soldier's responsibility as a father and husband suggested a moral and cultural set of assumptions that informed his prescription. He also saw the soldadera as the major problem and suggested that it was those women who were not legally wives who spread the disease between different soldiers in the garrison.[56] Somehow civil registration or a priest's blessing conferred a cure that prevented sexual diseases, or perhaps the lack of marital standing caused infection in the first place.

In the absence of mass marriage, maybe medicine could simply cure the issues of sexual diseases. Doctors could point to cases such as Lieutenant Francisco Pérez, whose third-stage syphilis included severe ulceration of the throat, and confidently claimed they had cured him in two months' time. As proof of their venereal mastery, they had brought to bear the finest in European treatments to bring soldiers back to an illusion of health.[57]

Despite advances, the normal treatment continued to consist of poisons and folklore. Discarding talk of inoculations, which remained unproven, doctors prescribed mercury pills that were, in 1893, all the rage in Montpellier, France.[58] Zurado y Gama found his troops resistant to medicines and to circumcision and seemed surprised that they should hide their symptoms from him—even though his principal treatment painfully cauterized genital sores.[59] Indeed, already in 1892, the most common operation in the medical corps was circumcision, but only about seventy were performed each year.[60] In addition, surgeons also performed three full castrations, presumably also related to venereal complications. In a Monterrey garrison, three men with what may have been syphilis suffered a round of treatment that combined strychnine, electric shocks, coffee, and cold baths.[61]

Notwithstanding the ineffectual results of these procedures, one can hardly blame the troops for avoiding them. Genital mutilation, no matter how well intentioned, did not lead soldiers to line up and volunteer. In an era new to antiseptic surgery and long prior to antibiotics, only the most desperate allowed surgeons to work below their waist.

The result of treatments did not instill great hopes, and reformers continued to lay the blame on the dubiously moral women of the garrisons rather than on gross medical ignorance and potentially dangerous malpractice.[62] For example, in the Tenth Regiment doctors publicly announced to everyone which women had syphilis. They felt the betrayal of confidence justified, since they limited their revelations to unmarried women and those only interested in money, thus indicating both the doctors' respect for barracks weddings and their disdain for "un-ordered" women.[63] But Lancereaux's prescriptive devices also connected the venereal outbreaks with their environmental causes, especially substance abuse and cleanliness. Indeed, diseases, cleanliness, and drug usage all connected the modernist discourses back to class expectations and the demands of modernity. It made little sense to treat chancres and symptoms, then, without also addressing the related perils of the barracks lifestyle. The doctors' assumptions that the "syphilitic affection [was] contracted from a disordered life" blamed women once again for the moral ills of the army.[64] Yet whether trooper woman, sexual partner, religious mother, or disease vector, soldaderas embodied vital roles within the Porfirian military and the nation it represented. The environment did not improve their predicaments.

The Perils of the Barracks

It was the ceaseless coughing that woke Salvador every time he almost drifted off amid the constant droning of a long humid night filled with buzzing clouds of mosquitos. Troops had carried out the tiny cadavers of two more children the previous morning, and his soldiers looked increasingly pale and unhealthy daily. The old former convent that housed them seemed each day more a prison with its darkness and its foul smells. As he looked down from his window, the overcrowded patio writhed with people. He shuddered; that vision exactly fit what Francisco had warned him about, the disgusting lot all huddled together with their foul habits and unclean bodies, breeding plagues on their petates. And, he felt, there was nothing he could do to help. Conveniently forgetting his own little embezzlements, he bemoaned the lack of funds that might bring in clean water or open up more living spaces, or even just improve the troops' diet. Down on the hard patio, Melchora cuddled in close to Diego for warmth and to comfort him as he coughed. Some of these nights, when the air grew still and the bugs gnawed, she hated this place. It would be worse for her, she knew, if she had not come here. The downtrodden women she saw in the markets and begging in the streets gave her daily affirmation that she had made the right choice. Still. If all of this illness continued, perhaps she would need to take little Rodrigo and move on for all of their sakes.

Visions of moral and physical hygiene echoed attempts by the medical officers to reform the barracks. Sexuality represented one set of behaviors that shaped soldiers, but disease and environment transformed them in other ways. Conditions in the aging barracks contributed to health issues that positivist hygienists believed they could control. Soldiers' habits and vices likewise raised concerns over the creation of modern citizens with both morality and vigor. The poverty of the barracks family also restricted the treatment of their illnesses, and some complained that the soldier's wage simply could not stretch to cover medicine for his family. For soldiers, too, the lack of pesos at times led to self-medicating with local remedies that were cheaper than scientific pharmaceuticals, and perhaps as effective.[65] They also sought out folk cures and herbal concoctions as they and their families had always done. Taking these alongside more modern or scientific remedies inspired better confidence in results and likely improved health, at least through placebo effects. Several of the botanicals and drugs they chose, including marijuana, alcohol, and opium, did work to alleviate pain and stress at the very least. Physicians and the elite had a different perspective. Understandings of the body changed as aspirations for science-based modernity built new, incorporeal demands. An unhealthy army suggested a sickly nation—the priorities of the regime made reforming bodies a national objective.[66] Biopower as a concept applies especially well here, as the elite made a conscious and overt leap in associating the physical health of the army with the moral robustness and potential of the nation. Taking Mexico as an organic whole, when cancers of disorder or physical disease threatened the garrison, they threatened to infect the entirety of the republic.

The complications of architectural inadequacy in their housing directly tied to troops' living quality. The barracks represented an enormous challenge and expense due to their shameful states of disrepair. Most had never been intended for the purpose, and the ex-conventos in particular made up the majority of these buildings. They had been built to house relatively few clerics rather than the large number of men, women, and animals that they then sheltered. The regime could not simply discard the buildings. In 1879 they totaled over 7.7 million pesos' worth of real estate.[67] On paper, the government budgeted some 300,000 pesos for the upkeep of eighty-three barracks buildings in 1899 and roughly the same for vital repairs. It was a losing proposition. Most buildings continued to disintegrate, and by 1920 those still standing required complete reconstructions that cost on average about 300,000 pesos per building.[68] The old cloisters simply could not work for this scale of usage, and the budget hemorrhaged.

Facilities also had to facilitate the spread of Porfirian power. In an era of expansion, the old convents simply did not have the coverage needed. The administration made use of hundreds of unofficial and temporary lodgings for which the army paid rent. Many times these rental properties came into use for only a short time, as they too proved inadequate for the army. The military increasingly found itself searching for quarters in places it had not previously garrisoned. As the national army extended its reach into the countryside and displaced local forces, the need grew to build or acquire quarters in previously ungarrisoned areas (see map 7.1 and chapter 7). This spread represented a form of self-colonization of the nation—areas often hostile to a distant federal government now housed rotating detachments of soldiers who brought with them Díaz's will.[69] Troops arrived throughout the hinterland, occupied territory, and settled it. Indeed, in between well-populated or well-traveled corridors regimes since Juárez's had established military colonies. These settlements, reminiscent of the old presidio-mission system, set up new towns under a military-appointed governor and inhabited by veterans and their families, in order to bring order to new places. They also cost a great deal, but since this funding came from the Departments of Hacienda (Interior) and Fomento (Development), the military saw this as a favorable move that offered a possibility for former soldiers. Scattered garrisons and temporary quarters nonetheless drained military coffers, and officers put off making improvements to buildings.

Despite increases made to budgets and to medical advice, persistent shortcomings made troops' lives uncomfortable and unhealthy. The military's facilities had many problems. Old, dilapidated, and not purpose-built, they fell far short as permanent, fortified homes for hundreds of men, women, and children. Old church buildings offered a choice of either ample living

FIGURE 5.2 Barracks at Piedad, 1921. Pascal Ortiz Rubio, *Los alojamientos militares en la República Mexicana* (México: Dir. de Talleres Gráficos, 1921), 70.

accommodations or basic working space for officers, and so soldiers had to make do with sleeping on the ground. Colonial structures rarely met modern standards. Nor had they been designed either for defense or for imprisonment, although this could at least be improvised. Among their many issues: poor lighting, stagnant ventilation, no beds, no tables, dirty or absent water supplies, and lack of either windows or mosquito netting.[70] Poor air flow made summers miserable, weak heat sources made winters awful.[71] Troops quipped that they could always tell the season by whether their drinking water iced up or steamed in the cup, since these represented the only options. The dismal environs and lack of illumination created a haven for mold and vermin, not to mention the bleak and depressive effect. Goals of civilizing recruits' behavior went unfulfilled as troops found themselves eating and sleeping on the dirt or stone of the patio, and they sometimes had to buy their own sleeping mats to ward off the chill at night. At times the cold prompted soldiers to light a fire despite the dangers of nearby powder magazines or flammable interiors.[72] The potential for massive explosions gravely worried officers, and troops compounded the peril of setting up braziers or campfires with their common smoking habits. Fire generally preoccupied the city elite, and soldiers clearly could not be trusted, so the army punished the men for endangering buildings and issued more blankets as a solution.[73]

The architecture also left men at the mercy of bloodsuckers, but they afforded a laboratory of sorts for physicians. Exposure to mosquitoes (not to mention lice and bedbugs) made for sleepless nights at best, and in some climates also led to *Anopheles*-induced malaria as well as yellow fever from *Aedes aegypti* or *Aedes albopictus* mosquitos.[74] Doctors followed their orders and their units, and so semipermanent postings to fixed hospitals had great appeal. The possibility of postings to less desirable regions prompted complaints and even resignations from some. The Yucatán, with its reputed unhealthy climate and ongoing warfare, nonetheless attracted a number of scientifically or morally minded doctors who saw the garrisons there as a challenge. The government also established new hospitals and clinics specializing in peninsular illnesses.[75] Malaria and yellow fever, as well as the more common typhoid and cholera, represented important puzzles for which the barracks, unfortunately, provided a possible testing ground.[76] Various theories appeared, some that came close to uncovering the connection between anopheles mosquitoes and disease. Mosquito nets, for example, they noted had "a salubrious (healthy) effect" for troops, but doctors felt that this stemmed from better resting conditions.[77] Others observed that in windier areas they saw fewer cases of the disease and drew the conclusion that something in the air must be to blame, but mosquitoes did not occur to them.[78] The final breakthrough would not come for another decade.[79] Similarly, yellow fever continued to take its toll, between 1883 and 1885 killing 581 men in the port garrisons of Veracruz, Mazatlán, Tepic, and Tampico alone.[80] Quite simply, the convents converted into barracks were not modern, healthy, or pleasant—poor supply and quality of water exacerbated their many problems.

Water shortage was a ubiquitous complaint of medical officers, thirsty garrisons, and neighboring civilians alike.[81] For many units, especially cavalry, even drinking water remained in short supply. Soldiers in hot weather required between six and eight liters a day just for hydration, and mounts needed a further twenty to forty liters depending on their activity level. Further, keeping horses clean required much more still, and the animals' health depended on some basic hygiene of this sort. On this issue the barracks often clashed with local communities. The residents near Santiago Tlatelolco barracks complained bitterly to the city government about the cavalry regiment's overuse of the neighborhood fountains as well as the demolition of parts of the fountain to help rebuild a wall in their barracks.[82] Nearly every garrison in Mexico City petitioned the municipal government for better water supplies. Like other residents, they had to apply and pay yearly for a *merced*, a grant allowing them to take a certain amount of water from the city supply. The merced represented a set quantity in liters per minute, measured by a standard bronze tube. The usual amount frequently failed to meet the requirements that hygienists called for, since per-man allotments still accounted only for soldiers, and not their families or animals, nor for bathing or laundry.

Poor supply caused issues of cleanliness, and contaminants in the drinking supply also had direct impact on the health of the barracks. Taken together, water quality ailments incapacitated 20–50 percent of ill soldiers and represented a possible vector for the infection of civilian populations as well. Typhus spread from dirty living conditions, as lice infestations infected hosts. Typhoid fever came from water supplies contaminated with *Salmonella typhi* bacteria and feces from those already infected with it. Some 5 percent of survivors also continued to carry the disease as asymptomatic vectors. Cholera likewise was transmitted through drinking feces-contaminated waters. Medical officers, with resulting public support, pushed engineers to improve potable supplies as part of the new, modern society, but with meager results. During the Porfiriato, despite the theoretical expansion of the water supplies available, the regime actually began to remove potential sources through the Gran Desagüe (Great

Drain) project, completed in 1900.[83] This public works achievement did reduce the endemic flooding that cross-contaminated the water table, but at the grave cost of ruining Lake Texcoco as an aquifer feed and the emptying of much of the subterranean supply. Still, improvements did reflect the government's prioritization of city hygiene. Attempts to repair waterpipes, dig wells, and pave streets came slowly, even in the Federal District, and remote areas waited even longer.

Health issues worried the army administration and the neighbors of garrisons. Local communities expressed concerns about the spread of disease from barracks, despite the somewhat lower rates of disease found there. Officers seemed especially bothered by reports of soldaderas and their children contracting typhus. Numerous letters to the president's office pleaded for assistance for families in the barracks whose health had suffered due to poor conditions. The lousy inhabitants spread the contagion in the close quarters of the patio, and while troops also suffered, the correspondence prioritized the innocent women and children as the chief victims. Anxiety over the barracks as a locus for immoral behaviors mirrored that regarding infections of the body. Assumptions of propriety and class attributed particular potency to a vision of the filthy and diseased soldier community.

The hygiene issues at times brought the military into political conflict with city officials. Secretary of War Felipe Berriozábal used common fears to threaten the Mexico City government in 1897, declaring that "the lack of water in the barracks must be mended with all haste to prevent a typhoid epidemic among troops, and thereby among all the inhabitants of the Capital."[84] The city said that the barracks' four square meters of water sufficed and denied any more grants, but the complaints continued for years. The barracks of the military police, with 150 men and 100 horses, did not obtain enough water to wash daily and frequently ran out. The Seventh Regiment used horse troughs for bathing and drinking by both man and mount.[85] In terms of hygiene this fell somewhat short, and it certainly put the men at greater risk for cholera and typhoid, not to mention dehydration among those with common sense. It also seems cruel to the horses. The First Battalion had faced over a year of inconstant water in 1878, despite having its garrison right at the heart of the city in the National Palace. They finally resorted to drinking directly from the cathedral's fountain sources, and much to the horror of clergy and bystanders, they stripped and bathed right out in the center of the Zocálo.[86] In this case the municipality gave way and granted better water access, if only to placate offended onlookers or as a nod to the unit's prestigious posting. Most often this conciliation did not occur.

The result: soldiers filthy at best, diseased at worst. Medical reports on infectious diseases indicate that compared to civilians, a soldier was somewhat less likely to contract fatal typhus (at rates of 1.2 percent versus 1.3 percent). This might have reflected the relatively more immediate attention of doctors or simply better prophylactic control over lice in the barracks than in most neighborhoods. The barracks nonetheless took a toll, and military men had roughly twice the rate of death from tuberculosis as did their civilian counterparts (7.6 percent compared to 3.3 percent). This makes sense, since overcrowding and poor nutrition closely associate with populations at risk for the disease, and alcoholism and tobacco use greatly increase one's susceptibility. Because tuberculosis had lower absolute fatality, military doctors focused on the typhus issue—not surprisingly, they once again concluded that the blame for disease in the barracks lay with soldaderas.[87] As with syphilis, the arguments of typhus prophylaxis insisted, to the point of frenzy, that women's promiscuity resulted in lower-class, unhygienic threats to the soldiers and the community. Again like syphilis, the treatment potentially did more harm than the disease, as typhus sufferers received an injection of strychnine.[88] Medically the toxin made sense. This potent poison can cause convulsions, paranoia, and respiratory failure if used in quantity, and this made it an effective solution for exterminating rats and stray dogs. Yet in smaller doses it causes muscular paralysis, which could alleviate the harsh hacking coughs of patients and provide some relief, at least for a time, from the self-destruction of the lungs.

Poor quality of water also aggravated disorders of the gastrointestinal tract, which were one of the most common causes of hospitalization and death during the Porfiriato. Hundreds of soldiers already afflicted with syphilitic damage added to the thousands more for whom bad water had inflamed or aggravated stomach issues. Dysentery and enteritis (intestinal infections) afflicted enormous numbers of soldiers and civilians in the capital, and annual flooding led to periods of higher disease rates. One cure of sorts, common in areas from China to London, came in the form of opium or tinctures of opium like laudanum, which cause constipation. These were often unavailable in Mexico City. Many soldiers, rightly leery of their water, attempted to drink only beer or pulque. Lack of sewage facilities made stomach ailments nightmarish, and the city of Mexico became renowned for its reek. To medical staff, the stinginess of civilian officials was seen as preventing the development of proper water supplies, and the refusal to dig artesian wells seemed a greedy ploy.[89] Control over the water supply presented municipal governments with opportunities for graft and significant influence over residents. Their monopoly over the merced system provided them an incentive to deny permits for well building, yet their concerns over the quality of the aquifer also came into their considerations. The wells did not always remain pristine, and the municipalities felt they could better monitor the supplies piped in from rivers and other sources.

Even when military units had sufficient water, other problems arose. From the Sixth Battalion in the Yucatán in 1902, General Victoriano Huerta wrote to the secretary of war that he could not convince his soldiers to wash their faces. In fact, he claimed that his soldiers were, for some mysterious reason, afraid to do so.[90] Perhaps the water smelled badly, perhaps a dirty face afforded troops some camouflage in jungle warfare, perhaps it discouraged mosquitos, but in any case Huerta jumped to his own assumptions. Other units, presumably less afraid of water, still complained of their dirty conditions and the omnipresent lice. For hygienists, filth of this sort was a concomitant symptom of the lower classes' behavior and their presumably aberrant morality and social diseases. Lack of washing represented both a symptom and cause for the problems they associated with what they called the life of disorder, the antihygienic. If cleanliness was next to godliness, the Mexican poor demonstrated a shocking lack of either, at least in the minds of other classes.

Adding to the problems of water supply, sewage treatment at many barracks presented a considerable issue, one made worse by the daily eviction of the soldaderas. For hours each day, the soldiers' wives and children were homeless, wandering the nearby streets while the barracks did its daily business. Unfortunately, most areas also lacked any public facilities. The city made attempts to provide residents an alternative to random urination with a number of *mingitorios* (urinals) that dotted the city center, particularly near long-established pulquerías and commonly visited parks. Newspapers nonetheless reported the less-than-pleasant habits of many people who chose expedience over modesty. Among these accounts, soldaderas featured with alarmed regularity, while ordinary drunks generally received only slight approbation.

In 1870 neighbors of the San José de la Gracia barracks complained to the city government about soldaderas' abuses against good health and public morality.[91] They claimed that the women left the sidewalks covered in fecal materials, turning their corner of the street into a literal dung heap. The deposits, solid and liquid, produced an awful stench and a public disgrace. In this incident, perhaps the most blatant irruption of barracks into street, the connections between class, hygiene, and morality once again focused public scrutiny on soldaderas as the embodiment of obstacles to modernity. The barracks again became the metaphor for national progress.

Conclusion

The barracks under the powerful gaze of a new medical corps attempted to shape a proper modern Mexican. The strength of the medical and scientific discursive systems of the late nineteenth century was apparent in barracks experiences. Experts, mostly from within the army's own educational institutions, applied all the newest scientific knowledge in breaking the scourges of typhus, cholera, syphilis, and immorality. They targeted the women of the garrisons for many cures, on some ailments they went after the troops, and on others they worked on architecture or environs. The doctors offended many they claimed to assist, but they did so from an irrefutable position of legitimate authority. One could dismiss or disdain their specific cures, but few challenged the value of medical advances generally. Within a mantle of connaissance, experts inscribed the subject population of the army with the instruments of modern assumptions and classist prescriptions. Doctors sought to make the soldier and his family "clean" in the most abstract of senses, and with whatever tools they deemed necessary.

Doctors envisioned denizens of the barracks as vermin of dubious morality but optimistically envisioned the possibility of transforming them. Applications of science would rebuild from generations of religion and tradition, and the facets of indigeneity would fade. With eugenic assumptions they attacked their "problem" by changing diet, dress, and environments. The soldiers and soldaderas did not willingly play along. Mexico certainly did not come to this circumstance alone among nations. Many countries in these decades brought to bear similar discursive and practical measures of hygiene against their populations. So what common factors impelled these policies transnationally at the turn of the century? The connaissance of hygienic racial environmental improvements went global alongside advanced capitalism. As mankind became a form of capital, individuals would (whether they liked it or not) face expert management to ensure fit within a societal whole; just as one shoe lodged in a gear may sabotage a factory, each part mattered *despite* its individual self. The medical field also had grown and become entrenched due to technological advances—people invented seemingly everything that made up modern life between 1870 and 1910, from remote controls to airplanes to elevators to zippers and so on. Similarly, doctors largely evolved from crude superstition and anecdotal research toward methodological soundness. Many exceptions to this continued, but on the whole the profession approached the point of helping more patients than they killed. This new credibility lent them power, especially in replacing non-professionals such as midwives. Finally, the nineteenth-century heyday of eugenics made an impact on increasingly capable governments. Social Darwinists and Comptean ideals shaped public policy. The idea of better breeding, promulgated by the elite and in no small way by world's fairs and expos, suggested dark solutions for unfit populations. Mexico followed along on all of these new paths and would reap their consequences.

Real limitations to the military medical projects came from the stubborn resistance of subjects and from the lack of resources the reformers required. Troops went hungry, or they ate the "wrong" foods. Women refused inspections for disease and rejected the blame for illnesses. Unhygienic buildings persisted and exacerbated epidemic conditions. Uncontaminated water came in quantities insufficient even for basic cleanliness. Cholera, typhus, typhoid fever, and tuberculosis ran rampant. The supposed supremacy of medicine failed. The blame fell on the women of the barracks. In explaining the failures of the modern state to remedy the disordered life, science inoculated doctors, and the perilous soldaderas and wild barracks evenings appeared to hold all the faults.

The medical discourse and greater knowledge systems had tremendous capacity to effect change, yet the garrison experience becomes all the more intriguing in the many ways ordinary people found to resist becoming lab rats in the national experiment. Women and families opted out of medical surveillance, even when doctors did not offer that as an official option. Forty-foot walls and armed guards could not control the environs of the garrison in meaningful ways. The eyes of the state encountered more blind spots than it dreamed, or feared, when it sought to bring this particular and mercury-tainted modernity to its captive subjects. It evinced a great deal of authority without much power.

The coughs and cholera passed with the end of the rainy season. Melchora stayed with her Diego, and Salvador gave up on his notion of expelling the soldaderas into the street. Everyone began to feel better, more energetic, but also somewhat pent up or bored. In the aftermath of illness and poor weather, entertainments drew the garrison back together in what outsiders called "the disorderly life."

The relief to so many punishments they [the troops] seek in marijuana and in alcohol, which numbs their members and drowns their faculties until they are useless for service.

—MANUEL MONDRAGÓN, *PROYECTO DE ORGANIZACIÓN*, 1910

Liberating Herb!, comfort of the overwhelmed, of the sad, and of the afflicted. You must be akin to death itself with the gift of making one forget the miseries of life, the tyranny of the body, and the malaise of the soul.

—FRANCISCO LUIS URQUIZO, *TROPA VIEJA*

CHAPTER SIX

The Disordered Life of Drugs, Drinks, and Songs in the Barracks

The nighttime wildness surprised Diego most in his military journey, and Melchora too, although she never would have admitted it aloud. Civilians spoke a great deal about how mad the barracks became at night, and how amoral their inhabitants. Diego remembered tales back home from the old veteran Tómas—every night a debauchery in his stories, much embellished for effect. Diego soon realized that while the tales were not quite true, and that while really chaotic or out-of-hand nights came rarely, the troops did enjoy some fun. The evenings did in fact mark a significant upending to the regimented order of the daytime. When the horns called Silence and officers retreated, a new world emerged among the patio denizens. The true campaign community formed there. Diego tried new habits, most already familiar to him from home, and some of them became routine. Some, like marijuana or gambling, intrigued him. Ultimately the barracks' inhabitants all found comforts and distractions where they could. Soldiers and soldaderas alike embraced the leisurely opportunities that came and accepted the usually mild consequences when these transgressed regulations.

The elite echelons of society and, even more so, the nascent middle classes gave far too much concern to the habits, vices, entertainments, and expressions of the poor and workers in Mexico. The realm of leisure, of recreation in a literal sense, demonstrated the cultural gaps that threatened national unity and progress.[1] As with hygienic projects, the government experts turned surveillance upon the barracks as a locus for improving the lower classes. They saw in leisure practices the elements of proof regarding social Darwinistic fitness, or more properly, they imposed these ideas on their subjects. At least, they tried to do so.

Ordinary Mexicans in the garrisons gave little mind to elite ideals of how to have fun. Soldiers did not bicycle or play baseball. They gambled, drank, smoked, and fought. They sang. They went to bullfights or cockfights. Sometimes they smoked marijuana. On the whole, they re-created self through leisure as they relaxed and built communities of gossip and as they bonded over laughter. Out of sight of the increasingly nosy state they had intimate lives. Their choices speak to the limits of power and to the hazy spaces outside army surveillance. And they give personality back to agents that the law and history have tended to obscure.

The life of disorder that concerned the hygienists and writers of the day associated the habits and practices of the lower classes, the *pelados* or *léperos*, with their lack of place in the modern nation.[2] Leisure has generally received short shrift as a measure of class identity and solidarity.[3] As personal experiences that shape worldviews, our chosen diversions build individually significant pieces of our ethnic, gendered, localized, and socioeconomic identities. An abiding love for rodeos says one thing; an addiction to mosh pits says another. In contrast to workplace or home address, leisure more often reflects a wider range of choices, even if ones bounded by economic means. This historically led the upper and middle classes to stigmatize selected kinds of inferior leisure as especially detrimental, or worse, *naco* (tacky). When they defined something as a lower-class activity, it was as much a part of creating their own, "better," class identity as it was a means of truly explaining what it meant to be poor or working class. The press, literature, government reports, and other discursive elements talked about leisure and class in ways that created hierarchy for all of society. Their disapprovals only strengthened class solidarity, which built around popular recreation, and segregated social groups. Sneering did little. The rich did their things, the middle class copied them as best they could, and the poor continued having fun as they always had.

Environmental and sexual factors aside, the health of the soldiers and soldaderas mostly degraded at their own hands. The contraband that garrisons obtained, much of it smuggled into barracks by the women, brought new opportunities to harm health and reputation.[4] Soldaderas acted as vivanderas, or venders, providing the things of life for a relatively small price. Among these items, they bought and sold cigarettes, marijuana, pulque, aguardiente, and on occasion even opium. Drugs, tobacco, and alcohol presented bored and desperate men with the means to escape the confinements of routine barracks life.[5] Broadly, the behaviors of the poor became associated with a traditional-seeming class identity. Drinking and other entertainments like gambling or blood sports demonstrated the vulgar or uncontrolled essence of the masses. Progress meant leaving behind such displays, or at least hiding them from the public spaces of the modern nation.

In this chapter I examine the ways that the disordered vida militar shaped identity and elite projects. Alcohol, tobacco, and other leisurely activities shaped the experience of soldiers and wives. What did this mean for them, but also for authorities seeing it from the outside? Did disordered lives present a genuine issue of discipline or merely another elite aspirational arena? Eventually, the rift between theoretical plans and simple fun fell in favor of men and women just trying to enjoy what life had given them.

The gente decente's preoccupations aside, the men and women of the barracks continued to intoxicate themselves as a normal and comforting custom. That these behaviors spilled regularly into streets from the supposedly sealed barracks only added to popular disdain for the army. If it occurred out of sight, the elite and others could comfortably ignore unruly activity. The poor suffered policing and jailing because of elite racism and the public exposure that came with poverty. Their experience as poor, as military, and as Mexicans did not exist separately from these relations. Power relations came through most strikingly in places and times of extreme disconnection between social classes and their basic worlds.

A Military Intoxicated

Diego remembered his first sips of pulque back home and how he had gagged on its slimy texture and acrid flavor. "If only they could see me now," he giggled, as he shambled unevenly down the side street he thought might take him home to barracks. Melchora had not accompanied him tonight, had asked him not go in fact, but she should mind her own business. He liked popping out for some pulque, and as a soldado de confianza, they even let him go out alone sometimes. Probably he had drunk a bit too much tonight, he admitted to himself, but some of his comrades took way more, every night! Deep in thought, Diego didn't even see the other man until they collided. The next day he dimly recalled swinging a fist and getting hit in the mouth at some point. He had a

somewhat hazy walk home afterward and barely recalled a sergeant hauling
him into lockup by his scruff. In the morning his sergeant told him, in far too
loud a voice, that he had earned a seven-day punishment, so at least he would
have plenty of time to think it over. Melchora also had ample time to express
her views on his drinking, which she shared freely and at length on the days
that she bothered to bring him any meals.

Bonding over booze was as old a custom among soldiers as bragging about it
later. There existed some rationales for allowing soldiers access to intoxicants, provided that it was intermittent and either supervised or kept hidden
behind garrison walls. Drinking in the barracks helped to ease tensions, if
done in moderation, allowing men and women a space to relax and enjoy
their otherwise hard lives. The social function of alcohol helped reduce
desertions, making life in the army a bit less onerous and also siphoning
away some of the cash a would-be deserter might use for his getaway. The
intoxication also represented an important rite of passage. In many military
systems the tradition of the "blowout" was considered necessary to foster a
sense of toughness, masculinity, and group solidarity.[6] In the case of the
Porfirian barracks, the community ties built by heavy drinking brought
together soldiers, NCOs, subaltern officers, and soldaderas.

In the Western world soldiers' use and reliance on certain drugs came
as a given. Much as for the new working classes, docility and obedience could
be fostered in these men with the appropriate mixtures of escapist, pain-
relieving, and euphoric ingredients. Drugs lubricate the modern world.[7] Karl
Marx's idea of a religious opiate of the masses made great sense in an era
when actual opiates and booze quieted resistance to harsh conditions and
exploitative environments. Allowing some abuse represented a compromise
for officials, but they only went so far.

Alcoholism became a prime concern of hygienic and scientific officials
during the Porfiriato, and this applied with special power in the military. As
a problem, it was certainly nothing new.[8] The violence and disobedience that
inebriation brought, especially again within the most regulated classes, had
long worried regimes. When it affected actual readiness and discipline, the
army responded but did so within a larger context. A new and scientific discourse on alcoholism corresponded with increased surveillance on the civilizing bodies of the army.

In the ranks, alcoholism and *escándalo* (uproar) represented the normal
state of affairs. Many men drank hard and often, and the women with them.

FIGURE 6.1 José Guadalupe Posada, *La terrible noche del 17 agosto de 1890*. Hoja suelta, pub. por A. Vanegas Arroyo.

Women smuggled in most of the alcohol; indeed, the term Spanish *vivandera*, from the French *vivandiére*, was often synonymous with *smuggler* in contemporary lexicons, relating the vender to her means. Old regulations called on officers to hire vivanderos to provide for troops and forage supplies that the government failed to supply on campaign. The modern soldadera made use of this long tradition in her own way, and in her role as sutler she brought both legitimate goods and lucrative contraband to "her" men. Hollowed-out loaves, soup pots, and concealed wineskins brought the full range of brews into the barracks: sotol, pulque, beer, aguardiente, *charanda*, and of course, tequila. They obtained locally fermented drinks from their usual producers, and normally this meant the women in nearby communities. The type of alcohol depended on region and season; for example, sotol in the north, tequila in the central regions, and charanda along sugar-growing coastlines. With little profit provided the manufacturers, soldaderas shopped out a supply knowing that troops would buy and consume everything they could get. This also could be an issue of health, since some drinks like pulque could cause serious ailments if improperly prepared and adulterated drinks might cause blindness. The risks dissuaded few people. No less than the men, the soldaderas also partook, of course. Every night in the barracks had the potential, depending only on the supply chain, to turn into a raging party.

Soldiers having a few drinks did not concern military administrators all that much. Officers could deal with most drunken shenanigans. Drinking to excess was not, in itself, the problem. Rather, alcohol abuse appeared officially as a problem only under certain circumstances, such as serious fights, public spectacles, or the undermining of military functions. In all cases, the violation of the dignity and morality of the ideal soldier, as much as his physical welfare, lay at the root of chastisements for inebriated troops. Rarely did officials show concern for the health of the offender. Instead they framed punishment as pseudoreligious duty to repair the evils of lower-class vulgar habits. Through a bit of confinement the men would learn to better control themselves and thus emulate the seldom arrested upper classes. And the women, fallen since Eve, rarely received any official attention.

Drunken brawling in the barracks occurred with routine frequency. Aponte remarked on the appearance of troops cut up and bloody, with knives still in hand and alcohol on their breath. He did not concern himself with the event, other than commenting that the officers of that garrison lacked the judicial knowledge to deal properly with their troops—the knife fight did not otherwise surprise him.[9] In personnel files, the great frequency of minor charges for wounding or assaulting bears up the general rough nature of garrison life, and the majority of these cases specifically mention drunkenness, suggesting that responsibility for violence was mitigated by alcohol.[10] Other questions arise from the reports: why did soldiers have knives, where did they hide them, and what instigated potentially lethal struggles? Officers said little, and trial records leave few details. From the scattered reports it seems most men had a blade available after only a month or two, and likely women held onto these during the daytime routine. Those who had knives, almost universally, used them to redress sexual rivalries. For the most part officers simply did their best to ignore this set of dynamics.

Accidents suffered by drunken soldiers, strangely enough, received official concern and investigation. This may have reflected an effort to control preventable events, which nonetheless suggests that the military did not see ordinary, nonaccidental injuries from alcohol abuse as preventable. For example, the 1898 death of soldier Timoteo Cisneros occasioned a full inquiry after a wall trestle crushed his skull while he was inebriated on pulque.[11] In another case, a soldier named Felipe Martínez fell and cut open his head in the street near his Mexico City barracks. It is remarkable that such an ordinary occurrence should gain the attention of military authorities, but this drunken soldier's case generated a full report all the way up the hierarchy to the regional commander.[12] Drunks suffering injuries required a response, or at least an investigation, so long as the wound did not come at the hands of NCOs or other drunken soldiers. What truly seemed to concern the army in these cases, it seemed, involved cases when the dregs of the barracks spilled into nearby communities.

Breaking the Seal between Streets and Barracks

Diego's luck held. The man he had beaten up turned out to be okay, just embarrassed, and better still, he worked as a policeman. Diego's sentence was shortened to a few days in confinement because the captain had little use for the police, as he proudly explained to the young soldier. Next time the whole battalion trooped out into the street Diego thought he saw people from the neighborhood shooting him smiles and winks. It was an odd thought, but he suddenly felt more at home here around the barracks than he ever had back in the village, where his family never prospered. Here he was a known quantity, Melchora too had earned at least the grudging acceptance of local women she dealt with each day at markets, and the presence of the couple usually attracted no special attention when they wandered through the area. As a soldier, his coin spent as well as any other and vendors knew where to find him if they had an issue. The people of the barrio turned an occasional blind eye to the odd fracas or lack of couth so long as the soldiers kept it within bounds. They provided good business, after all, and what could you expect from mere soldiers?

Numerous accounts of drunken soldiers from all ranks and branches encountered in the streets gave evidence of civilian prejudice and barracks leakage alike. Despite efforts to keep soldiers locked away in barracks, reports of alcohol-related crimes made it clear how the military frequently spilled into the community. The cantinas and pulquerías and their products brought out the worst side of the soldiers. It seems that after months of seclusion, soldiers had increasing opportunities to spend evenings out, especially in the company of junior officers who had similar habits. These expeditions did not receive official notice but rather they appear in records only in the context of other events or complaints. For example, two NCOs out on the town were nearly trampled by a carriage in a narrow alleyway and saved themselves only by striking the lead horse. Unfortunately, the carriage driver turned out to be their major and they then had to prove before a formal council of war that they had not deliberately and drunkenly attacked him.[13] Although technically prohibited from unescorted excursions, these and numerous other reports indicate that troops had access to the streets. When officers and soldiers mixed socially it complicated military discipline.

The issue of fraternization particularly worried senior staff. Junior officers on numerous occasions faced charges for taking their men to local bars in the evening, taking advantage of the opportunity to have a few drinks while also ingratiating themselves with the troops. Some officers courted favor in this way, dodging the potential charge that they gave too many leaves since they "supervised" the pulquería visits. This did not reassure their superiors, who commonly associated these types of bars with especially vulgar and low-class behaviors.[14] They would prefer that the public did not see officers of any rank entering such establishments. Yet for a young and impressionable lieutenant these field trips fulfilled an expectation of his troops and an important piece of his unwritten rules of duty that maintained morale. Their acquiescence to this peer pressure nonetheless led to the usual problems that drunken soldiers attracted.

In one case, a recently promoted officer went drinking with his sergeant, and they created uproar with obscenities and violent behavior. When confronted by police for his rude public behavior, Sergeant Antonio Quinines gave them a false name, claiming to be former president Manuel González. Not finished, he then instigated a fight. His sublieutenant received a minor castigation, but the unfortunate NCO earned a month in the military prison of Santiago.[15]

Some officers went further, eschewing trips out to the bar and embracing the opportunity that troops provided. One captain received complaints because the cantina he opened within the barracks had unfairly high prices.[16] His superiors did not prohibit his entrepreneurial idea; they simply condemned his exploitative business practices.[17] This also undermined the economy of women like the vivanderas, since they depended on troops' thirst for their living. Other officers in the barracks notably did not complain of this practice either, suggesting that a considerable degree of complicity among them permitted the cantina to function. Ultimately, this sort of cantina hurt unit discipline and blurred the hierarchal boundaries between the ranks and the officers.

Since soldiers represented a potentially lucrative market, civilian cantinas tended to proliferate in the same areas as barracks, and this brought inebriated troops into the awareness of the local community. Corner bars, improvised pulquerías, and alcohol-serving cafes popped up across the entire city. Much to the dismay of the city elite, the bars proved resistant to workable regulation. Cantinas opened directly across from barracks, for example at Peravillo, as market met demand. During the Porfiriato local entrepreneurs, mostly women, operated over 570 pulquerías in and around downtown Mexico City alone.[18] Most blocks had at least one, and this did not except zones dominated by wealthy homes or grand cathedrals. Not surprisingly this also included the densest area of barracks space in the whole country. Equally predictable, this combination of soldiers and bars led to clashes with civilian law keepers.

Fighting with police seemed almost a tradition. Conflicts rose between soldiers and civilians, as in the case of José Millan, who, in a drunken rage, refused to pay his bill in a cantina, beat up the owner, and fought the arresting police officers.[19] In 1898 two inebriated soldiers kept arresting officers at bay by throwing rocks at them.[20] In another instance, a soldier with nearby family began a lengthy brawl with a local storeowner, and with responding policemen, that eventually ended up in an uneasy siege of his barracks and a showdown between civil and military authorities.[21] This sort of clash appears to have been common enough to require a specific ordinance within the Military Penal Law, and soldiers insulting police faced up to eleven months in prison, or one to three years in the event of an assault.[22] Alcohol aggravated the charges. Officers discharged from service a presidential guardsman for insulting police in 1903, but only because of his previous arrest for drunkenness in the Hidalgo Theater a couple of months earlier.[23] His dismissal stemmed as much from his indiscretion as from his behavior. All of these highly visible misdeeds smeared the image of the military.

The reputation of the army as hard drinking and riotous became well entrenched, so much so that the rare unit that did not cause problems would be specifically noted for their morality. A letter from the Society of Farmers in the town of San Martín requested the removal of the officer in charge of their garrison. Rather than clearly laying out all of the man's misdeeds or slandering the unit itself, they remarked how the soldiers (as opposed to the officer) appeared moral and only rarely frequent the tavern.[24] The townspeople saw occasional drinking by the soldiers as not only normal, or inevitable, but as a positive boon to their cantina's business. That it became a sign of unusual moral rectitude for the troops to remain well behaved indicates a common acceptance of the stereotyped army.

Despite the seriousness of the alcohol issue, troops continued to receive a shot of hard liquor in the morning, and officers continued to lace their coffees with tequila.[25] While perhaps a delicious way to start their day, this seems to undercut the army's rhetorical stance against intoxication. The mixed message of condemnation and acceptance would have little effect on the barracks' drinking cultures. Civilians also expected little change in soldiers appearing in cantinas. Public censure instead focused on the taking of doña Juanita, the toasted tortilla, the *chupito*—marijuana.

Smoking in the Barracks

The business side of providing tobacco came as the first lesson for Melchora when she became a soldadera. The off-duty soldiers, bored and stressed, almost constantly smoked cigars or cigarettes and more rarely marijuana. From nearly the moment they arrived with the cuerda, if not during the trip, soldiers began lighting up. Diego smoked his first on the way to the city. Melchora took up the habit after sharing with him and other soldiers during the relaxed calm of the evenings. The patio had a smoky haze through much of the day, and certainly long into the night. Officers and medics occasionally tried to halt this practice but usually did so with their own cigarettes or pipes lit up. Marijuana, though, inspired dramatically different reactions. Diego and Melchora at times partook, lighting up in the hidden corners of the barracks, and found it wonderfully relaxing. They watched, perplexed, as a very few smokers seemed to go mad with hallucinations—usually the soldiers took care of these men themselves and hid them from superiors. Officers responded aggressively to those who met with "don Chupito." Diego had never seen them so harshly beat a soldier, throwing him in cold water and making him run until he vomited, among other things. So strange, he and Melchora whispered together, the smoke must not work for officers and so they are jealous. Maybe it had something to do with having paler skin? Of course, the drinks and smokes never went away. Diego and Melchora smoked and drank as a complement to other forms of entertainment in the garrison, but these were always a significant part of the military experience.

Marijuana represented a drug most uniquely associated with the Mexican army, by both press accounts and popular opinions. This, like other contraband, entered the barracks in sometimes-clever ways. Women concealed it in clothes, in food, and in their hair. Soldiers concealed it in hatbands and belts, and musicians commonly hid it inside their instruments. As with other contaminants, the officers attempted to prevent its entrance. In 1900 one commander ordered scrupulous inspection of all incoming women to prevent their trafficking in the dangerous herb to soldiers.[26] Considered in the press as the scourge of the troops, marijuana use was associated chiefly with barracks and with prisons, blending the two spaces in popular conception.[27] The use of the drug, nonetheless, long preceded the Porfiriato, and early corridos associated marijuana with the infamous Antonio López de Santa Anna, among others.[28]

The sale and use of marijuana, as with many drugs, became illegal only in 1884 in Mexico. Extraordinarily cheap in the street markets, it could be purchased for as little as fifty centavos per kilogram.[29] Particularly after it became illegal, it represented a lucrative commodity for those with access to barracks or prisons, and soldaderas sold it with a heavy markup, usually around ten centavos for a single cigarette.[30]

Not particularly well known in village or rural life, the drug became ubiquitous in garrisons and army facilities more generally. The soldaderas and soldiers learned of it quickly and became adroit at dealing drugs. The obvious demand among soldiers created a captive market (sometimes literally) with a clientele eager for relief. Some soldaderas gained a reputation for their ability to find better-quality marijuana or for procuring it with reliable regularity wherever the unit deployed. The practice did seem to set the army apart from neighboring communities in ways that drinking did not. For the most part, both press and popular opinion viewed the herb with disdain or fear. Public perceptions painted the marihuanero in the press as a dangerous figure, far worse than mere drunks.

As a "new" drug it threatened modern sensibilities and encouraged wild tales of psychosis and violence.[31] For example, three men and three women began a brawl in front of the pulquería La Montaña Rusa in 1895. The press attributed the difficulty the police had in subduing the inebriates to the one man who had apparently been smoking marijuana and claimed he became insane thereby.[32] Two months later the same paper reported a brutal attack on a sergeant by a soldier, who gave him blows to the head with a rock, and insisted the cause of the outburst was marijuana.[33] Five years later a different paper reported how two soldiers in the Twenty-First Battalion, intoxicated on marijuana, had slain a comrade in the barracks and now faced the death penalty. It reported that the drug had made the men lose control of their faculties.[34] The same paper commented outright that just as thieves were a lesser evil compared to murderers, rowdy drunks were less dangerous than marijuana smokers.[35]

This seemed true if press reports could be believed. In 1902 a woman screaming in the streets attracted the attention of pedestrians and police. She claimed that a nearby man had stolen from her and accompanied the police and unlucky man to the precinct. Upon further questioning, she revealed with perfect calm that the man had robbed her of her soul, and doctors determined she was afflicted by marijuana. The press also saw the drug in more a cosmopolitan light, if still a danger. In an 1895 article, the author compares it to Baudelaire's descriptions of hashish. He claims that while the coarse, smoking soldiers could not express the experience with French eloquence, they nonetheless became somewhat Oriental in a disheveled manner. The exotic origin of a drug from the Far East, with connections to the slave trade and to Caribbean migrants, created anxieties and fascinations. The newspaper reporter continues in a sarcastic tone to describe their harem of young, poor girls who then become involved with such men.[36] While everyone had experience with ordinary drunks, these emerging drug users had an air of mystery that suggested danger. They were, perhaps, modern. Dirty, vulgar soldiers smoking drugs made this impression that much more vivid. The popular image of the marijuana user thus emerged as insane, psychotic, vulgar, and violent. Expectations made this actually occur, as users reacted according to what they thought the drug would do to them.

This vision accorded with what some military officers wrote. The pernicious influence they attributed to the drug, exacerbated by alcohol, raised grave concerns about morality and discipline at least, and about crazed violence at worst.[37] Not content with degrading barracks, soldiers also contaminated the prisons that they guarded. One mayor's letter claimed that "government has not made jail a school of morality because soldiers introduce gambling, and marijuana."[38] Mondragón claimed that the drug dominated men, ruined their minds, and made their limbs weak.[39] Urquizo pointed to the marijuana smoker as the last stage of military degeneracy.[40] In one of his tales, when a group of soldiers encountered a *bruja* (witch) they sent in an ugly corporal because he might be a brujo too, or at least a marihuanero—suggesting that he was expendable. She turned him into a rooster for his troubles, and the other soldiers fled, one marijuana smoker fewer in number.[41] The humorous account mocked an unpopular NCO whose many failings included physical unpleasantness, dubious judgment, and drug smoking. The consequences play out as a morality tale against marijuana, yet likely troops enjoyed it more for its digs at the corporal, possibly while having a smoke themselves. Aponte described a more serious drug encounter in which a soldier hallucinating on doña Juanita saw an ocean scene and attempted to swim on the floor. He then imagined himself a condor and madly threw himself against walls trying to fly. To Aponte's shock, the officers beat the man severely, put him in a cold bath, and left him to sober up in a corner.[42] The medical establishment in the army appeared scarcely better informed and wrote nothing about marijuana until 1898, when they simply said that it seemed to have harmful effects similar to tobacco.[43] With no formal plans to combat pot smoking, the army simply discouraged the practice with brute force.

The troops themselves had a somewhat different take on the herb, sometimes called toasted tortilla or by other nicknames. Smoking it afforded a rare opportunity to relax, and importantly, to forget the hardships of service life, even more effectively than could be accomplished with alcohol alone. In the words of one, the freeing little herb was the consolation of the imprisoned, the eraser of miseries, and the music of the heart.[44] His compatriot described his experience as a descent into deafness and blindness to the mundane world, with senses suddenly sharpening to take in colors and sounds he had not noticed and a profound feeling of well-being. His thoughts turned to sex, to far-off family, and even to politics, flitting from topic to topic.[45] The experience, in short, fit far better with today's clinical descriptions of the effects of cannabis. Nonetheless, when discovered intoxicated by his officer and NCOs, they beat him and made him run around the patio until he sweated the drug out of his system. Their violent reaction seemed to come in default since no formal charges could be laid against the soldier. His escape from a bleak barracks reality proved brief.

The generally positive effects noted by soldiers clashed with the hysterical rhetoric printed in newspapers. So how then to explain the markedly different perceptions of marijuana between press and participants? The relatively mild symptoms of normal cannabis intake match closely with descriptions by the soldiers. Those engaged in the panicked discourse about drug fiends in the streets either spoke of a different drug entirely or exaggerated for effect. Another theory suggests that the marijuana's chemical content or the users' physiological responses, or both, cannot be accurately approximated a hundred years later—we must therefore take accounts of extreme intoxication as true symptoms.[46] Additionally, a compounding explanation would be that normal usage escaped notice, but occasional or first-time users sometimes either had preexisting mental conditions or encountered adulterated drugs laced with a hallucinogen such as opium, psilocybin, or peyote. The resultant hallucinations, psychoses, and paranoia could produce the kinds of episodes that newspapers reported. While many scientists deemed marijuana a minor nuisance, if one unseemly for soldiers, in this case moral outrage by the gente decente trumped medical opinion. As with conditions like syphilis or fears of typhus, middle classes manufactured a vision of the army as particularly infected, despite statistical evidence to the contrary. This allowed readers to share in a sense of superiority over the ragged conscripts. Other, more common drugs received far less disapproval.

Tobacco, although nonissue, entered barracks most easily. Smoking was only mildly discouraged despite contemporary studies that argued for its harms.[47] Dr. Joaquin Hernández claimed that immoderate use of tobacco harmed respiratory, circulatory, ocular, nervous, and digestive ailments, that its stink perturbed those around it, and that it made women lose their beauty. He nonetheless concludes that since it had become inveterate custom, doctors had to respect society's choice in using the drug. He also suggests that since smoking improves the morale and intelligence of its users, physicians should simply counsel moderation. He may also have been swayed by the money that the tobacco industry offered to quiet critics. In a second opinion, Dr. Alberto Escobar felt that tobacco, if taken with coffee, was perfectly acceptable.[48] Although some certainly died from tobacco use, smoking remained a normal practice in the army and in the streets.[49]

The long history of smoking and its prevalence in village and rural life meant that smoking did not become emblematic of a soldier's bond to service, as it had been in the French military. The French soldier-citizen, after his conscripted service, left the army with a newfound set of habits that set him apart from village life, including smoking. His cosmopolitan experience bonded him to fellow soldiers with a sense of solidarity that built on the imagined reality of nationhood.[50] By contrast, smoking excited little comment by either Mexican officers or society. Popular acceptance of the drug reflected in part the interests of the state and its addiction to the taxes that tobacco earned it.[51] Soldiers had been prime carriers and disseminators of smoking habits since the Colombian exchange began. Of all the common drugs, tobacco in many ways proved best suited to pacifying urban masses and easing soldiers' fears: "Troops with smokes were easier to control."[52] The Porfirian elite largely agreed.

Indeed, officers gave tobacco regularly to soldiers as a reward for good behavior or to mark festival days. This came cheap. One reform plan actually recommended an allowance for soldiers to buy their own soap, sundries, and tobacco, for a mere five centavos a day.[53] Ordinary brands of cheap cigarettes were accounted part of a soldier's daily expenses, indicating that smoking was endemic and as necessary as polish or other daily trifles paid for by the army.[54] Nonetheless, soldiers did appreciate the gift of cigarettes for festivities such as Independence Day and commented favorably when they received better brands such as Tabaco del Tigre or Canela Pura.[55] It seems that as an accepted vice smoking provided an exception to proscriptions on the disordered life and belonged to the realm of sociability and leisure.

The main prohibition on lighting up predictably applied to gunpowder magazines and other highly flammable areas. On a number of occasions this led to minor incidents and charges. But it had terrible potential for harm. After a serious troop and cargo train derailment at Cuautla soldiers pillaged the wreckage for its shipment of aguardiente. During the ensuing chaos either boilers or, more likely, careless smoking set off an explosion that killed over 150 people.[56] Despite its hazards, tobacco use remained a normal part of the army experience.

Cannabis, tobacco, and alcohol all constitute but a portion of the modern cornucopia of drugs available to the late nineteenth-century user. Daily use of various substances, coffee and tea and sugar and other physiologically affective consumables, formed one measure of modern life. Soldiers would find opium at times, even morphine, but on the whole these remained peripheral. Indeed, one should remember that the use of intoxicants in general did not on its own define the army experience. Since the archives focus on the criminal and deviant, it merely seems that all soldiers had problems. Far more usually they found other and safer means for entertainment.

Fun and Games

Not all spare time was filled with the imbibing of drugs. Diego loved the simple Sunday outings when he would stroll with Melchora, chat with friends, and maybe buy a treat in the marketplace. Merely getting out from behind the barracks' walls and away from the daily routine came as a relief. He had never before seen a city, let alone been to The City, nor had he seen anything quite like the great bullfights. The hot, sunny seats notwithstanding, he loved the roaring crowd and cheered the exhilarating bravado. Some evenings out they found cockfights in the neighborhood or even boxing matches. He began to gain

*a taste for gambling. It spices things up, he explained to Melchora. She knew
they had little coin but had to admit (if not to him) that the stakes for these
fights, or for card games, really did make them more exciting. Still, her favorite
activity, perhaps because she had a good voice, came when the barracks filled
with song.*

The upper classes' sense of danger and degradation in the barracks did not
come close to describing the full range of life or social experience for the soldiering classes. Card games, sports, theater, music, and promenades afforded
alternatives to less acceptable behaviors. Simply drinking and smoking left
men with attention and hands to spare for other activities. Leisure was an
important part of life and one that revealed much about individual and group
views of community. Their choices for fun and entertainment, though significant in their own rights, also reveal a sense of social unity, of fatalism, and of
resistance to military dictates. Fun built solidarity in ways that sometimes
countered official aspirations for discipline.

The lack of appropriate troop entertainments concerned authorities for a
number of reasons. Captain Rodolfo Casillas, after a three-year mission to Fort
Riley in the United States, made a lengthy report for the *Revista de Ejército y
Marina* in 1910.[57] Comparing the two armies, he argued that Mexican soldiers
absolutely lacked basic healthy distractions, which he felt would mitigate the
monotony that troops routinely suffered.[58] Sports appeared as the ideal type of
leisure activity that might counter what he referred to as the ennui and sadness
of barracks life.

Casillas recommended that the army impose practices that would instill
a taste for activity in the recruits. This could include passive pursuits such as
watching movies, circuses, theater, and bullfights. Other than the latter, he
suggested that these shows could come to the barracks and would also represent a properly national entertainment. His report also highly recommended increased free time for soldiers, expanding on the usual practice of
leaves on Sunday or for festivals, and noted that US soldiers were allowed to
spend nights at home with their families. Finally, he pointed out that the US
military provided shops, billiards, swimming pools, gyms, libraries, and
dances for their troops and had a correspondingly better record of morale
and low desertion. In particular, he claimed that sports contributed to health
and solidarity. The US Army encouraged participation in boxing, basketball,
baseball, football, polo, and track events. While some of these did not fit
Mexican tastes, Casillas's hope was that increasing opportunities to play

organized sports would vent soldiers' frustrations and build teamwork.[59] Perhaps requiring too much effort, perhaps too expensive, the army did not implement sports programs, although it had been slowly providing more spectator entertainments and leave time.

Entertaining the troops thus became a priority for better reasons than mere official benevolence. Leisure offered recreation in its broadest sense. Relief from mundane pressures and onerous tasks reduced feelings of isolation, alienation, and discontent. With small moments of leisure the army hoped, in a cost-effective way, to build docility among its distracted subjects. An occasional drunken night out seemed worth the bad publicity if it created a solid sense of morale and obedience on the drill square.

Soldiers did enjoy supervised leave on occasion and, as discussed earlier, also managed to exit barracks on their own at times. Officially, the prerogative of an "officer of the week" allowed him limited discretion to allow soldiers out into the streets by granting leave (dar franco). Those who abused this power went before superiors on charges.[60] A certain balance proved necessary. Too many leaves they charged as permissive and creating an environment that undermined discipline and facilitated desertions. Too few excursions hurt morale and also encouraged desertion attempts. Still, soldiers and their barracks families did spend time in local communities, if generally escorted by officers. These sanctioned excursions usually occurred on Sundays, as opposed to the individual drinking binges or clandestine escapes.

Those considered trusted soldiers (soldados de confianza) after three years' service also sortied out without supervision at times, provided they returned to the garrison by a certain hour. Officers created a notion of trust with this designation that incorporated legal ramifications. Those deemed worthy had privileges. They still faced limits, nevertheless, in a society where police and gendarmes had the legal right to arrest on "suspicion of desertion." These charges seemed to rarely appear before the courts, and this indicates a degree of conviviality as communities came to recognize their local soldiers and instead used these legal powers against vagrants or marginal characters. Excursions did create an interaction with the community that broke the idealized seal between barracks and streets.

The public spectacle of marching through towns and cities represented a way for the military to manage and control the ideal separation between barracks and streets. Civilians could not ignore, or pretend not to see, the soldiers and their women who regularly walked their streets and browsed in

their stores. Soldiers, for their part, likewise realized that life continued outside the high walls of the ex-convento. Troops out in public took the chance
to stroll through markets, to shop, and to loiter. Sugarcane and oranges seem
to have been common cheap purchases, although some less legitimate treats
undoubtedly also made it into pockets.[61] Controlled and supervised, the
troops could present civilians an unthreatening and orchestrated image,
making the army a normal part of public space without rigid formality.
Soldiers did feel themselves on display, and some bemoaned the state of uniforms or shoes that lacked what they envisioned as a properly modern or
prosperous appearance.[62] They also took this opportunity to relax with soldaderas and to announce their partnerships to the public and to comrades
by hand-holding during Sunday strolls.

The presence of troops as a normal spectacle diminished civilian anxieties about the army as something foreign or threatening. In theory, it had the
potential to build trust in national and public institutions, simply by removing the strangeness of their presence. In reality this did not always work since
civilians proved quite aware that the charming Sunday strollers included in
their files Friday night's drunken brawler and Tuesday morning's strike-
breaking thug. Still, as cheap public relations go, friendly daytime excursions
appealed to the army brass.

Long before Casillas's report, these afternoons sometimes included
attending a bullfight. Advertisements suggested an oddly patronizing and
perhaps educative element to this practice. For instance, bullrings offered
half-price tickets for children and for troops in formation, meaning under
supervision of officers.[63] This grouping hints at the idea of the outing as having a learning goal for viewers, particularly those seen as immature and
needing minders. As Casillas later suggested, these shows entailed a national
practice, perhaps one that would make mestizo or indigenous conscripts
more "Mexican." The Porfirian elite also made attempts to ban blood sports
as too primitive or barbaric for a modern, Europe-like nation, and so, at least
in Mexico City, the opportunity to see bullfights would be curtailed.[64] Yet on
this they vacillated. On the one hand these events drew crowds for good reasons. The traditions appealed to many audiences, in all classes, and issues of
morality or animal cruelty did not yet come into the picture. Pageantry made
of the bullring a grand spectacle of death and heroism, and to a lesser degree,
stoicism and fatalism. Lesser blood sports such as cockfights also drew
attendees and added gambling to the mix. Leisurely activities of various
types drew soldiers just as surely civilians. In any case, much of the soldier's

free time would occur inside the barracks walls, compared to these other, more rare excursions.

Gaming with cards and dice was a favorite activity in garrisons and nearby bars throughout the republic. Soldiers and officers alike played, in their own separate games and places, but women seem to have rarely joined in. As opportunities to gamble, these games required a bit of money and either the forty-card Spanish deck (*barajo*) or a set of bone dice.[65] Cards in the Spanish deck numbered one to seven with an additional three face cards (the *sota* or knave, the *caballo* or horse, and the *rey* or king). Some games they played in teams of four, others (like "Albures") offered card sharks an opportunity to fleece the unwary. The most popular game played in pulquerías as well as in barracks they called *rentoy*, which could be played by just two or by up to four pairs of gamers. The game required careful and discrete communication by gesture or mutter between the partners, which all expected but ran contrary to the rules. As historian Aurea Toxqui argues, the deeper game that coincided represented an interplay of memory and identity that bonded the players. It set a competition that depended on sociability and communications and revolved around how well you read your partner and your opponents. The game also included spectators, who had their own expected rules to follow and stood to gain since the losers had to supply winners and onlookers a round of drinks. The relatively high stakes and the deceptive nature of the game undoubtedly led to many outbreaks of violence and ill will, especially as the alcohol flowed freely.

The age-old practice of gambling among soldiers forged friendships and raised rivalries. The appeals of the games, at least at low stakes, included the relaxed social setting for talking and bonding, the possibility of occasionally feeling lucky, and the simple fun that filled idle hours. Yet the higher-risk aspects of a high-stakes game also created both more excitement and more conflicts. Gambling had long earned the disapproval of church and government. During colonial times the elite equated lower-class gambling with blasphemy given its insinuation of chance or luck, which ran against religious ideas of predestination by God's will. Worse still, passions that erupted from ill fortune made players proclaim in blasphemous ways, blaming God and the Virgin as a means of preserving their masculine status in the face of loss. Church officials believed that this offense threatened the whole colonial endeavor at worst and encouraged social disorder at the least. Of course none of this stopped the elite from playing their own games behind closed doors or the Crown from capitalizing on a monopoly over the sale of playing cards.[66] In barracks long afterward the gambling and cursing and strutting continued. The practice encouraged a particular flavor of masculine performance. Men exhibited courage, risk taking, deceptive skills, and acquired skills—and of course, sheer dumb luck or stoic sangfroid. Not all games ended well.

The exchange of money, goods, or debts among soldiers could lead to theft and violence, and officially, the military discouraged it. Officers and regulations could not easily prevent gambling, given the difficult of ascertaining at a distance a friendly game from one with stakes. Furthermore, the officers were among the worst offenders themselves, often too busy gambling and drinking to effectively police their own troops' behaviors.[67] For the most part, soldiers had too little money to get into much trouble, and perhaps better judgment than the army credited them. Relatively few charges or complaints appear in the records in comparison with the sheer numbers who played every day without problems. Still, some did stray. Men who lost too much became desperate, and numerous anecdotes connect a criminal reaction with the misfortunes caused by lady luck. At other times, fortune favored the prepared, and accounts warn of playing dice against the wily veterans of the army who came with loaded dice and card tricks.[68] When all else failed, song was free.

The Lyrical Play of the Barracks

Songs of tragic betrayals, glorious battles, brave executions, and strange events brought tears and laughter to the patio. Some nights the battalion band joined in or played instrumentally. Some nights new songs arrived with fresh recruits or from soldaderas' excursions. Diego sang along or applauded, but it was Melchora who really had the voice that earned her approval from the whole battalion. The music told old stories, from wars long past, but also brought the troops up to date on recent events like train derailments. Diego's favorites were the corridos of rail and of the army; both pointed out what seemed obvious things to him. Foreigners could not be trusted, for example, and the army had too many foolish officers. Particularly poignant to him, the tales of executed soldiers like Bruno Apresa or Juan Soldado always made him tear up. He recalled, all too vividly, the times he and his comrades had to witness the firing squad. One time still haunted his dreams and woke him in a cold sweat. His old friend from home, Pedro, had gone to another battalion and had fallen victim to what had to be a false charge of murder! There in the battalion patio, they marched the simpleton in and read his charges. Together the troops paraded him out the next morning, to the edge of the city. With little ceremony, a squad shot him dead. The last Diego saw of this man he had known since childhood was the still-confused look on his face.

Hearing music like corridos brought all Diego's feelings back to the fore. Along with a bit of pulque and some cigarettes, it brought together the soldiers and families that gathered there under the Mexico City sky with shared memories.

Soldiers in the ranks took to early corrido ballads to speak of their own army life and in lyrical play mocked the pretensions of the army in some not-so-hidden transcripts.[69] In contrast to the camouflaged resistance that some have proposed subject populations tend to enact, and regardless of whether we consider this true agency, the lyrics of corridos openly offered challenges only barely shaded in innuendo. Their format, often improvised informally as they were sung, gave the singer license to add even more criticism to lyrics, at a time when press and other media faced harsh censorship. Soldiers reimagined their comrades and deeds in ways that defied the regimes' carefully ordered narratives—reinserting rough masculinity, antiforeign sentiments, and racial identity where they had previously been stripped away. The shared language conventions exposed a common vocabulary with a mostly unified imagining of the patria invoked in terms of shared historical experience.[70] On one side, the military as an institution officially dedicated its efforts to a project of positivist modernizing and secular order, yet on the other, an alternative vision from within the ranks demonstrated the distance between rhetorical modernity and actual circumstances.

Music filled the Porfirian barracks by night. Neighbors recalled decades later how much they enjoyed the army bands as tunes spilled into streets.[71] The military bands also frequently performed for the public in arranged venues, but they were equally ready to accompany soldiers for less stilted material, chiefly corridos.[72] Whether with instruments or not, men sang in the evenings and during free times in garrison or on campaign. Their sad songs of tragedy and betrayal, of bandits and bullfighters, brought the outside world into army life.[73] The music of the lower classes represented their stylistic taste and also held deeper social meanings as they channeled rage and hostility into group solidarity.[74] Of course, there were occasional critics: one officer locked his band in a room and shot at their feet as a dance lesson, but his actions were likely due more to alcohol abuse than genuine criticism.[75] But the songs that allowed men and women the taste of home gave sufficient reason to sing. They were an acceptable way to express emotions and vent loneliness and were an important measure of cultural capital—every unit desired a good singer. And more, certain songs held special appeal, as they spoke to military life and, significantly, challenged it through subversive lyrics and subtle mockeries.

Ordinary soldiers often worried about the prospects of open warfare against the uprisings that continued to plague Díaz's nation. Chasing bandits or manning garrisons proved relatively easy duty in comparison with ongoing wars against the Yaquis of Sonora or the Mayas of the Yucatán. Their songs reflected pride in victory but also had telling elements of concerns over fighting against their own (50 percent of soldiers were of indigenous descent).[76]

An early corrido, "De los Tomochis" (Of the Tomochis), told the tale of a battle against a millenarian movement in the largely mestizo town of Tomochic in 1893.[77] The townspeople had risen in revolt against the state government through a religious movement that venerated a local girl blessed with visions, Santa Teresa. The uprising quickly escalated, and the federal army sent to quell it initially failed, thereby staining the repute of the Díaz military apparatus:

A esos indios del Tomochic,	To those Indians of Tomochic,
yo los quiero	I like them
porque saben morir	because they know how to die
en la raya,	on the line,
todititos murieron en la playa,	all died on plowed field,
combatiendo al Once Batallón.	fighting the Eleventh Battalion.

The lyrics speak of fighting against Indians, even though the uprising was by mestizos far up in the mountains. Making the place of the event ambiguous, the singers could build on the generalized plight of the indigenous soldier, even in an apparently patriotic song. The songwriter admired Indians for knowing how to die properly when the Eleventh Battalion went to war. The town, established as a military buffer against Indians in an important hub for mining traffic, was not populated by self-described Indians of any type. Where were all the Indians? Officers of the Eleventh Battalion had quite tellingly made up deficient numbers on the roster with aggressive conscription of Pima natives and had also taken a number of Yaqui prisoners of war into their ranks. In comparison with the followers of Santa Teresa in the mountain town, the army was indigenous. When the battle turned against the ill-prepared federal forces, the "indios del Tomochic" did indeed run and die:

Salieron los indios pimas	The Pima Indians came out
peleando de tres en dos,	fighting in threes and twos,
todos a una voz decían:	all in one voice said:
—¡Que viva el poder de Dios!	—Long live the power of God!
y que mueran los del Once Batallón.	and death to the Eleventh Battalion.
Salieron cinco tomochis	Five tomochis came out
peleando de tres en dos ...	fighting in threes and twos ...

This corrido also made an oblique reference to executions. The Indians died fighting in twos and threes, shot down with the same two-three pattern that repeatedly appeared in corridos about firing squads (see discussion of executions in chapter 2). With this twist, the only Indians in Tomochic, actually federal conscripts, faced heroic executions in the cause of government guns against God.

The popular lyrics and their interpretation of the fight ran contrary to the official military narrative of the campaign but also likely reflected popular lack of information on what truly happened so far from the urban centers. The official story told of a secular, modern nation quelling "savages" who threatened commerce, where initial setbacks were made right rationally and swiftly (see chapter 8).[78] It spoke of a contrast, a contradiction between a backward or traditional identity in the highlands and the secular, modern nation without. Yet religion did not come into the public discussion until subversive novels emerged and oddly worded corridos were sung.

The life of a soldier with all of its hardships and injustices is voiced in the song "Del desertor o Juan Soldado" (Of the deserter, or Juan the Soldier), apparently a favorite in some garrisons.[79] Even the title suggests a dual vision as it questions whether Juan embodies only a deserter or is instead a soldier—the possibility of existing as both was denied. Porfirian conscripts did not have an easy life. They faced dangerous conflicts with fellow troops, deprivation of comforts, and harsh punishments from their officers. Even worse for many soldiers was the boredom rising from incessant routine. The combination, even without the specter of actual combat, resulted in a desertion rate that sometimes reached 50 percent.[80]

Still, Juan's fall from grace was not inevitable. Indeed, he had wanted to be a soldier since childhood, lured by the pomp and music. He joined the army when taken by the leva at age fifteen. Despite his lack of choice in this, he came to love his regiment, became a corporal (cabo), and rapidly rose to sergeant but eventually chose to desert back to his land and his mother:

Ya no me gusto	I no longer enjoyed
seguir la Carrera	to follow my career
y me deserté y	and I deserted and
me fui pa' mi tierra.	went back to my land.

His homecoming did not last long. Making matters worse for Juan, he was captured and then abused by a mounted patrol of the Acordada. This infamously callous paramilitary force was a colonial vestige, and its presence in this song hints at the corrido's long pedigree, since the Acordada had been replaced by a new (and equally of poor repute) paramilitary police called the rurales in 1867.[81] The cavalry beat Juan and dragged him from his home in front of his poor mother:

Estando en mi casa	While in my house
con mi pobre madre	with my poor mother
llegó la Acordada	the Acordada arrived
tendiéndome el sable.	and took the saber to me.

His mother's weeping becomes the repeated lyrical counterpoint to the chorus, as the indifferent military band "toquen y toquen" (played and played). Music frames Juan's experience in the army; his mother's sobbing interjects. The juxtaposition of the music and the weeping emphasized the separate worlds of home and barracks.[82] Army periodicals often, in fact, asserted that the military was one Great Family with the president as father, suggesting that recruits might give up a past life and still retain this essential emotional connection, at least in theory. Yet Juan's two families did not easily coexist, and he could not legally abandon one or emotionally leave the other:

Y lo van llevando	And he was taken
para su cuartel	to their barracks
y la pobre madre	and the poor mother
llorando tras él.	was crying behind him.

After a brief trial and conviction of desertion in time of war, Juan faced execution by a firing squad of seven rifles (one loaded with blanks) and a coup de grace delivered to the head or heart by his immediate officer. The unfortunate man made his good-byes and faced his fate:

¡Adiós, mi cuartel . . .	Good-bye, my barracks . . .
¡Adiós, compañeros	Good-bye, fellows
los de zapadores![83]	of the sappers!
Toquen, toquen, toquen . . .	Play, play, play . . .
¡Adiós, mi teniente . . .	Good-bye, my lieutenant . . .
¡Adiós, mi sargento . . .	Good-bye, my sergeant . . .
¡Adiós, padre y madre,	Good-bye, father and mother,
adiós, hermanitos!	good-bye, my little brothers!
Aquí se purgaron	Here they will purge
todos mis delitos.	all of my crimes.

A shared colloquial language added meaning to lyrics beyond the obvious. A curious convention comes into play at this point. He faced death without blindfold or hesitation and without blame for the men who did the shooting (and might have sung this later). The issues that military communities faced were also whispered about in the shadows of the garrison.

Muttering and the Barracks Scuttlebutt

When Diego first met Melchora he had no idea what she had said to the other soldaderas around her. "It must not be good," he thought as he flushed with the attention, and they all looked his way and laughed. Some years later, he finally got the joke and could mostly comprehend the argot of the barracks dwellers. Strange new words for things strictly military like kepi hats, or acronyms, all became part of common military lore that even the officers understood. Other phrases, slang, and words borrowed from hometowns far away infiltrated the soldiers' conversations. Code words used to disguise contraband flourished. Innuendo and double meanings even let the cautious soldier make fun of superiors to their face, if only to a point. Melchora and Diego knew that the civilians and most officers couldn't make sense of their jargon filled with slang and insider jokes. It set them, the real army, apart from others. They had become part of a linguistic community of noncivilians, and they would retain this jargon for the rest of their lives.

Days before any movements or exercises, whispers and speculations began to circulate, always promising an event coming in "just three days." Always, painful and tantalizing, just three more godforsaken days. All the barracks were profoundly interested in any hints around potential changes of place, but scuttlebutt filtered through often-unreliable channels. These occasionally played out as rumored, but Diego fumed with impatience when, all too often, nothing came of it. When the unit went to war, troops had weeks of hints to build the anxiety. Other rumors likewise livened conversations and built community—Diego proudly recalled that he had broken the news about a certain lieutenant and his inappropriate relations with a local girl. Speculations lent him status; everyone assumed he knew what was happening around the battalion after that one.

Moving beyond song, conversation in myriad forms built community and filled leisure spaces.[84] From murmurs and complaints to rumors and obscenities, troops and families formed and gave expression to their circumstances.[85] The barracks developed its own language, a cant largely indecipherable to officers that wed a community of conscripts from various regions who may not otherwise have shared a common tongue.[86] A measure of autonomy and resistance in itself, barracks argot was significant to the expression of social hierarchy within the group, and mastery of cant indicated belonging and status. As soldiers and soldaderas gave it voice, they built their own sense of identity in the whispers and mutters of the old ex-convento.

Outside of formations the conversations did not cease. People shared rumors and scuttlebutt and complained as soldiers have throughout history. Little information trickles down to men in the ranks, and so men and women would speculate and dig into every hint. Making sense of life in the barracks required rumor, and those known for having good information enjoyed more popularity. This of course often meant NCOs, but soldaderas also had opportunity to put together talk from the streets with what they heard in barracks. Other conversations expressed feelings of sociability and solidarity. They swore at one another with the same terms favored by NCOs, but seemingly without the rancor.[87] Obscenities were markers of status, claims to power, that corresponded with other, more physical means to establish hierarchy and position.[88] As a class activity, cursing set aside suspicions of overeducation or pretension and made clear one's fit within the social strata—eloquence mattered far less than inventive imprecations.

Barracks talk also instructed newcomers. Officials reading regulations and penalties aloud stood in contrast with the whispered mutters and jokes of peers that fleshed out the real expectations of the conscript's profession. Learning the insider's lore made them and the soldaderas novitiates into noncivilian otherness. They became military through murmurs.

Rites of institution include group inculcation. The Porfirian army's failures to make fully modern soldiers by day stood in stark relief to the successful peer instruction by night. While love of patria and skill with arms had limited success, career soldiers transmitted their tricks and dodges to the rookies with the near perfection. Older troops, and in particular veteran soldaderas, taught their new comrades how to avoid trouble, how to break regulations, how to find a partner, and all of the other norms, vices, and trifles of army life.[89] This education succeeded where elite programs often did not. Among veterans of more than a few years' service, charges of ill conduct dropped off precipitously. They had not become rigid myrmidons or shiny saints, but they simply learned exactly how to dodge the worst charges.

Conversation could also be a means of resistance to erode authority and power.[90] Insolence and subversion were essential elements of barracks cant. Although NCOs promoted from ranks would be wise to the meanings, officers had to at least pretend incomprehension or stoop to a lower-class status. Soldiers prided themselves on clever wordplay that belittled their comrades and superiors, making use of *albures* and double entendre for subtlety. In sly wording they could make mockery without superiors calling them to account since doing so would acknowledge the hit. As an example, a dialogue in *Tropa vieja* pitted a soldier against his corporal.[91] The indigenous soldier Calequi pretended stupidity while managing to call his interrogator a gossip, an idiot, an animal, and a bastard, in the course of a dozen exchanges.

—¿Por qué te dicen Calequi?	Why do they call you Calequi?
—¿Qué?	What?
—¿Que por qué te dicen Calequi?	Why do they call you Calequi?
—¡Quén sabe!	Who knows!
—¿De dónde eres?	Where are you from?
—De un rancho.	From a ranch.
—¿Qué tan grande?	How large?
—Chiquito nomás.	Small, no more.

—¿Tú qué clase de indio eres?	What kind of Indian are you?
—Yo no soy indio, no seas hablador.	I'm not an Indian, don't be a gossip.
—¿Pues entonces?	Well, what then?
—Soy de Sierra de Ixtlán,	I'm from the Ixtlán highlands,
Estado de Oaxaca,	in Oaxaca,
de la merita miel en penca.	State from the honey lands.
—Eres de la tierra de Juárez.	You're from the land of Juárez.
—¿Cuál Juárez?	Which Juárez?
—Don Benito.	Don Benito.
—No lo conozco.	I haven't met him.
—¿Cómo se dice en indio	How do you say "what an asshole
"que *pendejo* eres"?	you are" in Indian?
—¿No te digo que no soy indio?	Didn't I tell you, I'm not an Indian?
—Entonces que, ¿eres español?	Then what, are you Spanish?
—Soy nomás tu padre,	No more than your daddy,
pa' que te lo sepas cabrón.	that's why you are a bastard.
—No, no; no te salgas por la tangente.	No, no; don't go off on a tangent.
—¿Qué gente?	What "gente"? [referencing *tangente*]
—¡No te digo! ¡Eres un animal!	Don't say that! You're an animal!
—Ya te dije que soy tu padre.	That's why you say I'm your father.
—No más eso sabes decir.	Say no more of this.

Humor, integral to the insolence of the hidden transcript, seems also to have been important to barracks life. Harsh realities of training, regimen, and war would later make soldiers and soldaderas reflect nostalgically on the fun times they stole on these better days.

Conclusion

The frenetic flailing of the elite to define their subjects through discipline led authorities to drown in the everyday waves of changes that came late in the century. Much of their program fell apart in the normal and everyday practices of ordinary folk. The activities of drinking, doing drugs, gambling, and singing gave meaning and depth to life. They disordered the ideal. Some practices undid discipline. Most only made people happier. The garrison became a barometer of normal activity.

The darkness of the evening barracks was a matter of perspective. Music flowed out into streets as men and women smoked, drank, gambled, sang, and talked. Itching from vermin and aching from disease, they inoculated themselves from the discomforts of unhygienic and uncomfortable surroundings. They made idle conversation, they complained, they spread rumors, and they discussed the raising of their children. Newcomers learned the ropes, veterans told lies and stories. Later still, sex and fights over sex filled the shadows. And in the process they created a community that frequently seeped out into local streets and broke the isolation of the barracks.

There came times when barracks life fell more lightly upon the soldiers and their families. In leisure activities and everyday diversions they found agency, solidarity, and a chance to relieve stress. Life had enjoyments and military order had limits. At times, serious abuses, for example with alcoholism or tainted drugs, led to official censure. Most times the soldiers entertained themselves in everyday ways with friends, family, and lovers. They expressed themselves in songs and gossip and learned from one another as they gambled, drank, or wandered the neighboring communities. In recreation, they created selves independent of authorities' visions.

For the military elite, repressing bad habits represented a class issue. Drug abuse did not represent a physiological predisposition. Their understandings, the connaissance that framed scientific yet traditional takes on the practices of the Other, made society within limitations that this chapter seeks to demonstrate. At the fin de siècle, an ill-defined sense of nature or essence manifested as class stereotypes. One's quality determined the appropriate explanation for excesses or deviance. The endemic issue of alcoholism, for example, applied to the lower class who could not help themselves, to the middle class who should know better, and to the upper class for their tragic disease. Thus, in considering alcoholics, the poor as "animals" needed leashing, the middle sectors needed better education, and the wealthy needed more discretion to hide their sad condition. The better classes faced no consequence provided they kept their drinking hidden behind household or private club doors. For officers, this meant at the very least that they leave their uniforms at home and try to stay somewhat behaved. If caught in cantinas they faced both public censure and up six months' imprisonment for inebriation in military clothes.[92] For NCOs, habitual drinking reflected a lack of judgment (rather than an illness) and could lead to destitución de empleo (dishonorable discharge). Proscriptions of drunkenness led officials to bring regulations and punishments to bear against the vices of the ebrio, or habitual drunkard.[93] Soldiers, on the other hand, many deemed simply unable to change, and so they received minimal punishments for exhibiting their true nature.

Efforts to have soldiers in the barracks become civilized individuals represented a grave disappointment, and to some degree officers simply gave up on truly impeding the flow of contraband into the barracks. Nor were young sublieutenants and lieutenants well suited to the task. By night many feared to enter the darker spaces of the barracks, and few officers had sufficient nerve to invade with the intention of seizing intoxicants from rowdy soldiers (see chapter 7). The elite belief in civilized (pseudo-European) behavior did not appreciably lead to a remedy for the rougher classes. Enjoyment of drinking trumped ill-enforced regulation. The attempts to deal with this issue changed over time. Through the modernizing era increasing attention to alcohol abuse led to new reforms and laws, yet the underlying eugenic assumptions remained quite stable. It might be, for example, that alcoholism in its symptoms and origins represents a disease with genetic roots. To Porfirians this ailment could infect only the poor and reflected their more general lack of moral and intellectual development. Other classes, when intoxicated frequently and problematically, suffered from social awkwardness or lack of gentlemanly decorum. Of course, to the general public this discourse had little relevance—they simply liked to relax.

The common perceptions of the superstition-bound peasants also face challenge here. Unimpressed by the training and by martial education, they chose the diversions of their comrades. Perhaps this might be seen as a success in bonding. They also paid little heed to religious proscriptions regarding gambling and seemed little interested in emulation of middle-class fads at all. On the whole, little evidence exists to suggest that they found recreation in ways unknown to the towns and villages of their origins. They represent considerable cultural continuity with their homes with only a few added opportunities, often differing only in scale. Even the new practices, like marijuana smoking, represented activities known to some newcomers and quickly made familiar to most through experimentation or vicarious enjoyment. This lay at the heart of the disordered life. That which seemed weird or backward to the elite became proof in their social Darwinist perspective of the basic failure of the soldier as a social being. Bad leisure played a role in "dooming" Mexican progress. Sometimes fun had grand stakes.

What outsiders disdained as the vida desordenada *served to bring Diego, Melchora, and their comrades together as a cohesive community. In leisure they also, if in occasionally debauched ways, made themselves a normal part of everyday life in the city streets. They became ordinary neighbors. Their solidarity with one another faced its ultimate test as the battalion marched to war.*

The wisdom of the congresses, the Machiavellian subtleties in the settlement of international questions, the intelligence in the classroom and the eloquence in the court, these represent much and are worth much; but to make a national greatness come together, the necessity lacked [is] the indispensable complement of an Army: show of power and emblem of the vitality and wealth of the people that arm and maintain it.

—*MEXICO HERALD*

CHAPTER SEVEN

The Lieutenant's Sally from Chapultepec

Junior Officers Deploying into Nation

Suddenly thrust into what seemed Dante's hell, the newly promoted Lieutenant Salvador descended into the barracks. All of his joy, pride, and enthusiasm from graduating now drained into the shadowy recesses of his surroundings, where every soldier was a mocked victim or a natural bandit. He had joined the ranks of their tyrannous jailers, perhaps even their eventual executioners. He soon confronted a situation shockingly different from the clean, sterile image his professors had given him. Knife-wielding drunks, marijuana-smoking thugs, filth-encrusted children, and pox-infected soldaderas presented a face of the barracks that no military college class prepared Salvador to meet. His shock at the promiscuity and filth in the garrison resonated with popular conceptions of the vulgar soldier. Salvador felt stunned when he met his fellow officers, all of them older, slovenly, and devious. Worse still, they had no appreciation for his stories about Europe! They constantly played him for a fool: they gave him orders that got him into trouble with the colonel, they stole his uniform, and they overcharged him on all his basic kit and equipment. There was nothing he could do, as they had seniority, and Salvador found that he was more preoccupied with handling the troops in any case. From all around him came the noises and reek of the horde, some with faces of decay or degeneracy, and all marked by the cruelty of the place. Of course, Salvador's perspective obscured the vital experiences of soldiers and families attached to a garrison, and their relationship with

the wider community around them. Yet his experience also demonstrated its
own truths regarding the vida militar.

Officers commanding small detachments occupied remote areas where federal troops had never previously deployed, and there they established direct
connections to the national regime. They broke down the barriers of intense
localism. Their conspicuous presence and interactions with local elites created new ties, if not always in positive ways. Other officers became part of
military colonies, garrisons that created an interstitial network in the unsettled spaces between towns. Still others, with different specialized training,
literally built the nation by undertaking engineering projects, constructing
buildings, and surveying territories.

Truly transforming the nation meant crying havoc and unleashing the
graduating officers of Chapultepec into the barracks and campaigns of the
republic. They sallied forth with better tools than any generation before: a
solid education, a national context in relative peace, powerful new weapons
like machine guns and telegraphs, and spaces compressed by railways and
steamships.

The officers dedicated their careers to the Porfirian slogan of "Order and
Progress." Roughly two in three became *prácticos* (line officers), who led troops
in the name of bringing order, while the remainder, called *facultativos* or
técnicos (technical or professional officers) labored in the name of progress.[1]
Both types of servants to the patria acted as agents of change, integral to constructing the nation. Their work hinged on the army's ability to invade, occupy,
and colonize the countryside.[2] The subaltern officers carried out these tasks.

This chapter moves from the individual and institutional application of
power to remake Mexican subjects to the broader plans by the government to
use young subalterns in managing populations, or even ways of life itself.[3]
Ties of steel and electricity held the modern nation in the tightening grasp of
the aged regime. The modern state made absolute demands, and these implied
violent measures. Prisons of discursive thought held personal identities in
check and in order with national priorities. The government relied on the
subaltern officer to accomplish these tasks as directed and as a role model.
This chapter delves into the results.

Once education as a cadet ended, the subaltern officers faced a serious
new learning curve. They sank into the barracks' vices and corruptions as
they became inured and saw them as normal. Some enjoyed meteoric rises in
technological services, while others languished as line officers. This chapter

seeks to illuminate the varying experiences of a new officer. How did the barracks change him? How did promotion opportunities and prestige twist interservice rivalries? How did corruption become embedded, and how did officers form families of their own? What role did the army play in the eradication of banditry? The careers of these men echoed elite aspirations and mirrored the deep fissures in the elite construction of nation.

Officers newly graduated from the Chapultepec system entered the nation laden with presumptions and perspectives shared among the elite. They carried this as baggage to their newly assigned posts. Some went to low-prestige commands within barracks, often in sharp contrast to their expectations. Some, better connected or simply lucky, took on commissions that afforded them prestige and possibilities of wealth. Yet all attempted to use what they knew and to make a life, and in so doing, to make Mexico better. This chapter follows the career trajectories that saw officers engage with troops, run garrisons, engineer projects, map barrens, and suppress the last waves of banditry. Their experiences and expectations demonstrated the role of a military not quite at war.

Promoting Fraternity

Salvador didn't really understand what had happened when he joined his battalion. Each day he stumbled through the motions and waited either for instructions or for someone to realize he had no idea what he was doing. He felt adrift and the men really didn't seem to respect him. What the devil? He had been to Paris! His fellow officers proved no better. Right from the moment he arrived they berated him as raw and inexperienced. Given their own disheveled and ignorant state, he had no doubts as to what had brought them to this unit, but he could never understand how he had ended up in such a place. Worse than either soldiers or officers, the soldaderas sneered, jeered, and openly laughed at him. Thrown into leadership with such unpromising materials as subordinates and outright obstruction from his peers, he began for the first time to doubt whether he could do this job. Salvador gazed around the patio. Large, scarred men, some obviously reeling from drink, scowled back at him from where they rested. Some saluted, but obviously sarcastically. These older men and their cold-eyed women did not respect him in the slightest. Salvador wished this merely embarrassed him, but he got the chills when he had to walk through the patio at night. Quite frankly, some of these people would happily knife him if they felt motivated, or so they let him believe.

When he took gate station as officer of the day for the first time, the sergeant whispered to him, "Some of these guys need to go out . . . ," and he listed names. Salvador, like all the other officers put in that place before him, nodded and signed off for the soldiers to take a leave in the city for the evening. When the numbers of troops seemed too high, which could lead to the young lieutenant facing charges, he simply nodded and took the extra soldiers out with him as personal supervisor, to their favorite bar. Sometimes he even bought some rounds. Not getting knifed is priceless.

The duties of the line officer in the field of battle had a certain restricted and straightforward nature. More confusing was the murky mess of roles in the garrison. The subaltern officer had an often ambiguous and complicated relationship with his troops. The upper brass expected these young men, with an average age of around twenty, to bully, to lead, to discipline, to educate, and to inspire large groups of generally older men from enormously different class and ethnic backgrounds. The usually poor training and attitudes of noncommissioned officers left the subalterns with limited options in enforcing their will.[4] While egregious insubordination held immediate consequences, it seems that more often an undisciplined laissez-faire relationship dictated normal interactions.

Fraternizing between the subalterns and troops stood out as a problem that concerned the higher command. The prospect of junior officers deserting along with their soldier friends warranted extra regulations, and the punishment for what they termed aggravated desertion invariably ran to years in prison. Orders distinguished between simple desertion (soldiers only) and aggravated desertion, where officers brought troops with them. The judges also noted that desertion requires intent—that is, one cannot accidentally desert—and this complicated a charge levied automatically upon three days of absence.[5] Far more usually, fraternization came with alcohol as young officers led soldiers on binges out of the barracks. Gendarmes caught Sublieutenant Antonio Manzano, for instance, drinking in a pulquería with four other officers and all of their troops.[6] At night, regulations required all officers below the rank of captain to return to the garrison to stand watch or be on hand. This created problems, as these men sometimes became involved in the evening's drinking, flirting, and socializing, thus undermining their distance from the troops and their women. Other officers tried, generally in vain, to keep the soldiers from their customary vices.

At the same time, many military college graduates, however friendly with their troops, opposed the promotion of soldiers to their ranks, whether as so-called mustang officers (common soldiers promoted to officer) or for those given abbreviated training at the Escuela de Aspirantes (Aspirants' School). *Mustang* was a somewhat derogatory term, as opposed to the French notion of "a marshal's baton in every backpack," a system that theoretically promoted officers for merit. The Escuela de Aspirantes had opened in 1905 and offered an abbreviated two-year program intended to produce much-needed line officers. Although it received favorable reviews from the press and from foreign observers, many officers felt it undermined overall quality and morale in the officer corps. Training at the escuela focused on practical tasks and skills, and at lower cost and with lower social capital needed for entrance, it proved attractive to the more humble classes. According to the press the instruction "appeals to those who want a career in arms without studying to highest grades."[7] The first graduates entered service in 1907, and from the records it appeared that they did no better nor worse than their slightly better trained counterparts. They boasted similar arrest records, similar commendations, and similar combat successes. Nonetheless, in the few years before the 1910 Revolution it seemed that promotion discrimination began to show.[8]

Attitudes toward the mustangs revealed some entrenched biases against the common soldier. Agreeing with the popular story of Juan Soldado, officers believed that an up-jumped soldier would soon return to his brutish nature and defile the honor of his acquired caste.[9] Resistance to rising from the ranks appeared in several forms, including denials of promotion and higher rates of incarceration and discharge among the mustangs.

Reviews for promotion often became political affairs, whether for generals and colonels reviewed by the Senate or for sergeants rewarded in battle. The Porfirian ideology and budget dictated efforts to reduce the number of officers on the payroll sharply, efforts that focused on those of higher ranks when possible but also hit subalterns.[10] In theory, promotions reflected time in service, merit by reviews, and passing of examinations. Retarded promotion nonetheless frustrated many officers, particularly among the prácticos, and especially in their mustang minority. One wrote to the president bitterly complaining that the army had consumed thirty of the best years of his life and now abandoned him to misery as he watched others pass him by for promotions.[11] Personnel records indicate that less than 1 percent rose from ranks to even the lowest grade, *alférez*, or sublieutenant.[12] Most of these had special skills or connections; for example, a good scribe might well move into a junior staff position in a cavalry unit as an alférez, or a skilled accountant might become a *pagador* (paymaster).

Still, line officers of any rank in the Porfirian army faced uncertain futures. Lieutenant Colonel José María García languished for over twenty years in and out of service and could never make the next promotion, despite his considerable talents.[13] His records suggest that, far from the armchair generals so common in deposit, he actually had real experience managing troops in combat and keeping them alive. He did not run museums or write editorials, yet at the premier task of the army, fighting, he excelled. In a suspiciously stifled career, Lieutenant Blas Garcilazo never received a second promotion in twenty-four years.[14] Many others experienced the same or gave up and left the army.

Long periods in a dreaded location or without promotions stifled officers' enthusiasm and created embittered or elderly officers who hurt the public's image of the army. In a cartoon from the *México Gráfico* (fig. 7.1), an older soldier asks what rank a young poet holds, to which another man replies sarcastically that the youth lacks the poetry even to call the old man colonel.[15] His resentment, and even shame, reflected the general public opinion about Díaz's aging senior officers. Some had gained ridicule in the fiasco at Tomochic, others typified the corruption at the top of government, and many more haunted the streets and pulquerías.

In some ways, the young line officer, for all his flaws, represented a man closer to the image of nation that Díaz desired than did his aged generals. The subaltern in charge of troops put an educated yet pragmatic face on the regime, a rejection of the *charro* (rural cowboy) tradition in his kepi and still *criollo* (European looking) rather than indigenous, although some thought this was in flux.[16] Photos reveal the rarity of darker-skinned officers, and race itself was a distinction erased from military auto recording (see chapter 8). The older generation of officers in deposit at times became an embarrassment to the government as they succumbed to vices and age. Of course, time solved the problem of their presence in its own ways, if at some cost to young subaltern officers and military resources.

Burying dead officers could be a complicated task. The ordinary military funeral presented a type of everyday public ceremony, but some had significantly more expense and effort, as with the funeral of Manuel Romero Rubio in 1895.[17] The army afforded honors in keeping with rank. For the top echelons, journals printed lengthy obituaries and panegyrics with full-page photos and

FIGURE 7.1 "Guerreros," *México Gráfico* (September 1891), 7. "How ranks this youth among poets?" "Enough to pain my tongue, saying 'my colonel' to this old relic."

even poetry. The aging officers of the Porfirian regime, many who had fought in the 1860s, began dying in droves by the 1890s.[18] Yet even for lowly subaltern officers the army regulations required special funeral arrangements, and this soon overcommitted the army. Official attempts to deal adequately with this, and to provide appropriate honors, stretched military manpower in Mexico City. As early as 1868, the officer of the day in Mexico City's central military command had complained that he simply lacked the troops, and especially the musicians, for the funerals.[19]

A number of factors came into play. Every time family or neighbors reported the death of an officer, the first priority became identification. During the 1890s, the ironically named Captain Alegría ("happiness" or "joy") worked incessantly to find the dead, identify them, and arrange for their funerals. As officer of the day, he needed to ensure who had passed away in order to assess accurately the pensions, the notifications, and the number of troops required for the honor guard. Complicating this, some of the dead had no family nearby or in contact, and neighbors might know only the rumored rank of the cadaver. Theft of pensions from the mentally ill senior officer Eduardo Arce, for example, had been possible only because of his isolated habitation. The 136-page file on his victimization traces the use of falsified documents by opportunistic junior officers who embezzled from him for years. Sadly, his death reflected a lonely life without family or friends—his neighbors discovered the corpse by scent.[20] The officer responsible for the theft deserted and made a run for the mountains, but the army captured and jailed him after a lengthy manhunt. Like Arce's, many cadavers remained undiscovered until they provoked complaints for decomposition odors, which made Alegría's task of identification more difficult. The officer also took inventory of the deceased's possessions. This painstaking list even included the make of their shoes and required signatures from two witnesses to the inventory process.[21] In the event that there was neither family nor a will, Alegría made appropriate arrangements. All of this required a lot of work, but more followed.

Once Alegría satisfied himself as to the name and rank of the dead he needed still to arrange an honor guard for next-day burials, a challenging organizational task at least. As an example, the October funeral of Brigadier General Jesús Sosa called on troops and officers from the General Staff, the Seventeenth Battalion, and the Tenth Regiment as a start. Under the command of Colonel Eugenio Barrón, this meant arranging logistics and directing four jefes, forty officers, almost five hundred troops, 151 horses, and around twenty band members. Sosa died at 7:30 p.m. and they buried him at nine the next morning, a mere fourteen-hour turnaround.[22] With some high-profile cases, politics determined the jefe in charge, as when Rocha led the honor guard for former president Sebastián Lerdo de Tejada, or in the funeral of Carlos Pacheco on the Independence holiday of September 15, 1891.[23] More often, they selected the officer in charge simply on availability. Funerals did provide another venue for the army to make public appearances. The nation put on display in parades, music, reviews, journals, and funerals built up the military as the primary exemplar of mexicanidad—setting the institution as an extension of the president, who had increasingly reworked the army into his own cult of personality.[24] Not all of the venerable officers played along with this, and some simply did not die when the regime might have hoped.

Some officers proved a nuisance for their vigor, as with Rocha, whose rough popularity he matched with a propensity for scandalously public dueling.[25] Quick to take offense, the aging Rocha publicly vilified fellow general and governor Francisco Cayntal y Arce in 1887. The matter reached the press, and soon letters arrived on the presidential desk asking him to forbid the duel. The question of Rocha's honor, in this case, was not at stake, but rather concerned officials thought the duel would prove a disgrace to the government and army and a potential tragedy for the nation.[26] Soon after this argument had been quelled, Rocha did manage to duel an unnamed opponent, killing him in September 1894. Facing a charge of murder, the old officer was acquitted on the grounds of immunity as a member of Congress.[27] All of this accorded with the former military college director's philosophy that the duel resolved conflicts more quickly, cleanly, and decently than a lengthy argument.[28] Dueling aside, Rocha gained a fearless reputation with his soldiers and among his peers. Challenged by a fellow officer about the loyalty of his men, Rocha in one case rode slowly across the foreground of an uncontrolled live-fire exercise, where any of his troops could have shot him without blame. He emerged unscathed and into legend; indeed, this story itself seems a recurrent tale among military anecdotes and may also have started as a legend. Nonetheless, as a relic of another age, Rocha continued to defy modern ways and assert his own sense of military personality until Captain Happiness took his cadaver away in 1897. The elderly general stood in stark contrast with an officer corps often marred by a lack of propriety.

Of Crime, Marriage, and Other Scandals

Salvador couldn't really have remembered exactly when it was that he started to get into trouble with superiors on a regular basis. Probably they couldn't either—the young man had merely become a normal subaltern officer, with all the troubles that entailed. He spent considerable time locked up in barracks for a whole range of faltas (missteps), which really seemed completely unavoidable. It all began with drinks, like so many good stories. At first just an odd evening out, but increasingly Salvador frequented the nearby cantinas with punctuality and regularity. Since he had the duty roster many evenings, he typically brought at least some of the soldiers with him. They pretended to like him; he pretended to tolerate the dirty pulquerías that they favored. Not so happy with the location, Salvador drank through his discomfort. He occasionally gambled with the men, usually when he had drunk too much, and never won. As he wrote home to his father, the troops had accepted him as a leader. If they never invited him to sit and drink with them, well, that just proved their good discipline!

In the dim lighting of yet another cantina, he met a pretty girl named Concepción. She seemed a bit young and poor, but he courted her attentions and spent time with her when her family chaperones absented themselves. He made her no promises and kept her around for months. All of these evenings began to wear on his wallet and meager pay. With the advice of fellow officers, he supplemented his income with las buscas, taking a bit here and there from army funds, or selling favors. Never much, though, just enough to buy drinks, get some decent food, and maybe buy a little trinket for Concepción at times. "What's the harm," he thought, "we all do it." He thought he heard soldiers mutter when pay came up short, but no concern to him if they felt jealous.

Things changed the week he finally received his promotion to second captain. Waking hungover in the Flag Room cell of the barracks, he saw his superior officer animatedly talking with Concepción's father. "This one dishonored my family," he said. A swift negotiation followed, without Salvador's input, and a deal was struck. No charges of rapto y estupro and in exchange Salvador would be a married man by the end of the week. After all, his superior growled at him, he was a gentleman, no? Didn't he want to be good example for the troops?

Various criminal problems appeared from within the officer corps that reflected sexual norms, ordinary alcoholism, and abused authority. The press vilified officers for public disturbances, seeing them as little different from the soldiers.[29] For all young officers, and again especially the mustangs, the threat of discharge dangled consistently overhead despite devoted services to the patria. Subalterns in garrisons commonly accrued charges and punishments, collecting them on their records at an amazingly consistent rate. Officers below the rank of captain, according to personnel records, typically collected two or three arrests each year, with average penalties of around a week in confinement to the Sala de Estandartes or Banderas (Flag Room) or to barracks. Among the subalterns charged or discharged, the mustangs stood out as easy targets for misconduct discharges, often dismissed for faults that their more educated brethren committed without consequence. Less often, and only after serious or repeated offences, the officers faced significant time in prison or discharge. This is certainly not to say they represented paragons of gentlemanly behavior. Complaints to police and army revealed a wide scope of misbehavior that extended from the National Palace to the tiniest rural garrison.

The army discouraged subalterns ranked lower than captain from marriage, mostly through offering poor pay and employing frequent transfers. Those with ranks of captain and up almost invariably married. This did not, in any way, mean that the road to marriage ran smooth. Superiors charged a significant number of subaltern officers with the crimes of rapto and estupro, and sometimes with rape, at the behest of fathers, and apparently most such disputes ended in settlement.[30] Second Captain Rosalio Salazar had been involved for some time with a sixteen-year-old girl, and officials eventually charged him based on the testimony of a number of workers in a hotel of ill repute.[31] After he confessed, the judge dropped the case without explanation. In another such incident, Alférez Porfirio Velasco's case saw him incarcerated for less than two weeks before the judge dismissed all charges.[32] The justifications for the reversals cited lack of merit, lack of information, or that the crime did not happen (*no paso*). It is likely that in some instances this demonstrated a negotiation between the family of the girl and the officer, with promises of either marriage or money. Many times the cases seem to coincide fairly closely with an officer's promotion, suggesting financial motive for the family to act.

Of course, even normal relationships had conflicts, and sometimes these became violent. Officers, like their troops, at times entered into less formal relationships with amasias (see chapter 3). Lieutenant Francisco Rojas chose an extremely tough lady. One night as he returned to barracks at Chapultepec with some NCOs, his drunken amasia took exception, threw him down, and beat him. When the sergeant and two corporals tried to help, she thrashed them too. Far more often, the violence came from the men. They most times escaped with only a fine for even the worst abuses. One charged with great "escándalo" frequently got drunk and abused his family, even cutting his wife's ear with a sword blow. Eventually a neighbor fired shots in the air to summon help from the police. Ultimately, the lieutenant paid a fine of twenty pesos, or about a week's salary.[33] One captain combined multiple faults of judgment when he drunkenly assaulted his family. He received a one-month sentence for making the band of the Fourteenth Battalion play against their will and for having then, with prostitutes in tow, ridiculed his family with obscene words in a "repugnant spectacle."[34]

Rampant alcoholism plagued the officer classes, just as it undermined the rest of society.[35] Extremely common incidents of disturbances filled the personnel records, and the jail cells. By the time they reached the rank of major, most officers either quit drinking or became relatively immune to arrest over simple matters. Minor displays of public drunkenness, if not too frequent, received short punishments. Serious charges came from the outrageous spectacles: brawls in theaters or at the bullfight, wild gunplay in the streets, or shrieking, loud profanities. Selling one's saber and pistol, threatening other officers' wives at sword point, and getting drunk in the archbishop's offices—"absolutely naked"—also seemed to aggravate the army justice system.[36] Intoxication created dangerous situations, but from the perspective of army reformers, the serious damage came to the military's public image. Newspapers, even those sympathetic to the regime, frequently published stories about the drunken antics of military men.[37] The propensity of officers to resist the police exacerbated the lack of decorum and extremes that their behaviors exhibited. Of course, all of these prostitutes and drinks did cost considerable money.

Drinking and troublemaking in proper style required more funds then low-paid officers typically earned. Along with a sense of opportunistic entitlement, this lifestyle led to the corruption and embezzlement that had become customary in the army.[38] The subalterns called their petty theft and skimming las buscas, or searches, and many considered it a normal bonus to their monthly pay. Indeed, complaints about low pay seemed justified, as men lacked even basic necessities, could not afford proper upkeep on equipment or mounts, and could not support families.[39] They received no additional funds for extraordinary expenses either, such as travel or medical costs, but the practice of giving obsequios appeared to be the most resented. Most graduates of the college or promoted sergeants immediately found themselves in debt, owing between 140 and 300 pesos just for their uniform, horse, and gear.[40] The army did not reimburse soldiers for dead or ill mounts either, and especially after campaigns, the officers slipped further into debt. What was a man to do? Military corruption in forms small and large had a long tradition and represented an area of Porfirian life that saw little progress.

The large-scale depredations of higher-ranking officers, particularly those with political office, included land speculation, accepting bribes, and even human trafficking. The lower-grade officers had to make do with modest schemes.[41] By far the most common means to earn a steady side income came from embezzling. Officers managing mounts and forage sometimes took the opportunity to adjust the accounts, showing nonexistent or low-quality horses and mules as officially purchased, fed, and doctored, and the embezzler kept the proceeds.

The possibilities these animals presented as a commodity that fluctuated in price, and one difficult to trace, led officers into numerous frauds. Horses and mules appeared on company records and invoices, only to later vanish when auditors came to call. The officers claimed the animals had died or been stolen. They cleverly blamed the sickliness of beasts on poor quality of feed and requested extra funds to remedy the situation. Forage proved even easier to embezzle. The official requisition rate for a horse was around forty-four centavos per day, depending on location, and officers inflated their requisitions seasonally or simply made claims for dead beasts. Inspectors, auditors, and veterinarians combated the practice to little avail.

Other small opportunities came to those who sought them. Officers sometimes drew pay for deserted or nonexistent men, but inspectors quickly noticed this. In la busca, officers accepted generously provided gifts from the soldiers, taken from the paychests, without bothering the troops for actual permission. Small bribes for entrance to the barracks or for allowing contraband further lined officers' pockets. The practice became normalized, and charges for "abuse of authority" required truly venal and outrageous excesses.[42]

How could inexperienced officers with such checkered records control their troops? Memoirs demonstrate a number of possible paths: violence, bribery, and apathy. Each garrison had its own personality, its tenor reflected location and often the efforts of the junior officers. Some units clearly lacked any real discipline from officers.[43] In Huerta's sycophantic correspondence with Bernardo Reyes he pointed out a number of junior officers he considered completely inept in dealing with troops. Some were too friendly and hence lacked the "moral fiber" to enforce dictates. Others he deemed simply too stupid to know how to lead. Among his own troops, he became known for a hard hand, and with support from their NCOs, a number of units gained reputations for harsh discipline and profligate use of the lash. This seemed a simple extension from how enemies saw him; Huerta admitted that in Sinaloa they referred to him as "animal carnicero" (butchering animal), in reference to his campaign style. This may not have been necessary. Some units appeared to have an orderly reputation without such harshness and earned praise in the military literature and press. Inspectors often cited the Ninth Battalion, the Seventh Regiment, and the Third Artillery as good examples to which other troops should aspire.

The officers sent to a new unit shortly learned to fit in with the general expectations of their counterparts. Rafael Aponte described the ordeal of a new artillery officer whose arrival at the garrison soon spiraled into fear of soldiers, hazing by officers, and a miasma of lowered expectations and apathy.[44] Far from working on commanding respect and order, he instead found himself focused on dealing with colleagues set on draining his wallet and embarrassing the new guy. His own expertise at duels or artillery mathematics did little to impress the hardened soldiers, let alone the jaded soldaderas. Ultimately, most new line officers attained little control over their factious soldiers beyond simple regulation keeping.

The subaltern of the line was more than a disciplinarian alone, but in many ways he also represented an exemplar of class and the educator of nationalism. Literacy programs (see chapter 2) required the práctico to become the primary school teacher as he read nationalist textbooks to, and with, his captive troops. The interpretation of the texts' materials and messages largely depended on him, an officer trained at a college that proudly claimed not to instruct cadets in historical interpretation or critique.[45] Daily, rote recitations of penalties and regulations also fell to the junior officers, as did drill instruction, although NCOs assisted with the latter. The great ennui such readings instilled in soldiers can only have been surpassed by that among officers who read them for years on end. Instruction at arms, on the other hand, seems to have been more entertaining, as it even brought senior officers out at times.

Beyond direct instruction, the army expected officers to provide their troops with a good example. Somewhat the antidote for geriatric eccentrics and vulgar conscripts alike, the regime displayed the junior line officer in public as proof of the nation's progress. In the face of low pay and high rates of alcoholism, this proved difficult. Superiors charged junior officers for providing a bad example, incurring a penalty of eight days in lockup, with some regularity.[46] Drinking to excess with one's troops, while barely acceptable within garrison walls, became a problem when translated to the city streets. Poor military demeanor, disheveled uniforms, and frequent lateness also demanded charges. Officers influencing soldiers through example seems possible, but the reverse seems more likely. Rafael Aponte and Manuel Mondragón's assessments agreed: the young officer, far from providing a good example, instead became mired in the vices and habits of his soldiers.

Professionals of Technical Progress

Now a respectable and married captain second class, Salvador began to think again about trying to improve his lot in the army. Even his drinks suddenly seemed more expensive as word of the promotion spread! His record, not spotless, at least did boast some of his cadet accomplishments, which he frequently pointed out to his superiors. His dozen or so faltas made him no more or less qualified than most officers in his battalion. He knew with certainty that the army did not actually work on merits, whatever it might claim. The chance to move up to artillery or other, better units existed but seemed unlikely. "The artillerists," he wrote to a friend, "they had it made." From their units one could move up into the really elite groups, like the Special Staff or the Planning Faculty. Had he been better at mathematics or engineering, he might even have joined the Geographic Scouting Commissions. All of those men, he believed, became wealthy and received all the best positions. Of course, many of them started wealthy, so it seemed quite unfair. Most of the surveyors came from the best classes of the Porfirian elite. Salvador scarcely knew what these units did, but it cannot have been very difficult. Didn't he deserve a little good luck too?

The scientific officers brought a broad résumé of skills to the tasks of building a modern nation. Some became medical staff and attempted to improve and control hygiene in the name of the army. Others built and sailed a new navy. Engineers worked to create a national arms industry, to harness nature, and to facilitate the colonization of the patrias chicas. They would proudly oversee ordinary Mexicans in the tasks of transforming and engineering the nation, as they depicted in an illustration from their journal (fig. 7.2). Chests thrust out and proudly mustachioed, they set out tasks for apparently willing and faceless subordinates. The officer-engineers embodied order, from their properly creased uniforms to their jaunty kepi hats. In their hands, the image suggests, work had serious overseers that made progress inevitable. These elite planners of the General and Faculty Staffs advised the president in how best to create his vision of Mexico.

The idea of a scientifically minded officer class did not purely appear as a Porfirian innovation but had antecedents reaching back at least to Santa Anna's conception of the military college.[47] As the century rolled forward, the curriculum changed to match the times. Specialty classes in new techniques of photography, in use of railways, and even in use of telephones soon appeared.[48] New explosives and chemistry entered the curriculum and required increased equipment and field experience. Sharp reforms in 1900 improved technical skills in the field, and seven-year graduates now earned the rank of second captain upon leaving the college. Technical officers learned from the timetabled precision of the Prussians and added to their arsenals new weapons that demanded new tactics, including the Whitehead torpedo and the machine gun.[49] New regulations and ordinances followed suit, and the Porfirians produced volumes of reforms to military law and procedure. The goal, as press and army alike announced, was to provide the nation with a modern, professional, and scientific officer. The same proponents also called for scientific NCOs.[50]

FIGURE 7.2 "Ingenieros militares," *Revista del Ejército* (1907), 224.

A number of significant institutional reorganizations and profound technological changes brought Díaz's army specialists to new levels of scientific professionalism. One crucial change came in the redefinition and organization of the Special General Staff (Estado Mayor Especial, EME) and its executive levels of the Professional Staff (PMF) and Department of Artillery. By the 1880s it became clear to military and civil planners that the technical leadership needed to direct modernization would likely come out of the military college. To be sure, not all officers had the required talents for specialization, nor could many be redirected away from actual troop commands. Those with the extra years of training in engineering, seamanship, medicine, or cartography, with proper family connections, became a vanguard in production of a rational nation.

The Presidential General Staff (EMP) of the PMF overlapped other services as an executive or planning group and included most of the CGE (Geographic Scouting Commission) favorites at some point or another. In theory, the staff served the president as orderlies, extra security, adornments, and liaisons to the army.[51] They also had an important symbolic role by adding a visual military presence with a youthful sheen to the old general. For Díaz, the younger men also included friends and family, a trusted coterie to assist him. Genuine respect and affection also come through in letters, as what seems sycophantic from others appears more heartfelt here.

For all of the dislike that the president professed for book-learned officers, his staff showed remarkable education and experience. These sixty-five officers conspicuously embodied the highest levels in their records and training. With few exceptions, they included graduates of the full seven years of the military college, and nearly all had field experience with the CGE or other specialized commissions. Most had traveled on military business or undertaken study missions to Europe and the United States. Some, like Lieutenant Colonel Francisco García, had considerable experience in directing civilian commissions like the Junta Directiva del Ferrocaril de Sonora (in Boston), which undertook the expansion of commercial rails in northwestern Mexico.[52] While critics of the regime bemoaned the cronyism and the persistence of ancient war heroes, the men staffing the presidential office suggested a significantly vibrant, if still military, alternative.

Engineering Changes

Engineering clearly was the branch of the specialist services with the greatest national prominence. It was roughly divided into three areas of expertise: construction, cartography, and artillery. The engineers represented, much like the medical staff, the finest in Porfirian education and families. The highest-ranking engineering officers tended to have highly recognizable names, coming from the clans of greatest political and economic influence. Many of the most successful families deemed engineering an appropriate and desired service for their children. The engineers had received a top-notch education at Chapultepec, sometimes supplemented at foreign academies, and excelled in mathematics especially. For some this represented true aptitude, such as with Felipe Ángeles, while others, like Díaz's son, struggled academically. Ultimately, many engineers enjoyed brief careers in the army before moving on to civilian life and higher wages.[53] This did not detract from the important work that many accomplished while in arms, nor did their future employments undermine the significance of the military as a prime institution in building a modern nation.

In the search for a scientific officer class, the engineers became essential to Porfirian shows of progress. The engineering units built on the historical duties of the sappers by adding modern techniques, and by 1900 they had largely relegated the Sapper Battalion to garrison tasks in the capitol. Sappers had traditionally focused their work on fortress construction or battlefield demolition and improving general fortifications. Battlefield engineering began to take second place to projects of greater civilian nature, or construction of military buildings. Cartography, statistics, and surveys increasingly fell under the aegis of army men. Likewise, they established control over waterways, if for somewhat different reasons.[54] Laying out roads, raising new barracks, installing fixed artillery, and charting exact borders became priorities for both sappers and engineers. These disparate and important duties at the heart of modernization belied the meager numbers of the specialists.

The new sapper-engineering officers differed in a number of other ways. Drawing on manpower from all available units and from criminal or hired levies, they played integral parts in the tremendous expansion of communication networks (roads, rails, and telegraph), in developing electrical services and dams, and in establishing both penal and military colonies.[55] Military engineers, in addition to their quality education, cost less than civilians did and accordingly were in high demand. They worked for a range of employers, as often drawing pay from the Secretariats of Development, Interior, or Government or from municipal and state governors as from their own secretary. The engineers remained under the overall command of planning officers from the PMF but clearly branched out from the army to direct the modernizing projects of Díaz and the elite.

They were not alone. Foreign engineers, especially from the United States and Great Britain, held lead positions in the largest public works projects across the country.[56] The Gran Desagüe, many railways, urban paving, and dam building depended on these foreign experts and the capital they carried.[57] Among the engineers brought in was Henry Ossian Flipper, the first African American graduate of West Point, who worked as a civil engineer following his dismissal from the US Army on trumped-up charges. He later also advised Senator Albert Fall on Mexican affairs during the Revolution.[58]

Men such as Weetman Pearson, Alfred Frisbee, and others drew on native talent, including military engineers, to oversee labor and for local guidance. Both credit and blame for the large projects generally ignored Mexican participation. Despite the importance of these outside experts, the demand for the military's builders continued to rise through the era.

Exotic projects absorbed only a small portion of the engineer's time, given the generally decrepit state of the army's facilities. Construction projects focused on military buildings: barracks, arsenals, hospitals, warehouses, and factories. Barracks repairs and maintenance (touched on in chapter 5) absorbed much of the army budget and left little for new housing. Still, new projects appeared from time to time.[59] With six large schools, eleven military hospitals, five factories, and more than eighty barracks, the engineers and construction companies had continuous work ahead.[60] The physical plant improvements drew on expertise and represented concrete achievements, but other projects held more cachet for the skilled engineers. Mapmakers remade a certain national reality.

Mapping the Nation

The modern nation required the overview of mapmakers. Cartographers and surveyors were important agents of change, especially those assigned to the CGE. Far out of proportion to their numbers, they affected wide territories. The military surveys combed the landscape for valuables, interfered in politics, rationalized navigation and communications, renamed thousands of towns, seized water rights, designed colonies, and, for themselves, found promotions and prosperity. One symptom of this impetus appears in the *Periódico Militar* (1889), which published a series renaming all towns and villages in Mexico, so that the army might have unique map notations appropriate for mail delivery and for military deployments.[61] These combined efforts made the fixed landscape of the Porfirians into a politically controllable space.

The slender ranks of surveyors proved thick with political connections. Even the dimmest sublieutenant in the army soon recognized that these men included an elite group of the PMF, staffed by such family names as Díaz, Treviño, and González. A military college graduate sent to command infantry would, if fortunate, attain the rank of major before retiring. In contrast, one sent to the PMF's engineers seemed rather unlucky if he did not make lieutenant colonel by his midthirties. Cartographers played a rather ambiguous role in local politics and in fixing the landscape, but equally important were their interactions with their fellow government and army actors.[62]

The primary task of the CGE came not in simply making places legible but rather in the active assertion of default claims on uncontrolled or locally ruled areas—in essence, a military occupation by mapping. With scattered deployments of garrisons and detachments across the nation, the surveyors served to simplify and fill spaces in between and enhance central government claims.

This did not occur without cynicism and profiteering, an example of which took place during a claim made on the Rio Hondo. In 1896 Licenciado Rebollar of the municipal government of Mexico City attempted to commission engineers to survey land to the southwest and possibly resolve the city's great deficiency of potable water.[63] A civilian engineer, Guillermo Puga, informed the city that it would require three engineers, two technicians, four servants, and six peons, as well as a budget of about 16,000 pesos. Unfortunately, upon assembling his group, he received serious threats from area residents hostile to his enterprise, and he requested an armed escort.[64] The *cabildo* government dismissed his services and requested that the secretaries of war and interior form a military commission from the Special General Staff, consisting of a jefe, two captains, four lieutenants, four peons, and whomever the local jefes políticos could spare. On behalf of the secretary of war, Manuel González Cosío responded in May that no army engineers were available but finally agreed in August to comply with a second request— provided that the city covered a substantial bonus of 70 percent of base salary for the officers.[65] Having held out for higher compensation, the Rio Hondo Commission continued to draw pay from the city for over two years, well after the survey was finished. Ultimately, the frustrated municipal governor contrived to cancel the parasitic commission only after a face-saving public declaration lauding the army's tremendous efforts, expertise, and service.[66]

The engineers of progress who carried cartography into all the dark corners of the nation found opportunities to make their task lucrative. Local actors, as Craib has shown, made use of federal surveyors to avoid, at least, falling victim to them.[67] Military authorities also controlled deployments to mitigate local advantage. When one town requested the service of several local-born army engineers fresh from the college, the president sent regrets. Scandals and lawsuits often dogged the tracks of the CGE, whose members at times discovered "unclaimed" or not officially titled and registered resources, set their stakes on it, and used soldiers to protect their claim.

This reputation added to local hostility and added an element of danger to the surveyors' tasks. A military escort, usually twenty men, protected the engineers as they pillaged by map. With conditions often horribly uncomfortable, officers reported great dissatisfaction among escorts to the Guatemala border commission and high rates of desertion. In another example, the president sent letters preceded a CGE mission by his nephew Félix Díaz, asking governors and local authorities to protect the survey team. The president asked specifically for his nephews Félix Díaz and Ignacio Muñoz to join the CGE for the good of their careers. He later asked for special help and escorts to help Félix, whom he sent to San Luis Potosí with a geographic commission.[68] In something of the reverse, when Treviño found a potentially profitable mining operation for which he had only a dubious claim, he wrote Díaz asking for a detachment of soldiers to "protect" it. He implied that there would be profit in it for the president, perhaps in the form of a kickback, but the old Oaxacan turned him down.[69] It is possible that the denial stemmed from purely political reasons or a disinclination to strengthen a regional caudillo, or even that the request offended the president's sense of propriety.

Military survey work in the Yucatán, perhaps more than anywhere else, revealed the martial nature of the engineer's task. The trackless and waterless jungles, at least for nonlocals, required new skills. The regime worked this out bluntly and brutally (see chapter 8). More immediately and obviously, powder and arms took on a new role for scientific officers.

The Science of Arms

The construction of factories to produce arms and ammunition had a central place in the nationalists' hearts. Since before Independence the army had depended on imported armaments, and with recurrent shortfalls in the treasury, the army often lacked weapons. Further, by the late nineteenth century the skilled engineering of tools of war emerged as the marker of well-educated and developed nations.[70] French and German arms makers held principal place as manufacturers of the highest quality in speçialist weapons, particularly artillery, while the United States had made tremendous gains as the producer of large quantities of rifles like the Remington.[71] The regime expected that the products of the newly renovated and expanded National Arms Factory and Fabrica Nacional Pólvora (National Powder Factory) in Mexico City would at least supplement purchases from abroad and help establish federal stockpiles. Of course, the cost and danger of such factories, especially when housed near the city center, gave pause to some, but the engineers insisted that they could manage the perils of proving their expertise. The meaning of gunpowder in the process of imperial expansion has garnered intense historical attention as the prime requisite of European colonization. This freight did not escape the Díaz regime's notice.

Properly under the Department of Artillery, the fabrication and storage of war materiel clustered around Mexico City. The National Foundry and National Arms Factory were located near Chapultepec, on the outskirts of Tacubaya. The location of the National Powder Factory caused problems finally resolved in 1895 when, after years of fear and pleas from the neighbors of Belem, near the center of Mexico City, they finally relocated to a spacious plant in Santa Fe, on the city's western outskirts. Among other problems, residents complained that the highly flammable National Powder Factory, still located in Belem at the time, lacked a proper water supply.[72] Ammunition magazines, going by old terms like Molino del Rey (the king's mill) or Casamatas (fortified arms vault), were more diffusely distributed. The largest supply caches and artillery hoards were kept in Almacenes (magazines), with their own subdepartment and controlled by the staff of the Parque General (General Arsenal). The only major establishment outside the environs of Mexico City remained the Arsenal Porfirio Díaz, which repaired naval vessels near Veracruz.

Mass production of armaments and rifles exceeded the capacity of the modest factories Díaz had built. At least in peaceful times, the army brass chose to purchase the best arms they could find, upgrading, for example, from their old US Remingtons to the high-quality German Mauser 98s. This rifle was so well engineered that it remained in military service in many countries until the mid-twentieth century. By 1905 more than fifty thousand had been purchased, compared to nineteen thousand of the US rifle.[73]

Early efforts to build a better artillery corps picked up speed as Europeans competed to control foreign sales. This also reflected the rapid improvements to technology, especially for weapons proven in wars across the globe, such as machine guns used in the Russo-Japanese conflict. In the early Porfiriato, the PMF relied mostly on the French firms of Schneider-Creusot and Schneider-Canet to restock depleted artillery stores. Simple field pieces at reasonable prices attracted a bare-bones army, but growing dissatisfaction with the quality of some of these weapons worried the engineers. Proving tests of these guns constantly impressed visitors to the factory in Europe, including Sóstenes Rocha, who wrote glowingly about them to his brother

Pablo in a letter published by the *Periódico Militar*.[74] Testing at Chapultepec, nonetheless, showed grave problems with reliability and durability among these and among the Bange Company versions that engineers examined. This, and considerable politicking, allowed General Manuel Mondragón to contract for his own patented guns thenceforth. Small arms aside, the big guns warranted big efforts.

Mondragón, a prolific arms designer, began to work with French foundries like St. Chamond to produce a new generation of artillery. A favorite of Díaz's, Mondragón was given great liberty to modernize arms and to reform the FNA. He also worked with his son, Enrique, an engineering graduate of the military college and of Drexel in Philadelphia.[75] Working from a college thesis on a project to fortify national coasts and ports, they first worked on establishing enormous cannons to protect places such as Vera Cruz and Salina Cruz. The father pushed through funding and production despite political opposition, and in 1907 the government held an inauguration in Salina Cruz. The army now boasted one of the largest cannons in the world, an eleven-meter fixed piece that drew wonder and consternation from US observers, who shortly thereafter installed similar defenses for the Panama Canal (1909).[76] At $75,000 a gun, this behemoth fired five-hundred-pound shells from a ten-inch muzzle—impressive, but not a very practical expenditure for the Porfirian government. Few ships of the line threatened the south of Mexico. When Mondragón and his son returned from a voyage in Europe in 1908, the *New York Times* commented favorably on their new coastal defense system.[77] The piece outstripped most naval counters as a true deterrent to attack and a threat to unwanted shipping. US diplomats saw a threat in such potent defenses, and negotiators from the two nations struck a deal for the removal of the Mondragón arms. Mexico sold them to Turkey for defense of the Dardanelles.[78] This proved a wise move for the United States, since in the invasion of Vera Cruz a decade later, their forces did not have to face what might have been formidable defensive firepower.

Other weapons of the Mondragón clan did enter service. The Porfirio Díaz sapper rifle, with special attachments for entrenching, was issued as a common arm for some units near Mexico City. Another variation, considered one of the world's first automatic assault rifles, had a more limited run of production in a Swiss factory. While few reached Mexico, German forces seized and used about ten thousand at the beginning of World War I before finding them too delicate for general battlefield conditions.[79] About fifty of another armament, the St. Chamond .75 cannon patented by Mondragón, remained in service until the Revolution (and became a staple of the French army, further memorialized as a cocktail). These relatively undistinguished pieces worked adequately well but the small arms never gained much affection from officers assigned to them.

What the arms produced by these factories had in common was that they illustrated the possibility for engineers to demonstrate a truly modern capacity and competitive status in the armaments trade. Offering proof of the military's ability to make its own weapons appealed to army planners and engineers, even if the plants did not yet operate at cost-effective scales. Engineers built new tools of empire in Federal District factories for a nation attempting to conquer itself. That larger task nonetheless required leadership to take the field.

Line Officers and the Bandit Threat

The horn call of Atención rang out abruptly at an odd hour that afternoon. Puzzled, Salvador formed up with his men on the muggy patio. "Amigos," announced the major, "pack your bags, you're hunting bandits!" His enthusiasm proved poorly founded.

Salvador and his men found themselves loaded aboard a third-class train car, with scarcely any air or room to stretch. They then rode up and down the length of Mexico for weeks at a stretch, with only brief breaks in tiny, dusty railway towns. They garrisoned the locomotive. At stops, local militias and ragged rurales tersely dismissed the federals and laughed as they filed back to their filthy train cars. On board, Salvador and the others all joked about how the militias lied and how feeble they seemed. They had heard of other units taking the fight into the hills, seeking out brigands in fierce combat, but their turn never seemed to come.

Salvador talked bravely but secretly felt relieved since he didn't relish the risk of fighting bandits on their home terrain. In the officers' separate car, another second captain, Dionicio, regaled him with tales of bandit chasing. He spoke of how these hardened gangs had constantly fended off serious attacks and embarrassed the units sent against them. He proudly explained that he had been on a mission himself, but in the late 1880s, when the army had solved the bandit problem. They had adapted. First, they sent out local scouts and rurales who identified possible lairs. Militias formed a periphery. The army then beefed up security on local targets (like mines) and fortified train lines. Finally, he had gone in with select forces, in overwhelming numbers, and

*driven the bandits into the arms of fixed garrisons. "Did you catch them?"
Salvador asked. "Absolutely," Dionicio laughed, "we identified them, heard all
their excuses, and once they had tied hands, each and every one of them made
a run for it. We had to shoot all of them!"*

*Two weeks later the train detachment disembarked at a small village to
answer reports that had come over the telegraph. The town jefe told them that
bandits had taken up in the hills. Scouts headed out and found an old campfire
and only a few dirty blankets. Salvador noted to himself, "Need to build this
up in my report." Suddenly they heard a shout. Salvador's unit finally caught
one of these brigands. He looked more like a skinny farmer really, but he had
come running from the right direction. The troops grabbed him, shook him,
yelled at him. He broke into tears, a clear indication, according to the older
captain, of guilt. Two veteran sergeants dragged the weeping peasant aside the
tracks, debated the use of the telegraph lines for a hanging (too high), and with
an echoing snap they simply shot him in the back. They hauled the corpse along
the trail and propped it up against a rock where it might be seen from the train.
They tied it in place to keep coyotes from dragging it off. Salvador's stomach
churned, but he carefully kept his face still. No use letting Captain Dionicio see
him flinch. As they all marched back to the train, Salvador heard the soldiers
idly chatting about next Sunday's bullfight. Finally having broken the bandit
gangs, the detachment could now triumphantly return to the Mexico City
barracks.*

To the many prácticos, line officers, fell the task of bringing the vision and
policies of the central government into the communities, towns, neighborhoods, and countryside—often to places that had scarcely seen the federal
presence previously. These officers often commanded small detachments and
garrisons, and they both embodied and enacted the infiltration of modern
governance from the center. Troops stationed away from the large cities
interfered with regional politics, suppressed dissent, and reduced banditry.
They also acted as a balance, not to rurales, as some have claimed, but to the
jefes políticos.[80] Line officers also facilitated the development of regional
economies by acting as labor supervisors in overseeing public works and
mining enterprises. In these as in other tasks, they ultimately obeyed their
commanders, who represented the central government; they only rarely
bowed to local elites. Progress and order, bread or the club, transformed from
motto to reality in the hands of these primarily low-level graduates from the
halls of Chapultepec.

The rurales and their promoters made it easy to romanticize what they accomplished in bringing order to the rural spaces of the nation. Resplendent in silver accoutrements, with long sabers, and on the best horses, they offered a traditional-looking spectacle of power and masculinity on parades and with the Wild Bill show abroad. At the same time referential to the past and making promises to the future, their image seemed at odds with the Mexican army's self-consciously modern presentation. One should not confuse image with realities. Aside from a few show units many rurales went unpaid and complained bitterly in letters, some had broken nags for mounts and many more lacked horses at all, and the corps, spread thin through the countryside, had no ammunition.[81] Far from grandiose mounted charges sweeping the mountains clear of outlaws, many rurales—ragged, afoot, and ill armed—worked in pairs to guard military supply depots in the hinterlands. The army, whose chief officers set a budget for the rurales drawn from the Development Ministry, used the rurales as scouts to find bandits or Indians in places known mainly to locals. Aside from a few odd collaborations, like Kosterlitzky's Eleventh Battalion (see chapter 8), the rurales in the field represented vestiges of old problems. By 1890, they chiefly existed as auxiliaries for federal forces, by providing a few hardened veterans who knew the terrain and had no strong local prejudices. Banditry required other solutions.

As a prerequisite to progress officers worked first to instill order throughout the country, and they made eradication of those labeled bandits their highest priority.[82] The long and storied history of highwaymen did not sit well with the new official image of a prosperous and modern nation.[83] Regardless of actual economic or security issues, the bandit hijacked the imaginations of foreigners and Mexicans when their thoughts strayed into the countryside. Their presence affronted ordinary people. The possibilities that their existence entailed of romantic resistance through unsanctioned violence became a terrible example of dissident action, and one that eventually prefigured the Revolution. Chasing bandit gangs thus occupied the attentions of many rural garrisons, particularly in the central states of the Bajío, throughout the first half of the Porfiriato (1876–1895). An image from the *Revista del Ejército* depicts a rare success in apprehending such a criminal, in this case a smuggler (fig. 7.3). The unrepentant man stands helpless as soldiers hold and search him, surrounded by well-mounted cavalry and under the stern gaze of officers. One of the troopers rifles through the man's belongings that lay strewn on the ground. The message of the picture stresses the overwhelming force that the army could bring against individuals. The soldiers, likely themselves somewhat sympathetic, obediently suppress the civilian, whose gun figures prominently among his seized personal effects.

In terms of armed brigandage, the army faced several problems in its efforts: identifying bandits, finding lairs, deploying troops, and public relations. Local populations often did not cooperate with federal forces, nor did they always agree that nearby gangs of armed men represented bandits in a pejorative sense. One man's bandit was another's wily smuggler, folk hero, eccentric neighbor, or local dissident. The regime first needed to neutralize the most notorious of brigands.

Two of the most famous bandits of the age were Heraclio Bernal, the Lightning Bolt of Sinaloa, and Jesús Arriaga, called Chucho el Roto. A number of historians have dealt with these figures (and others, like El Tigre) and analyzed their challenge to national order or their place as figures of social memory.[84] They presented a figurative identity that directly opposed the lettered city as center of civilization; they entailed a monster that could not be included or understood.[85] From the point of view of the military, these men represented a threat and challenge to controlling the expansion of the regime's power in the countryside and to the image that they deemed necessary to sell to investors. In short, they posed an unforgivable opposition to modernity as envisioned by government officials.[86] Both men robbed and resorted to violence, but the difference in methods and in setting (rural versus urban) reveals the great variety that the label of bandit can contain.

FIGURE 7.3 "Justicia militar," *Revista del Ejército* (1907), 340.

Both men attained some fame and popular respect from lower classes, and at least in the case of Chucho even the middling sectors appreciated his legendary daring. Defeating their predations was only one problem; indeed, Chucho proved apparently fairly easy to catch, as authorities captured him several times. Bernal raised official ire also for his purported links to revolutionaries like Juan Hernández y Marín, as alleged by nearby army officials.[87] An enduring problem for officials came in vanquishing the bandits' status as folk heroes in the process of eliminating their gangs. Never quite successful in this, the regime did its best to publish unflattering press pieces, ugly caricatures, and eventually quite crude and unromantic photographs of the two criminals.[88] Had these two been the only bandits they faced, the army would have rested content by 1888.

The challenge of these gangs did not surprise the army authorities. Many officers had fought as guerrillas against the French or had seen firsthand the skills of the rurales, whose ranks had initially included many men fresh from banditry. In fact, the small detachments that chased criminals through the hills differed little from their prey, and deserting soldiers regularly swelled the ranks of bandit groups. Worse, the deserters and "lost" (stolen or sold) military stores provided an ample supply of Remington and Enfield rifles to the bandits, as in the case of the Fierro Amarillos (Yellow Irons) gang.[89] Some bandit groups showed considerable expertise in the field. General Lorenzo García wrote to Díaz in 1892 to report that one of these organized bands had managed to surprise the Sixth Regiment at San Ignacio, Tamaulipas. The cavalry detachment not only could not catch bandits but also fell into an ambush where they lost horses and arms and left behind captives.[90] A relief unit sent to the rescue also failed and fled from a well-set defensive position. Bandit attacks came regularly through the early 1890s, but with increasing rail links, telegraph lines, and sustained efforts the armed forces at last eliminated the most notorious highwaymen.

Not all bandits truly fit the definition, however broadly phrased. As a publicity strategy and a discursive tool, the government made use of the negative associations of the bandit to justify the vicious elimination of broadly defined political rivals. The same elasticity of label could also affect rebellious generals, as in the 1880s, or with deserters in arms.[91] The principal means of carrying out this quick "justice" that the labeling demanded was the ley fuga, the antifugitive law that permitted use of lethal force against fleeing suspects at the discretion of the commander on the scene. The army generally did not question the appropriateness of this form of de facto execution, nor did many in the press or middle classes consider it extreme, so long as soldiers assiduously applied it solely to those deemed either savages or bandits. In a rare exception, the article "Ley fuga" in the radical periodical *Regeneración* reversed the usual rhetorical claim and called the authorities savages for their application of the policy.[92]

Impromptu executions made for bad press, unless properly justified. Indeed, this continues to haunt Mexico's contemporary armed forces. In the 1890s *savage* and *bandit* became interchangeable terms of careful exclusion, legal categories that permitted the most draconian action without besmirching the national honor. Nonetheless, the justification for the measure was tenuous, and Díaz took care to come out against it in his correspondence to regional commanders. His quashing of a naval mutiny in 1879 still dogged his reputation, and his final command to kill them in the heat of battle remained a common refrain in corridos and popular legend. His reluctance to take credit for ley fuga excesses came naturally, and his instructions to subordinates were clear. General Lorenzo García assured that his forces used the measure only in cases where victims clearly worked with bandits. The president informed him that this time the press would not report the shootings.[93] Most correspondence only declared the death of such bandits, hinting that the robber had been shot in the course of a crime and leaving vague the exact circumstances.[94] Lieutenant Ygnacio Esparzo García took it a step further, arguing that he shot a bandit only as a reflexive response to the sheer effrontery of being robbed, which according to him actually "insisted upon him that he give the thief a bullet."[95] The regime as a whole nonetheless did seek to distance itself from a practice widely considered illegal, illiberal, and perhaps worst of all, not modern. It loudly proclaimed that thinly veiled executions no longer happened. There is reason to believe this was a disingenuous dodge, mere lip service to the ideal, and officers continued to practice ley fuga out of the earshot of the president. They did so with impunity, and they continue in some ways to enjoy this in today's Mexico.

Powerful men in government could also remove political foes by having a detachment quietly execute a prisoner. In 1880 one Colonel Nicolás Caldera ran afoul of Rafael Cuellar, the governor of Guerrero with strong family ties to the military. Caldera had supported one of Díaz's first attempts at coup d'état in 1870 but had become a dissident and political rival of the regime. The army first tried him for repeated drunkenness and speaking ill of the government, a "crime against the common order" for which he went to the military prison of Santiago. After four months in jail, he was sent to Governor Cuellar (for unknown reasons) and somehow eluded his captors. The cavalry squads shot to death the unfortunate Caldera shortly after his "escape" over the high barracks walls.[96] In earlier reports the escort noted that the man's ill health and advanced age had made the journey slow—this did not seem to fit well with scaling buildings and outrunning cavalry and hounds. The escape attempt seems quite convenient for a government irritated by the dead man's criticism.

Savage or *barbarian* proved other labels that allowed military forces an unusual degree of latitude in dealing with opposition, whether armed or not. Three particular groups singled out for such treatment, the Mayas, the Yaquis, and the Apaches, faced murderous campaigns that leaned heavily on this discursive crutch (see chapter 8). The Apaches had long had a "barbaric" reputation that justified the army in its vicious campaigns of eradication. Worse still for border garrisons, as late as 1882 some units still lacked proper arms or ammunition to fight the incursions.[97] Since this did not fit Mexico's preferred self-image something had to change. So as proof of the nation's modern progress and civilized heights, the delegation that was sent to the Paris World's Fair in 1889 brought the head of the "savage" Apache chief Victorio in a jar. Astute observers did not miss the irony of a pickled head offered as evidence of civility and order.[98]

In most areas, the army garrisoned platoons and relied on swift reinforcement, if necessary, to keep order. The small detachments and sometimes-unconventional tactics used by the practical officers allowed the government to suppress wide-scale uprisings, but at a cost. Coverage of terrain, with scattered pockets of occupation, complemented the use of railways and telegraphs to move and coordinate larger units of reinforcements. The strategy was a type of armed reconnaissance in force, as small groups of twenty or thirty federal troopers could then coordinate with even smaller units of rurales to watch over large territories.[99] Where the gaps between garrisoned towns and railheads were too large, the government expanded on an older program of military colonies that were located between areas of normal coverage. Colonies were founded beginning in 1821 as rewards for soldiers who fought for Mexican independence. With time, governments established new colonies as a type of presido to defend the frontiers from "indios bárbaros" that threatened them. Later still the governments extended these to interior frontiers, for example, with colonies set up to protect the Yucatán in the late 1840s. For all of these communities, one motivation came from simply populating so-called deserted zones. The colonies expanded greatly under Juárez and spread under Díaz, as a response to Indian uprisings.[100] As with many military projects, the reality of

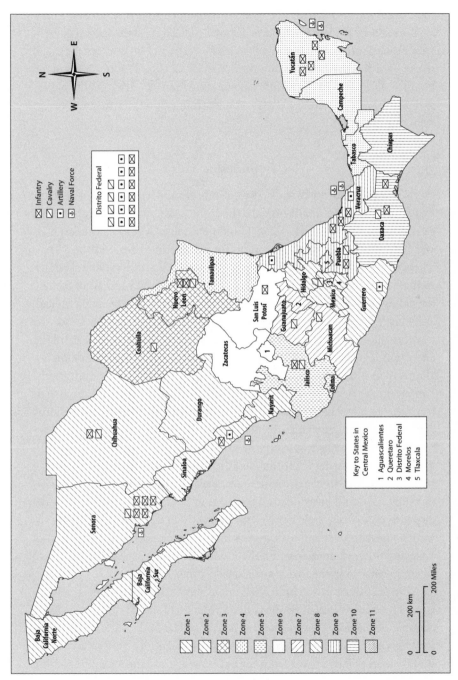

MAP 7.1 Military zones and deployment of main Mexican army and naval units, 1902.

the budget interfered with the vision of a pacified—garrisoned and populated—national landscape. Military colonies typically cost the federal government around 500,000 pesos annually to equip and maintain some six thousand troops, which often included a number of National Guard units. This cost did not include additional payments for providing medical care to both soldiers and their families. These scattered and underfunded units ultimately failed in pacifying the nation.

Conclusion

Once out of Chapultepec's walls, the line officers undertook myriad tasks for which no schooling could prepare them fully. Many moved from sterile classroom to filthy barracks. They found themselves sent to command hard and frightening men with reputations for drunkenness and violence. Their fellow officers hazed them, robbed them, and punished them almost daily. Actually leading troops out in the field against rebels and bandits confronted the young men with a steep learning curve. Some fell apart, some excelled, and most slid eventually into the opportunistic corruptions of la busca. By learning the army system, they found means to steal extra coins for drinking and gambling. Embezzling from forage accounts proved highly popular. For all prácticos, whether in garrisons of ten or a thousand, in city or jungle, the common experience included instability. By rapidly shuffling subalterns from post to post, the army attempted to sever federal officers from building local connections or loyalties. By making the officers move so often, the commanders hoped locals would see the army as faceless. Immunity to corruption from locals came from this mobility and unfamiliarity. The kinds of regional loyalties to charismatic officers that had propelled Díaz into his dictatorship would be avoided, if at a cost, to young men constantly on the move, in exile from their homes. Adherence to la Gran Familia, the army, would replace the subaltern officer's lingering memories of home and of a mother other than the patria. The modern military used these youths to re-create Mexico in the image envisioned by the elite.

The postitivist nation built itself on military sciences. Technical officers with three more years of training filled roles including army doctor, naval commander, factory overseer, land surveyor, and barracks builder. They constructed the nation's maps, roads, colonies, and fortresses. They set a military stamp on areas long absent from central control, un-naming and renaming them as they went. They pioneered the establishment or maintenance of military colonies in remote areas, facilitated recruitment and censuses, and protected foreigners' investments. They also surrounded, advised, and befriended the aging president. Modern stresses from new technological advances and rising social classes dragged old grievances into popular understandings. Sparks flew.

Perhaps one should pity the subaltern officer entering a real world he found harsh, unfamiliar, and beyond his limited experience. Many fraternized not due to weakness but due to genuinely liking and appreciating their men. Their positions, so clear in regulations, ran to chaos when they experienced real troops and their jaded fellow officers. When sent to the field they had to decide between clear laws on prisoners' rights, soldiers' expectations, and unspoken orders from superiors. Executions had become something of an anticipated duty without paperwork. Few in their early twenties could show the moral leadership that refusing illegal orders would require. Perhaps even harder, protecting prisoners might seem less than manly in front of the troops. Yet their choices nonetheless came to ultimately drain the legitimacy from authority and undermine their regime. Claims of moral weakness or poor training go only so far.

Junior officers must take some blame for areas where the nation failed to come together under their watch. It was their charge, even if the tools sometimes turned in their hands. Nevertheless, as young men without wholehearted support from superiors, or in particular from the national treasury, their experience reflected something more important than a mere pointing of fingers. They "succeeded" in some important regards. Under their influence the barracks replicated patriarchal norms and gave little space to those deviant in terms of sexuality, politics, or drug use. Few officers deserted. They took soldiers to the field with some successes, some failures, and rarely did the soldiers assassinate their officers. Against a horrible chance of promotion for merit, they persevered and some had decent careers. As agents of the consolidating nation, they, not at all unlike don Porfirio, failed to persuade citizens and dissidents of the virtues of modernity as they had ordered it. Subaltern officers mattered, then, not in their daily acts but rather as a lens through which to evaluate the relative strengths in Porfirian national consolidation. The task overwhelmed. The young officers underperformed. And hegemony, rule by consensus, remained elusive.

Salvador spat. "Always the same damn thing. Never a break for decent men like me," he muttered. The antibandit excursion had impressed none of his superiors.

His petition to join the Special Staff came back denied, again. No, the only chance for him to advance now, and incidentally to get away from Concepción and her complaining, would come from a combat-zone deployment. Teaching half-wits their left from their right had long since staled. If he only could prove himself on the battlefield, like the Old Man had done at Puebla so long ago, then surely he would fire up through the ranks. He prayed for a good little war. Nepotism could hardly matter out in the heat of battle. When the orders to deploy finally came, he could hardly believe the luck—they marched against mere savages, but still, this would finally give Salvador his chance to shine.

The Mexican people . . . have built a service which, if ever called upon again, will fill that enemy with bullets and favorable opinions, and it will not be dissipated by a defeat or two, as it was before it was reorganized—or better, recreated—by the soldier-statesman President Díaz.

—FREDERICK REMINGTON, "GENERAL MILES'S REVIEW"

CHAPTER EIGHT

Hatred in Their Mother's Milk

Savage, Semisavage, and Civilized Discourses of Nation

The garrison patio hummed with excitement for weeks as each night new rumors and speculations about the prospect of upcoming action preoccupied the troops and their families. Something was up. Proper packs and ammunition stores piled up precariously. Officers snapped more and murmured to each other out of earshot, until even Salvador had at least an idea of what the urgent need for constant inspections implied. Diego and Melchora, now stolid veterans of the barracks, had guessed that this all presaged that their battalion would move off to a war zone. Many possibilities of foes floated in idle conversations— some said that they moved against the United States to avenge Cuba, others claimed they had heard a major say that they would invade Guatemala. When the commanding officer called his restless battalion together and shouted down their muttering, he made clear that this was not a full-scale deployment and that only some few of them would be moving out. A detachment of sixty, the third cuadro, would march out with a string of mules and packhorses to reinforce the ongoing struggle against Indians in Sonora. Captain Salvador had command, Corporal Diego and his file would make up the troops. Melchora and her son, Rodrigo, as well as the other soldiers' families, immediately began packing their things, and that of the soldiers, as all assumed they would accompany the force. On a bright July morning they marched out of the barracks, loaded onto train cars, and sped for the Pacific coast. Diego restlessly went over his kit and rifle for the thousandth time, as did the troops around him, and found to his surprise that he looked forward to this adventure. They all stared out of the rumbling train car. He daydreamed a little about finding the enemy on some great flat battlefield wreathed in cannon smoke. He would get medals, even a promotion, and maybe a manly scar or two, and it would all be over in just a week or so. "Finally," he thought, "a chance to prove myself. And at least for a time, no more drill."

The regime largely pacified the countryside of its bandits by the 1890s, thanks to harsh applications of ley fuga aided by technology. Yet there remained a volatile element within the national body. The tendrils of government power did not reach all corners of the land. Rebels appeared from time to time. Barracks mutinied. But the greatest challenge to the fragile order still came in the form of indigenous uprisings, especially in the high Sierras and on the Yucatán Peninsula.

Long-standing grievances kept remote communities and indigenous peoples from embracing Porfirio Díaz's modern nation. The arrogance of central government made relations between core and periphery worsen. Many groups had halfheartedly joined the Independence Wars of the early nineteenth century with expectations for land, respect, and a voice.[1] The ensuing national regimes disappointed many of those far from the halls of government, and nearly all those with indigenous blood. Whether liberals or conservatives, mestizo rulers sought to pacify their indigenous subjects through assimilation, persuasion, or coercion. Rarely did the regimes offer *el pueblo* that which might have bound the nation together. Forms of hegemonic success nonetheless appeared, but the Porfirian modernizations persistently worked to reverse many of these gains.[2] Communities that demanded the preservation of lands, guarantees of subsistence, and maintenance of religious customs received little support from the federal government. A long century of conflict pitted regional interests—including municipal officials, indigenous tribes, important families, and adamant coreligionists—against outside factions and opportunistic foreigners, and against one another.[3] Sometimes, for a while, regional groups won concessions or guarantees. At others, they lost ground against the center. Their experiences demonstrated how Mexico as a young republic failed to establish a stable hegemony on a broad basis until the 1900s at best.[4]

This chapter investigates how the army met with organized uprising in Sonora, the Yucatán, and the Sierras and what that meant for power relations in the modernizing nation between the 1870s and the early 1900s. It is the first time in the literature that these have been directly compared. The suppression and reintegration of these rebels demonstrates a continuity and a developing institutional capacity tied to new variations of racism. Technological improvements met pseudoscience and ideology—looking at these uprisings not as separate affairs but as a process connected by military experience gives us a better sense of how nation building met indigenous challenges. After establishing context, this chapter demonstrates that the "enemy," broadly conceived, included terrain, climate, geography, and finally the expertise and cultural resilience of the indigenous foe. Concerted self-conquest employed tools of modern technology and traditional rhetoric to crush opposition as purpose shifted from punishing rebels to exterminating peoples. The elite sought to colonize their own country.[5] Furthermore, the reemergence and subsequent repression of the Yucatecan and Sonoran indigenous insurgencies illustrate how power relations in Mexico met with issues of biopolitics and governmentality. Among other things, the regime increasingly sought to manage populations on deep levels of identity through ridding them of place and eradicating their cultures.[6] The combinations of massacre, deportation, and the establishment of permanent bureaucratic controls brought the self-conquest into a modern transnational age.[7] Discourses embedded in beliefs, ideas, and symbolic languages shaped the process in ways that permitted the inhuman treatment of don Porfirio's enemies. In experiences of war, soldiers and soldaderas found tragedy and trauma as they came into bloody conflicts against civilians in the high hills and sweltering jungles of their nation. As agents of the neocolonial and self-colonizing apparatus of the modern regime, they brought a new order into being, justified by a permanent crisis, or "state of exception," and on the basis of new categories like the "semisavage," which became institutionalized through bureaucratic paperwork.[8]

It is my contention that this entire process presents crosscutting or a snapshot of the integral power relations that defined modern nation building at one of its frenetic points. The self-conquering impetus demonstrates how governmentality expressed itself.[9] The basic authority and legitimacy of the state, and its claims over populations, became naturalized as it sought to transform not just subject individuals but "life" or populations more broadly.[10] The object of power shifted from molding individual bodies or selves to instead applying discursive claims over groups, from the family level up to the community, the regional, and ultimately the national. Family, for instance, became both instrument and model for the new power-relations schema as society reproduced patriarchal hierarchies.[11] Power became visible only when

in its weakest formulation, and violence represented a symptom of power relations rather than their endpoint or cause. In other words, military actions
against indigenous or religious challengers came as only a facet of a broader
and often-incidental project that tried to compel acquiescence from disparate
and artificially connected populations.[12] The sole surviving vision, if all went
well, would be a shared historical experience and imaginary of what mexicanidad meant.

A fundamental reshaping of power relations in the country worked to
eradicate historical memories and religious worldviews at odds with the
regime. Press, literature, and laws did little to challenge the deeply held beliefs
of those living in far-flung frontiers. Whereas previous counterinsurgencies
moved to a largely political end, the Porfirian regime increasingly sought a
result suiting its ideological goals. If traditional ideas persisted in areas outside the grasp of government, the people who held to them faced obliteration
by all the means available to a modern regime.[13] After all, civilization would
not come until nonmestizo populations caught up to mainstream society.
Federal forces did not seek to pacify or castigate the "Indians" but to eradicate
their culture, history, and presence.

The Trajectory of Uprisings: Tomochic, Yaqui, and Mayan Contexts

*To Melchora the whole affair began with tremendous excitement as she boarded
her first-ever train and thrilled to the speed and noise and motion. By its end
the trip had lost much of its charm. The detachment arrived shortly at the port
in Acapulco. Bored troops, long out of booze and low on cigarettes, had mostly
exhausted their speculations about the fight to come, and an eavesdropping
Salvador had little to add. Older veterans spoke of how the fanatics of Tomochic
had made life miserable and short for troops just like these ones riding the railway. Some from the northern regions spoke of the heat and dust and rough
landscapes that they would find. Melchora began to lose sleep, waking every
night just to check that her Diego was still there beside her.*

*Melchora sighed with relief as they disembarked at the port and finally
enjoyed a brief break from the noise and wind of the train. After a few leisurely
days, the detachment and families loaded onto a cramped steamship transport
never designed for moving masses of men. Fortunately, the trip was mercifully
short and the overcrowded and seasick passengers tumbled ashore at Mazatlán.
Melchora gazed about in amazement at the apparent paradise they found in
the breezy and beautiful town. Clean streets and bustling markets filled with*

abundant seafood welcomed them. For a short time, the detachment relaxed there, hoping to stay, while Salvador and his fellow officers sent letters, organized gear, and ordered replacements. Melchora looked back over her shoulder, almost in tears, as they marched out and left behind the beauty of the coast on the hard, dry road inland. The scorching sun made her head pound, and the pack on her back seemed full of lead as they left behind the cool seaside breezes. Dust coated her throat, and Rodrigo in his sling complained nonstop in his discomfort. Water proved hard to find. After many days on the road, they finally marched into the newly constructed barracks at Torín. The worst, they told each other through chapped and bloody lips, must now be over.

The small detachment made their place in the barracks and in their own ways carved out their niches among the troops already there. Tussles between newcomers and old hands quickly settled the pecking order, and Diego and Melchora fit in immediately. Salvador found this adjustment much more difficult. Much to his surprise, he often thought about his wife and wished he could tell her of the voyage. He thought of writing but never seemed to have time. The other officers already in place left Salvador little opportunity to skim a few coins on the side. Those who already had combat experience never let him speak and did not appreciate his experiences in the salons of Paris, no matter how often he told his stories. It seemed that his peer officers soon gave up on offering him advice, but he did not mind. His troops began to filter out of the barracks the next day on patrols along the riverside and out to isolated farms. Melchora watched as the soldiers sharpened their bayonets and cleaned rifles, and she shuddered a little and pulled Rodrigo close.

Persistent conflict between mestizo elites and rural groups marked the majority of the republic's history. Bringing the most reluctant into sharing the national imagining nonetheless proved beyond the immediate reach of regimes. They neither shared a historical experience with their putative subjects nor offered them any substantial rewards for capitulating. Within a globalizing economy seeking materials, labor, and markets, the power brokers of Mexico turned increasingly toward capturing the "social assets" of their own nation in auto conquest. Requisites of global markets, as much as anything, drove the conflicts between intranational core and periphery. Serious revolts by the Yaquis and Mayas resurged in the late nineteenth century, but in a new context shaped by government reactions to the mestizos at Tomochic.

In 1879 a young lady named Teresa in the small highland town of Tomochic saw visions.[14] She and her father convincingly told their fellow villagers of the holy message, and mestizo and indigenous peoples from nearby came to hear her words and to seek solutions for crises of drought and famine. Her experience built on a long precedent of sacred visions within traditions of folk Catholicism from early in colonial history.[15] Never purely religious in their goals, prophets promoted moral economic concerns, religious autonomy, and local sovereignty, among many other underlying rationales.[16] They also represented a point of connection between broader communities of faith and specific indigenous identities. Although the people of Tomochic village largely came from mestizo stock (with some Tarahumara), Teresa's message drew in an indigenous audience from the Yaquis and other neighboring groups.[17] The challenge that the town rebellion embodied thus transcended mere political or purely religious significance due to its potent mixture of faith, region, and racial worldviews.

The Tomochics, inspired, rose against the secular will of the Porfirian regime and waylaid passing caravans laden with mined ore. They sought a new and holy polity, within their rights as an autonomous municipality, and prepared to meet the millenarian doom that they believed approached.[18] Federal soldiers responded in force under General José María Rangel, a dogmatic gentleman past his prime as a field officer.[19] On unknown terrain, poorly led, ill supplied, and shallowly trained, the troops failed and retreated wildly. The abashed government summoned overwhelming reinforcements and returned to ruin the town in a hail of gunfire. In the end some 350 villagers died, many of them women, children, or the elderly, while the federals lost nearly five hundred.[20] Santa Teresa de Cabora fled to Los Angeles, California, and into relative obscurity.

Mexicans remembered the tale in different ways. The surviving people of Tomochic told of their heroic and divine resistance against the halting military incursion. God demanded their martyrdom, while masculine pride and religious stoicism sustained their morale. The outcome, while tragic, also had its own honor and dignity. For communities in the Sierras, their rugged sense of manliness acted in concert with deep mysticism in impelling rebels despite the odds.[21] Those close to Teresa took her tale to the United States, where she became symbol and emblem of folk Catholic beliefs and eventually of a particular form of Chicana feminism.[22] The highest officials in the army perceived a lesson in the importance of dynamic and immediate assaults led by young officers and the need for better armaments and training among the common troops. Among soldiers and soldaderas and in popular quarters more generally, a different tale began to spread in the medium of the corridos.

Figure 8.1. José Guadalupe Posada, *Los sucesos de Tomóchic*. *Gil Blas*, 1892.

The communities' valiant and doomed defense inspired admiration and also a veiled criticism of the regime that ordered the assault. In corridos sung by soldiers and civilians the tragedy at Tomochic earned a common currency and built a shared sense of historical memory that blurred racial lines. Songs highlighted, for example, the indigenous origins of federal soldiers but alluded to a massacre of nonmestizo villagers. Sly references to the heavy losses incurred in the lopsided battle alluded to the deaths of soldiers rather than rebels. These lyrical tales of war allowed the sharing of experiences and military lore across a generation, for both soldiers and the Yaquis, who likewise shared these songs.[23] The most recent manifestation of the project in Sonora had not reflected well on the army—the 1893 fiasco at Tomochic embarrassed the regime for decades.

This millenarian revolt in the Sierras, the rebellion in the Yaquis' Eight Villages, and the long Mayan resistance tied together in complex ways. Considerable differences of ethnicity, race, historical experience, and specific grievances separated the rebels' causes. Faith, present in each, had significant cultural variations even if the Yaquis also venerated Santa Teresa. Nonetheless, all three uprisings represented part of a single larger process. The insurgent subjects aimed primarily to maintain a degree of local autonomy over labor and religion. The regime, fighting to build a coherent nation absent of such local aberrations, treated all challenges in consistent and excessive ways. It identified the challenges, defined the problem population, applied science (military and civilian), and set bureaucratic measures to make solutions permanent. Violence, as a manifestation of the power relations in progress, came as a mere symptom of larger strategies in play.

As the Apache threat in the north receded the pogroms against the Yaquis reached new levels.[24] Perhaps the greatest continuity for life in the Eight Pueblos was the long Yaqui and Mayo (Yoreme) history of armed resistance to government forces and outside peoples, whom they called *yori*. Uniting under the elected captain general, and at times allying with neighboring Mayos, the Yaquis fought for independence in several major revolts: they rose in 1740 (against the Jesuits), in 1826–1833 (the Banderas rebellion), in 1875–1885 (under Cajeme), again in 1893–1897 (under Juan Tetabiate), and in 1898–1900 (under Juan Maldonado).[25] In addition to these discrete uprisings, the Yaquis participated in the Wars of Independence, the Wars of Reform, the French Intervention, and the Revolution and undertook lengthy periods of insurgent or guerrilla warfare, particularly between 1885 and 1910, and again in the 1920s. These periods of open conflict generally followed increased government pressures or military occupations, and as a result, the Yaqui Valley saw few years of peace until late into the twentieth century. After 1883 the army had attempted what it called a slow squeeze of small occupations in the western Sierras rather than risking grand assaults that received negative press attention back in Mexico City.[26] After Tomochic in 1893, the military scaled up its efforts and once again built in force.

Taking the trail in 1899, reinforcements streamed into the Eight Village region along the Yaqui River.[27] Yet their task, to destroy the Yaquis and Mayos in the area came as only the latest step in a long, grinding process of outright wars and insidious laws that reduced the peoples there to subjects. The army would seek to avoid the errors of Tomochic, and military planning and use of advancing technology seemed central to this strategy. With this came a degree of caution. General José Montesinos wrote to General Carbó in 1898 making clear that he lacked the resources for a successful campaign against the Yaquis, and he urged diplomacy, asserting that the Yaquis "no se meten con nadie" (do not trouble anyone).[28] Dr. Fortín (Fortunato) Hernández also wrote the central government with a call to reject war, but the agents of conflict had already arrived.[29] The long war against the Yaquis had acted as a central component of a state strategy in controlling land and populace. This similarly described the case of the Mayas in the eastern Yucatán.

Both southern and northern uprisings had foreign elements of supply or support, both faced a major turning point in 1893 and an eventual smothering around 1900, and both featured many of the same officers and veteran troops using new technologies. The increasing bureaucratic sophistication of the army became apparent in these decades. Both conflicts hinged on terrain and on a construction of the enemy as barbarous noncitizens. Capitalist concerns for "proper" scientific use of land and developing the region drove both reconquests. Atrocity followed suit as *dzul* (non-Mayas) and *yori* (non-Yaquis) assaulted indigenous peoples. Not so unlike the Yaqui clashes, the Yucatán had a long history of unrest and federal intervention. Indeed, the Mayas had fought tooth and nail against dzul since long before Cortés or the Montejos managed to arrive, much as the Yaquis had struggled against the yori. The Mayan wars for survival have a deep historiography that needs no reinvention here.[30]

Divisions within Mayan ranks, and a hurried reinforcement of federal soldiers, defeated the rebels when the first phase of the Caste War of 1847–1855 came to an end. The elite worked to placate some of their discontented subjects and watched them with suspicion. For decades the Mayas simmered and watched their new overclass with well-justified suspicions. Industry came in the form of new sisal (henequen) plantations in the west, complementing the mahogany trade in the south and east.[31] A rough binding-cord fiber, sisal became an important substitute for other cordage and a commodity essential to shipping and agriculture.[32] As a highly labor-intensive crop it required a large and inexpensive supply of manpower if plantations were to thrive. Haciendas and timber concerns depended on Mayas termed *pacíficos*, while to the east resistance by bravos continued. Their resistance to peonage came as only one piece of their larger set of grievances.

In the decades that followed the war, skirmishes disturbed the peace and rumors began to emerge about a new movement by Mayan bravos centered in the deep brush south and east of the henequen-farming zone. Federal and state army units tensed. The earliest uprisings saw much the same reaction as in previous wars. Mexican soldiers marched out of garrisons and found their routes blocked by low stone walls, snipers firing on them from dense jungle, and towns emptied of populations who had fled while vulnerable plantations burned.[33] Calls for reinforcements brought up the remnants of the National Guard, the military colonies of the region went on alert, and worried elites in Mérida bought guns.[34]

The peninsula remained volatile, since these autonomous Mayas held a long stretch of refuge along the southeast coast and as far inland as the edges of henequen country.[35] They had, purportedly, a ready supply of arms from the south. Fears of a repeat of the Caste War continued to rise. The military governor worried that this time the dzul might lose, or at least face an embarrassing and protracted war. By 1893 and with the specter of millenarian uprisings like Tomochic in mind, the government began a campaign to destroy Mayan threats in a definitive way. A new treaty with the British promised to deny new arms or materiel for Mayan rebels along the southeast of the peninsula. The regime turned its attentions to quashing the ongoing millenarian uprising that centered on Chan Santa Cruz, outside of federal controls. The lands and peoples there needed Mexican rule, some argued, for their own good. More concerned about the image that rebels entailed, Huerta in 1902 pointed out that the uprising had offended "the Republic's prestige."[36] National sovereignty tolerated no rebels.

The three insurgencies together offered a singular challenge to Díaz's regime. They did not fit in the national story as told by the elite, to the elite. In order to apply power to what it deemed an existential problem the government had to overcome puissant warriors fighting on home territory, it had to withstand harsh climes, and it had to eradicate the rebels' cultures and memories.

The Many "Enemies of Civilization"

A flurry of activity came soon enough, with word from the scouts sent to the higher vantages. Diego and the other soldiers packed a full supply of rations, loaded up with more ammunition then any had ever fired in all their years of training, and set out on the road. This time, Melchora and her comrades stayed behind. None of the newly arrived knew quite what to expect, despite the stories they had heard, and Salvador and Diego alike pretended a calm they did not feel. Their column, some three hundred strong, marched into enemy territory with a long line of mules following behind. They had scarcely made a decent morning's march when the sharp whistle and angry crack of passing bullets sent them to cover behind rocks and trees. Maybe a handful of men risked exposure to fire back, but Diego had no idea where the attackers lay and simply kept low. Several hours of heat and sporadic fire drained the pinned unit's morale. Finally the shooting stopped, army horns called for the advance, and they all got up and moved on. Well, most of them. Two men returned to barracks on stretchers. One had taken a bullet in the side and would not live. The other had taken cover in a sunny ditch and mumbled madly in a curled-up position, red-faced and incoherent. Only a few kilometers out and already two men down, four men carrying them back, and a medic treating them along the way.

Neither Diego nor Salvador had yet seen the enemy. Diego tore into his rations and threw down his gear harder than he needed to. All around, troops cursed the cowards shooting at their friends and comrades from hiding. Salvador heard at length his major's disapproval with his not taking some more aggressive actions to flush out the enemy and displeasure at how Salvador's unit came to need a rescue. He promised to do better and lay sleepless that night planning how to get back to Mexico City. The slow advance continued, and the pattern repeated itself daily. It took weeks to arrive at the enemy's position. High above loomed a hill topped with a short wall and ringed with a ditch. Behind those simple wooden palisades the enemy awaited.

Taking on rebels in the arid Sierras and tropical jungles set the federals against numerous challenges. The able enemy included many skilled fighters. The environment and its diseases slaughtered outsiders. The enemy, moreover, had profound cultural and religious motivations that built on long historical memories. To defeat all of this, the government had to apply firepower, sciences, and guile. At times this meant facing those it had worked so hard to train.

The presence of capable federal veterans among the Yaqui forces contributed greatly to hard-fought and bitter campaigns. At the onset of the end-of-century fighting, Mexico City papers lauded the recruitment of some eighty Yaquis who had made up a significant part of the Twenty-Fourth Battalion in 1897.[37] Former rebels themselves, the new soldiers faced military service as "their sole punishment" for insurgency. According to the press, these men represented a new ideal for army men: they carried out orders perfectly; they seemed strong and robust; and they acted both submissive and even-tempered. Even better, the papers noted, these men had already demonstrated their skills as accurate sharpshooters, surefooted scouts, and hardy marchers, and they enjoyed the total trust of officers and sergeants, so much so that they could go out in the streets alone. They never deserted. In contrast to other soldiers, they seemed proud of their new station, and when they met civilians they showed off their military gear proudly and "manifestaban gran júbilo" (showed great happiness). As soldiers the Yaquis clearly excelled, and in the aftermath of the broken Peace of Ortiz in 1897, many returned to their homes to bring the fight to their former colleagues. This also applied to the Mayas, since no small number of their men also had spent time in national guards, militias, and even the federal army before joining the bravos.[38] The indigenous soldiers' skills, so lauded in the newspapers, were now turned against the federal army.

Insurgents mastered many skills and married these to old traditions of warcraft. In the late 1890s the Yaquis took advantage of shrinking assault groups suffering from illness. They established *loberas* (literally "wolf-dens," or foxholes) on hillsides that overlooked the marching routes from which they sniped at invaders.[39] Yaqui soldiers continued to use this tactic decades later in the Revolution with the addition of machine guns, making intruders pay a high price. From these points a pair of entrenched shooters could pin down and harass much larger enemy forces until eventually relief units came to outflank the snipers. Given the terrain and the lack of effective federal cavalry, the shooters generally managed to slip away from pursuit to fight again the next day. At more significant river crossings or larger forests the Yaqui forces set up more determined defenses and managed to hold the federals in check until lack of ammunition forced the defenders to retreat. Managing this proved a difficult task, nonetheless, since as soon as effective rebel fire slowed the army would move in quickly with bayonets to clear out the woods. According to one officer, the federals were fortunate that their tactics "worked well against Indians like the Yaquis."[40] Even though costly, this response allowed the federals to sweep up any injured or slow enemies. In a war of attrition the nation of thirteen million could afford losses much more readily than the thirty thousand or so who made up the entire Yaqui people.[41]

As with the Sierras, the Mayan jungle held many dangers. Dense foliage, hostile vermin, and punishing heat beat soldiers down and demoralized invaders. The army held mostly to the roads that permitted some ease of passage to supply trains and close-order columns.[42] Scouts kept close in order to avoid losing all contact with the troops. Communication and sight fell to extremely close distances in the dense woods. Snakes menaced the unwary, particularly the fer-de-lance, with its deadly hemotoxic bite. Jaguars and alligators menaced in the night. It is little surprising that few troops worried about mere bug bites. Behind the brush stalked enemies that had grown up hunting far more wary prey. They simply waited in cover and picked off soldiers unlucky enough to fall into the crosshairs. Just as with troops facing the guerilla tactics in the northwest, federals suffered serious losses to hidden foes that made the most of their knowledge of the land.

Mayan warriors maintained a long and effective guerrilla war that made excellent use of their jungle home as cover and refuge.[43] They employed simple but deadly traps, like punji sticks, and made use of their reputation as cannibals to frighten their enemies.[44] Their passage left few traces, and federal forces generally failed to discover the hidden sanctuaries where the

Mayas hid. Each day, soldiers made only limited headway through heavy brush or else suffered frequent ambush if they openly used the roads.[45] Cover rarely favored the invaders. Forces moved slowly forward, suffered from disease and snipers, and did not capture significant captives or camps for years.

These tactics nonetheless point to a particular weakness in the federal strategy for both the Yaqui and Mayan campaigns. Privileged and reserved for defending the centers of power, the main artillery units did not take the field with the other troops. Aside from fixed batteries in port cities, the army had a number of artillery regiments and a machine gun company, but these remained in Mexico City guarding the government at its source. These would have made a great difference in the campaigns, but the generals deployed only a few fast-firing smaller artillery pieces. The brush and forests would offer little cover to covering fire from 75-mm cannons, which would have pinned ambushers in place and allowed troops to maneuver into flanking positions. Fleeing indigenous fighters still could have avoided direct pursuit but would have paid a bloody price, taking indirect fire that they could not return. When the campaigning soldiers arrived at strongholds, artillery would have made havens into slaughterhouses. Even the medical officer Balbás saw that a lack of the heavy weapons had made the entire Yaqui invasion into a somewhat primitive and relatively even match.[46] This theater also saw federal forces meeting counterparts with federal expertise, a foreshadowing of much of the Revolutionary period in decades to come.

The leadership among the northern rebels featured a number of trained, modern Porfirian soldiers who had deserted from the army and brought skills with them. Men like Cajeme, Tetabiate, and Juan Maldonado understood the vulnerability of their high strongholds.[47] They scattered supply caches through the woods for the inevitable second phase of their war because they knew the fort would not hold. Balbás recounted, for instance, how scouts had discovered piles of ammunition, food, and water hidden in the bases of trees and in dugout spots hidden away and known only to the enemy.[48] The leaders thus established redundant and dispersed supply lines, infiltrated enemy terrain, and burdened invading troops with nonlethal casualties and noncombatant prisoners. The Yaquis learned from battlefields like Buatachive (1886) and Tomochic (1893) and replicated them at Bacahuete (1898). They used terrain effectively and sought once again to do so at Mazocoba in early 1900. Fortifications proved highly effective against federal and other enemy cavalry.[49] Such a stronghold presented a target too costly to attack, or so it had always been in the long history of the region. Their war extended into the political, as they assumed that costly assaults offered enough pressure that the politicians would give in to demands.[50]

All this might have succeeded scarce years earlier. The federal army of 1900 had improved since its 1893 failures. Troops carried better arms and ample ammunition and used them more aggressively.[51] Each soldier at Tomochic had only five rounds of ammunition, in part to discourage desertion and in part because a lack of standard equipment (thirty-four types of arms in service) led to logistics nightmares. This problem the quartermasters had solved in the interim years, and the soldiers now had good rifles and sufficient ammunition. More significantly, the army no longer lacked the support and numbers to press insurgents to a definitive end. Officers had considerable training in how to deal with fortifications from their Chapultepec days, and even if they lacked the artillery they preferred they did have some fast-fire light guns and a few machine guns.[52] The new army suffocated the uprising more thoroughly than its recent past would have augured.

Veteran warriors aside, the terrain and climate made the task of eradicating Yaquis a daunting one.[53] The rough hills and mescal scrub of the Sierras, the river crossings, and the steep crevices served the locals well. Ambushes and sniping ravaged federal army columns. Casualties needed ambulance carriers and doctors, so a single nonfatal injury potentially occupied several men's energies. While malaria and yellow fever had little purchase in the Sierras, the heat of the Sonoran sun took a toll on the army.[54] A large part of the invading forces fell to heatstroke and exhaustion, reported as *insolado* (sun-struck), including some key officers.[55] Little wonder that men fell to the sun. Packs and gear loaded a man down with some thirty kilograms, and daytime heat in the valley can reach the forties Celsius. Forces in the autumn of 1900, for instance, lost so many men to illness that they reduced their columns from seven to five and went from 180 to 150 men in each.[56] The continued need for good guides, especially ones acclimated to the heat, eventually led officials to bring in Opata and Pima natives to hunt the Yaquis on a bounty system in 1906.[57] At night the temperatures can drop precipitously, particularly atop the higher ridges. Clean water, relatively easy for locals to find, often eluded troops that strayed from the riverside. Dr. Manuel Balbás recounted how his charges often went days without sufficient fluids, made worse by activity, and how by contrast the enemy seemed never to lack.[58] Casualties mounted, and the advances began to falter and slow down. In Mayan lands, illness had even more fatal consequences.

Much as in Sonora, the Yucatán landscape fiercely fought human intruders. The dense lowland jungles gave cover to those who knew them, game animals fed the locals, and finding water supplies often required a native guide.[59] The higher prevalence of yellow fever and malaria made the region deadly for those ill prepared or foreign.[60] Troops on the march or in shoddy camps had little protection from diseases, inadequate food and water, and great discomfort. Some two thousand men eventually died in this campaign, most from diseases.[61] Military scientists very nearly made a precocious discovery upon finding that windy weather (when mosquitos cannot fly) led to fewer infections—but they never made the correct causal connection and continued to prescribe mosquito nets primarily to make sleep easier.[62] New sciences did focus increasingly on hygiene and some vaccines began to appear, but this came primarily to cities such as Campeche, rather than to all the troops in the field.[63] Many soldiers actually worsened their conditions, according to General Bravo, by self-medicating against the bad climate. The medics also proved unable to deal with the cadavers the disease left behind, and reports of shallow burials, far too close to hospitals, or shoddy cremations with petrol continued to fill reports sent back to the capital.[64] The regime called on its medical staff to remedy these ills, but in the meantime the government changed its approach.

Politics had shifted. The government had balanced its debts, reformed its legal codes, and generally mended many ills. As Díaz got his house in order he could no longer assuage his nation's indigenous issues with temporary treaties, as if with equals in status. Now instead, he would deploy the full weight of the military to obliterate his enemies regardless of cost. A new institution sallied against the frontiers.

In 1886 Porfirio Díaz wrote to his governor Abraham Baranda and told him that once the distraction of the Yaquis had ended, the nation would turn its full attention to the Yucatán.[65] A decade later—with the 1897 death of Tetabiate in the Sierras of Sonora and Tomochic four years settled—he indeed sent most of Mexico's armed strength southward to end the Mayan uprisings.[66] Among them came many veterans and officers, and after the 1900 battle of Mozocabo a second wave of experienced men (including officers like Brigadier General Victoriana Huerta) arrived in the Yucatán by the middle of May 1901.[67] The campaign proved costly, with thousands dead, thousands more injured, and a monthly cost of 9,117.63 pesos for garrisons alone.[68] Along with efforts to build infrastructure, the war absorbed over a quarter of the budget for Yucatán, even after the main fighting had ended.[69]

A Cultural Memory of Violence

Beyond terrain and tactics, the indigenous identity presented an enemy in its own right. Basic technologies and tactical reforms could overcome veteran indigenous warriors fighting on their own ground, yet this did not solve a more fundamental challenge. The insurgencies in both northern and southern arenas possessed a cultural worldview set within a shared historical memory. This culture posed a resistant foe that simple tactics could not defeat because the government simply could not compel loyalty from the indigenous. Or at least, no measure would suffice if any indigenous peoples survived.

The federal military arrived with a deadly and even genocidal mission that began in Sonora. In the words of the otherwise sympathetic Balbás, "Where there was one Yaqui Indian, there was an enemy of the government," and as he added later, "They are the enemies of civilization."[70] This notion suggested a strategic solution that is deeply horrific—mass murder. This made macabre sense in a situation where cultural and religious forces, more so even than armed insurgents, represented an enemy of the state. Deep adherence to millenarian folk Catholic fundamentals, embedded with indigenous lore, leadership, language, and identity and expressed in ritual practices of everyday life, represented an irreconcilable gap between the local community and the larger nation. Add to this historical memories of profoundly unjust treatment at the hands of the authorities, and the local sense of what was right could not be extinguished without a tremendously violent government pogrom—if even then.

A coherent oppositional historical memory underlay local identities, and it ran counter to a nationalist idea of what it meant to be Mexican. Closely held cultural loyalties rooted in the immediate community posed a stubborn foe to the homogeneity implied by a shared national imagining. Several facets of indigenous worldview led logically to a genocidal impulse when federals encountered peoples at the margins of citizenship.

The government used the military to eliminate the cultural presence of the peoples in the Eight Villages. The long religious traditions of the Yaquis had adapted and adopted Catholic and folk-Catholic elements, but shamans (*temastis*) continued to maintain their customary beliefs.[71] Women featured heavily among the pious who drove rebellions, so much so that military officers singled them out as the chief enemies among the Yaquis.[72] They and others who had heard the call from Santa Teresa de Cabora rallied the resistance to Díaz along lines of faith. General Abraham Bandala in 1892 saw this as a growing peril and wrote to the president that he wished to move in troops against the movement and "sofocarlo en su cuna" (suffocate it in its cradle).[73] The government's ignorance at times led to missteps in the campaign. For example, a folk figure in Yaqui beliefs, a mythic and mysterious leader named Odope, kept federal military leaders preoccupied and concerned for years, even though they never found convincing proof that the man existed.[74] As had occurred in mainstream Mexican culture, of course, the Yaquis also adapted to both the hardships of war and simply to modernizing and technological change.[75]

Some years later an anthropologist argued that the Yaquis and their culture represented "instinctive rebels" whose rejection of private property represented a threat to the capitalistic system.[76] This seems an oversimplification. Instead a pattern combining the best of modern and traditional ways marked their farming, family, and art. Common to all of these aspects of life was the strength and role of a community as incubator for daily practices. They pragmatically married new technologies to old ways of life, but underneath everything lay a sense of collective identity. This quality became a direct casualty of the government's arrival in their homes. The assault of the Porfirian military broke families, scattered survivors from Tucson to Belize, and prohibited gatherings to celebrate, mourn, or pray. It should not be surprising that this resulted in deep and lasting anger toward the regime. According to one military observer, "The Yaqui imbibed hatred of Mexico in their mother's milk and at their mother's knee."[77] Fundamental differences in national vision fueled the conflicts that led to genocides, particularly those reinforced with senses of historical injustice that infused tales of the past.

Rebellion, of course, did not rise solely from anger over contemporary events but carried on a strategy of armed resistance loaded with historical memory. In Sonora, for example, federal excesses at Bácum in 1868 became a rallying cry, as Yaquis remembered an entire village locked inside a church and burned alive.[78] Despite the 1876 change of regime under Díaz, the indigenous of Sonora did not suffer a surplus of trust in government. Their war captain Cajeme, whose name meant "the nondrinker," seemed an unlikely rebel, described by Governor Ramón Corral as mild-mannered, deeply religious, and reasonable man.[79] Himself a conscripted veteran of the federal army, his limited insurgency sought autonomy, especially in cultural matters, and the removal of foreign interlopers from the Yaqui valley. The army captured Cajeme and executed him by ley fuga in April 1887.[80] The rebellions built on these foundations of historical memory. Contemporary issues recalled not only government attacks on innocents like those at Bácum but also those against neighbors, as in Tomochic.[81] The execution of war leaders like Cajeme had relatively little effect on folk movements that saw all fighters as martyrs and had alternative leaders waiting in the wings. Genuine government solutions in favor of the Yaquis needed to redress all missteps, past and present. Instead, federal authorities sought to eliminate the memory by removing those who remembered.

Memories of the past articulated with faith in making a coherent and consistent cultural whole and a basis for rebellion beyond merely the Sonoran highlands. While Yaqui warriors openly invoked Santa Teresa in battle, events at Tomochic also had more in common with the resurgent Mayan uprising than might be apparent. Deep religious belief sustained the Mayan rebels in their seemingly eternal war against outside oppression. Holy sites took precedence over strategic ground.[82] The insurgents acted with persisting faith in destiny and a willingness for martyrdom if necessary. Mayan-imbued folk-Catholic religiosity therefore always undergirded the rationales and motives of these rebels, no less than it had for millenarians at Tomochic or for Yaqui warriors after 1893. Just as the regime had encouraged the deployment of Josephite missionaries to Sonora, missionaries also came to the Yucatán in order to bring a homogenous piety to the "savage" in a region where, some have argued, religion and the church play a consistently crucial role.[83] The soul became a battlefield for the national vision.

Faith therefore connected the insurgencies as a basic motivation and sustenance. The *cruzobs* (rebel Mayas) who followed visions of the flaming cross had much in common with the followers of Teresa. The mystical visions of their leadership explained the wars, and their claims offered them legitimacy in rule. For the cruzob a message transmitted by sacred means to their captains offered powerful motivation to withstand the hardships of campaigning.[84] The exact messages, or even the degree to which the bravos accepted them, mattered less than that the movement as a whole had the stamp of divine grace.[85] The armies that fought against them could not dissuade true believers, but they could remove bodies and dismantle families.

Faith could not save them from invasions, nor could walls. With the fall of the last indigenous fortifications, both federals and insurgents expected breathing room to seek a stable and political solution. The tragedy had only just begun.

The Civilized Discourses of Savage Nation

Salvador lit a cigarette with shaking hands and squinted into the sun as he looked up at the Yaqui fort early on a January morning in 1900. He tried to think of what his father would counsel him. Ahead at Mazocoba, according to scouts, some thousands of the Yaqui savages with modern rifles awaited. Two at a time they had paralyzed his men for weeks. No heavy cannons or machine guns had arrived with the expedition, throwing much of what he had learned at Chapultepec aside. He told his soldiers to leave behind their packs, sharpen their bayonets, and prepare their resolve. Diego knew at once that the man was insane. Hundreds of meters of open, steep terrain lay between where they huddled and where the enemy was set up with murder in mind. General Luis E. Torres's orders came, but the man never appeared in person. With a quick prayer, Diego crossed himself, loaded his Mauser, and fixed his bayonet. He breathed deep to steady his trembling hands. Fear began to turn to anger. He wished for some water to quell his intense thirst and wet his throat. When the horn call came, he charged ahead, with bullets buzzing past and raising puffs of dust ahead. From the corner of his eye he saw men alongside him fall or dive into cover, but he continued onward. Salvador watched from below and did not follow. Diego and his file mates leapt over the trenches, pushed through the crude walls, and shot toward the enemies. He screamed and cursed incoherently as they ran into the chaos of the overrun camp. He didn't recall killing anyone but later spent hours cleaning blood from the grooves of the bayonet.

He remembered how at the height of the fight he had heard considerable gunfire, all Mausers, coming from behind the low tents that dotted the plateau. He wondered why he heard no shots returned from their foe. Salvador eventually rejoined his sweating and spent soldiers and called them together in the ruins. Whispers had already begun about the officers' cowardice; some spoke of the Yaqui women and children who had jumped off steep cliffs to their death, while others also quietly hinted at the mass shooting of families. Diego never spoke of this with Melchora or with his comrades, other than brief mentions when deep in his cups. Salvador retold this story again and again, describing his place in front of the valiant troops, so many times that eventually he believed it. Like Diego, though, he never spoke of the march that came next.

When the modern state encounters a resistant historical "remnant," it brings it forcibly into the fold. Those who refuse to become sheep, the authorities label as wolves. The casting out of such inside outsiders pacified international capital that set a particular sort of stability (and homogeneity) as prerequisite for global ties of investment and recognition.[86] The offending population suddenly does not meet official standards for civilization, modernity, or national inclusion and becomes an "Other" and dangerous. The discourses shaped by urban technologically minded elites, that set of peculiar practices and beliefs that constituted "modernity," redefined the rebellious elements of the nation in terms of negative indigeneity, much as they had previously recast the bandit as national nightmare.[87] The management of populations through discourse preceded apparently normal and justified levels of force. This policy required that the Yaquis and Mayas appeared, to popular and official eyes, as outsider threats during a "state of exception." This often-artificial mode of crisis allowed authorities to apply extreme measures and marked a progression from efforts such as providing missionaries and schools to levels of violent oppression and symbolic erasure. Weary of piece-meal efforts, the government now sought the moral and scientific grounds for eradicating the indigenous challenge. Biopolitics, from discursive relabeling to massive bureaucratic policing, gave shape to a new and modern form of governmentality capable of meeting transnational requirements.[88]

The headlines of the late nineteenth-century Mexican and US press made much of "savagery" in their less than objective evaluation of the threat posed by the Yaquis rebelling in Sonora.[89] The campaign of civilization had little in the way of civil behavior. The press dehumanized the Yaquis to sell a narrative to a broad and largely middle-class audience. Initially, for example, Cajeme received favorable attention in US papers, but eventually they painted him and all the Yaquis as less than human.[90] The term "savage" appeared in newspapers and drew on old connotations with legal ramifications that defined "barbarians" versus good natives.[91] Much as with the Argentine gaucho or the Peruvian *montanero*, the dictates of modern society left little room for traditional natives in Mexico.[92] This precedent grew worse in the aftermath of Tomochic and in the context of a fin de siècle global image market. The discourse of savagery justified modernity's excesses and made indigeneity into a category of exclusion and "otherness."[93] With the Yaquis' significant military expertise and in the context of high labor demand, Mexicans added their own term to this discourse by making the Yaquis into "semisavages."[94] This identity permitted the regime a number of possibilities in refashioning its uses for, and relations with, the indigenous of Sonora as potentially becoming "social assets." It also extended, almost naturally, to later uses in the Mayan scenarios, with few differences.

Semisavagery developed in a sense specific to the Yaqui case. Apaches, Comanches, and Navajos retained their fully "savage" label with few exceptions, because the state had not tamed their violence and their peoples had not become useful to the modern nation.[95] In 1885 Bernardo Reyes wrote to President Díaz that the Yaquis and Mayos were "for the most part utilizable but have received much evil from the old government of Sonora." He went on to describe how they had been "kept from obedience to legitimate authority and from the influence of progress for so many years."[96] Other indigenous populations had integrated somewhat into society, as citizens sending children to schools, factories, and barracks, among other things. The Yaquis and Mayos remained more of a quandary. As cultivators of well-used lands, intelligent warriors, and pious (if occasionally heretical) communities, they seemed to have all the hallmarks of civilized Mexico.[97] Similar to the mestizo villagers of Tomochic, they did not overtly represent a completely alien or evil presence to the central government. Their bravery and capacity to resist the federal army gained them a further degree of respect from the broader public. Balbás commended their work ethic, which he claimed as exemplary, if only on "the rare occasion that they made use of it."[98] These peoples clearly did not fall into the "savage" category that endemic northern warfare ascribed to indigenous outsiders. But the respect this earned up to the 1880s did not prevent pogroms in the 1900s.

Those not fully harnessed to the modern national project became enemies by the turn of the century and occupied what has been termed a state of exception.[99] This idea describes a crisis situation where exclusions from the polity entail a strategic goal allowing for the regime to make use of a combination of ceremonial systems and policies (governmentality oriented) that make up power.[100] Populations excluded either by their own choice or by government fiat lost the dubious protections of law and custom that apply to the larger polity. Lives, bodies, and identities became subject to efforts to "fit" them into a system predetermined to leave their essential features out.[101] In the resulting limbo, any resorts to violence against the enemy (broadly conceived) take on the veneer of respectability, or at least of sad necessity. Porfirio Díaz's regime always valued such façades.

The army officially set out to destroy the opposition as rebellion, no longer comfortable in the rhetoric of savage versus civilized. The "savage" element permitted, even necessitated, the harshest of treatment. The "semi" recommended the managed acceptance of the population with optimistic aims. For the Yaquis, this liminal existence had no upside.

Violence in the modern state follows a certain logic and balance. The symbolic mode (à la Bourdieu) finds spaces for relatively free expression under the aegis of national need and natural authority.[102] This sort of violent intercession does not entail physical bodily pain but rather represents an expression of power and powerlessness. For soldiers, some examples included the shaving of recruits' heads, genital inspections, and their mandated spectatorship in execution rituals. The ultimate and most convincing facet of state competence came not in the visible manifestation of power but in these obscured and grudgingly accepted practices. For those outside of state protections, such as "savages" and the like, symbolic violence prefigured physical force. In other words, actual physical violence against bodies represented where state power fell as a last resort, but still fell. Before gaining an on-the-site governmentality, a shared sense of subjectivity based on individual acquiescence to rule, the government had to break bodies. Before breaking bodies, it needed to confine the populace in terms of discursive savagery, and it had to restrain them from escaping beyond the national reach. In both northern and southern insurgencies this proved problematic due to foreign interference.

Many Yaquis first became aware of federal forces' limits as they traveled back and forth across the loosely watched border into Arizona. They found much there to their liking; in particular, they purchased many cheap guns that they brought back to the Sierras to continue the guerrilla war.[103] And yet the US treatment of its own native population extended well beyond mere documentation, and by this time most American Indians faced clear discrimination, marginalization, and worse. Perhaps not a surprise, despite officials' misgivings over sovereignty, the US Department of Commerce and Labor agreed to deport all illegally Yaqui entrants from Arizona and refused to sell them any further arms or ammunition.[104] Decades worth of letters in the foreign relations archive attest to the helplessness of Díaz's government to stop this trade. Constant complaints from Sonoran and federal Mexican officials had eventually born at least some response, but with lack of enforcement it remained a somewhat rhetorical assistance.

The cordon around the First Military Zone had many gaps, but none so evident as the US border. Reciprocal treaties allowed soldiers of each nation to pursue enemies into border territories. Rhetorically this extended biopower or control over bodies beyond the boundaries claimed by nations or imagined on the maps. In reality, occasional clashes between police and soldiers and a relative lack of ongoing banditry had encouraged both sides to give the border zone some space.[105] They likely could not have closed things off in any case.

The border then, as now, spreads long, deserted, and mostly theoretical. Ultimately the controls on Yaquis there, as at home, did little to restrain their movement or autonomy, and so more extreme measures began. A forward-thinking American citizen sent a letter to Mexican officials with his own proposed solution to the ongoing 1907 Yaqui conflict, which he claimed could be resolved if only they purchased a dirigible to track the rebels.[106] Perhaps due to a lack of such zeppelins, the Sonoran government sought to restrain the indigenous with less finesse. Issues with their old adversary in the north supplying Yaqui rebels had a direct counterpart in the southeast with the Mayas.

Díaz had a long contention with his Yucatecan border. An earlier Mayan uprising had sputtered as enough forces moved in 1879 to push the bravos back toward British Honduras. There they rearmed. Numerous letters of complaint, much as those in later diplomatic letters about the Yaquis in Arizona, flowed between the early Porfirian government and the British in current-day Belize.[107] The British diplomats indignantly denied offering any aid to the Mayas. They admitted that some weapons did make it to them but insisted that they came only from smugglers and malcontents, not from any nefarious imperial purposes. Mexican officials had solid evidence, if largely circumstantial, but could not pin the blame on any specific government agents. Henequen and timber interests in the hands of friendly Mayas did appeal to the British, as did the notion of extending their protectorate northward, but the distraught Mexican officials never proved any wrongdoing. Since before the Caste War of the midcentury, government and business representatives in the Yucatán saw smuggling of arms from the British to Mayas as a chief cause of revolt.[108] In 1867 officials discovered a large cache of gunpowder on a ship intended to meet with natives at Bacalar, men the author of one letter referred to as "merciless savages and the scourge of civilized Yucatan."[109] Suspicions against the British supply of arms to "barbarians" continued, and in 1876 an accusation pointed to the presumably anti-Catholic stance of the English as reason for their hostility. Yet if Mexico removed this interference, as one man put it, "Little by little and without noise they [the Mayan Yucatán] will be absorbed into the national territory."[110]

By 1893 the Porfirians had found new diplomatic and discursive space to challenge indigenous insurgencies. Movements to punish dissent became drives to slaughter the unredeemable. Mayas and Yaquis now labeled in terms of savagery and lacking foreign assistance in arms and materiel became finally vulnerable to all modern measures of military force that Mexico could bring to its new auto-conquest.

Modern Solutions to Military Quagmire

The war ended. So at least it seemed to Diego and his comrades in arms as they gathered behind the shattered walls at Mazocoba, where a powerful stench lingered. Their enemy lay in piles attracting vultures, and while some Yaquis had surely escaped, hundreds more kneeled as prisoners under watchful eyes. Troops seized arms and some small supplies of ammunition and shoved the few remaining prisoners into lines. Along the cliff's edge sporadic gunfire presaged the heaving of bodies over the precipice. With a deep sense of unease, Diego helped push captives into line. Elderly or very young, with many women, the enemy filed out with bayonets on all sides. They marched for days and many Yaquis died of heat and exhaustion and wounds. Diego, like most soldiers, never saw a mercy killing but heard from his comrades of many. Salvador saw them but pointedly looked the other way and soon forgot about them. When Melchora and the other soldaderas rejoined the unit along the road to Guaymas, the column continued its slow, grinding march toward a distant coast. The soldiers, she noticed, seemed distant and no one sung in camp those nights. Diego privately wondered at this horrific voyage and who had ordered it. Why were they marching old women and little children, many no older than his own Rodrigo, down a road on which so many would clearly die? He said nothing and with his comrades closed ranks, kept the pace, did not look up. Few of them slept well, but they all blamed the heat. When they left Yaqui children behind, stiff in the ditches, he could not meet Melchora's eyes. In silence and under orders, the detachment moved on one cruel step after another.

One abstract level of dealing with resistance came in the form of the intangible recasting of indigenous peoples' status, but on the ground the staff and army also had to practically occupy territory, disarm rebels, and control the movement of peoples. By 1900 the enemies of colonizing—terrain, climate, illness, warriors, and historical memory—faced a regime with novel capacities. Tomochic, a mere seven years previous, truly represented a different century. Díaz's new tools of colonization, including his army, now set assiduously to the destruction of old enemies of order and progress.

Scientists preceded the army as vanguard for conquest in Sonora. Former federal soldier Cajeme's revolt sparked the first attempts to survey the valley accurately, in 1881, and upon his death the CGE entered in force by 1887.[111] Surveyors came first, as armed reconnaissance in the guise of simple cartographers and land-title experts, albeit with armed military escorts. They learned the overall topography, the hiding spots, the water holes, and the ambush points. They portioned out land that they found underused or vulnerably untitled. Under the Tierras Baldias law of 1885 a great part of lands suddenly fell under national title, despite Yaqui and Mayo claims that these had belonged to their communities since time immemorial, or *batnaaka*.[112] Old cultures clashed with scientific methods.

Occupying spaces and fixing cartography functioned to control the bodies within spaces now seen by the state and set in the record as fact.[113] Such actions offered a professional frame to biopower as it defined the terrain in which officials managed the population. Under the leadership of Colonel Agustín Díaz, surveyors moved through the region with military escorts as part of a strategy of scientific containment aimed at finishing the guerrillas and opening the area for foreign investment.[114] After initial surveys by the CGE, the specially designated Scientific Commission of Sonora arrived to map the valley definitively for railroads and large-scale agriculture. Faced with serious problems of climate and health, the engineers continuously upgraded the new barracks they had established. By the declared end of the first uprising in the late 1880s, military engineers had fully occupied the valley with examples of their trade.

Racial-scientific advances similarly permitted new efforts to control Mayan lands. Engineers and military physicians led the charge to colonize their own nation through science as they encountered hostile peoples and climates and tamed a previously splintered set of patrias chicas. To this effort, medical officers contributed against the infection-ridden climates of the pestiferous tropics, which they felt could be defeated with careful use of racial traits.[115] In other words, they desired specifically garrisons made up of Afro-Mexicans, who enjoyed slightly better immunity to malaria (at the cost of sickle-cell anemia), but since 1824 no official records on race had existed. The African heritage of many who fought for independence, made potent in the person of the second president of the republic, Vicente Guerrero, disappeared on paper. The unhealthy southern frontiers required "disease-resistant" forces to conquer territory on behalf of the nation. The larger project of homogenizing the people beyond racial difference made contortions of language a necessary element of medical discourse in the army. Officers attempted to make race disappear, as they deemed it divisive and non-European (i.e., nonmodern).[116] At the same time, by the 1890s the General Staff commonly assumed the need for soldiers genetically resistant to tropical ailments, particularly those with African or certain indigenous parentage. Army personnel records, rich with biometric details (for example, specific notes on scarring) and

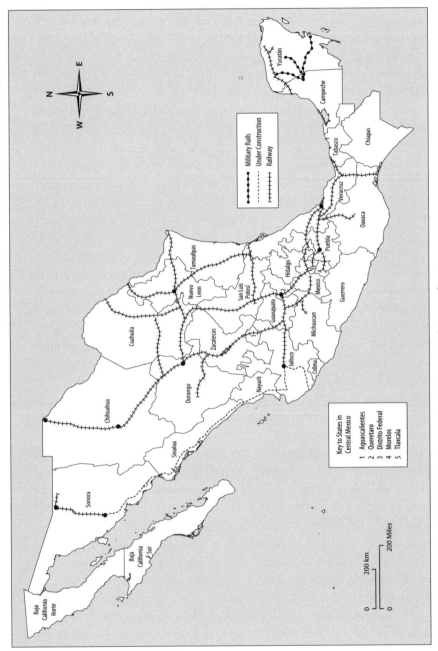

MAP 8.1 Major railways, rail links under construction, and military railways, 1902.

photos, assiduously avoided racial language or descriptions, silencing differences while noting distinctions. Recruits thus processed lost official acknowledgement of any racial identities, which suited the project of making them into national masses (see chapter 2).

Yet this created a problem for officers assigned the task of identifying appropriate men to garrison the Yucatán and Quintana Roo (after 1902) against indigenous uprisings. The author of one article advocated the replacement of colonies by specially selected troops acclimated to a region.[117] Maintaining a force required the identification and gathering of two regiments of what the army now termed "disease-resistant" soldiers in lieu of using racialized terms.[118] In 1906 frazzled officers put together the required units, but resistant did not mean immune, and with losses and discharges it became impossible to provide this garrison permanently. The officers delicately avoided racial language but faced additional challenges in finding men, given the personnel records' limitations. Recruiting from areas with larger Afro-Mexican populations, such as Veracruz, and skimming darker-skinned conscripts from random units simply could not restock the regional regiments, and they disbanded after 1908.[119] This even failed for purpose-created military colonies, and infectious diseases led to the failure of the two Yucatán colonies, which folded before the Revolution. Ordinary troops and their dependents thus faced possible death with every bite or itch. If medics fought diseases without clear victory, science did win important battles in otherwise making development of newly surveyed territory possible.

Various land speculators opportunistically took advantage of any new inroads into areas of the Yaqui Valley or in the Yucatán. In 1880s Sonora, foreign interests and Porfirian development officials followed hard on the heels of the CGE. Fearful natives, or at least cautious ones, retreated to the safety of the Sierras but did not relinquish claims. By 1888 officials redivided *ejido* (communal indigenous lands) lots into 3.04-hectare pieces.[120] Mormons, African Americans, Mennonites, and speculators arrived to settle and improve the vacant farmland.[121] They brought irrigation and new crops to modernize the valley and hoped to use the new railways to export their products to the southern United States. In 1896 Josephite missionaries arrived to bring orthodoxy to the Yaquis and quash pagan rites or folk-Catholic diversions. Development required modern homogeneity, and the indigenous continued to lose their ancestral lands. Officials in 1902 auctioned off some 221,364 hectares more at 6.6 pesos each.[122] An occupation of troubled lands by docile and productive peoples represented the perfect ending, from the government's perspective, of efforts to become modern.

Larger engineering projects drove the recolonizing of the Yaqui River valley in the wake of its forced depopulation and eventual repopulation. The First Military Zone now boasted updated maps and surveys, a railroad connection to the United States, three permanent garrisons with a military hospital, and a major canal and irrigation system.[123] Similarly, efforts to meet the challenges of the Yucatán stretched the expertise of the regimes' agents.

Military survey work in the Yucatán, perhaps more than anywhere else, revealed the martial nature of the engineer's task. New ports, especially at the aptly named Progresso and another near Santa Cruz, allowed yet another important tool of empire, the steamship, to help stitch the nation together.[124] Vast efforts and treasures went into designing, dredging, and protecting new harborages that drew the peninsula closer into the grasp of the central government. Not incidentally, these ports worked to help the army undermine the unwanted influence of Belize in the Mayan regions. The solution to foreign interference, military planners thought, would be the establishment of a guardable buffer zone. This region was populated by trusted pacíficos who harvested timber in a swath of the border region north of Belize and east of the henequen zone and had their own troubled relations with the cruzob to the north. Along the river line the federal army installed guard posts and barge-based weapons platforms intended both to quell smugglers and to deter bravos' raids, although that did not work out completely. Until broader changes came into effect the border remained porous. The subsequent political carving up of the peninsula with the establishment of Quintana Roo in 1902 complemented the 1893 treaties and finally permitted the local authorities of the military territory (the newly minted Tenth Zone) to block smugglers and consolidate power.[125] To these efforts, military engineers added an ambitious road and rail project that would tie together economic zones, and by 1905 they laid bare any potentially dangerous jungle interiors.

The challenges in building this southeastern infrastructure strained the Mexican government's capacities. Frequent letters to the secretary of war detailed problems with materials, lack of tradesmen, shortages of mules and rain suits, and even the troubling escape of some seventeen bulls into the jungle.[126] The letters also, nonetheless, charted the inexorable progress of the routes that crisscrossed the peninsula and the arrival of ever more reinforcements to build further. Porfirian roads, whose routes still exist today, matched the lines of military advance in late nineteenth-century campaigns.

General Pablo Rocha, as secretary of communications and public works, called on Reyes to assist in the building of the Yxtlan highway at military expense so that troops could move from San Marcos to San Blas in only six days. As an added set of benefits, he argued, it would not cost much, since he had so many starving bracero workers available there and thus it would also prevent depopulation. He sweetened his pitch by adding that Reyes would gain recognition and acclaim as the "Man of Progress."[127]

More than any measure, improved transport shackled insurgent regions with military control. The army primarily built its roads along the best paths between strategic goals, for example, connecting Mayan refuges at Chan Santa Cruz and Tulum to garrisoned towns like Valladolid or ports like Xcakek. The road between Progresso-Mérida and Chan Santa Cruz was a necessary umbilicus that connected two major projects while, not accidentally, slicing the region in two. This permitted federal armies swifter movement and better logistics as they sought their elusive enemies. For aggressive officers, especially Huerta, this also facilitated the deployment of small guerrilla-style troops who could rely on roads for resupply in between jungle excursions.[128] Forces under General Bravo also built a defensible set of permanent supply lines from which to scour the countryside. New ports in Xcakek, Progreso, and Cozumel allowed steamship access into local rivers where naval vessels provided fire support and logistics. This increasingly replaced the use of the semifixed barges that the navy had previously relied on to try to prevent river crossings of smugglers and insurgents.

Perhaps most crucial, the construction of a military railway system complemented the usefulness of the existing roads. These rails ran from Chan Santa Cruz (later named Santa Cruz de Bravo in honor of the general) to Peto and later to Vigio Chica.[129] Further rail lines between the coast and Valladolid, and extensions of civilian rails in the north of the peninsula, facilitated the swift movement of federal forces.

Building and maintaining such a network nonetheless proved difficult for Díaz's officers, many of whom spent years in the effort.[130] They saw clearly that the rails worked, yet the army had too few healthy hands to spare any for the grinding labor of laying new track. Local laborers either already worked on henequen or fell under military suspicion as possible rebels. The army turned to the same people thought to be arming their enemies, Belizeans, for a solution. While racial features disappeared from official rhetoric and army records, this prohibition applied only to national subjects, and so the army brought in black foreign laborers less affected by tropical disease and eager for pay. While the government had modernized its population beyond race, field officers found a ready supply of Afro-Belizean men next door whom they could use for the arduous toil of road and rail building.[131] They also brought in some African American workers from the United States, likely New Orleans, and in the case of both groups they needed to provide housing, health care, and education for the children and families of their hired hands.[132] Huerta, ever resourceful, also found his nearly three hundred prisoners of war useful not only for military rail work but also for the drainage of swamps and other hard labor. In the end, the rails successfully tied the region together for the federal forces.[133]

This resulting capacity to move swiftly did not in itself solve insurrection, but other technology also contributed. Wired communications featured heavily in both the Sonoran and Yucatecan campaigns. The military soon realized that despite British denials the arms that appeared in Mayan hands from the south remained an issue. New technology and bureaucratic measures sought to defuse this threat. Telegraphy worked hand in hand with railways to secure centralized power. In Chetumal, the gap across the bay challenged the regime to put in place an innovative wireless telegraph system to secure the area from smugglers who might aid the Mayas.[134] The installation of wireless telegraphy systems in the early years of the twentieth century permitted a defensive posture against the United States in the Sonoran Pacific, but in Quintana Roo the army oriented the system toward its efforts against Mayan rebels. By improving communications in the Bay of Chetumal the army sought to seal off the border and facilitate military deployment. Ultimately the measures do not seem to have improved the radio capacities of the navy before the Revolution, but regular telegraph lines sufficed for the task of finishing off the remnants of the cruzob movement. Segmented by rail and cut off from the sea by telegraph and aggressive naval patrols, the Mayan forces fell back and fell apart.[135]

The colonialist mission in the northwest and in the southeast, the self-conquest, seemed fulfilled—although peace never came easy or completely. Military garrisons continued to occupy key points and enforced the government's will. Postal service began too, and corporations intent on colonizing the territory increased in scale and activity, for example, with the Compañía Colonizadora de la Costa Oriental de Yucatán formed in September 1900.[136] Quintana Roo and Sonora now seemed civilized and secure enough to lure investments. This represented a façade, but a comforting one. Soldiers and residents began to see the uprising in terms not quite so threatening. Land claims burgeoned and the elite families of the regime took their rewards. In Yucatán, Rodolfo Reyes, the son of Bernardo Reyes, obtained 172,224 hectares, and Porfirio Díaz Jr. made a fortune on railroad speculations.[137] Many officers claimed, nonetheless, that the relative peace that made this possible came as a result not of technology so much as from their own efforts to implement updated tactics of counterinsurgency.

More veterans, especially from war against the Yaquis, and a well-disciplined local Twenty-Second Battalion made victory in the Yucatán a much more likely prospect after 1900. Likely not the architect of this success, although he claimed a central role, Victoriano Huerta laid out his ideal solution to make this work. From his many letters to Secretary of War Reyes a picture of modern counterinsurgency emerges.

Huerta's ideal method of counter-Maya warfare focused on swift deployment and ruthless assaults on populations. He proposed to Reyes that he would take four columns off the roads to "destroy all or most of the miserable pueblos." The short campaign, he urged, would be better for morale, would open good lines of communication, and would not waste time with excess soldiers, and he insisted that they deploy all solid veterans, since the mission was crushing the enemy and not training new soldiers. Pared of extraneous gear, they would have only the clothes they wore and leave at home their high chaco hats and huarache sandals. Thus they could move more quickly, and they would not stop, even in heavy rain, in order to deny the enemy any rest. Using the Vigía Chico to Santa Cruz de Chemal rail line, which he wanted guarded by otherwise useless National Guardsmen, Huerta would drive the enemy to their destruction. He also disdained the use of the Geographic Scouting Commission and its maps, which he claimed he did not need because they did not have sufficient accuracy or detail.[138] Instead, he suggested, his forces would move against the last Mayan refuges, whom he believed lay only a few kilometers off the rail lines and roads. In the meantime, he would secure his flanks by arming local dzul ranchers so that they would not be too frightened to guard their own property. With just three detachments, he argued that he could march from Chan Santa Cruz to Tulum, a distance of 150 kilometers, in only forty days and then turn inland to Valladolid and finally on to Puerto Morelos.[139] The plan, if only in general terms, described precisely how federal forces finally managed to end a tumultuous half century of fighting against the Mayas.

The ruthless edge of the army's leadership worked to break the enemy in more traditional ways. Rail and wire could not find the scattered war parties, but brute force had possibilities. Huerta, among others, took hostages and raided family homes in pacified villages. In one case, this meant capturing seven women, two boys, and one wounded man, and immediately they "divided the women among the officers."[140] The officers then used threats and torture to force information from the Mayas. Huerta insisted that after the female prisoners were interrogated, they "offered" to serve as guides to Mayan sanctuaries.[141] The federal forces deployed smaller search groups to hunt out isolated groups, often making coerced locals lead these at their own risk.[142] They employed scout dogs to find Mayan encampments.[143] Their ruthlessness uncovered many of the remaining rebels, and subsequently the army would remove any potential cruzob into exile.[144] When an officer wrote to Reyes that he felt unsure about the policy of exile for Mayan women and children, he was told that he should not worry, as they would become wards of the government. Furthermore, the families would be closely watched, and in any case, all of the officer's men would be receiving medals.[145] Overwhelmed, by 1901 the Mayan forces finally fell back to their last strongholds at Chan Santa Cruz de Chemal and near Tulum. Federal forces moved in. With the advantage of mobility and communication, and with ferocious tactics, the army quelled what remained of Mayan resistance—at least for a time.[146] Efficient tactics solved temporary problems, but long-term strategic goals required permanent solutions.

Genocidal Impulses and State Formation

Diego and Salvador rarely discussed the dead Yaquis they left on the roads from the Sierras. Sniper fire and hand-to-hand combat destroyed sentimental softness in the moment, and only much later would participants question actions that kept appearing in their nightmares. Melchora could tell the men were bothered, in a way, but never pressed her husband for details and simply held him when he had nightmares. The main campaign had ended, and the detachment received new orders to return by rail back to its headquarters in Mexico City. The trip passed uneventfully. They returned, and only a few days later rumors began again. Surely they could not be mobilizing again so soon? Orders came in, and this time the entire unit would sally forth once geared up for deployment. Since Salvador had still not earned any commendation, "This," he thought, "will mean salvation for my career!" Diego and Melchora slowly packed their gear once again, but they at least had survived one round of combat, so . . . the force moved out, the whole of the battalion, and took to the rail yards. Despite their numbers the train still held more spaces; Diego could have sworn he saw some of his former Yaqui captives huddled in another train car and, more amazing, some Yaquis in federal army uniforms packed yet another. The fears of the battalion grew as they realized their destination was the Yucatán—land of deadly Indians and mysterious diseases. They took ship from Veracruz for a very short trip in a more spacious steamer. The Porfirian instrument of order arrived in the port of Progresso and debarked on the piers a few hours north of Mérida. "Progress" fell behind as they marched inland.

So unlike the cool nights and warm days in Mexico City, the Yucatán greeted the battalion with heavy, humid air that seemed suffocating to the newcomers. The horizon closed in and they lost the sky to a dense canopy of leaves. The terrain changed, but the hardships of campaign seemed much the same to the veteran soldiers. Weeks of fighting, mostly moving skirmishes along the marching route and from rail lines, led into weeks of holding ground in strategic garrison points and at crossroads. With few fixed fortifications or army buildings, Melchora with the soldaderas and children followed along and foraged for food and water to keep the army going. She watched as her friends and their families wasted away with fevers and diarrhea, and she checked on Rodrigo constantly. The battalion withered as people died or headed back to the city hospitals, and none of them ever returned. The humid heat made everyone tense and irritable, and there was little laughter or song in camp at night.

Diego almost missed the hot, dry highlands of Sonora. Behind every tree, every bush, he began to see armed enemies or deadly serpents. Exhausted, Diego did not react when one of the captains took local Mayan women into a back room. Their screams made clear why the officer took them, but he just shook his head and kept cleaning his gear. The captain came out and ordered a new patrol of soldiers to prepare with light packs and plenty of ammunition. The woman, and her young sons, led the way as the unit moved into the thick jungle brush and shielded the force from enemy fire as they guided them to an enemy refuge. Diego and his comrades set out on this excursion, just one more of so many, with little excitement. It became commonplace: they burned villages, shot fleeing civilians, and then waited in ambush for Mayas attempting reprisal. Any nonsoldier who approached the railways or camps they shot on sight. More often, they waited in boredom and discomfort for hours and saw nothing but bugs. Had he read a map, Diego would have noted that the army had segmented the peninsula into small, manageable pieces and was inexorably pushing toward the coastline. He only knew how tired he had become, and how he hated this place. Diego realized that he had seen no enemies for some time, but he no longer cared. Resistance fell off.

The killing of rebels in action demonstrated merely the least persuasive of power relations in the toolkit of colonization. Permanent control over acquiescent populations, true governmentality, required measures from the extreme to the insidious. Populations ascribed with labels that dehumanized them in the context of the "state of exception" crisis could, and indeed had to, be excised to cure the national body of its infections.[147] For the good of most citizens, some not-quite-citizens must die. Those deemed to live in conditions of savagery or barbarism represented not the failures of the nation to improve their lot but rather an existential biological threat to the larger organism. They became alien. Survivors of the wars now faced genocide, and survivors of massacres confronted agents of the victorious state who attempted to erase cultural and historical identities, to destroy local loyalties, and to displace populations to areas where they might be better controlled. After massacres came murderous neglect coupled with malevolent bureaucracies. Violence lingered just below the surface of apparently benign measures of control, and power differences became immortalized by the paperwork that cemented a hegemonic apparatus.[148] To demonstrate this we turn first to the war in the north.

In the Sonoran highlands the refurbished military pressed its technological and ideological advantage by 1900. Using improved mapping and more experienced officers, the army seized highpoints and important terrain.[149] The battle at Mazocoba gave proof to this fundamental change. The army claimed the enemy lost some four hundred dead, eight hundred were taken prisoner, and perhaps nine hundred escaped.[150] Others' estimates made clear that a massacre had occurred.

When troops breached the defenses of the Yaquis they did not offer mercy or quarter to many. Machete in hand and bathed in blood, one Yaqui warrior stood alone and stunned in the ruins, and according to Balbás, an enraged soldier crushed his head with a rock.[151] One boy who had hidden from soldiers they summarily shot. Some observers reported that the wounded men, and some women and children, committed mass suicide by throwing themselves off a cliff.[152] This possibility seems unlikely in the context of the event. Some officials later implied that the "savage nature" of the Yaquis had led to their extreme reaction against capture.[153] The free and noble essence of this wild people, officials claimed, apparently overcame reason, and fanaticism drove them to leap. Foreign papers reported nothing of the deaths at all. More convincingly, Yaqui sources spoke of a massacre.[154] It would not be the last such occurrence.[155]

The soldiers who stormed the position did not restrict themselves to killing armed enemies, nor would officers expect them to show restraint. The ley fuga mentality had sunk into the army, and many soldiers assumed they would enjoy a degree of impunity and that officers would reward ruthlessness in action. Balbás's attitude, more progressive than most, still assumed that the indigenous at best could be termed "semisavage"—not quite so irredeemable as the Apaches, but not yet fully human either in the contemporary understanding.[156] In other words, discourses shaped events on a concrete level of practice. Soldiers frustrated by the long, hot campaign, angry and frightened and unrestrained, broke into the stronghold and into hand-to-hand combat. As had happened at the end of sieges since before the fall of Troy, the attackers took out their anger on defenders. Theoreticians describe this sort of reactive and infectious violence in terms of moral holidays (where normal rules are suspended due to high-stress contexts) or as forward panic (where terror and group consciousness lead to excessively violent reaction to a frightening or stressful situation).[157] Hundreds of civilian children and women died that afternoon in fusillades not officially recorded.[158] Officers did not punish or constrain the troops, and if they spoke of the events at all, they stuck to the claim that staunchly Catholic women had taken their children and committed the mortal sins of suicide and murder as they willfully jumped to their death.

Outright massacres and open genocide nevertheless should not be confused with power but rather seen as a symptom of power relations fluctuating in areas the state could not control. The capacity to kill, if practiced, reflects desperation. The objects of violence in this case, dehumanized and dislocated from a society in a "state of exception," lost personhood in the eyes of those who dispatched them in the name of expediency, ideology, and "mercy." The indigenous opposition to the national idea had proven too costly to overcome in normal discursive and political ways.[159] When the elite could not shape the populations' ideas, they sought instead to rid the country of the peoples themselves. In the literal breach, individual soldiers also acted out violence in ways foreign to their normal states of mind and morality. Interpersonal violence is rare, brief, and difficult even for soldiers trained for war. Yet common soldiers did commit atrocities, or permit atrocities, and theories about forward panics or cultural impunity do not fully explain why this was possible. It is plausible that they fought for the man next to them, and if that soldier made questionable decisions, then they spread through the ranks. In the end, the violence might be regretted and mysterious, but it nonetheless happened with official approval.

This likewise took place in Mayan territories as the army raised "the red flag of extermination."[160] Control over the land, taming the terrain, allowed the army to pacify the cruzob populace. The military combined draconian traditional measures with technologies of movement, communication, and sudden violence. The incoming General Ignacio Bravo took much of the credit for renewed successes, although the records leave some doubt as to his actual impact.[161] From his point of view, this conflict transcended mere pacification, and when he wrote to the president he bluntly asserted that the cruzob, as a race, must be extinguished for humanity's sake.[162] Explicit calls for eradication by veterans of Yaqui wars came as an echo of policies long since underway in the north.

When the dust from Mazocoba cleared the president and governor enacted a new policy in Sonora. Federal troops marched the despondent Yaqui captives toward the coast, over fifteen days away. Many did not survive. The road, according to the army, had proven too long for the women and children they shepherded.[163] Few questioned the movement or the migrations, at least in the press, or asked why so many people fell alongside the road. "Savages" or "semisavages" could not always keep up with progress. At the end of the military campaigns, development became the highest priority, and according to General Luis Torres, the way was clear to colonize and populate the area, to take advantage of its great land and climate. He asked the government to expedite rail building in order to connect the state to markets. His unbounded optimism in 1901 laid out Sonora's possibilities for a new era in civilization.[164] Military historian Francisco Troncoso felt that the regime could solve Yaqui insurgency through extermination, deportations, or colonization. While he deemed the first two options too inhumane, the third necessarily awaited an "empty" landscape.[165]

The regime culled many Yaquis in this phase of the military campaign. Eyewitnesses remarked with little credibility on the suicide of many captives at Mazocoba. Many more died on the grueling march out of the Sierras. They fell exhausted, neglected at the roadside by passing troops, and there they died. Corpses littered the route. Some children they shot.[166] When one young child grew increasingly ill and weak, the soldier who had previously carried him knocked his brains out on a rock. Dr. Balbás neither intervened nor helped, although he was only steps away. He wondered in his memoirs whether this had not in fact been a simple act of mercy, but the fact that this incident stuck with him and merited lengthy inclusion suggests that he recognized it as mere brutality.[167] His experience on that long and horrible march seemed to haunt him decades later. Yet another captive attempted to escape by swimming out into the Sea of Cortés, prompting two soldiers to strip down and swim out to retrieve the drowned body. Those Yaquis who survived the trek or had not participated in the war in any way still faced the new measures of control that limited their options.

Between 1897 and 1902 the government largely focused its efforts on managing the remaining captives with ideas and workplaces but began to consider moving the population to better controlled areas.[168] Tentative use of deportation began by 1899 under Bernardo Reyes, who justified the policy as using work in other states to "proportion to them [the Yaquis] a certain well-being, to begin to accustom them to civilized peoples."[169] In 1901 Victoriana Huerta recommended to Reyes the sending of all Yaqui prisoners to work in the Yucatán.[170] Minister of Development Olegario Molino and Minister of War Francisco Z. Mena, both of whom owned henequen plantations in the southeast, saw the Yaqui population as a potentially ideal solution for labor demand.[171] Between 1902 and 1907 some five to eight thousand Yaquis, by a conservative estimate, shipped out of Sonora in shackles and under military guard to work the plantations of the Yucatecan lowlands.[172] Balbás, writing years later, disagreed with this measure since he believed that for the Yaquis mass deportation incurred a powerful "nostalgic consumption" that quickly led to their deaths. This, he felt, represented a tragic waste since a healthy Yaqui, once educated and civilized, would represent a physically and intellectually superior citizen for Mexico.[173] A few returned many years later after a difficult and dangerous trip homeward. Far too many did not get this chance. An unknown number, in fact, the military "disappeared" rather than guard the whole way to the south. A ship in 1906 left port at Guaymas destined for the railhead at Acapulco, some four days away, with some two hundred souls on board. The vessel returned two days later, empty.[174] Disappearing, as military regimes of the twentieth century found, represented one of the ultimate demonstrations of power over populations.

Of course, outright murder robbed the state of important labor resources. Breaking up the population and dispersing them to new regions became the official policy for civilizing the recalcitrant. General Torres wrote to the secretary of war in 1900 that he did not deem it "convenient to leave in this state any warrior Yaqui who surrender," as he had nowhere to keep them, and so he would send them out as conscripts to disparate battalions across the nation.[175] In Bernardo Reyes's reply, he proposed rather to send them all to the Yucatán since he thought it would be too much of a bother to guard and feed prisoners and their families otherwise. Already by 1889, only about a thousand Yaquis remained in the pueblos out of the approximately twelve thousand who had lived there in 1872, and the scattered remnants soon faced genocide through deportation.[176] Governor Rafael Izábal, in particular, became the feared despotic agent of this new policy.[177] The Sonoran elite deemed that the indigenous had finally proven unsalvageable, or at least, were far from being prepared for civilismo (civilized in behavior and belief). By this logic, the Yaquis as a people became an obstacle to modernity and accordingly required excision.

After 1900 this became immanently practical. According to the official military historian of the Yaqui campaigns, Francisco Troncoso, President Díaz and his advisors had declared the idea of mass deportation still completely inappropriate and unworkable in 1902.[178] Nonetheless, it is telling that they already had considered the option and undoubtedly had drafted some plans for its implementation. In the wake of the US campaigns that had been forcing Indian peoples onto reservations since the 1830s, it should not be surprising that Mexico would consider the option. Indeed, one Emilio Kosterlitzky became the chief architect of the military and rural police operations against the Yaquis by 1904 (in a combined unit put together as the Eleventh Battalion).[179] Aside from his colorful personality, Colonel Kosterlitzky contributed a transnational combination of military experience to the enterprise, having served with the US and Russian armies previous to his desertion to Mexico. The "Mad Russian" thus provided his direct experience with suppressing and relocating native tribes to Governor Izábal, and by 1906 the New York Times lauded him as "a terror to evildoers both savage and civilized."[180] The increasingly draconian measures taken by the government, moreover, directly benefited the biggest henequen plantation owners of the Yucatán, including a number of men at high levels of the regime. In this sense, the policy change derived in part from pragmatic desperation, in part from indifferent racism, and in part from capitalist ambition.

The regime's declarations of the Yaqui nature as inherently uncivilized gained momentum as a military strategy as the demands for coerced labor increased. By 1907, efforts by Izábal had achieved the deportation of most of the Yaquis who had not managed to flee the country. The nationwide economy as one interconnected system benefited from the creation of a permanent and dependent underclass of labor that managers could move to meet needs in any area. The regime primarily deported adults as workers, and given the mortality from disease, the Yucatán plantations had continual hunger for more. Children generally stayed behind, given as servants to wealthy families or simply left in camps to fend for themselves.[181] By separating families in this fashion, the regime also undermined the cultural integrity of the Yaquis and further destroyed what it regarded as a problem culture.[182]

The process of the forced migration traumatized Yaqui families with deprivations and a degree of official indifference normally reserved for the mistreatment of army recruits. Two Yaqui women, Chepa Morena and Dominga Ramírez, recounted their remarkably similar memories for the anthropologist Jane Holden Kelley.[183] Both recalled soldiers rounding them up like livestock and allowing them to gather only a few clothes as they left. Chepa, pregnant and carrying an infant son, suffered terrible army-supplied food of watery beans, tasteless bread, a little pozole—but never in sufficient amounts. They endured cramped, unsanitary quarters in cells or billeted near to barracks where their husbands remained prisoners. Perhaps surprisingly, the army gave them about sixty centavos a day for the needs of their families, but Chepa found this barely enough for her and her husband and pitied larger families. Once sufficient prisoners had been gathered, the government agents loaded them in train cars for shipment, in Chepa's words, "stuffed in like goats."[184] By boat, and train, and marching, they made their ways to the center of Mexico, where brokers for the Yucatecan hacendados purchased them outright, again "sold like so many goats."[185] Along the way, Chepa lost her young child to starvation and thirst. Both women arrived finally at henequen holdings and, once there, endured beatings and in the case of Chepa (now in advanced pregnancy), a significant flogging. In the harsh conditions of the plantation, both Chepa and Dominga lost infants to disease.[186] Both had to bury the baby without the comfort of a priest. Such was the reality of the deportation process.

More insidious than Mausers and railways, the modern age offered an ideologically loaded weapon to officials seeking a stable and permanent solution for indigenous resistance. Those who survived the blunt instruments of the armed invasions found themselves increasingly enmeshed in the fetters of bureaucratic regulation and at the mercy of an indifferent and faceless form of state power.

The Bureaucratic Instruments of Power

Salvador's company deployed from camp early, before first light, into an already warming morning. The battalions of the expedition had become quite adept after long months of maneuver, and their columns swiftly sorted out and sallied along their designated routes. Almost all the soldiers now had experience as veterans of the lengthy wars against the indigenous and could do these kinds of sorties without thinking. Despite Salvador's exclamations, as a new cabo Diego felt little confidence that this day's assault on whatever "stronghold" it turned out to be would actually prove to be the conquest that won this frustrating war. He and his fellows recalled all too well that this had been said before when Santa Cruz fell, or later when Bacalar surrendered. Supported by fast-fire artillery and naval gunships, those assaults seized for-tifications already largely abandoned by Mayan fighters suffering from their own epidemics of disease. The soldiers mocked, but the generals always seemed to come out with a record of victory and then move on to politically advantageous positions. The troops, of course, stayed in the jungle. Diego could not remember the last time he had worn the shoes moldering in the bot-tom of his pack.

The military network extended further, but it was difficult for Diego to see this effect when all he faced was more of the same marching and skirmishing and sweating. Disease and exhaustion depleted Mayas and federals alike—Salvador despaired of ever getting all his troops to take the unpleasant quinine tonics that might help them out. This morning the mop-up forces approached yet another stronghold, or so the rumors had it. Artillery cracked overhead, and in the distance sporadic fire from the river echoed. As they neared the site, Diego ordered fixed bayonets. With a shout, they broke from the tree line toward the shattered huts and stonework ahead. Sweat pouring and heart pounding, he crossed the open ground and over a low wall. Nothing waited for them but a few dead cows. By this time in 1905, few Mayas remained in arms. Salvador cursed another wasted morning while Diego and his comrades quietly crossed themselves in thanks.

As events at Bácum and during the Caste War demonstrated, massacres alone had never sufficed to stifle rebellious impulses. The discourses of press and in government correspondence similarly failed to persuade insurgents that they and their communities needed to change and keep up with the national vision. A more consistent, coherent, and visceral demonstration of state power given at a local and personal level worked to weave hegemonic claims of legitimate government into accepted knowledge. Objects upon whom violence and power had acted became subjects shaped by power as the regime made its administration tangible in Sierras and selvas. The invisible power of the state, invested in bureaucratic regulation, created a changed reality in Mexico's newly occupied territories.

The regime not only sought to control its subjects at profound levels in the context of the barracks making soldier-citizens but also extended this to the streets and villages where civilians lived. Thorough internal peace remained an ultimate goal for a military without genuine foreign foes. Framed by theorists as the discursive force of "civilizing" or of "enclosure," the modern government exerted power over its subject populations through institutional weight and by restricting mobility.[187] This constituted one of the crudest modes of biopower, in the form of control over places and bodies' access to them.[188] It was applied en masse, and this represented a shift from obtaining power over people as individuals to a broader sense of allowing a sense of place to define, through the subjectivity of the self within it, those who could exist within. Individuals thus become irrelevant and inconsequential as the mass of bodies, located in space and power relations, becomes the focus object for control and surveillance. Mobility controls offered governments the most certain means by which to channel opposition and rule over the individual.[189] They parted subjects from the support of communities, robbed them of the sense of place, and transformed individuals on basic grounds. Migration and exodus only do so much. Those controlled in one location do not always remain so, unless further measures, modern ones, come into play.

Díaz's regime did not aim at a temporary solution for the Yaqui or the Mayan situation. It sought absolute control, and in the words of Reyes the government needed "to bring the Yaquis under the dominion of the laws," whereby they would lose all autonomy.[190] A clear slate suited the needs of land speculators, state politicians, and scientific progressives alike. Luis Torres, as general of the expeditionary army, wrote to the capital in 1902, stating, "We are disposed to tear out [arrancar] the race [of Yaquis] whatever it may cost us."[191] As governor of Sonora six years later, he threatened remnants of rebellion in 1908 with outright "extermination."[192] By 1909 they employed a former Yaqui leader named Bule to hunt down his former compatriots, and the government also offered a sizable bounty for any rebel captured in arms, ranging between 100 and 500 pesos.[193] Officials like General Bravo had directed similar rhetoric toward the indigenous of the Yucatán. In attaining their goals against both the Yaquis and Mayas officials emulated the well-honed Western techniques of colonial conquest current with imperialists of the day.

The citizen-subject does not carry identification papers for self-benefit but for the government's convenience and for the law enforcer's exercise of power. Many thousands of Yaqui and Mayo captives of war became laborers for the hacendados in the lowlands of Sonora.[194] Some others worked on railways or in towns. In either circumstance, the government required them to stay within the First Military Zone (Sonora, Sinaloa, and Baja California). The military applied its power here through jurisdiction, while civilians managed a bureaucracy that set workers to tasks under an ever-increasing surveillance. The government oversaw the indigenous with new tools, especially making use of documentation to control the captive populace, with passports required for all Yaquis over fifteen years of age.[195] State representatives could stop and force any indigenous person traveling in the First Military Zone to show his or her papers. Those who would not, or could not, faced a number of potential punishments, ranging from fines and beatings to jail time and military service.[196] As collateral damage, many non-Yaqui indigenous peoples in the area also faced arrest and deportation due to official ignorance.[197]

The use of documentation as part of an oppressive surveillance system to control questionable populations had precedence in both national and imperial experiences. A lively historiography on the meanings of colony, empire, power, and surveillance offers some insights into the Yaqui experience of military rule.[198] As global empires did elsewhere, the Mexican government sought through positivist sciences and administration to manage "its" population. New, if primitive, biometrics dehumanized and categorized constructed racial types through photography, phrenology, and papers.[199] Documents remove legitimacy of identity from individual and family to official record. They limit where one may go, at what job one may work. Only the government, properly, could vouch for the individual's genuine claim of who he or she was. The documents made state fantasy into reality. They provided a shortcut to national imagining by insisting on one basic, shared bureaucratic identity. Documents fixed and stabilized individual identity.

The Yaquis and Mayos first, and later the Mayas, were transformed from armed insurgents to documented aliens. Apart and distinct, the required papers set them aside from "normal Mexicans." Doing so made the quality of mexicanidad more, not less, natural seeming. Real citizens need not prove otherwise. It left the indigenous outside of the political whole, "reserved" from the main nation, and implied that during the state of exception their only legitimate place appeared on their papers, subject to federal revision. The step toward isolating and "reservations" had its own rhetorical power and historical precedents.[200]

Documentation offered a compromise to the harsher measures that incited political rivalries in Sonora. Not all in Sinaloa or Sonora agreed with Governor Ramón Corral or his successor Rafael Izábal's convictions about the Yaquis.[201] The governors' caudillo impulses did not thrill many of their constituents. Some Sonorans felt great discomfort with the relegation of long-time neighbors into forced labor. They criticized both the government's excessive harshness and its failures to protect against Yaqui attacks on rails and haciendas.[202] Acceptable solutions to the state's security issues seemed scarce as the iron glove approach failed, but installing a bureaucracy had fewer critics.

Just as in Sonora, the end of open hostilities opened the Mayan regions to stabilizing measures of bureaucratic control. With the practical end of the rebels in force the military set out create a secure region as it envisioned it, thereby extending the campaign into new areas of power relations. It would make the Tenth Zone fit for the progress of global capitalism and administered the area with the same crude touch it brought to the First Military Zone. Villagers fell under scrutiny, and prisoners filled out the labor forces in henequen farms. The nonhenequen side of the peninsula became Quintana Roo, a territory under direct military control intended to suppress the Mayas and keep out the British. The new territory became a military-bureaucratic fiction created to control the enemy within. Under the shelter of a new regional administration came an influx of speculators, investors, and government officials. The dividends of peace lined many pockets, few of them Mayan.

Ultimately, a long and local history of resistance and faith clashed with a national vision. Challenges of race, ethnicity, terrain, disease, beliefs, and memory met with science, technology and violence. Survivors wore permanent discursive labels and bureaucratic leashes. The Mayas and the Yaquis had not, nonetheless, fired their lost shots in this battle for a place in Mexico.

Conclusion

With an aching head Salvador sat in his tent to write yet another of the seemingly endless review reports his superiors demanded from a company commander. His hand shook from what he hoped was hangover and feared might be malaria. His men had been decimated in this damn place and he still had no commendations on his own record. He had feverishly sent countless strongly worded letters to Mexico City hoping for transfer—either his or that of his incompetent fellows—but never earned more than platitudes. He paused a moment in his writing. "Was it three dead or five this month?" He tried hard to remember; at six pesos per month per soldier he could draw this extra pay for his own needs until the next full inspection required honesty. The new cabo (David or Diego or some such) poked his head into the tent:

"Señor Capitán, will you be taking a patrol out this morning?"

"Cabo, how many we lose last month?" said Salvador.

Diego paused. "Twenty-two, sir."

"No, no! Soldiers!"

"Three then, señor," replied Diego.

Salvador scribbled this down with a frown and looked up, surprised, to see the NCO still there. "Take a dozen men," he ordered, "you take them yourself and don't go too far." The cabo saluted and went off to gather his men, musing to himself how this captain must surely be the worst and laziest in the whole battalion.

The squad moved out and patrolled along the edges of the military railway. Dense foliage stretched like a curtain to either side of the path. In truth, the troops all watched for fer-de-lance vipers out on the track sunning themselves more than for Mayan guerrillas by this point in the campaign. The jungle birds fell quiet a moment as a loud crack sounded from the brush ahead. Diego felt confused as he stared up at the sky and tried to catch his breath.

Melchora heard the bad news from a red-eyed soldier a few hours later. When Diego's squad carried his body home to the camp Salvador mentally revised his action report to read "four dead." He couldn't remember the man's name; he would have to ask the cabo later. He bitterly muttered, "This campaign will be where my career dies."

Uprisings against the president, against the nascent nation, represented a reaction against the presumed meanings that underlay the widely shared ideas of what the regime meant when it claimed to be modern and civilized. Scientific knowledge held pride of place over traditional lore, and if secular humanism had little purchase outside of rhetoric, religious orthodoxy at least remained assumed as the only appropriate Catholicism. A rule of law that presumed efficient (if not necessarily just) legal enforcement became the norm for ordinary citizens as banditry faded into legend. So when thousands of indigenous rebels rose to challenge the modern order, they did so in a context in which they may not have realized that their presence came as an existential threat to building a nation. They reasserted a faith loaded with local practices and historical memory as they rejected modernizing impulses that offended a deeply held sense of community and identity. Framing its efforts in terms of race and civilization, the regime reconstructed the recalcitrant with labels including *barbarian, savage,* and *semisavage.* The state then sent in not only armies but also surveyors, missionaries, and scientists. Through crude measures they reestablished a preferred type of order. They exterminated their opponents' cultures. They extinguished land rights. They eradicated populations. The military experience lay at the heart of this process that dragged Mexico into the new century.

Stability marked a precondition for foreign investment and drove the government to establish Mexico as a modernized and orderly place. The formal army's conflicts with indigenous so-called savages dovetailed with a liberal assault on religious communities. The last decades of the century continued the process with significant violence and military action, as outright wars of eradication targeted rebels and natives across the frontiers.

The meaning of citizenship and of "savagery" shifted over the century as the state consolidated and the nascent nation began haltingly to consolidate. It did so within a context of increased globalization where new technologies and ideas from abroad reframed models for prosperity and governance. Díaz's regime built consensus as often through raw force as sensible persuasion. His armed forces proved central to building order, and reproducing it, in the manner the positivists hoped. The army moved against those who saw ancestral lands as inherently "theirs" and soldiers quieted those who insisted on autonomy from Díaz's will. A shift in basic discourse matched with practices as the military moved from castigation to extermination, as Díaz urged his future minister of war to "punish, as examples, those that try to perturb the peace."[203] Resistance became proof of "uncivilized" behavior in the shrill rhetoric of government officials and everyday press. The military brought progress and order at bayonet point and carried out orders as the flag bearer of a modernity deemed broadly as a strategic piece in a larger state-formation project. It attempted to break the obstacles to national unity and centralist hegemony. The efforts of the regime to settle, calm, pacify, exploit, and populate the farthest corners of Mexico represented self-targeting colonialism. Quelling the natives came as part of this drive as the "nation" conquered its own lands for the first time.[204] This took on shades of holy war as elites set the army against religiously motivated populations.

The rebellious Yaquis and Mayos of Sonora and the Mayas of Yucatán had fought against (and sometimes for) the federal government ever since

the Wars of Independence, and their periodic guerrilla wars also connected
to other regional struggles, such as that in Tomochic in 1893. These insurgencies rose from long conflicts within Mexico between unregulated frontiers and central power. The Mayas and Yaquis represented profoundly
religious worldviews embedded in indigenous identity and practices,
enflamed by incursions against land rights. The nonindigenous Tomochic
struggle came in a turning-point year and suggested that ethnic differences
held only relative importance. The modernizing capitalist-driven positivists
found nothing redeemable in the peoples they faced—indeed, to a degree,
the rejection of "old ways" defined modern identity. The insurgencies stood
in the way at a time and in a circumstance where the nation-state demanded
domination over internal opposition. Pseudoscientific racism and liberal
anticlericalism provided discursive ammunition to those seeking control
over populations and justified excessive violence when such seemed appropriate. They made measures of surveillance and bureaucracies appear neu-
tral and impositions of development seem benign.[205] Neocolonialism had
its own logic.

The clash represented what modern meant in terms of biopower and the
capacity to govern populations. Beyond the individual subject, "life" itself
became the object for power relations. Horrifying massacres and open violence marked one end of a continuum of power enacted against resistance,
and on the other end quiet measures of paperwork and racist language made
assumptions into common sense. From this basis the nascent nation formed
in regions previously only weakly held.

The army at war against indigeneity reflected a number of not so coincidental connections and built legacies that echoed long into the new century.
The wars against Yaquis, Mayos, and Mayas did not succeed with totality or
for long. The peoples assaulted held to some customary beliefs and adapted
to modern ways. Inasmuch as the indigenous failed, they did so as a result of
renovated and modernizing national military apparatus. These forces did not
act nicely as civilizing agents—they tortured, they executed, and they acted
in "savage" ways. If the elite failed to overcome the many contradictions
within the national body, it may not have been simply a failure of its apparatus. Rather, the strength of the Mexican people and the depths of community
resources and memories maintained hope in the face of tremendous repression. This lesson also applied to Díaz's soldiers. The auto-conquest shuddered
under the brutality of the imperializing state and its enforcers. Science and
medicine provided the elite one model for bringing nation and citizens into

modernity. Clouds of gunpowder blasted another, apparently easier, pathway toward full national hegemony. This strategy, and its proponents' misdeeds, ignited the approaching Revolution.

"It seemed the whole thing happened, the whole damn war, just to kill my Diego," thought Melchora. She presided at the gravesite of her beloved with sickly Rodrigo at her side. Most of the battalion came, listened solemnly to her simple eulogy, and when prompted confirmed their Christian duty to care for Rodrigo's upbringing as compadres. She felt strange standing in for an absent priest but had come to accept this as the army way. The men and their families shuffled back to camp, packed their gear, and began moving to the rail yard. Díaz's war against the "savages" had concluded, or at least for them. They soon returned home to barracks in the capital. Surely they had not ensured national peace with so fruitless a campaign? It did not feel like victory.

Epilogue

RAVAGED, UNSETTLED, AND BANKRUPT, MEXICO CONFRONTED AN uncertain future when Porfirio Díaz seized power in 1876. Urban and rural criminals worsened the country's reputation and quality of living, and creating an image of stability became a priority in order to restore international credit. Regional power brokers and caudillos undermined the legitimacy of the government, and an uneducated populace felt little loyalty to a still poorly defined nation. The advent of a modern age marked by new technologies and transformative sciences seemed poised to skip Mexico and leave the country dependent and vulnerable. For over three decades, the regime attempted to reconstruct the nation from the center, a task complicated by indigenous and military rebellions. To all of these challenges, Díaz chose to apply his surest tool—a federal army forged for the task. And yet within these ranks violence all too often called into question both the government project and the price that soldiers paid to serve their nation.

Sentenced to death, Second Captain Clodomiro Cota of the Twelfth Battalion reportedly faced his firing squad with cold blood and serenity in early July 1897 at the garrison in Torín, Sonora.[1] Officials had caught him in the act of murder, and he confessed all. It seems that he had gone seeking his superior officer one night in September 1896 with a weapon in hand and had shot Major Luis D. Trens four times. One of the first bullets pierced the victim's gun hand, and the final one hit him in the brain. The charge of murder of a superior officer during an active campaign had aggravating factors, specifically that the major had been effectively disarmed and that the disturbance counted as raising a false alarm in the camp. Additionally, the judges found that the twenty-five-year-old Cota had not drunk enough alcohol for them to consider him in a state of madness, and indeed, he had not even drunk sufficiently to betray a state of nervousness in the premeditation of his act of murder. Cota claimed that he acted in revenge for how the major abused him, including the time Trens slapped him for singing too loudly with a group of civilians Cota had invited into the barracks. The trial record further suggests that previously the two soldiers had dueled to mutual minor injuries but had obviously not resolved their differences. Perhaps most troubling to the military court was that this case "countered the faith that the Señor Trens undoubtedly had, that all officers had, in the loyalty and subordination of their inferiors" and, worse, that after the incapacitating shot to Trens's hand Cota acted without honor, it "being notable and very rare that a Mexican soldier attacks a defenseless enemy." The judges sentenced him to death.

In another instance in the same theater of war, only miles away and in the same months, a soldier named Remegio Gallegos faced his own firing squad.[2] In the Fifth Regiment in Potán, Sonora, a sergeant named Antonio Martínez had ordered Gallegos to harness a mule and when the soldier balked, beat him with several blows of a stick. Shortly after, a corporal asked the soldier where Martínez had gone, and he answered that the man had gone off to "evacuate a necessity" and that it did not matter anyway since Martínez was good for nothing. The corporal sent him off to fetch the sergeant, but Gallegos soon returned without his quarry and in a fresh change of clothing. Suspicious, the regiment's alférez and two more sergeants searched until dawn the next day, and a full search then continued for three more days. When they found Martínez, he lay partially buried at the foot of a mesquite tree. The paper reported that the body was in fearful condition and that vultures had torn open the chest, devoured the entrails, taken the muscles, and removed the eyes from their sockets. Even worse, the body had been half burned in an attempt to destroy the evidence. Despite Gallegos's protests of innocence, investigators found his military hat (kepi) in the grave, tracks exactly matching his shoes led straight to it, and blood stained the soldier's underclothes. He claimed the latter came from previous injuries, but ultimately no one could account for his whereabouts between eleven that night and one in the morning. The judges sentenced him to face the firing squad.

Are these simply tales of crime and justice? Of interclass conflict? Of masculine overreactions? Of tensions in becoming modern, or of military relations, or of random violence? Of sensational press accounts tailored to sell papers to a growing middle class? The story of the soldier's world was that of Mexico entering the twentieth century. The new age arrived with violence, with boredom, with community, and with transformation; lives in the barracks and on campaigns demonstrate a sharper view of Porfirian life. Drinking to excess, escaping barracks walls, knife fights, immodest sex, hunting bandits, and finding lovers—all the adventures of the everyday soldier, and so too the mundane routines of drill, of family, and of parade. The soldier's tale becomes a lens to see into a changing nation in the last decades of the century.

The quotidian experience of military life in the lower ranks reveals the presumptions and failures of broader elite attempts at enacting their own modern and cosmopolitan version of the nation. This work examines the Porfirian military at individual levels and through social and cultural history, including training, recruitment, family, gender, hygiene, and warfare as experienced by junior officers, soldiers, and their families. It looks at the military as a metaphor for the nation more broadly, as it was acted upon by a multiplicity of forces and power relations. Its purpose, to tie together experience with broader processes, connects to notions of nation formation and, generally, with how the personal ties together with the social. The broader sweeps of power, as experienced in daily lives of soldiers and their community, depicted a vision of late nineteenth-century society from atop the barracks wall. There they told a story of power relations, of nation, and of ordinary men and women.

Power relations with citizens changed when nations became "real" and when the elite entered into the global compact of liberal-seeming capitalism. The ability of the state to project change on populations, whether captive or wild, became an uncontrollable current. Transformations came, but none knew where they would lead. This proves nowhere more evident than in examining the military as subject role model, symbolic example, and violent enforcer. Violence itself did not simply mean power but served as a symptom of power relations in an active state. Just as with the "nation," "sexuality," and other abstractions, the military experience was symptomatic of the national pathway into modernity. The soldier's experience incarnated the messy and contradictory nature of an imposed modern system and pointed to disciplinary failures in nation formation.

In some similar senses I hope my reductions and simplifications do not mislead regarding the prevalence of vices within the army ranks. This definitely runs me into the rocks of discretionary balance and source bias. Many of the archival records exist solely for the charting of the missteps, minor crimes, and bad habits of the military men. This made it easy to write their stories as a series of alcohol-driven or marijuana-inspired events happening to thugs, as if this were the normal state of affairs. The soldiers' misdeeds did warrant the trouble of recording and charging and so on. Although interesting, and occasionally correct, this did not represent the everyday. The troops would not have impressed saints, but they also did not fit the stereotypes of an old spaghetti Western. The tenor of this book, especially in chapter 6, might lead a reader to suppose all or most soldiers were drunken, drugged, knife-brandishing brutes. This represents a source issue. Vices did appear in all ranks, and with some frequency. Yet the soldiers and soldaderas who merely lived ordinary lives and avoided trouble, those invisible in written complaints, would represent a vast majority of the military. Nonetheless, I seek fire so I looked for smoke. The minor and major criminal complaints that received press and were recorded in military records have been preserved. These provide insight into the unusual and so, I presume, into what is more normal as well. They are not meant as a slur or a judgment but rather simply as a tool to illuminate the limits of the acceptable.

Additionally, my study could not hope to cover all possible military actors. This work largely limits itself to troops in the central command, mostly between 1880 and 1905, and omits the navy and other specialists. These years struck me as the most significant and reliably chronicled and, I hope, the best in terms of generalizing to broader processes. A further limitation, that this work gives short shrift to senior officers and staff, also invites an explanation. They honestly do enter into this book more often than I would like, as the sources of reforms, as modernizers, and as prosecutors of charges. In my defense, they wrote all the books of literature and politics in the era. They have had their say. Their shade lies over the lives of the barracks I have tried to describe here.

Finally, the inclusion of an unconventionally "fictive" set of narratives frames this work. The stories of Diego, Melchora, and Salvador become at times disjointed, leave things out, and do not clearly fit with the analytical threads I have followed. This is intentional. In building a story line with clean starts, climaxes, and denouements one finds rather soon that even a manufactured reality does not correspond with records. This made an incidental point of its own. Their lives would not conform precisely to my examination, especially of the army at war, where story lines diverged from the objective framework of analysis, and for this I am perversely proud. They took on their own lives. I hope their stories made this work relatable and imbued it with the social historical perspective that sources alluded to but that often eluded my academic voice.

Legacies

This work emerged from over ten years of thought and research during which a shadow loomed large over the topic. How does one write a fair history of an institution that has so often been the antagonist of civil society in the wake of drug wars, ideological conflicts, and human rights abuses? In the immediate aftermath of the Mexican army's self-proclaimed centennial anniversary, it has come under increasing and deserved fire for the ongoing conflagration in Michoacán, where the Ayotzinapa massacre of forty-three student teachers reminds us of a century and more of armed forces' violence and atrocities. There are legacies both positive and negative in the military experience, many rooted in Porfirian efforts, which deserve attention in order to understand where the army and society have arrived today.

The first great heirloom of the military, and one often hidden, was the Porfirian military's role in the Revolution. My intent has been, as far as I might, to avoid playing into teleology and thereby simply discussing the Porfirian military as the reason for, and loser of, the 1910s Revolution. None saw the Revolution coming and none foresaw the military folding (apparently) in such a sudden way. In 1910 none would associate the army with this, and so I too avoided doing so. Yet it is worth a few comments.

Far from the Revolution representing purely a military failure, one could point to some questionably successful demonstrations of the prowess of Porfirian soldiers and their training. Deserters and turncoats in a few limited areas did orchestrate a successful rebellion against an initially larger federal force, due at least in part to finally having the funding and arms that they had fought for when in service. Yet before Díaz's resignation in 1911 the remaining army crushed many rebel forces without much difficulty. Furthermore, officers from the Chapultepec College and European exchanges lent their expertise as much to federals as they did to others, including to Pancho Villa and various revolutionaries. The well-educated officers of the military college did not simply disappear into the maelstrom of the Revolution; while many fought for Díaz, some quite well, many others would turn to his opponent Francisco Madero. After Díaz, nothing illustrated this ambivalence better, perhaps, than the Decena Trágica, which pitted his officer factions against one another in the streets of the capital. Notable Revolutionary officers' writings have appeared throughout this study, including those by Rafael Aponte, Francisco Luis Urquizo, and Rodolfo Casillas, and some like Felipe Ángeles appear as exemplars of the Porfirian army.

In other words, the entire struggle tapped into the developed, modernized military system on all sides. A case in point: when the forces of Villa, absent the advice of Ángeles, faced the educated generalship of Álvaro Obregón at Celaya, the worth of a military college education and training proved evident. In 1915 Villa foolishly charged his cavalry headlong into barbed wire, defensive trenches, and machine guns—manned largely by men trained in Porfirian barracks at some point or another. Equally, one might point to the skilled insurgencies of resurgent Yaqui and Mayan veterans, and how the Porfirian leva had seeded the country with a cadre of a quarter of a million trained former soldiers, which the regime now faced with twenty-five thousand regular troops. The latter fought effectively for half a year, and when the first wave of revolution ended it came as an acknowledgement of a new political economic order—the Ciudad Juárez and El Paso commerce far outweighed strategies to defend the parapets of Chapultepec castle. While it may obviously then stretch a point to claim that political collapse and the prowess of deserters shows the success of the military system, it at least suggests that military skills had spread well beyond the walls of federal barracks. If the federal forces had truly been as fragile as critics claimed, the wars of revolution would have claimed far fewer lives in those terrible years.

Moreover, the old federal military remained a force and made a comeback in 1913 under the hard-edged Victoriano Huerta, at least until foreign invasions and embargoes uprooted his fragile government. And, I would argue, at least some of the old military still reemerged as preeminent in the 1920s as Joaquin Amaro, under US counsel, staked military modernization on Porfirian presumptions and brought home old exiles to resume their ranks in the "reformed" army. Porfirio Díaz's army lost little status in the end and fought well on both sides of the civil wars. The Revolution therefore does not change my general argument. Some soldiers and soldaderas and officers changed sides, many did not, but power relations had already made their marks on their places in the nation. The Porfirian military, sadly for the up to two million people who died in the Revolution, scarcely failed but simply reinvented itself and folded old personnel into the winners' ranks. Many faces in the top and middling ranks remained much the same, and the ill repute of the army followed them into the new era. Another event also adds to doubts about how many Porfirian soldiers continued in service under the Revolutionary government. Reportedly, after the fall of the Díaz regime an unknown number of soldiers and officers raided the military archives, where they altered or destroyed their personnel files. They sanitized their previous service and at times claimed more battle honors.[3] Accordingly, scholars have likely underestimated the continuity of those in army service, to some unknown degree.

A second legacy describes the relative failure of the army as an institution to modernize the country as a whole. Beyond its issues of image, it is dubious that the armed forces were ever a suitable means of constructing a modern nation. The military quite simply proved to be the wrong tool for a complex job, whether in self-colonizing Mexico or in a more contemporary example, for instance in Afghanistan since 2001. Few tools in the soldier's *mochila* backpack sufficed. He could march and look polished, perhaps thereby inspiring patriotism to a predisposed audience. This is a slow process and only marginally helpful, and only then in relatively peaceful environs. On the other hand, he could use brute force of arms. Two options—look good or get bloody. The Porfirian military, as is so often the case, had few protocols to build the nation, and it likely should not have been its task. It directed modernizations poorly, engineered for military purposes, and saw, if one can forgive the cliché, all problems as nails for its hammer. Modernizing asks for a certain subtlety beyond the army's usual methods. Military men could plot artillery coordinates and cartographies but they could rarely find inroads into civilians' hearts and minds. Military reconstructions worked best when they left an area in the hands of allies, but the Porfirians often failed to find such assistance in the scorched ground where the army had marched.

Beyond revolution and nation building, the Porfirians exemplified a particular sense of how Western militaries seized a place in politics seemingly insulated from complaints of its illiberal or antidemocratic nature. This study engages in specific ways the wider history of the Latin American military and the global nineteenth century. The majority of midcentury Latin American nations saw the success of liberal oligarchic regimes' drive for power, eliminating or diminishing conservative or democratic options from competition. With their immediate political troubles under control, regimes began the delayed project of modernizing their military forces with new arms, regulations, training, and tasks. European contractors (especially the Germans of Krupp and the French of Schneider-Kreusot) aided a number of militaries across the region, including those in Argentina, Brazil, Peru,

Chile, El Salvador, and Guatemala. Efforts by the Germans in Mexico fell short of the advisors' expectations, due in part to the difficulty recruits had in learning German marching songs. The Mexican experience had a different trajectory in several ways.

The Latin American process of professionalizing the military never precluded its intervention in politics (as in Brazil in 1889), nor did it always produce uniform success (for example, compare 1870s Argentine victories against indigenous Mapuches to Mexican attempts to control the Mayas). By the last decades of the Porfiriato (1890–1910), significant advances in military sophistication still had not remedied the lack of popular enthusiasm for military service, and recruitment continued to be an issue. Yet an important renovation had occurred almost universally across the region as militaries reformed and centralized power and shared their ideas with the international community. They brought a modern touch to an old politics.

Contrary to perceptions based on formal party politics, the Latin American military and its contemporaries never sat apart from power. Armed forces routinely intervened in politics, especially in the management of new social classes appearing in mines, factories, and cities. All history, as Marx taught, is the history of class struggle, and the New Military History no less. For militaries across the region, these changes meant dealing increasingly with what Brazilian and Chilean politicians called "the social question," or maintaining order against a population becoming urban, industrial, and frighteningly radical. Early in the century, governments exerted brute force to quell labor in its tracks, resulting in massacres in Chile (Valparaiso 1903, Santiago 1905, Antofagasta 1906, Iquique 1907), Mexico (Cananea 1906, Rio Blanco 1907), Argentina (Buenos Aires 1919), and later in Colombia (Santa Marta 1929). A direct result, the army responded to this modern circumstance through efforts to manage labor—it became the fulcrum of balance between the wealthy and new sectors of working-class society and justified its interventions as the its modern mission. Industrialization pressures increased socioeconomic disparity and land tenure issues and, along with other factors, contributed to the unrest turning revolutionary in Mexico (1910) and Brazil (1930), while in Argentina (1930) the Infamous Decade saw the rise of a conservative regime and in Chile (1927) General Carlos Ibañez de Campo seized power for four years.

So in a third legacy, the Porfirian army continued involvement of the military in civilian politics, just as other Latin American militaries had. All of these cases saw the military move into politics either as broker for the middle class or at least acting in its name while claiming apolitical objectivity. Aside from a few brief interludes, Mexico kept generals (whether federal or not) in the presidency from 1824 until 1946. Across the larger nations of the region, demands of new classes by 1900 gave the military a new mission, at least for a time. The army as institution did not sit outside of class struggle as an apolitical spectator, despite its proclamations, but represented an integral piece of restructuring class relationships.[4] The early twentieth century eventually witnessed the demise of many liberal oligarchic regimes, replaced in turn by somewhat more inclusive and popular forms of government. Nonetheless, for a long time military leaders held tightly to their place at the political table.

During the reign of Díaz the nation had extended its hold over parts of Mexico previously unburdened by persistent federal presence. The army enacted a symbolic and physical occupation that represented to civilians what modern Mexico meant, using the persuasive evidence of technology and force. By 1911 a pattern had set in place. The national government, whatever else it might be, became associated with the army and its worst practices, including leva, graft, and brutality. This perception of the oppressive military would only be made worse by the revolutionary excesses of various armies, as all claimed legitimacy and killed freely.

This meant that the modern military retained an ill repute and that many Mexicans (especially rural populations) remembered a shared experience of army oppression and corruption, a memory that continues to shape public opinion.[5] Nor did the army's attempts to provide a basic education or literacy to a broad portion of the male population bear fruit until well into the century, and then more because of general primary schooling than army service. These failures play into an important old historiographic question. Given its geography and wealth of natural resources, why did Mexico not prosper and develop in a manner more like the United States or Canada?[6] A 2005 World Bank study contends that the fundamental determinants that limit the socioeconomic development of a country can be traced to poor education levels and to distrust of public institutions.[7] This research suggests that a fourth legacy of the Porfirian army was that, in setting a modern context for the rising public fear of the military and resignation to widespread governmental corruption, it also did, and would continue to, hinder national prosperity. Had the Revolution changed the basic perceptions of the armed forces, rather than adding to their ill repute in historical memory and myth making, a different trajectory might have been taken. Despite all the credit given the Mexican army for not overthrowing government since Huerta in 1913, it remained an important element in the weaving of political culture throughout the twentieth century.[8] Today, with massacres at Ayotzinapa lingering, the taint of fear and distrust seems entirely rational, if also tragic. Organizational reforms and new missions permitted armies to slip quietly into the political shadows, with their ancient fueros (legal immunities) and general impunity intact.

In this realm the military legacy of Mexico presents stark failures. Systematic and frequent violations of human rights mark an institutional culture in which impunity continues to undermine public trust and breed deep anger. Violent crimes by soldiers against civilians have sadly been the norm throughout Mexican history, appearing in accounts of the Aztecs, during the colonial period, throughout the nineteenth century, and from the Revolution on until today.[9] Brutality, not only unpunished but encouraged, continues. In the wake of revolutionary civil wars, the army turned against Cristero rebels, against fascist groups, and ultimately against any challengers to the regime. For instance, the SEDENA ordered the army in 1971 specifically to "locate, harass, capture, or exterminate gangs" in Guerrero, against an enemy composed of students, teachers, activists, women, children, indigenous, and the elderly.[10] The "Drug Wars" of the twenty-first century have seen ongoing reports of death, rape, and torture: in 2013 alone 1,921 complaints of human rights violations against the armed forces led to a mere eight trials, and those in military courts rather than civilian.[11] In 2014 the massacre of twenty-two people in Tlatlaya not only has escaped convictions, but the military has been accused of torturing witnesses (at the urging of officials) in order to compel them to change their testimony and to cover the murderers' tracks.[12] Public faith reaches new lows.

This all connects back in some ways to Porfirio Díaz's army and its missed opportunities. The old warhorses, at the top of government and military, enacted few reforms that might undermine their glorious army. Young officers, overwhelmed by their duties, did not instill changes to military culture. Conscripted soldiers did not have any means to challenge their orders, even if it occurred to them. Military courts and jurists found themselves working against a constant backlog and unable to step back and reflect on reforms that might have been good for the nation and army alike. Ultimately, for all of the Porfirian efforts to reorganize and retrain the army, little shifted in the crucial area of setting permanent limits to military self-rule or jurisdictional autonomy. As a result, the framers of the revolutionary 1917 Constitution enshrined in Article 13 an incredibly hazy definition of military jurisdiction for crimes—any "failure to abide by military discipline"—and it passed without subsequent amendments.[13] For the army, this represented safety from civil interference, since virtually any violence or criminal action would naturally be deemed a disciplinary issue. This resonated with Porfirian remnants and veterans and seemed normal enough to the new insurgent elite. It represents a lost chance and a choice that continues to draw criticism from outside observers, including the Inter-American Court and Amnesty International. Impunity remained the sacred right of soldiers, brutality followed, and public intimidation has continued. The modernizing army failed to reform in this critical area and has never, therefore, truly become the "servant of the nation."

Final Thoughts

This study has followed and explored the lives of those in the Mexican military's lowest ranks from barracks to war. Their experiences as individuals and as part of an institution describe a relatively unknown but common facet of Porfirian Mexico in a time of accelerating social and technological change as well as increasing enmeshment into a global capitalist system. The barracks provided the regime, if at times inadvertently, a laboratory in which to construct an ideal type of modern citizen and subject. These attempts spilled over into the lives of the women of the troops, and their offspring, and demanded a great deal of young and inexperienced junior officers. Many times the experiment failed. At times the subjects burned down the laboratory. Much more significant than the regime's fantasy, the barracks community reveals the way that ordinary people resisted and ignored prescriptions and reenvisioned how to live in a modern nation all on their own. While Díaz and his advisors shared Elysian dreams of Parisian boulevards, the "servants of the nation" ate atole, drank pulque, and wore huaraches. They held to their religion, they married without priests, they fought over honor, and they rejected the seemingly arbitrary boundaries that army or society set upon them. At the same time, when the time came, the military and its adherents successfully battled banditry and quashed insurgency across the countryside. Their world, I have tried to show, had more depth, nuance, and meaning than history has credited them.

The Porfirian military found that it could not, in the end, inculcate the precise nationalism that it sought. While officers intended that military service would make raw recruits into men filled with patriotic fervor, instead most troops evinced a grand disinterest and hostile resentment. The critical problem, already visible in the colonial period, was that impressment and poor training, coupled with societal disdain, left the soldier with little incentive to become the kind of man that the modern army demanded. Rather, in the face of emasculating or infantilizing treatment by superiors, he too often opted to act in the ways men of his class had been expected to do since colonial times—drinking, fighting, and visiting prostitutes. Furthermore, there was no discontinuity between home and barracks life in terms of gender, which might have encouraged soldiers to become disciplined and less resistant to authority. Instead, women, the soldaderas, lived in barracks and shuffled on the march, and in their presence soldiers continued in a performance of gender learned in the home. Finally, the continuing presence of civic militias with colonial roots, and weakness of federal forces, meant that there existed no universal male experience of levée en masse to inculcate modern nationalism. It did not fail entirely.

Did the army actually transform soldiers? Whereas many communities resented and rejected the leva, the hatred it inspired and instilled did not reflect in the soldiers' attitudes. Young men forced into hardships sought relief, but more than a few also found great pride in their new careers. Despite crudeness of method many did come to feel exceptional or at least noncivilian in a genuine way. The soldaderas, too, when their men died or deserted, often remained in the army by choice. It seems that on some quite real and important levels a military identity had been successfully inculcated. Many recalled ritual exercises fondly as stirring moments of emotional connection. They became basically different from those who had not served and kept a sense of difference their whole life. They did not fit in when they returned to small-town life, and perhaps knowing this, many men reenlisted. To be sure, some of those did so for lack of other options, or as a substitution for criminal punishments, and yet not all. Hatred of recruitment and public suspicions of the army did not necessarily fill soldiers with depression. Once enlisted, many made it a home. In this much, the military experiment succeeded at remolding peasant into soldier or soldadera. If the army's intended battlefield skills, or troops' discipline, or general barracks hygiene, did not meet high standards, than a likely culprit can be found in budgets. Few resources for training, little to entertain troops, ancient and decrepit facilities, miserly and missing pay all made real reforms unlikely or haphazard. Díaz got what he paid for: an army of paper tigers suitable for repressing labor unrest or native insurgencies. They strutted well and showed few qualms in applying ley fuga justice. When he needed more, a counterrevolutionary elite force, he soon found himself on the *Ypiranga* steamship bound for France. Modern soldiers outlasted the old guard.

The army represented one of the great engines for transforming inhabitants into citizens. It could, in the right circumstances, add a particular value to its membership. Service lent pride and reshaped identities. Those taken into the service of arms changed. How this met with the reconfigurations of the nation in an era of accelerated technological and social changes has dominated this work. This highly gendered process acted to, in the words of some, "make men of them" and helped to create a modern sense of patriarchy within the nation-state and its version of mexicanidad.

I prefer to end on a different note. At heart, these protagonists represented men of war and not merely an abstract social engineering experiment. For many thousands of young men, their families, and their communities, the experiences of Porfirian army service determined their entrance into modernity and their reference point to the nation. At the heart of elite projects of colonizing or modernizing rested a human element, making individual understandings and adaptations to a changing world all around them. It is my sincere hope that this study has given due credit to the people and times examined. It was their lives, hopes, and struggles that built the modern nation. When called on, they rode out from barracks, they fought for Mexico, and many knew they would not all return from battle.[14]

Con horrido estruendo	With a horrid roar
Sonando los sables	Ringing of sabers
Golpeando los cascos	Striking of helmets
El suelo, al trotar,	The ground, at the trot,
Alzadas las bridas,	Raised bridles,
Cubierto de polvo	Covered in dust
Pasó el regimiento	The regiment passed
Como un huracán.	Like a hurricane.
Se van á la guerra	They go to war
Ya no volverán!	They will not return!

Notes

Abbreviations Used in the Notes

AGN	Archivo General de la Nación
AGN, CMDF	Archivo General de la Nación, Fondo Guerra y Marina, Comandancia Militar de DF
AGN, CMDF, EP	Archivo General de la Nación, Fondo Guerra y Marina, Comandancia Militar de DF, Expedientes Personales
AGN, FgyM	Archivo General de la Nación, Fondo Guerra y Marina
BAHDF	Biblioteca del Archivo Histórico del Distrito Federal, Mexico City
BR	Bernardo Reyes
CDX	Condumex/Carso
CPD	Universidad Iberoamericana, Colección Porfirio Díaz
Memorias	*Memorias de Secretaría de Guerra y Marina* (1876–1910)
PD	Porfirio Díaz
PHO	Instituto Mora, INAH Proyecto de Historia Oral
SER	Secretaría de Relaciones Exteriores

Introduction

1. Janvier, "Mexican Army," 818.
2. For instance, see James Kelley, "Professionalism"; Alexius, "Army and Politics"; Bazant de Saldaña et al., *La evolución de la educación militar*; Hernández Chávez, "Origen y ocaso del ejercito porfiriano."
3. This impulse ranged in manifestations from the microphysics of power (controlling things such as diet, dress, language, housing, and so on) to the broad application of biopower (managing populations, ways of living, modes of thinking), and these implications drove much of the writings of Michel Foucault, whose work closely influenced my analysis.
4. McNamara, *Sons of the Sierra*; Mallon, *Peasant and Nation*; Vaughan, *Cultural Politics in Revolution*.
5. Foote and Horst, *Military Struggles and Identity Formation*, 1–4; McNamara, *Sons of the Sierra*, 2–11, 12,13, 205, 20–21.
6. Centeno, *Blood and Debt*.

7. Archer, *Birth of Modern Mexico*; Manuel Chust, "Armed Citizens: The Civic Militia in the Origins of the Mexican Nation State, 1812–1827,"in Rodríguez O., *Divine Charter*, 235–54.

8. Rodríguez O., *Divine Charter*; Tenenbaum, *Politics of Penury*; Stevens, *Origins of Instability*; Costeloe, *Central Republic in Mexico*; Santoni, *Mexicans at Arms*; Josefina Vázquez, "War and Peace with the United States," in Meyer and Beezley, *Oxford History of Mexico*, 339–69; Santa Cruz, *Armies, Politics, Revolutions*.

9. Stephen Neufeld, "The Mexican Military and National Change, 1821–1920," in Beezley, *Companion to Mexican History*, 390–404; Arrom, "Popular Politics."

10. Rodríguez O., *Down from Colonialism*; DePalo, *Mexican National Army*.

11. See, for example, Levinson, *Wars within Wars*.

12. Hale, *Transformation of Liberalism*.

13. Beezley and Lorey, *¡Viva Mexico!*

14. Centeno, *Blood and Debt*, 146, 148.

15. Camp, *Generals in the Palacio*; see also Rath, *Myths of Demilitarization*.

16. Vanderwood, *Disorder and Progress*.

17. G. Thompson, "Bulwarks of National Liberalism"; Lloyd, *Porfirio Díaz frente al descontento*.

18. McNamara, *Sons of the Sierra*.

19. On the Porfiriato generally, see Garner, *Porfirio Díaz*; Cosío Villegas et al., *Historia moderna de México*.

20. Cota Soto, *Historia militar de México*, 87–90.

21. See Alonso, *Thread of Blood*; Hu-DeHart, *Yaqui Resistance and Survival*.

22. Archivo General de la Nación, sección Gobernación, Rurales; also see chapter 7, note 81.

23. The book describes, through various approaches, the broader functions of power systems as conceived in systems of knowledge (connaissance) and as the regime sought to control its subjects' ways of living (as biopolitics and governmentality). The fissures in this experience reflect how halting and contradictory power relations can be in the context of an imperfectly capable state, where hegemony fell short in part due to flawed fundamental building blocks.

24. Lieuwen, *Arms and Politics*; and Lieuwen, *Mexican Militarism*. Lieuwen, previously funded by the US Department of Defense, sought to explain, and perhaps prescribe, the causes of military interventions in politics. His studies became even more important as scholars tried to understand stabilizing influences in the region in the wake of the Cuban Revolution (1959). As he supervised thirty-five graduate students over the course of his career, numerous dissertations came out that looked to the roots of military professionalism in the early twentieth century across Latin America (among them: José Ferrer, "The Armed Forces in Argentina Politics"; and Allen Gerlach, "Civil-Military Relations in Peru"; as well as publications by Winfield Burggraaf on Venezuela, Michael Meyer on Mexico's General Huerta, Robert Potash on Argentina, and Frederic Nunn on Chile). Among other works, see Nunn, *Time of the Generals*; Loveman and Davies, *Politics of Antipolitics*; Loveman, *For the Patria*; Pion-Berlin, *Civil-Military Relations*; also see L. Rodríguez, *Rank and Privilege*.

25. "Introdução," in Castro, Izecksohn, and Kraay, *Nova história militar brasileira*; Morgan, "Revolt of the Lash"; Kraay, "Reconsidering Recruitment"; Beattie, *Tribute of Blood*. John Keegan is also considered by some to be a New Military Historian; see Keegan and Holmes, *Soldiers*.

26. For example, see Pion-Berlin, *Civil-Military Relations*, 1–35.

27. B. Anderson, *Imagined Communities*.

28. Brading, *Los orígenes del nacionalismo mexicano*.

29. Beezley, *Mexican National Identity*.

30. Anna, *Forging Mexico*; French, "Imagining"; Xavier-Guerra and Quijada, *Imaginar la nación*.

31. Castro-Klarén and Chasteen, *Beyond Imagined Communities*.

32. Foucault, *Discipline and Punish*.

33. See, for Latin America generally, Centeno, *Blood and Debt*; for France, the classic is Weber, *Peasants into Frenchmen*.

34. Centeno, *Blood and Debt*, 29.

35. The term Juan Soldado, or John Soldier, represents a generic type, as G.I. Joe did in the United States.

36. Weber, *Peasants into Frenchmen*, 298.

37. See Barman, *Brazil*.

38. Snyder, *Citizen Soldiers and Manly Warriors*, 15–16; G. Thompson, "Bulwarks of National Liberalism"; Stephen Neufeld, "Behaving Badly in Mexico City: Discipline and Identity in the Presidential Guards, 1900–1911," in Rugeley and Fallow, *Forced Marches*; Cañeque, "Theater of Power."

39. Savage, *Standing Soldiers, Kneeling Slaves*; Beattie, *Tribute of Blood*; Mosse, *Image of Man*.

40. Meaning Afro-Mexican, part African, indigenous, or half African. See Vinson, *Bearing Arms for His Majesty*; Young, *Minorities and the Military*, 19, 27–28; Wickham-Crowley and Kraay, *I Die with My Country*; Beattie, *Tribute of Blood*.

41. Snyder, *Citizen Soldiers and Manly Warriors*, 52, 55.

42. Weber, *Peasants into Frenchmen*, 297, 292, 302.

43. Paz, *A dónde debemos llegar*, 18–19.

44. Unlike in other places and times, Mexican recruits rarely brought family along with them. For contrast, see Stavig, *World of Tupac Amaru*.

45. Alexius, "Army and Politics," 34; on transvestites, see Irwin, McCaughan, and Nasser, *Famous 41*.

46. Alexius, "Army and Politics," 68.

47. Vanderwood, *Disorder and Progress*.

48. French, *Peaceful and Working People*; and Robert M. Buffington and William E. French, "The Culture of Modernity," in Meyer and Beezley, *Oxford History of Mexico*.

49. Gellner, *Nations and Nationalism*.

50. Centeno, *Blood and Debt*, 163–66, 168–72, 241, 235, 257.

51. See a similar argument in Tenorio-Trillo, *Mexico at the World's Fairs*.

52. See Gramsci, Hoare, and Nowell-Smith, *Selections*.

53. William Roseberry, "Hegemony and the Language of Contention," in Joseph and Nugent, *Everyday Forms of State Formation*, 355–66.

54. Like *nation*, *modernity* can be a slippery term, often rendered insensible in confusions with stylistic modernism and technological modernization. The definition of modernity here asserts that, first, modernity as an idea is an inclusive process, saturating daily life and forming historical consciousness, and second, that it is a polysemic, indeterminate, and often-ambivalent manifestation of a cultural consciousness. It is not always evident at the time it emerges and it is often rife with contradictions, yet it still becomes a common refrain among all parts of society. Additionally, modernity comprises both discourse and practices and invents both the modern and the traditional at the same time and in a specific context. Real life, the phenomenological, happens between these rhetorical bookends. Felski, *Gender of Modernity*, 9; Giddens and Pierson, *Conversations with Anthony Giddens*, 90–94; Hall, *Modernity*, 1–18; Berman, *All That Is Solid Melts into Air*, 15–16; Jervis, *Transgressing the Modern*.

55. Scott, *Weapons of the Weak*; and Scott, *Domination and the Arts of Resistance*, ix–16.

56. Tenorio-Trillo, *Mexico at the World's Fairs*, 158–80.

57. Schama, *Dead Certainties*, 325; others supportive of this idea include Karen Halttunnen, "The Challenges of Narrativity," in Bonnel and Hunt, *Beyond the Cultural Turn*, 165–80; and Ginzburg, "Proofs and Possibilities," in *Threads and Traces*, 54–71. For two examples of other histories making use of this conceit, see Wunderli, *Peasant Fires*; and Sullivan, *Xuxub Must Die*.

58. On this fine line, see White, "Introduction," 153.

59. Frías, *Battle of Tomochic*; Urquizo, *De la vida militar mexicana*; and especially Urquizo, *Tropa vieja*, as well as various other short stories and memoirs, including Urquizo, *Memorias de campaña*; Urquizo, *Fui soldado*; Aponte, *Empirismos*.

60. Quite inadvertently, this work also follows and demonstrates the trajectory of Michel Foucault's career writing on power relations. His vision of how society encounters fields of power, augmented with the works of thinkers like Michel de Certeau, Pierre Bourdieu, and Giorgio Agamben, fits within the arc of this book. I would love to claim some particular strategy in this, but it occurred accidentally, or perhaps simply as a structural quirk that happens when you examine identity and power in a modernizing institution. The first two chapters, on recruitment and training, discuss the efforts of the regime to shape soldiers as subjects or objects through articulated discourses and visible disciplines, with the aim of creating what Foucault called "le militaire." Chapter 3 offers an expansion on this as it examines disciplinary biopower applied against gender and family in the figure of the soldadera women among the troops. Chapter 4 likewise examines institutional means of power in the education of the young officer. Chapters 5–7 begin to move beyond discipline over the individual to address the broader sense of power as knowledge systems, the *connaissance*, as agents working for the state sought to control bodies through hygiene, race, and criminology. The final chapter moves definitively into the late stages of Foucault's philosophies on biopolitics and governmentality, the control over large populations based on subjective "life" itself. This thought also ties back to the first chapter and the discussion of community politics of recruitment and resistance to the idea of the military life. This represents how the processes of power intertwined and had a

continuity of scope and scale. No one manifestation of power worked without the others; Foucault, *Security, Territory, Population*; Foucault *Birth of Biopolitics*; Burchell, Gordon, and Miller, *Foucault, Effect*; Deleuze, *Foucault*; Foucault, *History of Sexuality*; de Certeau, *Practice of Everyday Life*; Agamben, *State of Exception*; and an update in Agamben, *Kingdom and Glory*; Bourdieu, *Outline of a Theory*.

Chapter One

1. I take my cues from the New Military History; see Beattie, *Tribute of Blood*; and Castro, Izecksohn, and Kraay, *Nova história militar brasileira*.

2. On imagining and nationalism theory, see Xavier-Guerra and Quijada, *Imaginar la nación*; B. Anderson, *Imagined Communities*; Castro-Klarén and Chasteen, *Beyond Imagined Communities*; and Hobsbawm, *Nations and Nationalism*.

3. The leva took citizens by force into service in arms for five years minimum. It differs from a draft or conscription in that it was selective, arbitrary, and unconstitutional. It included elements of recruitment, in that some did willingly enlist. Here I use the terms *recruit* and *conscript* interchangeably, even though the press-gang nature of this service suggests that other terms might also apply, like *impressee*. The system was at times both arbitrary and bureaucratically impersonal. See also Beattie, *Tribute of Blood*, xx–xxi.

4. Foucault, *Discipline and Punish*, 143–44, 298–99; Foucault, "Spaces, Knowledge, and Power," in Rabinow, *Foucault Reader*, 243. These also specifically affect the army, which Foucault defines as a technique of power over social bodies (collectively) in the form of the "militaire"; see Foucault, *Discipline and Punish*, 179–86.

5. James Kelley, "Professionalism," 14–38; Alexius, "Army and Politics," 8–67.

6. Frazer, *Bandit Nation*.

7. Garner, *Porfirio Díaz*, 56–65.

8. Fowler, *Forceful Negotiations*, esp. chapters 11 and 12.

9. A wide literature on this suggests that some liberals did see a role in politics for the lower classes, albeit often limited in practice. For a discussion, see Knight, "El liberalismo mexicano."

10. James Kelley, "Professionalism," 137; despite impressive progress, the number of geriatric officers continued to be far beyond feasible or sustainable.

11. Luís González y González, "El liberalismo triunfante," in Cosío Villegas et al., *Historia general de México*, 1:635–705.

12. See Alonso, *Thread of Blood*; Delay, *War of a Thousand Deserts*.

13. See chapters by Rugeley, Haworth, and Smith in Rugeley and Fallaw, *Forced Marches*.

14. On the evolving National Guard, see Manuel Chust, "Armed Citizens: The Civic Militia in the Origins of the Mexican National State, 1812–1827," in Rodríguez O., *Divine Charter*, 235–55; Santoni, "Fear of the People"; and, during the Porfiriato, Garner, *Porfirio Díaz*, 55–58.

15. McNamara, *Sons of the Sierra*, 93–121.

16. James Kelley, "Professionalism," 40; also in Garner, *Porfirio Díaz*, 110–15.

17. Díaz's and his generals' attitudes are seen in Gen. G. Palomino to PD, 1/22/89, CPD, Legajo 14, Caja 2, Doc. 598.
18. Chuchiak, "Indigenous Sentries and Indios Flecheros"; on regular forces' numbers at Independence, see von Humboldt, *Ensayo politico*, 554–57.
19. Cosío Villegas, *United States versus Porfirio Díaz*, 146.
20. Ibid., 209, 214, 215.
21. On the early lack of budget, see *Memorias de Secretaría de Guerra y Marina* (1876–1910) (hereafter *Memorias*); and Archivo General de la Nación, Fondo Guerra y Marina, Comandancia Militar de DF, Expedientes Personales (hereafter AGN, CMDF, EP), various expedientes (1867–1880).
22. Hernández Chávez, "Origen y ocaso del ejército porfiriano," gives low figures supported by Alexius, "Army and Politics," 20; higher press figures included Porfirio Díaz's in the *New York Times* (June 13, 1881, sec. 3, 3); and the *Memorias'* yearly totals and detachment reports, which tended to be high.
23. Ward Stavig, "Conflict, Violence, and Resistance" in Hoberman and Socolow, *Countryside in Colonial Latin America*, 222–28; and Archer, *Army in Bourbon Mexico*.
24. See Lopez, "Cadaverous City."
25. Lear, *Workers, Neighbors, and Citizens*, 13–86.
26. Foucault, *Discipline and Punish*, 135–70; Buffington, *Criminal and Citizen*, 32–37; Xavier-Guerra, *Le Mexique*, 212–22, 312–16.
27. "La esclavitud en Yucatán," *Regeneración*, January 31, 1901, 4, refers to the soldiers as proletariat.
28. On Cananea and Rio Blanco, see James Kelley, "Professionalism," 83, 84; Koth, *Waking the Dictator*, 1–40; also see "Los sucesos de Rio Blanco," *El Imparcial*, January 10, 1907, 1.
29. For example, *Memorias*, 1902, Anexo 23, Bernardo Reyes, July 1–June 30, 1901–2; and Anexo 24, July–December 1902. This was not without exception, particularly when they captured skilled Maya or Yaqui warriors; see chapter 8.
30. On similar processes in Brazil, see Beattie, *Tribute of Blood*, 99–122.
31. On deportations, see Hu-DeHart, *Yaqui Resistance and Survival*, 134–35, 165–70; Troncoso and Ministerio de Guerra y Marina, *Las guerras con las tribus Yaqui*.
32. Universidad Veracruzana, *Memorias e informes*, 15.
33. "Estadístico de reconocimiento de reemplazos," *Gaceta Médico Militar*, 1889, 123–25.
34. G. García to PD, May 6, 1887, CPD, Legajo 12, Caja 11, Doc. 5102.
35. AGN, CMDF, Caja 360, Florentín Morín and Lázaro Mendoza.
36. On the politics of recruitment, see Beattie, *Tribute of Blood*, 81–151; Alexius, "Army and Politics," chapter 2.
37. Paz, *A dónde debemos llegar*, esp. 74, 75.
38. Vázquez Gómez, cited in Ibid., 76.
39. For example, this was the opinion of Paz in *A dónde debemos llegar*, 31, 32; and of the Flores Magón brothers in "Más sobre bizarría militar," *Regeneración*, May 7, 1901, 15, 16.
40. French, "Prostitutes and Guardian Angels."

41. José Almeida Alderete, interview by Ximena Sepulveda, October 30, 1973, Instituto Mora, INAH Proyecto de Historia Oral (hereafter PHO), 1/27, 5.

42. French, "*Te amo muncho*"; Alonso, "Love, Sex and Gender," 1–10; and Kathryn Sloan, "Runaway Daughters: Women's Masculine Roles in Elopement Cases in 19th-Century Mexico," in Macías-González and Rubenstein, *Masculinity and Sexuality*, 53–78.

43. Altimirano, *El Zarco.*

44. Kathryn Sloan, "Runaway Daughters: Women's Masculine Roles in Elopement Cases in 19th-Century Mexico," in Macías-González and Rubenstein, *Masculinity and Sexuality*, 54–58.

45. Léon Martínez to PD, September 28, 1880, CPD, Legajo 5, Caja 7, Doc. 003464.

46. Pedro A. Ehlera to PD, January 26, 1885, CPD, Legajo 10, Caja 3, Doc. 1445.

47. AGN, Caja 359, Ep-M, Antonio Vásquez.

48. Miguel Jiménez to PD, November 2, 1891, CPD, Legajo 16, Caja 29, Doc. 14130.

49. Poverty inspired some: Andrés Frías to PD, August 18, 1880, CPD, Legajo 5, Caja 4, Doc. 1595; Enrique Mayer to PD, July 21, 1880, CPD, Legajo 5, Caja 5, Doc. 2223; I. Gómez Cárdenas to PD, March 18, 1885, CPD, Legajo 10, Caja 6, Doc. 2630.

50. Arcadio Ramírez to Pedro Hinojosa, November 30, 1885, CPD, Legajo 10, Caja 25, Doc. 12118-a.

51. AGN, CMDF, Caja 358, Capt. 1 Marcial Madero.

52. Pedro Galván to PD, September 1, 1885, CPD, Legajo 13, Caja 4, Doc. 1917.

53. Pablo Pantoja to PD, July 6, 1889, CPD, Legajo 14, Caja 15, Doc. 7371.

54. Pablo Pantoja to PD, August 2, 1889, CPD, Legajo 14, Caja 18, Doc. 8591.

55. Trinidad Vega interview, PHO 1/26; also mentioned in PHO 4/15.

56. Tnt. Crl. Ignacio Súarez, interview by Alexis Arroyo Daniel Casas, January 1961, PHO 1/85.

57. *El Partido Libertad*, July 21, 1887, 3, 4.

58. "El batallón 24," *La Patria*, March 23, 1884, 5.

59. "Bizarría militar," *Regeneración*, April 23, 1901, 12, 13; and "Más sobre bizarría militar," *Regeneración*, May 7, 1901, 15, 16.

60. On press readership, see Díaz, "Satiric Penny Press"; Ramos, *Divergent Modernities*, 78–150. Among many, many more examples, see "A los militares," *El Combate*, May 9, 1879; "En gran escandolo," *El Nacional*, September 25, 1895, 3. For a full listing of incidents surrounding inebriation, see Campos-Costero, *Home Grown*, esp. 91–110.

61. Garza, *Imagined Underworld*, 1–11, 179–81.

62. Foucault, *Discipline and Punish*, 16, 26–27, 235–45.

63. Neufeld and Matthews, *Mexico in Verse*, 11–12, and chapters 2, 3, 5 especially.

64. "La esclavitud en Yucatán," *Regeneración*, January 31, 1901, 4; AGN, CMDF, Cajas 50–400; and AGN, Estado Mayor Presidencial, Cajas 92–98.

65. James Kelley, "Professionalism," 79; Pavía, *El ejército y la política*, 3–6; *México Nuevo* (Mayo, 1909) published lists of Reyistas sent to Yucatán.

66. AGN, CMDF ,Caja 359; see Condumex/Carso (hereafter CDX), fondo DLV, Bernardo Reyes letters.

67. Víctor Macías-González, "The Bathhouse and Male Homosexuality in Porfirian

Mexico," in Macías-González and Rubenstein, *Masculinity and Sexuality in Modern Mexico*, 25–52.

68. AGN, CMDF, Caja 334, 1867–97, Subtnt. Manuel Cataneo.
69. Irwin, McCaughan, and Nasser, *Famous 41*, 1–21.
70. AGN, CMDF, Caja 360, Capt. 2 Artillería Antonio Navarro.
71. For example, Anexo 23 BR in *Memoria*, 1901–1902, reports falling 50 percent short of recruitment goals.
72. Bishop, *Old Mexico*, 155.
73. Scott, *Weapons of the Weak*.
74. See a great discussion in Alexius, "Army and Politics," chapter 1.
75. See "Reclutamiento del Ejército," *Revista Militar*, September 15, 1880, 532–39, on sorteo. Regarding state and militia regulations, see Serrano Ortega, *El contingente de sangre*.
76. Sec. Guerra Bernardo Reyes, Dept. de Estado Mayor, Circulo 314, January 28, 1902, Anexo 2, *Memorias*, 1902.
77. Arellano García, *El juicio de amparo*, 134–37.
78. French, "Prostitutes and Guardian Angels."
79. Eduardo F. Marín to PD, September 2, 1889, CPD, Legajo 14, Caja 20, Doc. 9587 (3908).
80. Anexo 23 BR, *Memorias*, 1901–1902.
81. See *Memorias*, 1879 (5824–25), which calls for constitutional reforms; Alexius, "Army and Politics," 50–66.
82. Lomnitz, *Deep Mexico, Silent Mexico*, 95–98; Rabinow, *Foucault Reader*, 171.
83. Mondragón, *Proyecto de organización*, 21–23.
84. Bernardo Reyes, "Ensayo de reclutamiento," 185–89, in *Revista Militar*, April 15, May 15, June 1, 1889.
85. See Stephen Neufeld, "Behaving Badly in Mexico City: Discipline and Identity in the Presidential Guards, 1900–1911," in Rugeley and Fallow, *Forced Marches*, 87–88.
86. PD to Bernardo Ruiz Sandoval, 1884, CPD, Legajo 9, Caja 2, Doc. 861.
87. Gen. Carlos Fuero to PD, October 10, 1885, CPD, Legajo 14, Caja 21, Doc. 10469.
88. Gen. Julio Cervantes to PD, July 11, 1889, CPD, Legajo 14, Caja 14, Doc. 6766.
89. AGN CMDF Caja 359, for various examples of these evil clerks and difficulties they created.
90. Hernández to CMDF, March 20, 1899, AGN, CMDF, Caja 359
91. Crl. Rosalino Martínez to PD, July 7, 1886, CPD, Legajo 11, Caja 16, Doc. 7833.
92. Clementina de Calapis to PD, May 26, 1889, CPD, Legajo 14, Caja 9, Doc. 4434.
93. Antonia García de Bueno to PD, October 4, 1885, CPD, Legajo 14, Caja 22, Doc. 10563.
94. Alexius, "Army and Politics"; Mondragón, *Proyecto de organización*, 13.
95. Urquizo, *Tropa vieja*, 54; Jefe de Fuerzas Federal, Bonifacio Topete to PD, May 14, 1883, CPD, Legajo 8, Caja 1, Doc. 74, 75.
96. Janvier, "Mexican Army," 818.
97. AGN, CMDF, Caja 323, Tnt. Joaquin Ayala, 1879.
98. Among many examples, see Abraham Pimental to PD, January 11, 1889, CPD, Legajo 14, Caja 2, Doc. 660.
99. On complaints and problems at Hospital Juárez with guards, see AGN, CMDF,

Caja 329, 67–97, Capt. 2 Luis G. Calderón; on the doctor disguise, see AGN, CMDF, Caja 350, Victorio Vicente Garza, January 20, 1902.

100. AGN, CMDF, Caja 318, 67–97, Capt. 1 José María Aguirre, 1892.

101. Sgt. Miguel Himénez to PD, November 2, 1891, CPD, Legajo 16, Caja 29, Doc. 14130.

102. AGN, CMDF, Caja 350, (trial of) Teófilo Gutiérrez y Socios, November 1, 1894.

103. AGN, CMDF, Caja 318, 67–97, Luis Airaldi.

104. Clarke, "Mexican Armies and Generals."

105. AGN, CMDF, Caja 359, José Millán, January 24, 1898, and Nicasio Villaseñor and Luciano Martínez, músicos, November 26, 1898.

106. AGN, CMDF, Caja 351, Subtnt. Alfonso Hong, 1875; on the search for a deserter in atrial record, see AGN, CMDF, Caja 321, Crl. Eduardo Arce, May 8, 1889.

107. Janvier, "Mexican Army," 818.

108. AGN, CMDF, Caja 350s, misc. folders on soldiers' trials; Alexius counts some three thousand deserters per year, "Army and Politics," 108; on modern discipline and the floating population, see Foucault, *Discipline and Punish*, 141.

109. In *A donde debemos llegar*, 28, Eduardo Paz gives a national population figure of 13 million in 1910, among which 1.7 million were men of military age (18–36) and derives from this that, assuming 15 percent of eligible men were enlisted, the nation could, in extremis, field 255,000 total mobilized troops. Given population growth and relative peace, I contend that the hundreds of thousands who did get military experience remains a very significant figure for the thirty-five years of the era, approaching most of Paz's on-call emergency contingent.

Chapter Two

1. On time inculcations, see E. P. Thompson, *Customs in Common*, 352–404; on Mexico, see French, *Peaceful and Working People*.

2. On similar nationalist attempts, albeit in an extremely different context, see Fahmy, *All the Pasha's Men*.

3. Bunker, *Creating Mexican Consumer Culture*, 1–12.

4. See Foucault, "Spaces, Knowledge, and Power," in Rabinow, *Foucault Reader*, 243; on the "militaire," see Foucault, "Discipline and Punish," in Rabinow, *Foucault Reader*, 179–86. The symbolic persona or role that le militaire played connected to the apparatus of power and discourse that Foucault mentions largely in passing. Perhaps Foucault's brevity resulted from the self-evident or obvious centrality of le militaire as the wielder of a great deal of state power.

5. See Eduardo Paz, Instrucción, *Boletín Militar* (weekly installments of two to three pages from February 1, 1900, to March 23, 1900); and Mílada Bazant de Saldaña, "La modernización en la educación militar, 1876–1910," in Bazant de Saldaña et al., *La evolución de la educación militar*, 183–84.

6. On the daily lives of soldiers in Brazil as comparison, see Beattie, *Tribute of Blood*, esp. 125–51.

7. On habitus versus understandings, see Bourdieu, *Outline of a Theory*; on totalizing institutions, see Goffman, *Asylums*; on inscribed subjectivities, see Foucault,

Discipline and Punish; and Rabinow, *Foucault Reader*; tying them together, see Shilling, *Body and Social Theory*.

8. See *Periódico Militar*, weekly, January 16–March 30, 1880, for a summary of this renaming process in publication.

9. Edward Casey, "How to Get from Space to Place in a Fairly Short Stretch of Time: Phenomenological Prolegomena," in Feld and Basso, *Senses of Place*, 13–52.

10. On the presence of these women, children, and others, see chapter 3.

11. See Porfirio Valderrain to PD, December 29, 1884, CPD, Legajo l9, Caja 2, Doc. 577 1884; Gen. Albino Zertuche to PD, May 8, 1885, CPD, Legajo 10, Caja 11, Doc. 5135.

12. José del Valle to Pedro Hinojosa, February 22, 1890,CPD, Legajo 15, Caja 3, Doc. 1064–65; see chapter 7.

13. Bernardo Reyes to Jefe de Hacienda de Edo. Sonora, February 23, 1881, CPD, Legajo 6, Caja 1, Doc. 422; and Manuel González to PD, 1882, CPD, Legajo 7, Caja 2, Doc. 441.

14. "Reclutamiento del Ejército," *Revista Militar*, September 15, 1890, 535.

15. AGN, Gob. s/s, Caja 760, Exp. 8. Trinidad Vega recalled that the Revolutionary general Pascual Orozco was popular in part for paying an extravagant three pesos per day. PHO 1/26, 13; Bunker, *Creating Mexican Consumer Culture*, 126; Francois, *Culture of Everyday Credit*, 160.

16. On soldaderas, see chapter 3; on expenses, see Aponte, *Empirismos*, 82, 83. Common expenses are covered in *Memorias* 1879, Circulo 92, 354–55.

17. Aponte, *Empirismos*, 82, 83.

18. For but a few examples (see chapter 5 for more), see Biblioteca del Archivo Histórico del Distrito Federal, Mexico City, Ayuntamiento Gobierno de DF, vol. 34, exp. 92, March 19, 1874, May 28, 1884, exp. 96, 98, 99, 121, 126; on potable water problems for hygiene, see Masilla, *De cómo Porfirio Díaz dominas las aguas*.

19. PD to Aurelio Melgarejo, Mexican consul in Belgium, April 11, 1891, CPD, Legajo 16, Caja 8, Doc. 3769–72.

20. For an example, translated from the French, see "El ataque á la bayoneta en las próximas guerras," *Revista Militar*, May 1, 1889, 314.

21. AGN, Gobernación, sin sección, Caja 757, 745; *Memorias*, Anexo 51, Circ. 356, December 22, 1903; Keegan and Holmes, *Soldiers*, 66, 70.

22. Frías, *Battle of Tomochic*; and Vanderwood, *Power of God*.

23. Tenorio-Trillo, *I Speak of the City*, 168–72.

24. Escobar, *Manual de higiene militar*, 94.

25. AGN, Gobernación, sin sección, Circulo 252, Caja 745, gobernación s/s E11, February 14, 1900.

26. Hardie, "Mexican Army," 1211; Janvier, "Mexican Army," 822.

27. AGN, Gobernación, sin sección, Caja 745, Gobernación ss, e11; also see Frías, *Battle of Tomochic*, 39.

28. Trinidad Vega, interview by Ximena Sepúlveda, October 29, 1873, PHO 1/26, 6.

29. Ibid., 6–7.

30. On the particulars of his visit, see Remington, "General Miles's Review."

31. On Remington's art in Mexico, see Neufeld, "Performative Army."

32. McNeill, *Keeping Together in Time*, 132. For an extension of this to military cultures from ancient Greece through the modern day, see Desch-Obi, *Fighting for Honor*, 6–12.
33. Urquizo, *Tropa vieja*, 56.
34. Capt. Francisco Macías, interview by María Isabel Souza, January 22, 1974, PHO 1/54, 26, 35.
35. Scott, *Weapons of the Weak*.
36. Grossman, *On Killing*, 81–82.
37. Mondragón, *Proyecto de organización*, 14.
38. Urquizo, *Tropa vieja*, 43.
39. Roughly, the terms mean: fucker, asshole, fairy, son of a bitch, and bastard, respectively.
40. Urquizo, *Tropa vieja*, 59–60.
41. Robert Buffington, "Homophobia and the Mexican Working Class," in Irwin, McCaughan, and Nasser, *Famous 41*, 193–226, 221.
42. Also part of military discipline as meticulous ordering; see Rabinow, *Foucault Reader*, 170, 181.
43. AGN, CMDF, EP, Caja 358, Agapito Maldonado, 1898, sentenced to one month in the military prison of Santiago rather than limpieza.
44. *El Imparcial*, May 1908, cited in Pavía, *El ejército y la política*, 31.
45. See Burkhart, "Mexica Women," 33–38.
46. Irwin, McCaughan, and Nasser, *Famous 41*, 8; McCrea, *Diseased Relations*.
47. Creelman, "Porfirio Díaz."
48. Bill French, "'I'm Going to Write You a Letter': Coplas, Love Letters, and Courtship Literacy," in Neufeld and Matthews, *Mexico in Verse*, 145–80.
49. Rodríguez O., *Divine Charter*, 1–34.
50. Kourí, *Pueblo Divided*.
51. Robert Buffington and William French, "The Culture of Modernity," in Meyer and Beezley, *Oxford History of Mexico*, 408–11.
52. *Memorias*, 1905, 25.
53. Mílada Bazant de Saldaña, "La modernización en la educación militar, 1876–1910," in Bazant de Saldaña et al., *La evolución de la educación militar*, 181–85; Sánchez Rojas, "La educación del ejercito porfiriano."
54. Secretaría de Guerra y Marina, "Reglamentos para las escuelas de enseñanza primaria elemental," *Memorias*, 1898, 5; for ordenanzas, see México, *Manual de oficial subalterno*.
55. Bernardo Reyes, Circulo 268, July 20, 1900, AGN, Gobernación, Caja 745, Exp. 11 s/s 1900.
56. Sec. Guerra y Marina, Anexo 15, "Reglamento para las escuelas de enseñanza elemental," *Memorias*, 1906, 170.
57. Ibid., 183, 184; Mílada Bazant de Saldaña, "La modernización en la educación militar, 1876–1910," in Bazant de Saldaña et al., *La evolución de la educación militar*, 193, 194; on literacy, see Matthews, *Civilizing Machine*, 18; P. Smith, "Contentious Voices," 38.
58. Súarez Pichardo, *Hechos ilustres*; Fuentes, *Historia patria*; Prieto, *Lecciones de historia patria*.

59. Fuentes, *Historia patria*, 9.

60. Ibid., 29, 30, 31.

61. Ibid., 231.

62. Creelman, "Porfirio Díaz," 244, 245.

63. Súarez Pichardo, *Hechos ilustres*, 6.

64. Ibid., 16.

65. Ibid., 101.

66. Weber, *Peasants into Frenchmen*, esp. 292–303 on the military.

67. Hardie, "Mexican Army."

68. Beezley, *Mexican National Identity*, ix–xii.

69. Beezley, Martin, and French, *Rituals of Rule*, xv–xx; on nation as natural seeming, see the introduction to Barman, *Brazil*.

70. Urquizo, *Tropa vieja*, 73–74.

71. Mosse, *Image of Man*, 51–53, 78; Beezley, Martin, and French, *Rituals of Rule*, xiii–xx; Bell, *Ritual*, 23–60; Kertzer, *Ritual, Politics, and Power*, 1–15, 77–102.

72. On confessions, see Foucault, *History of Sexuality*, vol. 1, esp. 58–65; and, in application, Serge Gruzinski "Individualization and Acculturation: Confession among the Nahuas of Mexico from the Sixteenth to the Eighteenth Century," in Schwaller, *Church in Colonial Latin America*, 103–20.

73. Urquizo, *Tropa vieja*, 53; on the social body, see Foucault, "Discipline and Punish," in Rabinow, *Foucault Reader*, 184, 199.

74. de Certeau, *Practice of Everyday Life*, xiv.

75. Ibid., xiv–xvii, 37–38, 45–56.

76. "Ejecución militar," *Vanguardia*, February 4, 1891, 1, 2.

77. "Ejecución militar," *Vanguardia*, June 27, 1891, 2.

78. "El Coroneta Bruno Labastida," *Revista Militar Mexicana*, 2 (November 1890): 660–62.

79. Mendoza, *El corrido mexicano*, 150.

80. Piccato, *City of Suspects*, 250–51.

81. Esposito, "Memorializing Modern Mexico," 1–67; Beezley, *Mexican National Identity*, 53–98.

82. From Sec. Guerra y Marina, *Ordenanza General del Ejército* (1890), Articulo 9220; Urquizo, *Tropa vieja*, 80–81.

83. Urquizo, *Tropa vieja*, 55.

84. On this concept, see Foucault, *Subjectivité et vérité*, and the insightful discussions by Stuart Elton on his blog Progressive Geographies (www.progressivegeographies.com) regarding the development of Foucault's thought.

85. For a few examples, see Matthews, *Civilizing Machine*; Alexander, "Quotidian Catastrophes"; Toxqui Garay, "El Recreo de los Amigos"; Bunker, *Creating Mexican Consumer Culture*.

Chapter Three

1. E. P. Thompson, *Customary Practice*, 478–79, 500–501.

2. Tenorio-Trillo, *Mexico at the World's Fairs*.

3. French, "Prostitutes and Guardian Angels."

4. Michel Foucault, "Governmentality," in Burchell, Gordon, and Miller, *Foucault Effect*, 91–101; C. Taylor, "Foucault and Familial Power."

5. Urquizo, *Tropa vieja*, 110.

6. Súarez Pichardo, *Hechos ilustres*, 52.

7. Mondragón, *Proyecto de organización*, 11.

8. Stephen Neufeld, "Sly Mockeries of Military Men," in Neufeld and Matthews, *Mexico in Verse*, 67–69.

9. Urquizo, *Tropa vieja*, 61; also see chapter 1.

10. Shilling, *Body and Social Theory*, 156.

11. Salas, *Soldaderas in the Mexican Military*.

12. Van Creveld, *Men, Women and War*.

13. Ibid., 227.

14. Lynn, *Women, Armies, and Warfare*, 93.

15. Van Creveld, *Men, Women and War*, 96.

16. See Eduardo Ángeles Meraz, interview by Alicia Olivera de Bonfil, 1972, PHO 1/31; and Francisco Macías Rodríguez, interview by María Isabel Souza, 1974, PHO 1/54.

17. Salas, *Soldaderas in the Mexican Military*, 82–101, 120–22; Poniatowska, *Las Soldaderas*; chapters by Mary Kay Vaughan, Gabriela Cano, Anne Rubenstein, and Julia Tuñón in Vaughan, Cano, and Olcott, *Sex in Revolution*; Soto, *Emergence of the Modern Mexican Woman*, 43–46.

18. Ben Fallaw, "Eulogio Ortiz: The Army and the Antipolitics of Postrevolutionary State Formation, 1920–1935," in Rugeley and Fallaw, *Forced Marches*, 136–171; and Thomas Rath, "Revolutionary Citizenship against Institutional Inertia," in Rugeley and Fallaw, *Forced Marches*, 172–209.

19. Aponte, *Empirismos*, 68–72.

20. For an example of this emotional support from Europe, see Lynn, *Women, Armies, and Warfare*, 92.

21. Agostini, *Monuments of Progress*, 26; Buffington, *Criminal and Citizen*, 69.

22. Aponte, *Empirismos*, 71; Ortiz Rubio, *Los alojamientos militares*.

23. Lynn, *Women, Armies, and Warfare*, 67.

24. Agostini, *Monuments of Progress*, 68; Toxqui Garay, "El Recreo de los Amigos," 215, 250; Lynn, *Women, Armies, and Warfare*, 124–25.

25. Frías, *Battle of Tomochic*, 18–19; Lynn, *Women, Armies, and Warfare*, 55.

26. Porter, *Working Women in Mexico City*, especially chapter 1; Frías, *Battle of Tomochic*, 114–15.

27. AGN, CMDF, EP.

28. A wealth of sociology exists on the topic of labeling and stigma. See, for example, Link and Pubert, "Conceptualizing Stigma"; Goffman, *Stigma*.

29. Two published examples are "Un escándalo," *Diario del Hogar*, April 22, 1903; "El reconocimiento médico de las mujeres de los soldados," *Diario del Hogar*, June 10, 1903, 7–9.

30. AGN, CMDF, Caja 366, Alberto y Portilla, June 25, 1897; by military regulation: México, Secretaría de Guerra, *Ordenanza general*, Article 2440, 274.

31. Frías, *Battle of Tomochic*, 39.

32. AGN, FGyM, Subseries Battalón, (14th Batt.), Caja 1265, Exp. 1319, December 10, 1891.

33. Aponte, *Empirismos*, 71.

34. Urquizo, *Tropa vieja*, 77.

35. See, for example, AGN, CMDF, Caja 360, Tnt. Reynaldo Nila October 17, 1895.

36. AGN, CMDF, Caja 360, July 4, 1898.

37. AGN, CMDF, Caja 373, Subtnt. Juan R. Solorsano, November 22, 1881.

38. "Formaciones militares," *Vanguardia*, March 9, 1891, 1–2, and April 1, 1891, 1.

39. Examples of this are seen in accounts in Urquizo, *Tropa vieja*, and Aponte, *Empirismos*, and in various expedientes with complaints by officers against violent soldiers.

40. AGN, CMDF, Caja 364, Tnt. Pérez, s/f.

41. Aponte, *Empirismos*, 69–71; Mondragón, *Proyecto de organización*, 15.

42. AGN, CMDF, Caja 352, Mayor Cdte. Antonio E. Herrera, January 7, 1888.

43. Frías, *Battle of Tomochic*, 18.

44. Ibid., 12, 13.

45. Ibid., 12.

46. Stephen Neufeld, "Sly Mockeries of Military Men," in Neufeld and Matthews, *Mexico in Verse*, 96–98.

47. See Toxqui Garay, "El Recreo de los Amigos," 268–70; "Crónica negra," *El Partido Liberal*, July 27, 1887.

48. For one example, see AGN, CMDF, Caja 357 Ep-m, Soldado Antonio Martínez, March 14, 1889.

49. AGN, CMDF, Caja 352, Alférez Manuel B. Herrera, 1886.

50. AGN, CMDF, Caja 359, Agapito Maldonado, December 21, 1898.

51. AGN, CMDF, Caja 359, Soldado Antonio Martínez, March 14, 1889.

52. AGN, CMDF, Caja 356, Soldado Pedro Lara, May 17, 1880.

53. Urquizo, *Tropa vieja*, 44.

54. Ibid.

55. Ibid., 85.

56. Ibid., 96–97.

57. Ibid., 76.

58. Ibid., 60.

59. AGN, CMDF, Caja 366, Juan Pevedilla, June 24, 1879.

60. Frías, *Battle of Tomochic*, 113.

61. Lynn, *Women, Armies, and Warfare*, 92.

62. Salas, *Soldaderas in the Mexican Military*, 64; Urquizo, *Tropa vieja*, 60.

63. Lynn, *Women, Armies, and Warfare*, 105; Robert Buffington, "Toward a Modern Sacrificial Economy: Violence against Women and Male Subjectivity in Turn-of-the-Century Mexico City," in Macías-González and Rubenstein, *Masculinity and Sexuality*, 157–96.

64. Stephen Neufeld, "Performing the Masculine Nation: Soldiers of the Porfirian Army and Masculinity, 1876–1910," in Kraay, *Negotiating Identities*, 49–69.

65. AGN, CMDF, Caja 359, Agapito Maldonado, December 21, 1898; for a lengthy investigation of knife fighting over women, see AGN, FGyM, Caja 1218, Exp. 1102, 1886.

66. Mondragón, *Proyecto de organización*, 13; Frías, *Battle of Tomochic*, 112 (on pecking order); Urquizo, *Tropa vieja*, 41 (on hazing).

67. Mendoza, *El corrido mexicano*, 150. Also see chapter 2 for a discussion of Bruno and chapter 6 for songs and executions.

68. Piccato, *City of Suspects*, 14–15, 216–19; Baudry, *From Chivalry to Terrorism*, 202–3; Herrera-Sobek, *Mexican Corrido*, xiii, 64.

69. AGN, CMDF, Caja 360, Sgt. 1 Pio Gutiérrez and Sgt. 2 Candelario Carrillo, Report to Primero Juez, May 28, 1896.

70. A (very) rough translation with spelling errors approximated: "yer vury bitchy and reel son of a slut and vury whorish . . . if u don't fuck me when I tells you, u is a vury stubbirn bitch," followed by a few variations of "yo momma."

71. Agostini, *Monuments of Progress*, 16; Toxqui Garay, "El Recreo de los Amigos," 232; Aponte, *Empirismos*, 70; Mondragón, *Proyecto de organización*, 30; Frías, *Battle of Tomochic*, 18; Buffington, *Criminal and Citizen*, 58; AGN, CMDF, Caja 343 ep-g, Tnt. Alberto González, Seventeenth Battalion, Report of First Demarcación to CMDF, October 19, 1885.

72. Tenorio-Trillo, *I Speak of the City*, 64–65.

73. Urquizo, *Tropa vieja*, 41.

74. AGN, CMDF, Caja 341, Francisco Franco, November 13, 1880 (letter of E. Flores to CMDF).

75. Bunker, *Creating Mexican Consumer Culture*, 217.

76. Beattie, *Tribute of Blood*, 177–204.

77. Nesvig, "Lure of the Perverse," 3–4, 35, 37.

78. Lynn, *Women, Armies, and Warfare*, 90.

79. Buffington, *Criminal and Citizen*, 193–95; da Matta, *A casa y a rua*, 11–28.

80. Mondragón, *Proyecto de organización*, 21; Frías, *Battle of Tomochic*, 18 (on campaign).

81. Johns, *City of Mexico*, 96, 97.

82. An understudied topic for the nineteenth century in Mexico, these indigenous attitudes toward sex were presumably some continuation of differing notions during colonial times. See as examples Clendinnen, *Ambivalent Conquests*; Gruzinski, *Conquest of Mexico*.

83. Urquizo, *Tropa vieja*, 48.

84. Salas, *Soldaderas in the Mexican Military*, xi, 123n1.

85. Knight, *Mexican Revolution*, 1:18–19; also see chapter 1.

86. AGN, CMDF, Caja 321, Cipriano Andrade, June 23, 1887.

87. AGN, Gobernación, sin sección, Caja 760, Expediente 2,Círculo 342, 1903, by Francisco Mena, August 26, 1903.

88. Agostini, *Monuments of Progress*, 78; see also *Memorias*, yearly, 1878–1910, which lists all military buildings.

89. Lynn, *Women, Armies, and Warfare*, 88.

90. Urquizo, *Tropa vieja*, 97 (on weddings), and 113 (on engagements).

91. E. P. Thompson, *Customs in Common*, 493.

92. Salas, *Soldaderas in the Mexican Military*, 77; Urquizo, *Tropa vieja*, 113.

93. *Memorias*, 1878, "Documento 39," 92 (on hijos naturales).

94. Urquizo, *Tropa vieja*, 67.

95. Ibid., 84–85.
96. Ibid., 83–84.
97. Ibid., 171.
98. On prayers for the dead, see Frías, *Battle of Tomochic*, 109; on masses, see Frías, *Battle of Tomochic*, 115; praying is also mentioned in Urquizo, *Tropa vieja*, 117.
99. Urquizo, *Tropa vieja*, 68; Mondragón, *Proyecto de organización*, 13.
100. Aponte, *Empirismos*, 83; see chapter 5.
101. French, "Imagining."
102. On street versus home, see Freyre, *Casa-Grande y senzala*; da Matta, *A casa y a rua*; Beattie, "The House, the Street, and the Barracks"; Wells and Joseph, *Summer of Discontent, Seasons of Upheaval*, 148.
103. "La vida del calle," *México Gráfico*, no. 235 (January 1, 1893): 3–6.
104. Giddens, *Modernity and Self-Identity*, 2, 5, 80–81.
105. Lynn, *Women, Armies, and Warfare*, 110–17.
106. On efforts to discipline, see chapter 2.

Chapter Four

1. See Joseph and Nugent, *Everyday Forms of State Formation*.
2. Fausto Becerril, interview by Eugenia Meyer, March 1974, PHO 1/61.
3. Rath, *Myths of Demilitarization*.
4. Chavarri, *El heroico Colegio Militar*, 16, 241.
5. Sánchez Lamego, *Generales de ingenieros*, 193–97.
6. Ibid., 81–94; AGN, CMDF, Caja 370, Sóstenes Rocha.
7. Sánchez Lamego, *Generales de ingenieros*, 195.
8. Chavarri, *El heroico Colegio Militar*, 249, 250.
9. "Boletín Militar," *Revista Militar Mexicana*, July 1, 1890, 1–2.
10. H. Reed, "Mexican Military Academy," 811–18.
11. L. Zafra to PD, January 1880, CPD, Legajo 5, Caja 10, Doc. 4532–33.
12. Gen. Francisco Naranjo to PD, January 1882, CPD, Legajo 7, Caja 1, Doc. 62.
13. Jerónimo Treviño to PD, CPD, Legajo 9, Caja 6, Doc. 671–72; on Zertuche, see Luis Luna García and PD, CPD, Legajo 10, Caja 2, Doc. 589–90; *Revista Militar Mexicano*, June 1, 1890.
14. Rojas, *Un gran rebelde*, 21–32.
15. H. Reed, "Mexican Military Academy," 814.
16. Mílada Bazant de Saldaña, "La modernización en la educación militar, 1876–1910," in Bazant de Saldaña et al., *La evolución de la educación militar*, 184–85.
17. Mier de Terán to PD, March 8, 1885, CPD, Legajo 10, Caja 6, Doc. 2831.
18. Hardie, "Mexican Army," 1203; Janvier, "Mexican Army," 816.
19. Deák, *Beyond Nationalism*, 85–88; H. Reed, "Mexican Military Academy," 816.
20. H. Reed, "Mexican Military Academy," 816.
21. *Mexico Militar*, 1900, 429.
22. "La Vida de un Cadete," *El Imparcial*, January 1, 13, 1907; "Equilibria," *Boletín Militar*, November 1, 1899, 1.
23. James Kelley, "Professionalism," 62–65.

24. Deák, *Beyond Nationalism*, 86, 87; "Proyecto de escuelas," *Revista Militar Mexicana*, December 1, 1889, 16–20.
25. Rocha, *Estudios*.
26. Sánchez Lamego, *Generales de ingenieros*, 81–94.
27. A. Fernández Merino, "El General Sóstenes Rocha," *Periódico Militar* 1 (November 1879): 1–5 (republished from an unnamed Spanish periodical).
28. *Periódico Militar* 1 (February 1, 1879): 3–4.
29. See, for instance, González y González, "El liberalismo triunfante," 652–706.
30. Janvier, "Mexican Army," 818.
31. Frías, *Battle of Tomochic*.
32. Stephen Neufeld, "Sly Mockeries of Military Men," in Neufeld and Matthews, *Mexico in Verse*, 58–65, 97–98.
33. Tnt. Cor. Eduardo Ángeles Meraz, interview by Alicia Olivera, December 8, 1972, 1, PHO 1/31.
34. Rodolfo Casillas, interview by Alexis Arroyo, March 1961, 6, PHO 1/104.
35. Meraz, interview, 6, PHO 1/31.
36. Rojas, *Un gran rebelde*, 27–28.
37. Meraz, interview, 21, PHO 1/31.
38. Some examples: AGN, CMDF, Caja 353, Subtnt. Ángel Jíménez deserts military college; AGN, CMDF, Caja 342, Capt. David de la Fuente, alcohol smuggling; AGN, CMDF, Caja 341, Daniel de la Fuente; "Noticias militares," *Vanguardia*, February 17, 1891, 8.
39. Janvier, "Mexican Army," 816–17.
40. H. Reed, "Mexican Military Academy," 818.
41. Becerril, interview, 17, PHO 1/61.
42. Stealey, *Porte Crayon's Mexico*, 103, 922.
43. AGN, CMDF, Caja 95, Capt. Porfirio Díaz.
44. AGN, FGyM, Estado Mayor, Expedientes Personales—Estado Mayor Presidencial 1824–1912, Caja 96, Félix Díaz.
45. Juan Villegas and PD, October 3, 1891, CPD, Legajo 16, Caja 27, Doc. 13303–4.
46. AGN, CMDF, expedientes personales; Léon Martínez to PD, September 28, 1880, CPD, Legajo 5, Caja 7, Doc. 3464.
47. For common military attitudes toward the deposit, see "El depósito," *La Vanguardia*, June 6, 1891), 2
48. Escudero, *El duelo en México*, 156.
49. Ibid., 157–58.
50. Ibid., 160.
51. Ibid., 164–65; Piccato, *Tyranny of Opinion*, 83–93, 225–51.
52. Tovar, *Código del duelo*; on various duels and outcomes, see Escudero, *El duelo en México*.
53. Antonio Tovar to PD, January 19, 1891, CPD, Legajo 16, Caja 2, Doc. 976–79.
54. México, Secretaría de Guerra y Marina, Estado Mayor, and Reyes, *Ley orgánico*, 1900, Articles 3607, 3011.
55. *Diario Oficial*, June 2, 1897, details cost of legations to the UK, Latin America, and Germany.
56. Neufeld, "Servants of the Nation," 269–88.

57. Tnt. Cor. Porfirio Díaz [Jr.], Tnt. Cor. Gustavo Salas, Tnt. Cor. Francisco García, and Tnt. Cor. Davila Fortino, all in AGN, FGyM, Estado Mayor, Expedientes Personales—Oficiales y Tropa, Guardia Presidencial, Caja 94.

58. "Mexico Wants No Loan," *New York Times*, February 26, 1893.

59. Schell, *Integral Outsiders*, 74.

60. Robert R. Symon to PD, December 15, 1892, CPD, Legajo 17, Caja 37, Doc. 18213: an offer to have Díaz Jr. go to England, joining either the Royal Artillery or the Royal Guards under the Duke of Cambridge, Edmund Conmerrel.

61. Secretaría de Relaciones Exteriores (hereafter SRE), Agregados en EUA, T 421, Legajo 1049, Porfirio Díaz Jr. (20 fojas).

62. "Oficiales en Francia," *Boletín Militar*, May 1, 1900), 5; translated and reprinted from *Le Voltaire*.

63. AGN, CMDF, Caja 318, Mayor-Medico Federico Abriego, July 17, 1893; AGN, CMDF, ep-g Caja 345, Tnt. Cor. Medico Eduardo R. García; AGN, CMDF, Caja 347, Cor. Bodo von Glümer; AGN, CMDF, Caja 375, Mayor-Medico Daniel Vélez, 1895; *Memorias*, 1900, Doc. 21.

64. Matías Romero to PD, December 25, 1890, CPD, Legajo 15, Caja 29, Doc. 14344; Juan F. Cahill to PD, January 27, 1890, CPD, Legajo 15, Caja 27, Doc. 13207.

65. J. Johnson, "Latin-American Military," 108.

66. Co. des Hauts-Fourneaux to PD, January 30, 1885, CPD, Legajo 10, Caja 4, Doc. 1853 (Banges cannons).

67. "Correspondencia extranjero," *Boletín Militar*, April 27, 1899, 3 (report from St. Chamond, Manual Mondragón to Samuel García Cuellar, March 24, 1899).

68. "Algo sobre las municiones," *La Vanguardia*, May 14, 1888, 2.

69. Bernardo Reyes (hereafter BR) to Crl. Gilberto Luna, May 8, 1902, CDX BR, vol. 34, Doc. 6747; Dir. General of Societé Anonyme Capital to BR, June 11, 1901, CDX BR, vol. 35, Doc. 7471–74.

70. Schiff, "German Military Penetration into Mexico."

71. Max A. Philipp to PD, October 7, 1890, CPD, Legajo 15, Caja 26, Doc. 12643–4; AGN, CMDF, Caja 349, 1891; AGN, CMDF, Caja 368; *Periódico Militar*, July 1879), 7; Rocha, *Estudios*.

72. Sgt. Francisco Ramírez to PD, December 25, 1884, CPD, Legajo 9, Caja 2, Doc. 804.

73. "Ventajosas opiniones extranjeras sobre nuestra ejército," *Mexico Herald*, cited in *México Militar*, 1900, 157–58.

74. Ibid., 158.

75. *México Militar*, October 1900, 200.

76. Joaquín Gómez Vergara to PD, April 18, 1881, Legajo 6, Caja 2, Doc. 772.

77. SRE, Archivo Histórico, Legajo 13, expedientes of Cor. Carlos Gagern, August 29, 1882, September 13, 1882.

78. Bryan, "Mexican Politics in Transition," 74.

79. Tnt. Cor. Pablo Escandón, AGN, FGyM, Estado Mayor, Expedientes Personales—Estado Mayor Presidencial 1824–1912, Caja 96.

80. "Comisión militar en Francia," *México Militar*, December 4, 1900, 299–300.

81. Bryan, "Mexican Politics in Transition," 71.

82. Tnt. Crl. Porfirio Díaz, AGN, FGyM, Estado Mayor, Expedientes Personales—Oficiales y Tropa, Guardia Presidencial, Caja 94.

83. For example, see Tenorio-Trillo, *Mexico at the World's Fairs.*
84. "Desde Buffalo," *México Militar,* June 15, 1900, 61–62.
85. "Los rurales en Buffalo," *México Militar,* August 1, 1900, 128–29.
86. AGN, Estado Mayor Presidencial, Exp. Caja 98, Expediente de Samuel García Cuellar, letter of August 15, 1901.
87. AGN, CMDF, EP; and see Brenner, *Juventino Rosas.*
88. SRE, A Agregados en EUA, T 170, Legajo 252, Exp.10 (Jamestown).
89. "Millions Cheer Martial Pomp," *New York Times,* October 1, 1909.
90. SRE, Agregados en EUA, T 170, Legajo 252, Exp.10 (Jamestown), letter from president of Jamestown Exposition Company to Ambassador Joaquin D. Casasus, April 11, 1906.
91. Ibid., Ambassador Casasus to Jamestown Expo Co., May 10, 1906, and subsequent report by special commissioner for Latin America.
92. Ibid., Elihu Root to Leg. Mexico, March 26, 1907.
93. Ibid., sec. relaciones exteriores to Jamestown Exposition, March 27, 1907, and US secretary of state to embassy of Mexico, April 8, 1907 (on transport).
94. SRE, Agregados en EUA, T 170, Legajo 252, Exp. 9 (San Antonio).
95. Roosevelt speeches in "President Opens Jamestown Fair," *Washington Herald,* April 24, 1907, 2–6.
96. Gutiérrez Santos, *Historia militar de México,* 2:20–22.
97. Ibid., 2:23.
98. James Kelley, "Professionalism," 69–72.
99. *Boletín Militar de Asociación Mutualista,* March 12, 1884, 1.
100. Schiff, "German Military Penetration into Mexico," 578–79.
101. México, *Documentos históricos constitucionales,* vol. 2.
102. As comparison, see also Deák, *Beyond Nationalism,* 4–9, 73–189.

Chapter Five

1. On connaissance, see Foucault, *Archeology of Knowledge,* 15; Deleuze, *Foucault,* 74–75. On the discourses of criminology emerging in Mexico, see Buffington, *Criminal and Citizen.*
2. McCrea, *Diseased Relations,* 2–3, 4; on the claim that medical was political, see McCrea, *Diseased Relations,* 7–8, 14. See also Arnold, *Imperial Medicine and Indigenous Societies*; Lindenbaum and Lock, *Knowledge, Power and Practice*; Nash, *Inescapable Ecologies.*
3. Figueroa, *Higiene militar,* 1–10.
4. After a number of scandalously mishandled horse purchases, the veterinarians were assigned their own branch of service.
5. See DePalo, *Mexican National Army,* 51.
6. De Lizardi, *Mangy Parrot,* 152–64.
7. For examples of the latter, see Azuela, Jorgensen, and Munguía, *Underdogs,* 27, 30–32.
8. B. Álvarez to PD, May 21, 1887, CPD, Legajo12, Caja 8, Doc. 3541.
9. AGN, CMDF, Caja-Ep V, Daniel Vélez, March 23, 1895; see also *Memorias,* parte expositivo, 1906, 45–47.

10. This was reflected in the medical school theses produced: A. Rodríguez, *Profilaxis de las afecciones venereo-sifiliticas*; Ortega, *Breves consideraciones*; Figueroa, *Higiene militar*; Domingo y Barrera, *Ligero estudio*.

11. AGN, CMDF, Cajas 357–59, Montes de Oca.

12. Balbás, *Recuerdos del Yaqui*.

13. Ibid., 116.

14. Escobar, *Manual de higiene militar*.

15. Varios revolucionarios to PD, February 1911, CPD, Legajo 36, Caja 7, Doc. 3241.

16. Escobar, *Manual de higiene militar*.

17. Ibid., 95–156.

18. *Memorias*, 1883, 343 (rations for the day).

19. Also in regulations for 1883; see Escobar, *Manual de higiene militar*, 121.

20. Buffington, *Criminal and Citizen*, 38–63.

21. Pilcher, *¡Que vivan los tamales!*

22. "Porte de campana de la infantería alemana," *Revista del Ejército y Marina*, 1906, 195.

23. Pilcher, *¡Que vivan los tamales!*, 45–77.

24. Escobar, *Manual de higiene militar*, 95, 120, 125.

25. Gen. Ignacio Bravo to Bernardo Reyes, July 12, 1900, CDX, Fondo BR, vol. 29, Doc. 5771; Governor of Yucatán to Bernardo Reyes, June 1, 1900, CDX, Fondo BR, vol. 29, Doc. 5757 (on the eating of cattle).

26. Crl. Lorenzo Fernández to PD, September 14, 1890, CPD, Legajo 15, Caja 22, Doc. 10644 (on food for San Juan de Ulúa); PD to Sabás Lomelí, January 10, 1889, CPD, Legajo14, Caja 1, Doc. 446.

27. Urquizo, *Tropa vieja*, 36, 43, 58.

28. Ortiz Rubio, *Los alojamientos militares*, 67.

29. Pilcher, *¡Que vivan los tamales!*, 59, 83; AGN, CMDF, Caja 359, Agapito Maldonado, December 21, 1898.

30. Agostini, *Monuments of Progress*, xiii, 23, 62–63, 71.

31. Pérez Montfort, Castillo Yurrita, and Piccato, *Hábitos, normas y escándalo*, 148; Agostini, *Monuments of Progress*, 87 (public works budget). Agostini claims the average life-span is 25.5 years, which must overemphasize infant mortality; *Monuments of Progress*, 78.

32. Á. Rodríguez, *Profilaxis de las afecciones venereo-sifiliticas*, 26.

33. A comparable protest rose from camp followers of the American Revolutionary forces; see Lynn, *Women, Armies, and Warfare*, 113.

34. Á. Rodríguez, *Profilaxis de las afecciones venereo-sifiliticas*, 25.

35. Lancereaux, *Treatise on Syphilis*, vol. 1.

36. Ibid., 1:8, 272 (on soldiers), and 1:58–59 (on Mexico).

37. Ibid., 1:61, 92.

38. Ibid., 1:63. See Foucault, *Birth of the Clinic*, 13.

39. Lancereaux, *Treatise on Syphilis*, 1:92: gonorrhea was mostly known as separate, although there was not a complete international consensus on this; for one example, Charles Knowlton, who believed nocturnal ejaculation related to venereal disorders under a blanket term, see "Gonorrhoea Dormientium" [1842], in Lefkowitz Horowitz, *Attitudes toward Sex*, 85–88.

40. Lancereaux, *Treatise on Syphilis*, 1:66, 127.
41. Ibid.,2:228, 230–32, 239, 245.
42. Ibid., 1:26.
43. Oriel, *Scars of Venus*, 201.
44. Lancereaux, *Treatise on Syphilis*, 1:274, 275; Á. Rodríguez, *Profilaxis de las afecciones venereo-sifilíticas*, 28.
45. Oriel, *Scars of Venus*, 78. Serum tests were started in 1906 but they were not perfected until 1949.
46. Bliss, *Compromised Positions*, 28; also see Lara y Pardo, *La prostitución en México*, on prostitution rates and contemporary attitudes.
47. Lancereaux, *Treatise on Syphilis*, 2:243, 286–302, 290; Oriel, *Scars of Venus*, 88–89.
48. Á. Rodríguez, *Profilaxis de las afecciones venereo-sifilíticas*, 24.
49. "Memoria y mejoras en Hospital Militar de Instrucción 1889," *Gaceta Médico Militar* 2 (1889): 329; Quétel, *History of Syphilis*, 176–77, 231.
50. AGN, CMDF, Caja 372, Subtnt. Díonicio Silva, December 5, 1877.
51. Ibid.
52. AGN, Gob. s/s Dep. Cuerpo Médico, Caja 653, Exp. 8, Sec. Guerra y Marina, August 3, 1888; see also Mayor Zurado y Gama, "Algunos consideraciones sobre la profilaxis de los enfermedades venereo-sifilíticas en el ejército," *Gaceta Médico Militar* 4 (1893): 176–86.
53. AGN, CMDF, Caja 344, Tnt. Crl. José P Gayón, May 12, 1891.
54. Á. Rodríguez, *Profilaxis de las afecciones venereo-sifilíticas*, 7.
55. Mayor Zurado y Gama, "Algunos consideraciones sobre la profilaxis de los enfermedades venereo-sifilíticas en el ejército," *Gaceta Médico Militar* 4 (1893): 182.
56. Ibid., 180.
57. AGN, CMDF, Caja 363, Tnt. Francisco Pérez, December 31, 1893.
58. "Tratamiento de la sífilis," *Gaceta Médico Militar*, 1893, 361 (mercury pills delivered 10–20 cg/day).
59. Mayor Zurado y Gama, "Algunos consideraciones sobre la profilaxis de los enfermedades venereo-sifilíticas en el ejército," *Gaceta Médico Militar* 4 (1893): 183.
60. *Gaceta Médico Militar*, 1889, 330.
61. Jesús M. González to Alberto Escobar, *Gaceta Médico Militar*, 1893, 352–53.
62. Bliss, *Compromised Positions*, 43, 53–61.
63. *Gaceta Médico Militar*, 1893, 360.
64. AGN, CMDF, Caja 71, 1897, Mayor Médico Cirujano J. Hernández, *Gaceta Médico Militar*, 1893, 329.
65. Gen. Ignacio Bravo to BR, August 14, 1900, CDX, Bernardo Reyes, Carpeta 29, Doc. 5775; on funds, see Aponte, *Empirismos*, 83.
66. Rabinow, *Foucault Reader*, 17–20; Foucault, *Birth of the Clinic*, 33.
67. *Memorias*, 1879, "Informe," 110–12.
68. Ortiz Rubio, *Los alojamientos militares*.
69. Matthews, *Civilizing Machine*.
70. Felipe Ángeles, *Revista del ejército y marina*, 1908, 228.
71. Ortiz Rubio, *Los alojamientos militares*, 17.
72. AGN, CMDF, Caja 319, Ramiro Alvado.
73. Alexander, "Incendiary Legislation."

74. Reyes to PD, January 6, 1904, CDX BR, carpeta 35, doc. 6850.
75. Luis Mier y Terán and PD, August 31, 1886, CPD, Legajo 11, Caja 17, Doc. 8327 (on problem of doctors leaving service); "Cuerpo médico," *Memorias*, 1903, 251–53.
76. McCrea, *Diseased Relations*, 1–4, 20–57.
77. Crl. Hipolito to PD, November 1885, CPD, Legajo 10, Caja 22, Doc. 10683.
78. "Ligeras reflexiones sobre infección," *Gaceta Médico Militar* 2 (1889): 337–43.
79. "Campana de Yucatán," *México Militar*, 1901, 329.
80. *Memorias*, 1886, Doc. 82, signed E. Cacho, March 3, 1886.
81. On civilian complaints, see Víctor Macías-González, "The Bathhouse and Male Homosexuality in Porfirian Mexico," in Macías-González and Rubenstein, *Masculinity and Sexuality in Modern Mexico*, 34.
82. Originarios del pueblo to Sr. Pres. de Ayuntamiento, October 10, 1878, BAHDF, Ayuntamiento del Gobierno DF, Vol. 1312, Exp. 453, 461.
83. Tenorio-Trillo, *I Speak of the City*, 6, 69.
84. Felipe Berriozábal to Ayuntamiento DF, May 14, 1897, BAHDF, Ayuntamiento del Gobierno DF, Vol. 34, Exp. 92.
85. Cdte. Luis Figueroa, October 9, 1900, BAHDF, Ayuntamiento del Gobierno DF, Vol. 34, Exp. 153.
86. Jefe de 1 Batallón to Fomento to Ayuntamiento, February 16, 1878, BAHDF, Ayuntamiento del Gobierno DF, Vol. 1312, Exp. 416.
87. *Gaceta Médico Militar*, 1891–1893, 326–29; on civilian rates, see Agostini, *Monuments of Progress*, 67.
88. *Gaceta Médico Militar*, 1891–1893, 328.
89. Johns, *City of Mexico*, 43–46; AGN, Gob. s/s, Salubridad, Caja 791, Exp. 4, 1906, "Informes" for January and June 1906.
90. Victoriano Huerta to BR, March 31, 1902, CDX BR, Carpeta 34, Doc. 6741.
91. Inspector de Cuartel #11 to Gobierno DF, July 22, 1870, BAHDF, Ayuntamiento del Gobierno DF, Vol. 3669, Exp. 98.

Chapter Six

1. On culture and leisure, see Conway, *Nineteenth-Century Spanish America*, 2–3.
2. On similar concerns in the late colonial period, see Viqueira Albán, *Propriety and Permissiveness in Bourbon Mexico*.
3. Two exceptional works that discuss the working class and leisure in historical context are Espana-Maran, *Creating Masculinity*; and DeLotinville, "Joe Beef of Montreal."
4. Lynn, *Women, Armies, and Warfare*, 138; Urquizo, *Tropa vieja*, 41; Van Creveld, *Men, Women and War*, 94.
5. Aponte, *Empirismos*, 49.
6. Higate, *Military Masculinities*, 22, 26; on Mexico see Toxqui Garay, "El Recreo de los Amigos," 69, 70, 113.
7. Courtwright, *Forces of Habit*; Schivelbusch, *Tastes of Paradise*.
8. See W. Taylor, *Drinking, Homicide, and Rebellion*; Pablo Piccato, "No es posible cerrar los ojos," in Pérez Montfort, Castillo Yurrita, and Piccato, *Hábitos, normas y escándalo*, 75–142; and in Toxqui Garay, "El Recreo de los Amigos."

9. Aponte, *Empirismos*, 78.

10. Collins, *Violence*, 259–70.

11. AGN, CMDF, Caja 335, Timoteo Cisneros.

12. AGN, CMDF, Caja 360, Soldado Músico, 12 Regt. Felipe Martínez, July 6, 1898.

13. AGN, CMDF, Caja 330, Mayor Agustín Camacho y Arrayo, Tuesday, February 17, 1891.

14. Two examples: AGN, CMDF, Caja 357, Subtnt. Antonio Manzano, Tuesday, January 7, 1879; AGN, CMDF, Caja 368, Subtnt. 11th B, Jesús Rivas, Monday, January 6, 1879.

15. AGN, CMDF, Caja 335, Subtnt. Cleofas Córdova.

16. Geronimo Treviño to PD, March 8, 1891, CPD, Legajo 16, Caja 7, Doc. 3064–66.

17. As a random note, Richard Nixon operated a small casino while in service in World War II, and the money he won later helped fund his political campaigns.

18. For examples, see Frías, *Battle of Tomochic*, 8; Toxqui Garay, "El Recreo de los Amigos," 198.

19. AGN, CMDF, Caja 359, Soldado José Millan, January 24, 1898.

20. AGN, CMDF, Caja 360, Soldados Porfirio López and Severiano Marín, Monday, July 4, 1898.

21. AGN, CMDF, Caja 355, Alf. Genaro Lozero, February 22, 1884.

22. The Ley Penal Militar of 1897, chapter VI, article 286, charges "ultrajes" against civil police with eleven months, with assault earning up to one to three years.

23. AGN, Estado Mayor Presidencial, Exp. Caja 96, Expediente de Leopoldo Palacios.

24. Letter from Sociedad de Agricultores de San Martín, AGN, Gob. s/s, Caja 362, Exp. 1, June 22, 1893.

25. Frías, *Battle of Tomochic*, 21.

26. "Vigilancia en los cuarteles," *La Patria*, March 1, 1900,2.

27. Campos-Costero, *Home Grown*, 81–121; on smuggling, see Urquizo, *Tropa vieja*, 78.

28. Pérez Montfort, Castillo Yurrita, and Piccato, *Hábitos, normas y escándalo*, 186;"Décimas Dedicated to Santa Anna's Leg," in Joseph and Henderson, *Mexico Reader*, 213–17.

29. Pérez Montfort, Castillo Yurrita, and Piccato, *Hábitos, normas y escándalo*, 187–88.

30. Urquizo, *Tropa vieja*, 70; *La Patria*, December 16, 1894, 3.

31. Isaac Campos-Costero details many of these tales in *Home Grown*.

32. "Escándalo y agresión a la policía," *El Nacional*, September 25, 1895, 3.

33. "Otro delito militar," *El Nacional*, October 28, 1895, 3.

34. "El drama en 21 Batallon," *La Patria*, October 25, 1900, 3.

35. "Escarceos," *La Patria*, Friday, December 21, 1900, 1.

36. "Fuegos Fatuos," *El Nacional*, December 5, 1895, 1.

37. AGN, CMDF, Caja 360, Soldado 16th B, Cruz Sira, May 28, 1898.

38. Alcalde to gobernador, AGN, Gob. s/s, Caja 760, Exp. 3, December 30, 1903.

39. Mondragón, *Proyecto de organización*, 11.

40. Urquizo, "Juan soldado," *De la vida militar mexicana*, 49.

41. Urquizo, "Una historia de brujas," *De la vida militar mexicana*, 60.

42. Aponte, *Empirismos*, 81.

43. *Gaceta Médico Militar*, 1898, cited in Pérez Montfort, Castillo Yurrita, and Piccato, *Hábitos, normas y escándalo*.

44. Urquizo, *Tropa vieja*, 70.

45. Ibid., 71–72.

46. Campos-Costero, *Home Grown*, 103–22.

47. "El abuso del tabaco," *Gaceta Médico Militar*, 1889–1893, 20–21.

48. Escobar, *Manual de higeine militar*, 144, 153.

49. Although suggested by rates of lung disorders, the only specific death I discovered was recorded in AGN, CMDF, Caja 374, Capt. Ygnacio Tirado, July 21, 1882.

50. Weber, *Peasants into Frenchmen*, 292–303.

51. On tobacco advertising and industry, see Bunker, *Creating Mexican Consumer Culture*, 14–56.

52. Courtwright, *Forces of Habit*, 141, 152–57.

53. Urquizo, *Tropa vieja*, 37, 82.

54. Mondragón, *Proyecto de organización*, 37.

55. Urquizo, *Tropa vieja*, 82.

56. Bishop, *Old Mexico*, 190. On similar train incidents, see Matthews, *Civilizing Machine*, 143–98.

57. Capt. Rodolfo Casillas, "Vida del soldado americano," *Revista del Ejército y Marina*, June 1910, 36–44.

58. Rodolfo Casillas, interview by Alexis Arroyo, 1961, PHO1/104.

59. Ibid., 40–41; Shilling, *Body and Social Theory*, 166 (on sports versus violence); Frey and Eitzen, "Sports and Society."

60. The position of officer of the week rotated among junior officers and denoted responsibility for the garrison in ordinary matters. AGN, CMDF, Caja 351, Tnt. Jorge Holzinger, August 1, 1878.

61. Urquizo, *Tropa vieja*, 54.

62. Trinidad Vega, interview by Ximena Sepúlveda, October 29, 1973, PHO 1/126.

63. Urquizo, *Tropa vieja*, 54.

64. Beezley, *Judas at the Jockey Club*, 16–17.

65. For specific games and their meanings, see Toxqui Garay, "El Recreo de los Amigos," 114–16; Urquizo, *Tropa vieja*, 67.

66. "On Divine Persecution: Blasphemy and Gambling," in Villa-Flores, *Dangerous Speech*, 77–103.

67. Frías, *Battle of Tomochic*, 113, 140.

68. Urquizo, *De la vida militar mexicana*, 49.

69. Scott, *Weapons of the Weak*.

70. Castro-Klarén and Chasteen, *Beyond Imagined Communities*, xvii–xvix.

71. Becerril, interview, PHO 1/61, recalls listening to the music of the barracks across from Ildefonso, in downtown Mexico City; yet these tunes scarcely received academic interest, for example, only the briefest mention in Stevenson, *Music in Mexico*, 162–63.

72. For example, see the official repertoire of the Seventeenth Battalion in AGN, CMDF, Caja 323, Exp. Capt. Santiago Avadaño.

73. Frías, *Battle of Tomochic*, 39, 114.

74. Thompson, *Customs in Common*, 485.

75. AGN, CMDF, Caja 95, personnel file of Capt. Luis Delgado, March 2, 1877: "dar cañonazos a banda."

76. This estimate comes from Hardie, "Mexican Army." Official statistics on race in the army were not kept by the regime.

77. Mendoza, *El corrido mexicano*, 23, 24; on Tomochic, see Frías, *Battle of Tomochic*; see also Vanderwood, *Power of God*.

78. It also confused the Yaqui and Tomochic campaigns in Mexico City newspapers; see Vanderwood, *Power of God*, 245.

79. Urquizo, *Tropa vieja*, 101 (singing "Juan Soldado" in barracks); lyrics in Mendoza, *El corrido mexicano*, 147–50. Juan Soldado is the equivalent to GI Joe, a generic term used to describe average soldiers. This corrido prefigured and was reused in 1938 in the case of Juan Castillo Morales, examined in Vanderwood, *Juan Soldado*, although his much later Juan was shot after being forced to flee, and without trial (51).

80. Vanderwood, *Power of God*, 242–45.

81. Ibid., 40–42, 144–46.

82. On street versus home, see Freyre, *Casa-Grande y senzala*; da Matta, *A casa y a rua*; Beattie, "The House, the Street, and the Barracks."

83. *Sapper*, or *zapador*, is the archaic term for a combat engineer whose task was originally to undermine fortifications with tunneling and then burning of the support beams, called saps.

84. Urquizo, *Tropa vieja*, 47.

85. For examples, see Frías, *Battle of Tomochic*, 12–13.

86. Of course, some officers did know better but pretended not to understand. On the spread of common parlance and, in particular, *palabras brotas* (broken words) among the educated and ordinary alike, see Tenorio-Trillo, *I Speak of the City*, 369–82.

87. Frías, *Battle of Tomochic*, 39; Urquizo, *Tropa vieja*, 123, 140.

88. For a contemporary history on the topic, see Sharman, *Cursory History of Swearing*, 11–21; on the colonial era, see Villa-Flores, *Dangerous Speech*, 10–52.

89. Urquizo, *Tropa vieja*, 68.

90. Scott, *Weapons of the Weak*, 289–95; and Scott, *Domination and the Arts of Resistance*, 140–62.

91. Urquizo, *Tropa vieja*, 98.

92. Ley Penal Militar, 1897, Tit. 2, Cap.1, on "embriagues"; Art. 236–40, on drinking; Art. 238, on officers in uniform; and Art. 239, on sergeants or cabos. See also "Oficiales en las cantinas," *Diario del Hogar*, April 29, 1903, 24.

93. "Embriaguez," *Derecho Militar*, May 4, 1895, 1–2. This term also could include marijuana use.

Chapter Seven

1. James Kelley, "Professionalism," 57.

2. Headrick, *Tools of Empire*, 4–12.

3. As described by Foucault, this is a shift of scope from biopower to processes of governmentality and biopolitics.

4. Aponte, *Empirismos*, 71, 78.

5. AGN, CMDF, Caja 334, Soldado Rafael Cervantes: trial, November 23, 1897.

6. For one example, see AGN, CMDF, Caja 3567, Subtnt. Antonio Manzano, January 7, 1879.

7. "Escuela de Aspirantes," *El Imparcial*, January 6, 1907.

8. AGN, CMDF, expedientes personales.

9. Urquizo, "Juan Soldado," *De la vida militar mexicana*, 43–50.

10. Alexius, "Army and Politics," 69–124.

11. Léon Martínez to PD, September 28, 1880, CPD, Legajo 5, Caja 7, Doc. 3464.

12. The alférez was the lowest rank of cavalry officer, equivalent to second lieutenant or sublieutenant of infantry. Etymologically it comes from Moorish borrowings and means, simply, rider.

13. AGN, CMDF, Caja 343, Tnt. Cor. José María García.

14. AGN, CMDF, Caja 345, Tnt. Blas Gracilazo.

15. *México Gráfico*, September 1891, 7.

16. For example, see Janvier, "Mexican Army," 816, where he notes officers' indigenous features as a positive sign.

17. Esposito, *Funerals, Festivals, and Cultural Politics*, 100–103, 138–43.

18. Xavier-Guerra, *Le Mexique*, 53–61.

19. AGN, CMDF, Caja 371, Capt. Fermín Sada, 1868.

20. AGN, CMDF, Caja 321, Crl. Eduardo Arce, May 8, 1889.

21. See, for example, AGN, CMDF, Caja 372, Capt. 1 Alejandro Silvestrini.

22. AGN, CMDF, Caja 372, Gen. de Brig. Jesús S. Sosa.

23. CPD, guía, efímeras: May 13, 1889, former president Lerdo de Tejada's body returned to Mexico, Rocha commands honores; September 15, 1891, Grl Carlos Pacheco dies; January 9, 1900, Felipe Berriozábal dies.

24. Stephen Neufeld, "Behaving Badly in Mexico City: Discipline and Identity in the Presidential Guards, 1900–1911," in Rugeley and Fallow, *Forced Marches*, 85–88; Víctor Macías González, "Presidential Ritual in Porfirian Mexico: Curtsying in the Shadow of Dictators," in Brunk and Fallaw, *Heroes and Hero Cults*, 83–108.

25. Piccato, *Tyranny of Opinion*, 83–93.

26. Cor. Juan N. Malda to PD, July 23, 1887, Legajo 12, Caja 14, Doc. 6537.

27. AGN, CMDF, Caja 370, Sóstenes Rocha.

28. Escudero, *El duelo en México*, 159.

29. For a few examples, see "Oficiales en las cantinas," *Diario del Hogar*, August 13, 1890, 3; "Un oficial consignado," *Diario del Hogar*, January 9, 1902, 3; "Los militares en las pulquerías," *Diario del Hogar*, May 25, 1906, 3; "Otro jefe de batallón suspendido," *Diario del Hogar*, July 18, 1903, 3.

30. French, "*Te amo muncho*"; also see his forthcoming monograph.

31. AGN, CMDF, Caja 372, Capt. 2 Rosalio Salazar.

32. AGN, CMDF, Caja 375, Alférez Porfirio Velasco, 1890.

33. AGN, CMDF, Caja 374, Cdte. Guillermo Thompson, 1885.

34. AGN, CMDF, Caja 346, Capt. 2 Rafael Guitian June 4, 1880.

35. Pérez Montfort, Castillo Yurrita, and Piccato, *Hábitos, normas y escándalo*, 75–121.

36. AGN, CMDF, Caja 320, Subtnt. Zacarías Álvarez del Castillo, June 27, 1896; AGN, CMDF, Caja 358, Capt. 2 Herminio Montenegro; AGN, CMDF, Caja 372, Subtnt. Luis San German, May 3, 1872.

37. Pérez Montfort, Castillo Yurrita, and Piccato, *Hábitos, normas y escándalo*, 26–37, 82–97.
38. James Kelley, "Professionalism," 81; Didapp, *Gobiernos militares de México*.
39. "Gratificaciones," *Revista Militar Mexicana*, December 15, 1889, 39–44.
40. Ibid., 42.
41. Alexius, "Army and Politics," 90–124.
42. CDX BR, Vol. 34, 6735, Juan D. Brijar to BR, March 7, 1902; CDX BR, Vol. 34, 6753, V. Huerta to BR, August 31, 1902; CDX BR, Vol. 29, 5772, Juan A Hernández to BR, July 13, 1900; Ignacio Escudero to José del Valle, February 21, 1890, CPD, Legajo 15, Caja 3, Doc. 1065; PD to Gob. Alejandro Prieto, August 19, 1891, CPD, Legajo 16, Caja 19, Doc. 9105; Prieto reply, October 29, 1891, CPD, Legajo 16, Caja 28, Doc. 13771.
43. Ongoing diatribes in CDX BR, Vol. 34, letters from Huerta to BR, Docs.6733, 6741, 6743, 6745, March–May, 1902, and in Vol. 34, 6636, May 16, 1901, Huerta in Sinaloa.
44. Aponte, *Empirismos*, 81.
45. James Kelley, "Professionalism," 63–64.
46. For one example, see AGN, CMDF, Caja 95, Tnt. Antonio Díaz, July 15, 1892.
47. México, Secretaría de Guerra, *Examenes de Colegio Militar*.
48. México, Secretaría de Guerra, *Reglamento de Colegio Militar*; Chavarri, *El heroico Colegio Militar*, 195–237.
49. *Memorias*, parte expositivo, 1906.
50. For one example, see "Todo es empezar," *La Vanguardia*, April 9, 1891, 1, 2; April 16, 1891, 1; April 23, 1891, 1–2.
51. On the Presidential Guards, see Stephen Neufeld, "Behaving Badly in Mexico City: Discipline and Identity in the Presidential Guards, 1900–1911," in Rugeley and Fallow, *Forced Marches*, 81–109.
52. AGN, FGyM, Estado Mayor Especial, Caja 94, expedientes persónale, Tnt. Cor. Francisco García.
53. James Kelley, "Professionalism," 132.
54. Waterways were mostly federalized by 1888. See Masilla, *De cómo Porfirio Díaz dominas las aguas*.
55. For various examples, see career accomplishments in Sánchez Lamego, *Generales de ingenieros*; and México, Secretaría de Fomento y Olegario Molina, *Memorias*, 1906–1907.
56. Garner, *British Lions and Mexican Eagles*, 88–89.
57. Luis Espinosa, "Reseña histórica y técnica de las obras del desagüe del Valle de México, 1856–1900," in Gonzalez Obregón, *Memoria historica y técnicade*, vol. 1; Schell, *Integral Outsiders*.
58. For a full biography, see Flipper and Taylor, *Colored Cadet at West Point*.
59. *Memorias*, 1900–1902.
60. *Memorias*, December 31, 1902, 12.
61. Ramona Falcón, "Force and the Search for Consent: The Role of the Jefaturas Políticas of Coahuila in National State Formation," in Joseph and Nugent, *Everyday Forms of State Formation*, 124; see chapter 1.
62. Craib, *Cartographic Mexico*, 127–92.
63. R. Rebollar to Ayuntamiento DF, December 31, 1896, BAHDF, Ayuntamiento del Gobierno DF, Vol. 1323, Exp.1254.

64. BAHDF, Vol. 1323, Exp. 1254, Guillermo Puga to R. Rebollar, April 3, 12, 1897.

65. BAHDF, Vol. 1323, Exp. 1254, Secretaría de Guerra to Ayuntamiento, May 1, August 12, 18, 1897.

66. BAHDF, Vol. 1323, Exp. 1254, Ayuntamiento to Sec. Guerra, December 20, 1899.

67. Craib, *Cartographic Mexico*, 8–17.

68. Agustín Díaz to PD, January 24, 1889, CPD, Legajo 14, Caja 1, Doc. 230; PD to Gen. Carlos Diez Gutiérrez, October 2, 1890, CPD, Legajo 15, Caja 25, Doc. 12034.

69. Jerónimo Treviño to PD, May 10, 1885, CPD, Legajo 10, Caja 11, Doc. 5395 (response 5396): from near Monterrey.

70. Nunn, *Yesterday's Soldiers*.

71. Hogg and Weeks, *Military Small Arms*, 116–52; PD to Aurelio Melgarejo (in Liege), April 11, 1891, CPD, Legajo 16, Caja 8, Doc. 3769–72 (expresses his preference for purchase of more German rifles).

72. BAHDF, Ayuntamiento del DF, Vol. 34, Exp. 96, May 6, 1898.

73. *Memorias*, 1906, 15.

74. "El ultimo colosal cañon Krupp," *Periódico Militar*, January 1, 1880, 7–8.

75. AGN, CMDF, Caja 359, Capt. Enrique Mondragón.

76. Casasola, *Biografía ilustrada*, 115.

77. "New Guns for Mexico," *New York Times*, September 5, 1908, 4.

78. Becerril, interview, 17, PHO 1/61. It is not clear whether this artillery piece saw action in World War I in defense of Turkey at Gallipoli and so forth, as most of the heavy guns that took such a toll on British and French vessels appear to have been Krupp made. It remains something of a mystery for now.

79. Hughes, *Mexican Military Arms*, 19–20.

80. Ramona Falcón, "Force and the Search for Consent: The Role of the Jefaturas Políticas of Coahuila in National State Formation," in Joseph and Nugent, *Everyday Forms of State Formation*, 107–34.

81. AGN, sección Gobernación, Rurales, Caja 662, Exp. 2–21; Caja 665, Exp. 11–20 (1890); Caja 681, Exp. 8 (1892); Caja 686, Exp. 2–26 (1893); Caja 703, Exp. 1–10 (1895); Caja 707, Exp. 3 (1896), among others.

82. The classic study is Vanderwood, *Disorder and Progress*.

83. Frazer, *Bandit Nation*.

84. Buffington, *Criminal and Citizen*, 33; Robinson, "Mexican Banditry"; Irwin, *Bandits, Captives, Heroines, and Saints*.

85. Dabove, *Nightmares of the Lettered City*, 1–42.

86. Robinson, "Mexican Banditry," 8, 9.

87. Juan M. Flores to PD, July 5, 1887, CPD, Legajo 12, Caja 13, Doc. 6299–6300.

88. CPD, Legajo 13, Caja 7, Doc. 3112-a (photo of cadaver of Heraclio Bernal).

89. AGN, CMDF, Caja 336, loose note.

90. Lorenzo García to PD, December 14, 1892, CPD, Legajo17, Caja 39, Doc. 19370.

91. James Kelley, "Professionalism," 79n43.

92. "Ley fuga," *Regeneración*, March 15, 1901, 5–6.

93. Lorenzo García to PD, July 19, 1882, CPD, Legajo7, Caja 2, Doc. 702.

94. Lorenzo García to PD, November 5, 12, 1891, CPD, Legajo 16, Caja 29, Doc. 14271–72; Aniceto López to PD, December 14, 1884, CPD, Legajo 9, Caja 4, Doc. 1812.

95. AGN, CMDF, Caja 347, Lt. Ygnacio Esparzo García.

96. AGN, CMDF, Caja 329, N. Caldera, 1880.

97. Lorenzo García to PD, July 19, 1882, CPD, Legajo 7, Caja 2, Doc. 702.

98. Tenorio-Trillo, *Mexico at the World's Fairs*, 84.

99. Hernández Chávez, "Origen y ocaso del ejército porfiriano."

100. "Colonias militares," *Revista Militar Mexicana*, October 15, 1890, 587–91.

Chapter Eight

1. J. Hernández, "From Conquest to Colonization"; Savarino Roggero, *Pueblos y nacionalismo*, 61–71.

2. For two examples of how an early sense of hegemony was built, won, and ultimately lost in different regions of the nation during the early nineteenth century, see Mallon, *Peasants and Nation*; and Guardino, *Peasants, Politics*.

3. Rodríguez O., *Divine Charter*, 22; and Alicia Hernández-Chavez, "From *Res Publicae* to Republic: The Evolution of Republicanism in Early Mexico," in Rodríguez O., *Divine Charter*, 35–64.

4. Frazer, *Bandit Nation*, 14–15, 133–39; Beezley, *Mexican National Identity*, vii–xii, 147–49.

5. On self-targeting imperialism and hegemony, see Richard, *Nuevas fronteras Mexicana*; William Roseberry, "Hegemony and the Language of Contention," in Joseph and Nugent, *Everyday Forms of State Formation*, 355–66; Gruzinski, *Images at War*, 3–6, 32–60; Headrick, *Tools of Empire*, 3–16, 209; Parsons, *British Imperial Century*, 1–3, 5–8.

6. See Edward Casey, "How to Get from Space to Place in a Fairly Short Stretch of Time: Phenomenological Prolegomena," in Feld and Basso, *Senses of Place*, 13–52.

7. Matthews, *Civilizing Machine*, 11–20, 250–55; Adas, *Machines as the Measure of Men*, 199–270, 402–18.

8. Savarino Roggero, *Pueblos y nacionalismo*, 19–27.

9. Foucault, *Security, Territory, Population*; Foucault, *Birth of Biopolitics*; Burchell, Gordon, and Miller, *Foucault Effect*, 2–3; Deleuze, *Foucault*, xxix; Foucault, *History of Sexuality*, 6:148.

10. Colin Gordon, "Government Rationality: An Introduction," in Burchell, Gordon, and Miller, *Foucault Effect*, 3; Foucault, *Society Must Be Defended*, 240–42.

11. Michel Foucault, "Governmentality," in Burchell, Gordon, and Miller, *Foucault Effect*, 99.

12. Deleuze, *Foucault*, 29; Gilles Deleuze and Félix Guattori, "Savages, Barbarians, and Civilized Men," in Lawrence and Karim, *On Violence*, 478, 480–84, 489.

13. Robins, *Native Insurgencies*, 154–72.

14. Vanderwood, *Power of Gods*.

15. Gosner, *Soldiers of the Virgin*; Lamadrid, "El Corrido de Tomóchic"; Frías, *Battle of Tomochic*; Vanderwood, *Power of God*; Gruzinski, *Images at War*, 170–72.

16. CDX BR, DLI, Carp. 1, Legajo 15876–77.

17. Taibo, *Yaquis*, 101–6; Vanderwood, *Power of God*, 190.

18. For a Brazilian counterpart of the same era, see Da Cunha, *Os sertões*.

19. Vanderwood, *Power of God*, 248–53.

20. Lamadrid, "El Corrido de Tomóchic," 443–44.
21. Vanderwood, *Power of God*, 281–93; Alonso, *Thread of Blood*, 21–50.
22. Vanderwood, *Power of God*, 294–306, 317–29.
23. Lamadrid, "El Corrido de Tomóchic"; Stephen Neufeld, "Sly Mockeries of Military Men," in Neufeld and Matthews, *Mexico in Verse*, 94–98.
24. Truett, *Fugitive Landscapes*, 57–63; Vanderwood, *Power of God*, 112–16; Julia O'Hara, "'The Slayer of Victorio Bears His Honors Quietly': Tarahumara and the Apache Wars in Nineteenth-Century Mexico," in Foote and Horst, *Military Struggles and Identity Formation*, 224–42.
25. Troncoso and Ministerio de Guerra y Marina, *Las guerras con las tribus Yaqui*, 235; Hu-DeHart, *Yaqui Resistance and Survival*, 73.
26. CDX BR, DLI, Carp. 1, Legajo 54, BR to PD July 31, 1883.
27. Troncoso and Ministerio de Guerra y Marina, *Las guerras con las tribus Yaqui*, 239; to the existing Eleventh and Twelfth Battalions and Fifth Regiment, the government now deployed the Twentieth, Seventeenth, and Fourth Battalions, along with elements from other units as detachments and auxiliaries.
28. CDX BR, DLI, Carp. 1, Legajo 15708, José Montesinos to General Carbó.
29. CDX BR, DLT, Carp. 34, Legajo 6705, Dr. Fortín Hernández to Bernardo Reyes.
30. See, among others, Farriss, *Mayan Society under Colonial Rule*; Clendinnen, *Ambivalent Conquests*; Wells and Joseph, *Summer of Discontent, Seasons of Upheaval*; Eiss, *In the Name of El Pueblo*; Dumond, *Machete and the Cross*; N. Reed, *Caste War of the Yucatán*; Rugeley, *Yucatán's Mayan Peasantry*; Rugeley, *Rebellion Now and Forever*; Evans, *Bound in Twine*.
31. Joseph, *Revolution from Without*, 33–69.
32. Evans, *Bound in Twine*, 33–39.
33. Dumond, *Machete and the Cross*, 319–22; Reed, *Caste War of the Yucatán*, 224–300.
34. Richard, *Nuevas fronteras Mexicana*, 30.
35. Ibid., 19.
36. CDX BR, DLT, Carp. 34, Legajo 6733, Victoriano Huerta to Bernardo Reyes, March 4, 1902.
37. "80 Yaquis en 24 Batallón," *El Imparcial*, July 4, 1897, 1.
38. On Mayan capabilities as soldiers, see Richard, *Nuevas fronteras Mexicana*, 23–28; *Mexico Militar*, various reports throughout 1900–1901; Morris, *Story of Mexico*, 136.
39. Balbás, *Recuerdos del Yaqui*, 33, 39.
40. Ibid., 18–19; CDX BR, DLT, Carp. 34, Legajo 5723, Luis Torres to Bernardo Reyes, March 8, 1900.
41. Hu-DeHart, *Yaqui Resistance and Survival*, 91.
42. CDX BR, Carp. 29, Legajo 5775, Bravo Peto to BR, August 14, 1900; CDX BR, DLT, Carp. 34, Legajo 6750, Victoriano Huerta to Bernardo Reyes, May 20, 1902.
43. Wells and Joseph, *Summer of Discontent, Seasons of Upheaval*, 52.
44. Reed, *Caste War of the Yucatán*, 288–99.
45. CDX BR, DLT, Carp. 34, Legajo 6733, Victoriano Huerta to Bernardo Reyes, March 4, 1902, and Victoriano Huerta to BR, March 31, 1902.
46. Balbás, *Recuerdos del Yaqui*, 18.
47. Taibo, *Yaquis*, 33–37, 84–88, 89–94.

48. Balbás, *Recuerdos del Yaqui*, 7.

49. Spicer, "Military History," 59.

50. CDX BR, DLT, Carp. 34, Legajo 6738, Luis E. Torres to Bernardo Reyes, March 18, 1902.

51. Vanderwood, *Power of God*, 247.

52. Troncoso and Ministerio de Guerra y Marina, *Las guerras con las tribus Yaqui*, 245.

53. CDX BR, DLT, Carp. 34, Legajo 5723, Luis Torres to Bernardo Reyes, March 8, 1900.

54. The Sierras were not absent of malaria and yellow fever; for example, see Taibo, *Yaquis*, 57.

55. Balbás, *Recuerdos del Yaqui*, 28.

56. CDX BR, Carp. 29, Legajo 5793, L. E. Torres to BR, September 30, 1900.

57. "Mexico Will Use Indians to Fight Indians," *New York Times*, June 24, 1906, SM3.

58. Balbás, *Recuerdos del Yaqui*, 7; Troncoso and Ministerio de Guerra y Marina, *Las guerras con las tribus Yaqui*, 268. Other reports also supported this. See "Mexico Will Use Indians to Fight Indians," *New York Times*, June 24, 1906, SM3.

59. Eiss, *In the Name of El Pueblo*, 27, 218–43.

60. On malaria as a chief obstacle to imperialism, see Headrick, *Tools of Empire*, 58–82; and, for Yucatán, McCrea, *Diseased Relations*.

61. Wells and Joseph, *Summer of Discontent, Seasons of Upheaval*, 50.

62. McCrea, *Diseased Relations*, 133–62.

63. CDX BR, Carp. 41, Legajo 9976, Pedro Baranda to BR.

64. CDX BR, Carp. 29, Legajo 5775, Gnl. Bravo to BR, August 14, 1900; CDX BR, Legajo 6743, Victoriano Huerta to BR, April 6, 1902; Kenneth Turner cited in Richard, *Nuevas fronteras Mexicana*, n57.

65. PD to Baranda, CPD 7, Legajo 11, Doc. 3351, 1886.

66. Richard, *Nuevas fronteras Mexicana*, 31.

67. CDX BR, DLT, Carp. 34, Legajo 6636, Victoriano Huerta to Bernardo Reyes, May 16, 1901.

68. CPD 5, Legajo 8, Caja 10, Doc. 4054, Tnt Crl Francisco Matos to PD.

69. Wells and Joseph, *Summer of Discontent, Seasons of Upheaval*, 50.

70. Balbás, *Recuerdos del Yaqui*, 6, 69.

71. Lamadrid, "El Corrido de Tomóchic," 450–55; Spicer, "Military History," 56; Vanderwood, *Power of God*, 190; Gruzinski, *Images at War*, 197–99; Troncoso and Ministerio de Guerra y Marina, *Las guerras con las tribus Yaqui*, 236.

72. Troncoso and Ministerio de Guerra y Marina, *Las guerras con las tribus Yaqui*, 236.

73. Gen. A. Bandala, May 16, 1892, cited in ibid., 196.

74. Spicer, "Military History," 59; Troncoso and Ministerio de Guerra y Marina, *Las guerras con las tribus Yaqui*, 287.

75. Spicer, "Military History," 59–112; Moisés, Kelley, and Holden, *Yaqui Life*, 30–69.

76. Fabila, *Las tribus Yaqui de Sonora*, xi, 184–88.

77. Spicer, "Military History," 56.

78. Spicer, "Military History," 58; Taibo, *Yaquis*, 30–32.

79. Spicer, "Military History," 55.

80. Taibo, *Yaquis*, 33–37, 84–88.

81. Troncoso and Ministerio de Guerra y Marina, *Las guerras con las tribus Yaqui*, 181, 196, 236.

82. Dumond, *Machete and the Cross*, 355–58; Reed, *Caste War of the Yucatán*, 266; Savarino Roggero, *Pueblos y nacionalismo*, 97.

83. Richard, *Nuevas fronteras Mexicana*, 17; Savarino Roggero, *Pueblos y nacionalismo*, 173.

84. For example, see José María Rosado, "Not as a Prisoner but as One of the Family: The Captivity Narrative of José María Rosado," in Rugeley, *Mayan Wars*, 68–78.

85. Gruzinski, *Images at War*, 170–72, 197–99.

86. Aníbal Quijano, "Coloniality of Power, Eurocentrism, and Social Classifications," in Maraña, Dussel, and Júaregui, *Coloniality at Large*, 181–221.

87. Dabove, *Nightmares of the Lettered City*.

88. Foucault, *History of Sexuality*, 1:76; Michel Foucault, "Questions of Method," in Burchell, Gordon, and Miller, *Foucault Effect*, 20–38.

89. A few such examples include "Indians of North America," *New York Times*, July 4, 1885, 4; "Gov. Ortez's Quarrel with Federal Gen. Reyes," *New York Times*, October 28, 1882, 5; "Mexico," *New York Times*, December 29, 1885, 3; "Mexico-Yaqui Indians; Government Troops and Tax Collectors Attacked," *New York Times*, December 28, 1892, 1.

90. Spicer, "Military History," 61.

91. SRE, Archivo Histórico, Tomo 3, Legajo 1689, Correspondencia Diplomática, *Revista de Mérida*, January 1874.

92. De la Fuente, *Children of Facundo*; J. Rodriguez, *Civilizing Argentina*; Larson, *Trials of Nation Making*, 49–52, 111, 152, 214, 63–65; Mallon, *Peasant and Nation*; Lynch, *Massacre in the Pampas*, 9–37, 195–205.

93. Agamben, *State of Exception*; and an update in Agamben, *Kingdom and Glory*.

94. Spicer, "Military History," 54; Vanderwood, *Power of God*, 135–40; Troncoso and Ministerio de Guerra y Marina, *Las guerras con las tribus Yaqui*, 22.

95. Alonso, *Thread of Blood*, 21–50; Hämäläinen, *Comanche Empire*, 306–7, 319–20, 355–60.

96. CDX BR, DLI, Carp. 1, Legajo 164, BR to PD, March 24, 1885.

97. See, for instance, civilization lauded in the official textbook of the Colegio Militar (between 1886 and 1901), Prieto, *Lecciones de historia patria*, 448.

98. Balbás, *Recuerdos del Yaqui*, 9.

99. Agamben, *State of Exception*, 85–88.

100. Agamben, *Kingdom and the Glory*, 3–4, 109–11.

101. Michel Foucault, "Governmentality," in Burchell, Gordon, and Miller, *Foucault Effect*, 87–88, 99–104; Deleuze, *Foucault*, 92; Foucault, *Society Must Be Defended*, 245.

102. Bourdieu, *Outline of a Theory*, 191–93.

103. SRE, Archivo Histórico, Tomo 170, Legajo 266, Robert Bacon to Amb. Enrique Creel, April 10, 1907, and Mexican consul (Tucson) to SRE, April 19, 1907; Truett, *Fugitive Landscapes*, 80, 118–19.

104. Hu-DeHart, *Yaqui Resistance and Survival*, 88; SRE, Archivo Histórico, Tomo 170, Legajo 266, Arizona governor Joseph H. Kibley to SRE, April 23, 1907.

105. See, for example, *US v. Benavides*, testimony of Francisco Morales and various others, taken by US Commissioner L. F. Price, February 16–19, 1893, in SRE, Archivo Historico, Tomo 421, Legajo 197; E. Young, *Catarino Garza's Revolution*.

106. SRE, Archivo Histórico, Tomo 170, Legajo 311, Ricardo Johnson to Enrique Creel, January 7, 1908.

107. Various reports in SRE, Archivo Histórico, Tomo 3, Legajos 1689, 1835, and 1383, from 1874 to 1880s.

108. SRE, Archivo Histórico, Tomo 3, Legajo 1669, letter to Ministro de Negocios Extranjeros, July 28, 1874.

109. SRE, Archivo Histórico, Tomo 3, Legajo 1669, Y. L. Vallarta to Minister of Foreign Affairs, 1867.

110. Richard, *Nuevas fronteras Mexicana*, 12.

111. Hu-DeHart, *Yaqui Resistance and Survival*, 74–75.

112. Spicer, "Military History," 48.

113. Craib, *Cartographic Mexico*, 7–17, 127–92.

114. México, Secretaría de Fomento y Olegario Molina, *Memorias*, 1909–1910, vi–viii and 40–74 (report for Comisión Científico de Sonora, by Tnt. Cor. Antonio F. Torres).

115. McCrea, *Diseased Relations*, 154–61; on the concept of medicalized race, see Peard, *Race, Place, and Medicine*, 81–108.

116. Wells and Joseph, *Summer of Discontent, Seasons of Upheaval*, 153.

117. "Colonias Militares," *Revista Militar Mexicana*, October 15, 1890, 587–91.

118. "Territorio de Quintana Roo," *Memorias*, 1906, 12.

119. *Memorias*, 1909, 57.

120. México, Secretaría de Fomento y Olegario Molina, *Memorias*, 1909–1910, 69–71.

121. CDX BR, DLI, Carp. 1, Legajo 164, March 24, 1885; Hu-DeHart, *Yaqui Resistance and Survival*, 76; Spicer, "Military History," 60 (import of colonists); Dabdoub, *Historia de el Valle del Yaqui*, 64; México, Secretaría de Fomento y Olegario Molina, *Memorias*, 1909–1910, 73; Taibo, *Yaquis*, 59.

122. México, Secretaría de Fomento y Olegario Molina, *Memorias*, 1909, 1074.

123. Troncoso and Ministerio de Guerra y Marina, *Las guerras con las tribus Yaqui*, 264–80.

124. Headrick, *Tools of Empire*, 17–18.

125. Vallarta Vélez, *Los payobispenses*, 369–428.

126. CDX BR, DLT, Carp. 34, Legajo 6736, March 13, 1902, Bernardo Reyes to José María de la Vega.

127. CDX BR, Carp. 29, Legajo 5730, Pablo Rocha to BR, March 14, 1900.

128. PHO 1/31, Meraz, 6.

129. *Memorias*, 1902, 447.

130. Sánchez Lamego, *Generales de ingenieros*, 116, 240, 247, 266, 273.

131. CDX BR, Carp. 34, Legajo 6743, Victoriano Huerta to BR, April 6, 1902.

132. CDX BR, Carp. 34, Legajo 6745, Victoriano Huerta to BR, April 27, 1902; CDX BR, Carp. 34, Legajo 6743, Victoriano Huerta to BR, April 6, 1902.

133. CDX BR, DLT, Carp. 34, Legajo 6754, Victoriano Huerta to BR, September 3, 1902.

134. Castro, "Wireless Radio, Revolution, and the Mexican State," 61–89; Dabdoub, *Historia de el Valle del Yaqui*, 304–5; Troncoso and Ministerio de Guerra y Marina, *Las guerras con las tribus Yaqui*, 277; Vallarta Vélez, *Los payobispenses*, 369–428.

135. CDX BR, Carp. 34, Legajo 6743, Victoriano Huerta to BR April 6, 1902 (asserting need for telegraph installed soonest at Tulum).

136. CDX BR, Carp. 34, Legajo 6748, Victoriano Huerta to BR, May 28, 1901; CDX BR, 29, A. Barrios to BR, September 13, 1900; Richard, *Nuevas fronteras Mexicana*, 146.

137. Richard, *Nuevas fronteras Mexicana*, 48; Wells and Joseph, *Summer of Discontent, Seasons of Upheaval*, 46.

138. CDX BR, DLT, Carp. 34, Legajo 6733, Victoriano Huerta to Bernardo Reyes, March 4, 1902.

139. CDX BR, DLT, Carp. 34, Legajo 6750, Victoriano Huerta to Bernardo Reyes, May 20, 1902.

140. CDX BR, Carp. 34, Legajo 6743, Victoriano Huerta to BR, April 6, 1902; PHO 1/31, Eduardo Angeles Meraz, 6.

141. CDX BR, Carp. 34, Legajo 6744, Victoriano Huerta to BR, April 8, 1902.

142. CDX BR, Carp. 34, Legajo 6750, Victoriano Huerta to BR, May 20, 1902; CDX BR, Carp. 34, Doc. 6754, Victoriano Huerta to BR, September 3, 1902.

143. Reed, *Caste War of the Yucatán*, 298.

144. Wells and Joseph, *Summer of Discontent, Seasons of Upheaval*, 155.

145. CDX BR, DLT, Carp. 34, Legajo 6739, Molina to Bernardo Reyes, March 25, 1902.

146. See "Campaña de Yucatán," *México Militar*, 1900, 17–20; James Kelley, "Professionalism," 68–71.

147. Foucault, *Archeology of Knowledge*, 43; Foucault, *Society Must Be Defended*, 257–58; Cobb, "Archeology and the 'Savage Slot'"; Robert Cover, "Violence and the Word," in Lawrence and Karim, *On Violence*, 303.

148. Parsons, *British Imperial Century*, 27–32; Savarino Roggero, *Pueblos y nacionalismo*, 24, 43–53.

149. CDX BR, DLT, Carp. 34, Legajo 5713, Luis E. Torres to BR, February 27, 1900; and CDX BR, DLT, Carp. 34, Legajo 5723, Luis E. Torres to BR, March 8, 1900.

150. Hu-DeHart, *Yaqui Resistance and Survival*, 79; Troncoso and Ministerio de Guerra y Marina, *Las guerras con las tribus Yaqui*, 284–86.

151. Balbás, *Recuerdos del Yaqui*, 48–55.

152. Ibid., 54; Spicer, "Military History," 49.

153. Troncoso and Ministerio de Guerra y Marina, *Las guerras con las tribus Yaqui*, 287.

154. Taibo, *Yaquis*, 154–57, 182–86, 227–36; Moisés, Kelley, and Holden, *Yaqui Life*, xvii–xx; 2–34; Jane Kelley, *Yaqui Women*, 83–84, 131, 159; F. Hernández, *Las razas indigenas*, 174–80; Dabdoub, *Historia de el Valle del Yaqui*, 155.

155. For example, another massacre took place at Mazatán two years later. Taibo, *Yaquis*, 182–86.

156. Balbás, *Recuerdos del Yaqui*, 103.

157. See Collins, *Violence*, 19–20, 76–78, 83–99.

158. Taibo, *Yaquis*, 154–57.

159. Colin Gordon, "Governmental Rationality: An Introduction," in Burchell, Gordon, and Miller, *Foucault Effect*, 38; Sharon Welch, "Dangerous Memories and Alternate Knowledges," in Lawrence and Karim, *On Violence*, 363–76.

160. Richard, *Nuevas fronteras Mexicana*, 64.

161. Richard, "El territorio de Quintana Roo."

162. Ignacio Bravo to Porfirio Díaz, cited in Wells and Joseph, *Summer of Discontent, Seasons of Upheaval*, 46.

163. Troncoso and Ministerio de Guerra y Marina, *Las guerras con las tribus Yaqui*, 260, 287; Spicer, "Military History," 140; McCrea, *Diseased Relations*, 153.

164. CDX BR, Carp. 34, Legajo 6640, LE Torres to BR, May 2, 1901.

165. Troncoso and Ministerio de Guerra y Marina, *Las guerras con las tribus Yaqui*, 342.

166. Spicer, "Military History," 60.

167. Balbás, *Recuerdos del Yaqui*, 60–61.

168. On both the deportation and conditions in Yucatán, see Evans, *Bound in Twine*, esp. 62–82.

169. *Memorias*, 1900, 3–4.

170. CDX BR, DLT, Carp. 34, Legajo 6636, Victoriano Huerta to Bernardo Reyes, May 16, 1901.

171. Hu-DeHart, *Yaqui Resistance and Survival*, 83; on Molino's career in Yucatán, see Wells and Joseph, *Summer of Discontent, Seasons of Upheaval*, 3–6; Savarino Roggero, *Pueblos y nacionalismo*, 151–80.

172. Government figures said 2,000 from 1903 to 1907; Hu-Dehart, *Yaqui Resistance and Survival*, 83. J. K. Turner says 15,700; cited in Spicer, "Military History," 47. Galeano said 10,000 but lacked research materials when doing so; Galeano, *Open Veins of Latin America*. A conservative estimate suggests that a number no greater than 8,000 and no fewer than 5,000 went south; Spicer, "Military History," 160–61. For an excellent discussion of varying estimates, see Evans, *Bound in Twine*, 62, 77, 78.

173. Balbás, *Recuerdos del Yaqui*, 108, 114–16.

174. "Mexico Will Use Indians to Fight Indians," *New York Times*, June 24, 1906, SM3.

175. CDX BR, Carp. 29, Legajo 5770, L. E. Torres to BR, July 7, 1900.

176. Spicer, "Military History," 160–61; Troncoso and Ministerio de Guerra y Marina, *Las guerras con las tribus Yaqui*, 24. Total population figures varied; for example, twenty thousand total is claimed in "Yaquis at Last Conquered," *New York Times*, June 1, 1908, 4.

177. Hu-DeHart, *Yaqui Resistance and Survival*, 83, 94–109.

178. Troncoso and Ministerio de Guerra y Marina, *Las guerras con las tribus Yaqui*, 24–26, 235.

179. C. Smith, *Emilio Kosterlitzky*; Truett, *Fugitive Landscapes*, 139.

180. SRE, pt. 2, 7340–43, April 10, 1907; "Col. Milio [sic] Kosterlitzsky," *New York Times*, June 6, 1906, 2.

181. Hu-DeHart, *Yaqui Resistance and Survival*, 187, 188.

182. Dabdoub, *Historia de el Valle del Yaqui*, 150–54.

183. Jane Holden Kelley provides two Yaqui accounts of the hardships deportation entailed in *Yaqui Women*, 134–36, 159–61.

184. Ibid., 134.

185. Ibid., 136.

186. Ibid., 134–36, 159–61.

187. The classic text on this is Elias, *Civilizing Process*.

188. Michel Foucault, "Governmentality," in Burchell, Gordon, and Miller, *Foucault Effect*, 99–100; Deleuze, *Foucault*, xxvii, 76, 92; Foucault, *Society Must Be Defended*, 256.

189. Harris, *Resettlement of British Columbia*, xii, 92–102, 157–60, 191–93; Dumond, *Machete and the Cross*, 389; Foucault, *Society Must Be Defended*, 242, 250.

190. CDX BR, DLI, Carp. 1, Legajo 7, BR to Manuel González, May 14, 1881.

191. CDX BR, DLT, Carp. 34, Legajo 6738, Luis E. Torres to Bernardo Reyes, March 18, 1902.

192. Hu-DeHart, *Yaqui Resistance and Survival*, 88; Spicer, "Military History," 56.

193. Hu-DeHart, *Yaqui Resistance and Survival*, 90.

194. Ibid., 83.

195. Evans, *Bound in Twine*, 77–78; Hu-DeHart, *Yaqui Resistance and Survival*, 80.

196. Hu-DeHart, *Yaqui Resistance and Survival*, 83.

197. Spicer, "Military History," 53.

198. Torpey, *Invention of the Passport*; Salter, "Global Visa Regime"; Dutton, "Commonwealth Investigation Branch."

199. On numerous efforts to modernize criminology, see Piccato, *City of Suspects*, 50–72; Buffington, *Criminal and Citizen*, 38–63; Garza, *Imagined Underworld*, 12–38; Mark Overmyer-Velazquez, *Visions of the Emerald City*.

200. US prejudices crossed into neighbors' relations with indigenous populations, too. See Sullivan, *Xuxub Must Die*, 159.

201. Hu-DeHart, *Yaqui Resistance and Survival*, 83, 92.

202. Hu-Dehart, *Yaqui Resistance and Survival*, 73; CDX BR, DLT, Carp. 34, Legajo 6738, Luis E. Torres to BR, March 18, 1902.

203. Porfirio Díaz to BR, October 27, 1882, in Troncoso and Ministerio de Guerra y Marina, *Las guerras con las tribus Yaqui*, 96.

204. Gustavo Verdesio, "An Amnesiac Nation: The Erasure of the Indigenous Past by Uruguayan Expert Knowledge," in Castro-Klarén and Chasteen, *Beyond Imagined Communities*, 196–224; Larson, *Trials of Nation Making*, 8, 10, 17, 117–20.

205. Parsons, *British Imperial Century*, 27–32.

Epilogue

1. *El Imparcial*, July 21, 1897, 1, 2. Also see Posada's depiction of this execution, figure 2.2.

2. *El Imparcial*, July 23, 1897, 1.

3. I found a number of duplicated files where soldiers added a new, cleaner version but failed to find and destroy their old records. This particularly marked the transition to Huerta's regime in 1913.

4. For one example, see Plasencia de la Parra, *Personajes y escenarios*.

5. Camp, *Generals in the Palacio*. Distrust lay at the basis of demilitarization efforts that continued well after the 1940s; see Rath, *Myths of Demilitarization*, 2–3; and chapter 5 on popular responses.

6. Three prime examples: Rodríguez O., *Down from Colonialism*; Tenenbaum, *Politics of Penury*; Haber, *How Latin America Fell Behind*.

7. Hamilton, *Where Is the Wealth of Nations?*

8. William S. Ackroyd, "Military Professionalism and Nonintervention in Mexico," in L. Rodríguez, *Rank and Privilege*, 219–35.

9. Clendinnen, "Cost of Courage"; Daniel Nugent, "Reflections on State Theory through the Lens of the Mexican Military," in Rugeley and Fallaw, *Forced Marches*,

238–68; Aviña, *Specters of Revolution*; and see Rath, *Myths of Demilitarization*, esp. 172.

10. Laura Castellanos, "Ordenó la SEDENA exterminio en 1971," *El Universal*, January 16, 2015.

11. See Amnesty International, "Annual Report on Mexico, 2013" http://www.amnestyusa.org/research/reports/annual-report-mexico-2013#.

12. José Miguel Vivanco, "Letter to Barack Obama," January 15, 2015, Human Rights Watch, www.hrw.org.

13. Lieuwen, *Mexican Militarism*, 28, 40–45, 155; Knight, *Mexican Revolution*, 2:450–53, 474, 491.

14. Frías, "Presentimiento," *México Militar* 1, no. 15 (December 1900): 284.

Bibliography

Archives and Libraries

Archivo General de la Nación, Mexico City
    Ramo Gobernación
    Ramo Secretaría de Guerra y Marina
Archivo Histórico del Agua, Mexico City
Archivo Histórico del Estado de Guanajuato
Archivo Histórico de Secretaría de la Defensa Nacional, Mexico City
    Acervos Históricos
    Biblioteca del Ejército
    Biblioteca "General Francisco L. Urquizo" (Museo de Betlemitas)
Biblioteca del Archivo Histórico del Distrito Federal, Mexico City
Biblioteca Miguel Lerdo de Tejada, Mexico City
    Fondo Reservado
    Hemeroteca
Centro de Estudios de Historia de México, CARSO, Mexico City
    Biblioteca
    Fondo de Bernardo Reyes, DLI
    Fondo de Félix Díaz
    Acervos Históricos
Instituto de Investigaciones Dr. José María Luis Mora, Mexico City
    Biblioteca "Ernesto de la Torre Villar"
Instituto Nacional de Antropología e Historia
    Sistema Nacional de Fototecas (SINAFO)
Museo Histórico Naval de la Armada de México, Veracruz
Secretaría de Relaciones Exteriores, Instituto Matías Romero, Mexico City
    Acervos Históricos
Universidad Autónoma de México, Mexico City
    Fondo Reservado
    Hemeroteca Nacional
Universidad Iberoamericana, Mexico City
    Colección Porfirio Díaz
University of Arizona, Tucson
    Special Collections

Periodicals

Boletín Asociación Mutualista Militar/Vanguardia
Boletín de Instrucción Pública
Boletín Militar
Derecho Militar
Diario del Hogar
Diario Oficial
El Chisme
El Combate
El Gráfico (Mexico City)
El Hijo de Ahuizote
El Imparcial
El Nacional (Mexico City)
El Observador
El Partido Liberal
El Tiempo
El Universal (Mexico City)
El Universal Gráfico (Mexico City)
Excélsior (Mexico City)
Gaceta Medico-Militar
Graphic (London)
Juventud Literaria
La Ciudad de Dios
La Patria
La Revista Moderna
La Vanguardia
México Gráfico
México Militar
New York Times
Periódico Militar
Regeneración
Revista de Ejército y Marina (1901–1910)
Revista Militar Mexicano

Books, Articles, Dissertations

Adas, Michael. *Machines as the Measure of Men: Science, Technology, and Ideologies of Western Dominance*. New York: Cornell University Press, 1990.

Agamben, Giorgio. *The Kingdom and Glory: A Theoretical Genealogy of Economics and Governmentality*. Translated by Lorenzo Chiesa. Stanford, CA: Stanford University Press, 2011.

———. *State of Exception*. Translated by Kevin Attell. Chicago: University of Chicago Press, 2005.

Agostini, Claudia. *Monuments of Progress: Modernization and Public Health in Mexico City, 1876–1910*. Calgary: University of Calgary Press; Boulder: University Press of Colorado, 2003.

Alexander, Anna. "Incendiary Legislation: Fire Risk and Protection in Porfirian Puebla." *Mexican Studies* 29, no. 1 (Winter 2013): 175–99.

———. "Quotidian Catastrophes in the Modern City: Fire Hazards and Risk in Mexico's Capital, 1860–1910." PhD diss., University of Arizona, 2012.

Alexius, Robert M. "The Army and Politics in Porfirian Mexico." PhD diss., University of Texas at Austin, 1976.

Alonso, Ana Maria. "Love, Sex and Gender in Legal Cases from Namiquipa, Chihuahua, Mexico." Unpublished conference paper, 2004.

———. *Thread of Blood: Colonialism, Revolution, and Gender on Mexico's Northern Frontier*. Tucson: University of Arizona Press, 1995.

Altimirano, Manuel Ignacio. *El Zarco*. 2nd ed. 1901; repr., México: Berbera Eds., 2009.

Anderson, Benedict. *Imagined Communities*. New York: Verso, 1983.

Anderson, Rodney. *Outcasts in Their Own Land: Mexican Industrial Workers, 1906–1911*. DeKalb: Northern Illinois University Press, 1976.

Anna, Timothy E. *Forging Mexico: 1821–1835*. Lincoln: University of Nebraska Press, 1998.

Aponte, Rafael. *Empirismos de cultura, moral, social y militar*. México DF: Tip. H. Barrales Sacr., 1924.

Archer, Christon I. *The Army in Bourbon Mexico, 1760–1810*. Albuquerque: University of New Mexico Press, 1977.

———. *The Birth of Modern Mexico, 1780–1824*. Wilmington, DE: Scholarly Resources, 2003.

Arellano García, Carlos. *El juicio de amparo*. México DF: Porrúa, 1974.

Arnold, David. *Imperial Medicine and Indigenous Societies*. New York: St. Martin's Press, 1988.

Arrom, Sylvia Marina. "Popular Politics in Mexico City: The Parián Riot, 1828." *Hispanic American Historical Review* 68, no. 2 (May 1988): 245–68.

———. *The Women of Mexico City, 1790–1857*. Stanford, CA: Stanford University Press, 1985.

Ashplant, T. G., Graham Dawson, and Michael Roper, eds. *The Politics of War, Memory, and Commemoration*. New York: Routledge, 2000.

Aviña, Alexander. *Specters of Revolution: Peasant Guerrillas in the Cold War Mexican Countryside*. New York: Oxford University Press, 2014.

Azuela, Mariano, Beth Ellen Jorgensen, and E. Munguía. *The Underdogs: A Novel of the Mexican Revolution*. New York: Modern Library, 2002.

Balbás, Manuel. *Recuerdos del Yaqui: Principales episodios durante la campaña de 1899 a 1901*. México, DF: Sociedad de Edición y Librería Franco Americano, 1927.

Barman, Roderick. *Brazil: The Forging of a Nation, 1798–1852*. Stanford, CA: Stanford University Press, 1988.

Baudry, Leo. *From Chivalry to Terrorism: War and the Changing Nature of Masculinity*. New York: Alfred A. Knopf, 2003.

Bazant de Saldaña, Mílada, et al. *La evolución de la educación militar de México.* México, DF: Secretaría de la Defensa Nacional, 1997.

Beattie, Peter M. "The House, the Street, and the Barracks: Reform and Honorable Masculine Social Space in Brazil, 1864–1945." *Hispanic American Historical Review* 76, no. 3 (1996): 439–73.

———. *Tribute of Blood: Army, Honor, Race, and Nation in Brazil, 1864–1945.* Durham, NC: Duke University Press, 2001.

Beezley, William H., ed. *A Companion to Mexican History and Culture.* New York: Blackwell-Wiley, 2011.

———. *Judas at the Jockey Club and Other Episodes of Porfirian Mexico.* 2nd ed. Lincoln: University of Nebraska Press, 2004.

———. *Mexican National Identity: Memory, Innuendo, and Popular Culture.* Tucson: University of Arizona Press, 2008.

Beezley, William H., and David E. Lorey, eds. *¡Viva Mexico! ¡Viva la Independencia!: Celebrations of September 16.* Wilmington, DE: Scholarly Resources, 2001.

Beezley, William H., Cheryl English Martin, and William E. French, eds. *Rituals of Rule, Rituals of Resistance: Public Celebrations and Popular Culture in Mexico.* Wilmington, DE: Scholarly Resources, 1994.

Bell, Catherine. *Ritual: Perspectives and Dimensions.* New York: Oxford University Press, 1997.

Berman, Marshall. *All That Is Solid Melts into Air: The Experience of Modernity.* New York: Penguin Books, 1982.

Bishop, W. H. *Old Mexico and Her Lost Provinces.* New York: Harper & Brothers, 1883.

Bliss, Katherine Elaine. *Compromised Positions: Prostitution, Public Health, and Gender Politics in Revolutionary Mexico City.* University Park: Pennsylvania State University Press, 2001.

Bonnel, V., and L. Hunt, eds. *Beyond the Cultural Turn.* Berkeley: University of California Press, 1999.

Bourdieu, Pierre. *Outline of a Theory of Practice.* New York: Cambridge University Press, 1977.

Brading, David. *Los orígenes del nacionalismo mexicano.* México, DF: Edit Era, 1980.

Brenner, Helmut. *Juventino Rosas.* Warren, MI: Harmonie Park Press, 2000.

Brunk, Samuel, and Ben Fallaw, eds. *Heroes and Hero Cults in Latin America.* Austin: University of Texas Press, 2000.

Bryan, Anthony. "Mexican Politics in Transition, 1900–1913: The Role of General Bernardo Reyes." PhD diss., University of Nebraska, 1970.

Buffington, Robert. *Criminal and Citizen in Modern Mexico.* Lincoln: University of Nebraska Press, 2000.

Bulnes, Francisco. *El verdadero Díaz y la revolución.* México, DF: Editora Nacional, 1960.

Bunker, Steven. *Creating Mexican Consumer Culture in the Age of Porfirio Díaz.* Albuquerque: University of New Mexico Press, 2012.

Burchell, Graham, Colin Gordon, and Peter Miller, eds. *The Foucault Effect: Studies in Governmentality.* Chicago: University of Chicago Press, 1991.

Burkhart, Louise. "Mexica Women on the Home Front." In *Indian Women of Early Mexico,* edited by Susan Schroeder, Stephanie Wood, and Robert Haskett, 25–54. Norman: University of Oklahoma Press, 1997.

Camp, Roderic Ai. *Generals in the Palacio: The Military in Modern Mexico.* New York: Oxford Press, 1992.

Campos-Costero, Isaac. *Home Grown: Marijuana and the Origins of Mexico's War on Drugs.* Chapel Hill: University of North Carolina Press, 2012.

———. "Marijuana, Madness, and Modernity in Global Mexico, 1545–1920." PhD diss., Harvard University, 2006.

Cañeque, Alejandro. "Theater of Power: Writing and Representing the Auto de Fe in Colonial Mexico." *Americas* 52 (1996): 321–43.

Carvalho, José Murilo de. *A formação das almas: O imaginário da república no Brasil.* São Paulo: Companhia das Letras, 1990.

Casasola, Gustavo. *Biografía ilustrada del General Porfirio Díaz.* México: Editorial G. Casasola, 1994.

———. *Seis siglos de historia gráfica de México, 1325–1925.* 4th ed. Vol. 3. México: Editorial Gustavo Casasola, 1971.

Castro, Celso, Vitor Izecksohn, and Hendrik Kraay, eds. *Nova história militar brasileira.* Rio de Janeiro: Editora Bom Texto, 2004.

Castro, Justin. "Wireless Radio, Revolution, and the Mexican State, 1897–1938." PhD diss., University of Oklahoma, 2013.

Castro-Klarén, Sara, and John Chasteen. *Beyond Imagined Communities: Reading and Writing the Nation in Nineteenth-Century Latin America.* Baltimore: Johns Hopkins University Press, 2003.

Caulfield, Sueann. *In Defense of Honor: Sexual Morality, Modernity, and Nation in Early-Twentieth-Century Brazil.* Durham, NC: Duke University Press, 2000.

Centeno, Miguel Angel. *Blood and Debt: War and the Nation-State in Latin America.* University Park: Pennsylvania State University Press, 2002.

Chavarri, Juan N. *El heroico Colegio Militar en la historia de México.* México, DF: Libro Mex. Editores, 1960.

Chuchiak, John, III. "Indigenous Sentries and Indios Flecheros, or How the Maya Saved the Port of Campeche: The Importance of Maya Indigenous Militias and Coastal Guards in the Defense of the Port of Campeche, 1550–1750." Paper presented at the annual meeting of the American Ethnohistory Society, Springfield, MO, November 9, 2012.

Clarke, A. Conquest. "The Mexican Armies and Generals." *Galaxy* 4, no. 6 (October 1867): 691–700.

Clendinnen, Inga. *Ambivalent Conquests: Maya and Spaniard in Yucatan, 1517–1570.* 2nd ed. Cambridge: Cambridge University Press, 2002.

———. "The Cost of Courage in Aztec Society." *Past and Present* 107 (1985): 44–89.

Cobb, Charles R. "Archeology and the 'Savage Slot': Displacement and Emplacement in the Premodern World." *American Anthropologist* 107, no.4 (2005): 563–74.

Coerver, Don M. *The Porfirian Interregnum: The Presidency of Manuel Gonzalez of Mexico, 1880–1884.* Fort Worth: Texas Christian University Press, 1979.

Collins, Randall. *Violence: A Microsociological Theory.* Princeton: Princeton University Press, 2008.

Conway, Christopher. *Nineteenth-Century Spanish America: A Cultural History.* Nashville: Vanderbilt University Press, 2015.

Corrigan, Philip, and Derek Sayer. *The Great Arch: English State Formation as Cultural Revolution.* Oxford: Basil Blackwell, 1985.

Cosío Villegas, Daniel. *El Porfiriato: La vida política exterior, parte primera.* Edited by Fernando Vizcaíno. México, DF: Clío, 1998.

———. *The United States versus Porfirio Díaz.* Translated by Nettie Lee Benson. Lincoln: University of Nebraska Press, 1963.

Cosío Villegas, Daniel, Francisco R. Calderón, Luis González y González, Emma Cosío Villegas, and Moisés González Navarro. *Historia moderna de México.* 9 vols. México DF: Editorial Hermes, 1955.

Costeloe, Michael. *The Central Republic in Mexico, 1835–1846.* Cambridge: Cambridge University Press, 1993.

Cota Soto, Guillermo. *Historia militar de México.* México DF: n.p., 1947.

Courtwright, David. *Forces of Habit: Drugs and the Making of the Modern World.* Cambridge, MA: Harvard University Press, 2002.

Craib, Raymond. *Cartographic Mexico: A History of State Fixations and Fugitive Landscapes.* Durham, NC: Duke University Press, 2004.

Creelman, James. "Porfirio Díaz." *Pearson's Magazine,* March 1908, 231–77.

Dabdoub, Claudio. *Historia de el Valle del Yaqui.* México, DF: Lib. Manuel Porrúa, 1964.

Dabove, Juan Pablo. *Nightmares of the Lettered City: Banditry and Literature in Latin America, 1816–1929.* Pittsburgh: University of Pittsburgh Press, 2007.

Da Cunha, Euclides. *Os sertões.* Translated by Samuel Putman. 1901; repr., Chicago: University of Chicago Press, 1957.

da Matta, Roberto. *A casa y a rua: Espaço, cidadania, mulher e morte no Brasil.* São Paulo: Brasiliense, 1985.

Deák, István. *Beyond Nationalism: A Social and Political History of the Habsburg Officer Corps, 1848–1918.* New York: Oxford University Press, 1990.

de Certeau, Michel. *The Practice of Everyday Life.* Berkeley: University of California Press, 1984.

de la Fuente, Ariel. *The Children of Facundo: Caudillo and Gaucho Insurgency during the Argentine State Formation Process, La Rioja, 1853–1870.* Durham, NC: Duke University Press, 2000.

Delay, Brian. *War of a Thousand Deserts: Indian Raids and the U.S.-Mexican War.* New Haven, CT: Yale University Press, 2008.

Deleuze, Gilles. *Foucault.* Translated by Seán Hand. Minneapolis: University of Minnesota Press, 1988.

de Lizardi, José Joaquín Fernández. *The Mangy Parrot: The Life and Times of Periquillo Sarniento, Written by Himself for His Children.* Translated by David Frye. Indianapolis: Hackett, 2004.

DeLotinville, Peter. "Joe Beef of Montreal: Working-Class Culture and the Tavern, 1869–1889." *Labour* 8/9 (1981–82): 9–40.

DePalo, William A. *The Mexican National Army, 1822–1852.* College Station: Texas A&M University Press, 1997.

Desch-Obi, Thomas J. *Fighting for Honor: The History of African Martial Art Traditions in the Atlantic World.* Columbia: University of South Carolina Press, 2008.

Díaz, María Elena. "The Satiric Penny Press for Workers, 1900–1910: A Case Study in the Politicisation of Popular Culture." *Journal of Latin American Studies* 22, no. 3 (October 1990): 497–526.

Didapp, Juan Pedro. *Gobiernos militares de México: Los ataques al ejército y las maquinaciones políticas del partido científico para regir los destinos nacionales.* México DF: Tip. de J. I. Guerrero y Comp., 1904.

Domingo y Barrera, Francisco. *Ligero estudio sobre higiene de cuarteles e indicaciones de los condiciones que guardan los de la capital.* México, DF: Tip. Literaria de Filomeno Mata, 1880.

Dublán, Manuel, and José María Lozano, eds. *Legislación mexicana, o colección completa de los disposiciones legislativas expedidas desde la independencia de le República.* 34 vols. México, DF: Imprenta del Comercio, 1876–1904.

Dumond, Don. *The Machete and the Cross: Campesino Rebellion in the Yucatán.* Lincoln: University of Nebraska Press, 1997.

Dutton, David. "The Commonwealth Investigation Branch and the Political Construction of the Australian Citizenry, 1920–40." *Labour History*, no. 75 (November 1998): 155–74.

Eiss, Paul. *In the Name of El Pueblo: Place, Community, and Politics of History in the Yucatán.* Durham, NC: Duke University Press, 2010.

Elias, Norbert. *The Civilizing Process.* 1930; repr., New York: Wiley-Blackwell, 2000.

Escobar, Alberto. *Manual de higiene militar.* México: Imprenta de Ignacio Escalante, 1887.

Escudero, Angel. *El duelo en México.* México: Imprenta Mundial, 1936.

Espana-Maran, Linda. *Creating Masculinity in Los Angeles' Little Manila: Working-Class Filipinos and Popular Culture, 1920s–1950s.* New York: Columbia University Press, 2005.

Esposito, Matthew. *Funerals, Festivals, and Cultural Politics in Porfirian Mexico.* Albuquerque: University of New Mexico Press, 2010.

———. "Memorializing Modern Mexico: The State Funerals of the Porfirian Era, 1876–1911." PhD diss., Texas Christian University, 1997.

Evans, Sterling. *Bound in Twine: The History and Ecology of the Henequen-Wheat Complex for Mexico and the American and Canadian Plains, 1880–1950.* College Station: Texas A&M University Press, 2007.

Fabila, Alfonso. *Las tribus Yaqui de Sonora: Su cultura y anhelada en autodeterminación.* México, DF: Dept. de Asuntos Indigenes, 1940.

Fahmy, Khaled. *All the Pasha's Men: Mehmed Ali, His Army and the Making of Modern Egypt.* Cambridge: Cambridge University Press, 1997.

Farriss, Nancy. *Mayan Society under Colonial Rule.* Princeton, NJ: Princeton University Press, 1984.

Feld, Steven, and Keith Basso, eds. *Senses of Place.* Santa Fe, NM: SAR Press, 1996.

Felski, Rita. *The Gender of Modernity.* Cambridge, MA: Harvard University Press, 1995.

Figueroa, Agustin García. *Higiene militar: Causas de la frecuencia de la sífilis en el ejército y medios de disminuirla.* México DF: Imprenta de Ignacio Escalante, 1874.

Flipper, Henry Ossian, and Quintard Taylor Jr. *The Colored Cadet at West Point.* Lincoln: University of Nebraska Press, 1998.

Florescano, Enrique. *Etnia, estado y nación: Ensayo sobre las identidades colectivas en México.* México, DF: Taurus, 2001.

Foote, Nicola, and René D. Harder Horst, eds. *Military Struggles and Identity Formation in Latin America: Race, Nation, and Community during the Liberal Period.* Gainesville: University Press of Florida, 2010.

Foucault, Michel. *The Archeology of Knowledge.* 1972; repr., New York: Vintage, 1982.

———. *The Birth of Biopolitics: Lectures at the Collège de France, 1978–79.* Edited by Michel Sennellart. Translated by Graham Burchell. New York: Picador, 2004.

———. *The Birth of the Clinic.* New York: Vintage, 1994.

———. *Discipline and Punish: The Birth of the Prison.* New York: Pantheon Books, 1977.

———. *History of Sexuality.* 6 vols. New York: Picador, 2004.

———. *Security, Territory, Population: Lectures at the Collège de France, 1977–78.* Edited by Michel Sennellart. Translated by Graham Burchell. New York: Picador, 2004.

———. *Society Must Be Defended: Lectures at the Collège de France, 1975–76.* Edited by Maruo Bertani and Alessandro Fontana. Translated by David Macey. New York: Picador, 1997.

———. *Subjectivité et vérité.* Paris: Seuil, 2014.

Fowler, Will, ed. *Forceful Negotiations: The Origins of the Pronunciamiento in Nineteenth-Century.* Lincoln: University of Nebraska, 2010.

Francois, Marie Eileen. *A Culture of Everyday Credit: Housekeeping, Pawnbroking, and Governance in Mexico City, 1750–1920.* Lincoln: University of Nebraska Press, 2006.

Frazer, Chris. *Bandit Nation: A History of Outlaws and Cultural Struggle in Mexico, 1810–1920.* Lincoln: University of Nebraska Press, 2006.

French, William E. "Imagining and the Cultural History of Nineteenth-Century Mexico." *Hispanic American Historical Review* 79, no. 2 (1999): 249–67.

———. *A Peaceful and Working People: Manners, Morals, and Class Formation in Northern Mexico.* Albuquerque: University of New Mexico Press, 1996.

———. "Prostitutes and Guardian Angels." *Hispanic American Historical Review* 72, no. 4 (November 1992): 529–53.

———. "'Te amo muncho': The Love Letters of Pedro and Enriqueta." In *The Human Tradition in Mexico,* edited by Jeffrey Pilcher, 123–36. Wilmington, DE: Scholarly Resources, 2003.

Frey, James H., and D. Stanley Eitzen. "Sports and Society." *Annual Review of Sociology* 17 (1991): 503–22.

Freyre, Gilberto. *Casa-Grande y senzala: Formação da família brasileira sob o regime de economia patriarcal.* 13th ed. Rio de Janeiro: J. Olympio, 1966.

Frías, Heriberto. *The Battle of Tomochic: Memoirs of a Second Lieutenant.* Translated by Barbara Jamison. 1893; repr., New York: Oxford University Press, 2006.

Fuentes, Ernesto. *Historia patria, obra adoptada por la secretaría de guerra y marina para servir de todo en las escuelas de tropa del Ejército Nacional.* México DF: Sec. de Fomento, 1909.

Galeano, Eduardo. *Open Veins of Latin America: Five Centuries of the Pillage of a Continent.* New York: Monthly Review Press, 1997.

García, Gustavo A. "In Quest of a National Cinema: The Silent Era." In *Mexico's Cinema: A Century of Film and Filmmakers,* edited by Joanne Hirshfield and David Maciel, 5–16. Wilmington, DE: Scholarly Resources, 1999.

Garner, Paul H. *British Lions and Mexican Eagles.* Stanford, CA: Stanford University Press, 2011.

———. "The Politics of National Development in Late Porfirian Mexico: Reconstruction of the Tehuantepec National Railway, 1896–1907." *Bulletin of Latin American Research* 14 (1995): 339–56.

———. *Porfirio Díaz, Profiles in Power.* Harlow, UK: Longman, 2001.

Garza, James Alexander. *The Imagined Underworld: Sex, Crime, and Vice in Porfirian Mexico City.* Lincoln: University of Nebraska Press, 2007.

Gellner, Ernest. *Nations and Nationalism.* Oxford: Blackwell, 1983.

Giddens, Anthony. *Modernity and Self-Identity: Self and Society in the Late Modern Age.* Cambridge: Polity Press in association with Basil Blackwell, 1991.

Giddens, Anthony, and Christopher Pierson. *Conversations with Anthony Giddens: Making Sense of Modernity.* Cambridge: Polity Press, 1998.

Ginzburg, Carlo. *Threads and Traces: True False Fictive.* Translated by Anne and John Tedeschi. Berkeley: University of California Press, 2012.

Goffman, Erving. *Asylums: Essays on the Social Situation of Mental Patients and Other Inmates.* Chicago: Aldine, 1962.

———. *Stigma: Notes on the Management of Spoiled Identity.* New York: Prentice-Hall, 1963.

Gonzalez Obregón, Luis. *Memoria historica y técnicade las obras del desagüe del Valle de México 1449–1900.* México, DF: n.p., 1902.

González y González, Luís. "El liberalismo triunfante." In *Historia general de México—Versión 2000*, edited by Josefina Z. Vázquez, 633–706. México: Colegio de México, 2005.

Gordon, C., and P. Miller. *The Foucault Effect: Studies in Governmentality.* Chicago: University of Chicago Press, 1991.

Gosner, Kevin. *Soldiers of the Virgin: The Moral Economy of a Colonial Mayan Rebellion.* Tucson: University of Arizona Press, 1992.

Gough, Terrence J. "The Root Reforms and Command." US Army Center of Military History. http://www.army.mil/cmh-pg/documents/1901/Root-Cmd.htm.

Gramsci, Antonio, Quintin Hoare, and Geoffrey Nowell-Smith. *Selections from the Prison Notebooks of Antonio Gramsci.* New York: International Publishers, 1972.

Grossman, David. *On Killing: The Psychological Cost of Learning to Kill in War and Society.* New York: Little, Brown, and Company, 1995.

Gruzinski, Serge. *The Conquest of Mexico: The Incorporation of Indian Societies into the Western World, 16th–18th Centuries.* Cambridge: Blackwell, 1993.

———. *Images at War: Mexico from Columbus to "Blade Runner," 1492–2019.* Durham, NC: Duke University Press, 2001.

Guardino, Peter. *Peasants, Politics, and the Formation of Mexico's National State: Guerrero, 1800–1857.* Stanford, CA: Stanford University Press, 2002.

Gutiérrez Santos, Daniel. *Historia militar de México, 1876–1914.* México, DF: Ateneo Press, 1955.

Gutmann, Matthew C. *The Meanings of Macho: Being a Man in Mexico City.* Berkeley: University of California Press, 1996.

Haber, Stephen, ed. *How Latin America Fell Behind: Essays on the Economic Histories of Brazil and Mexico.* Stanford, CA: Stanford University Press, 1997.

———. *Industry and Underdevelopment: The Industrialization of Mexico, 1890–1940.* Stanford, CA: Stanford University Press, 1989.

Hale, Charles. *The Transformation of Liberalism in Late Nineteenth Century Mexico.* Princeton, NJ: Princeton University Press, 1989.

Hall, Stuart. *Modernity: An Introduction to Modern Societies.* Oxford: Blackwell, 2000.

Hämäläinen, Pekka. *The Comanche Empire*. New Haven, CT: Yale University Press, 2008.

Hamilton, Kirk. *Where Is the Wealth of Nations?: Measuring Capital for the 21st Century*. New York: World Bank, 2005. As cited in Ronald Bailey, "Our Intangible Riches," *Reason*, August/September 2007, http://www.reason.com/news/show/120764.html.

Hardie, F. H. "The Mexican Army." *Journal of the Military Service Institution of the United States* (1892): 1203–8.

Harris, Cole. *The Resettlement of British Columbia: Essays on Colonialism and Geographical Change*. Vancouver: UBC Press, 1997.

Hart, John Mason. *Empire and Revolution: The Americans in Mexico since the Civil War*. Berkeley: University of California Press, 2002.

Headrick, Daniel R. *The Tools of Empire: Technology and European Imperialism in the Nineteenth Century*. New York: Oxford University Press, 1991.

Henderson, Peter V. N. *In the Absence of Don Porfirio: Francisco Léon De La Barra and the Mexican Revolution*. Wilmington, DE: Scholarly Resources, 2000.

Hernández, Fortunato. *Las razas indigenas de Sonora y la Guerra del Yaqui*. México, DF: Talleres de la Casa Editorial J. De Elizalde, 1902.

Hernández, José Ángel. "From Conquest to Colonization: Indios and Colonization Policies after Mexican Independence." *Mexican Studies/Estudios Mexicanos* 26, No. 2 (Summer 2010): 291–322.

Hernández Chávez, Alicia. "Origen y ocaso del ejército porfiriano." *Historia Mexicana* 39, no. 1 (1989): 257–96.

Herrera-Sobek, María. *The Mexican Corrido: A Feminist Analysis*. Bloomington: Indiana University Press, 1993.

Higate, Paul. *Military Masculinities: Identity and the State*. Westport, CT: Praeger, 2003.

Hoberman, Louisa Schell, and Susan M. Socolow, eds. *The Countryside in Colonial Latin America*. Albuquerque: University of New Mexico Press, 1996.

Hobsbawm, E. J. *Nations and Nationalism since 1780: Programme, Myth, and Reality*. Cambridge: Cambridge University Press, 1990.

Hobsbawm, Eric, and Terence Ranger, eds. *The Invention of Tradition*. Cambridge: Cambridge University Press, 1983.

Hogg, Ian V., and John Weeks. *Military Small Arms of the Twentieth Century*. Northbrook, IL: DBI Books, 1981.

Hu-DeHart, Evelyn. *Yaqui Resistance and Survival: The Struggle for Land and Autonomy, 1821–1910*. Madison: University of Wisconsin Press, 1984.

Hughes, James B., Jr. *Mexican Military Arms: The Cartridge Period, 1866–1967*. Houston: Deep River Armory, 1968.

Irwin, Robert McKee. *Bandits, Captives, Heroines, and Saints: Cultural Icons of Mexico's Northwest Borderlands*. Minneapolis: University of Minnesota Press, 2007.

Irwin, Robert McKee, Edward J. McCaughan, and Michelle Rocío Nasser, eds. *The Famous 41: Sexuality and Social Control in Mexico, 1901*. New York: Palgrave Macmillan, 2003.

Janvier, Thomas. "The Mexican Army." *Harper's Weekly* 79, no. 474 (November 1889): 818–42.

Jervis, John. *Transgressing the Modern: Explorations in the Western Experience of Otherness*. Oxford: Blackwell, 1999.

Johns, Michael. *The City of Mexico in the Age of Díaz*. Austin: University of Texas Press, 1997.

Johnson, John J. "The Latin-American Military as a Politically Competing Group in Transitional Society." In *The Role of the Military in Underdeveloped Countries*, edited by John J. Johnson, 91–130. Princeton, NJ: Princeton University Press, 1962.

Johnson, Lyman L. "Dangerous Words, Provocative Gestures, and Violent Acts: The Disputed Hierarchies of Plebian Life in Colonial Buenos Aires." In *The Faces of Honor: Sex, Shame, and Violence in Colonial Latin America*, ed. Lyman Johnson and Sonya Lipsett-Rivera, 127–51. Albuquerque: University of New Mexico Press, 1998.

Joseph, Gilbert. *Revolution from Without: Yucatan Mexico and the United States, 1880–1924*. Durham, NC: Duke University Press, 1988.

Joseph, Gilbert, and Timothy Henderson, eds. *The Mexico Reader: History, Politics, Culture*. Durham, NC: Duke University Press, 2003.

Joseph, G. M., and Daniel Nugent, eds. *Everyday Forms of State Formation: Revolution and the Negotiation of Rule in Modern Mexico*. Durham, NC: Duke University Press, 1994.

Keegan, John, and Richard Holmes, eds. *Soldiers: A History of Men in Battle*. New York: Elisabeth Sifton Books, 1986.

Kelley, James R. "Professionalism in the Porfirian Army Corps." PhD diss., Tulane University, 1971.

Kelley, Jane Holden. *Yaqui Women: Contemporary Life Histories*. Lincoln: University of Nebraska Press, 1978.

Kertzer, David I. *Ritual, Politics, and Power*. New Haven, CT: Yale University Press, 1988.

Knight, Alan. "El liberalismo mexicano desde la Reforma hasta la Revolución (una interpretación)." *Historia Mexicana* 35, no. 1 (1985): 59–92.

———. *The Mexican Revolution*. 2 vols. New York: Cambridge University Press, 1986.

Koth, Karl. *Waking the Dictator: Vera Cruz, the Struggle for Federalism, and the Mexican Revolution, 1870–1927*. Calgary: University of Calgary Press, 2002.

Kourí, Emilio. *A Pueblo Divided: Business, Property, and Community in Papantla, Mexico*. Stanford, CA: Stanford University Press, 2004.

Kraay, Hendrik, ed. *Negotiating Identities in Modern Latin America*. Calgary, AB: University of Calgary Press, 2007.

———. "Reconsidering Recruitment in Imperial Brazil." *Americas* 55, no. 1 (July 1998): 1–33.

Lamadrid, Enrique. "'El Corrido de Tomóchic:' Honor, Grace, Gender, and Power in the First Ballad of the Mexican Revolution." *Journal of the Southwest* 41, no. 4 (Winter 1999): 441–60.

Lancereaux, Etienne. *A Treatise on Syphilis, Historical and Practical*. Vols. 1–2. Translated by G. Whitley. London: New Syndenham Society, 1866.

Lara y Pardo, Luis. *La prostitución en México*. México, DF: Librería de la Vda de Ch. Bouret, 1908.

Larson, Brooke. *Trials of Nation Making: Liberalism, Race, and Ethnicity in the Andes, 1810–1910*. Cambridge: Cambridge University Press, 2004.

Lawrence, Bruce, and Aisha Karim. *On Violence: A Reader*. Durham, NC: Duke University Press, 2007.

Lear, John. *Workers, Neighbors, and Citizens: The Revolution in Mexico City*. Lincoln: University of Nebraska Press, 2001.

Lefkowitz Horowitz, H., ed. *Attitudes toward Sex in Antebellum America*. Boston: Bedford–St. Martin's, 2006.

Levinson, Irving. *Wars within Wars: Mexican Guerrillas, Domestic Elites, and the United States of America, 1846–1848*. Fort Worth: Texas Christian University Press, 2005.

Lieuwen, Edwin. *Arms and Politics in Latin America*. 2nd ed. New York: Praeger, 1961.

———. *Mexican Militarism: The Political Rise and Fall of the Revolutionary Army, 1910–1940*. Albuquerque: University of New Mexico Press, 1968.

Lindenbaum, Shirley, and Margaret Lock, eds. *Knowledge, Power and Practice: The Anthropology of Medicine and Everyday Life*. Berkeley: University of California Press, 1993.

Link, Bruce G., and Jo C. Pubert. "Conceptualizing Stigma." *Annual Review of Sociology* 27 (2001): 363–85.

Lloyd, Jane-Dale, ed. *Porfirio Díaz frente al descontento*. México, DF: Universidad Iberoamericana, 1986.

Lloyd, Jane-Dale, et al. *Visiones del Porfiriato, visiones de México*. México, DF: Universidad Iberoamericana, 2004.

Lomnitz, Claudio. *Deep Mexico, Silent Mexico: An Anthropology of Nationalism*. Minneapolis: University of Minnesota Press, 2001.

Lopez, Amanda. "The Cadaverous City: The Everyday Life of the Dead in Mexico City, 1875–1930." PhD diss., University of Arizona, 2011.

Loveman, Brian. *For the Patria: Politics and the Armed Forces in Latin America*. Wilmington, DE: Scholarly Resources, 1999.

Loveman, Brian, and Thomas M. Davies, eds. *The Politics of Anti-politics: The Military in Latin America*. 2nd ed. Lincoln: University of Nebraska Press, 1989.

Lynch, John. *Massacre in the Pampas, 1872: Britain and Argentina in the Age of Migration*. Norman: University of Oklahoma Press, 1988.

Lynn, John A. *Women, Armies, and Warfare in Early Modern Europe*. Cambridge: Cambridge University Press, 2008.

Macías-González, Victor M., and Anne Rubenstein. *Masculinity and Sexuality in Modern Mexico*. Albuquerque: University of New Mexico Press, 2012.

Mallon, Florencia. *Peasant and Nation: The Making of Postcolonial Mexico and Peru*. Berkeley: University of California Press, 1995.

Maraña, Mabel, E. Dussel, and C. Júaregui, eds. *Coloniality at Large: Latin America in the Postcolonial Debate*. Durham, NC: Duke University Press, 2008.

Martínez Peláez, Severo. *La patria del criollo: Ensayo de interpretación de la realidad colonial guatemalteca*. Guatemala: Editorial Universitaria, 1970.

Masilla, E. *De cómo Porfirio Díaz dominas las aguas*. México, DF: Concurso CIESAS, 1994. Available at Archivo Histórico del Agua, Mexico City.

Matthews, Michael. *The Civilizing Machine: A Cultural History of Railroads, 1876–1911*. Lincoln: University of Nebraska Press, 2013.

McCrea, Heather. *Diseased Relations: Epidemics, Public Health, and State-Building in Yucatán, Mexico, 1847–1924*. Albuquerque: University of New Mexico Press, 2010.

McNamara, Patrick. *Sons of the Sierra: Juárez, Díaz, and the People of Ixtlán, Oaxaca, 1855–1920*. Chapel Hill: University of North Carolina Press, 2007.

McNeill, William. *Keeping Together in Time: Dance and Drill in Human History.* Cambridge, MA: Harvard University Press, 1995.

Mendoza, Vicente T. *El corrido mexicano.* México, DF: Fondo de Cultura Económica, 1954.

México. *Documentos históricos constitucionales de las fuerzas armadas mexicanas.* Vol. 2. México, DF: Edición del Senado de la Republica, 1966.

———. *Manual de oficial subalterno.* México, DF: Talleres de Ramón de S. N. Arraluce, 1900.

México. Secretaría de Fomento y Olegario Molina. *Memorias presentado al Congreso de la unión por el secretaría de fomento.* México, DF: Imprenta y Fototipia de la Secretaría de Fomento, 1910.

México. Secretaría de Guerra. *Examenes de Colegio Militar.* México, DF: n.p., 1838.

———. *Ordenanza general para el ejército de la republica de México.* México, DF: Imprenta de I. Cumplido, 1882.

———. *Reglamento de Colegio Militar.* México, DF: De M. Murguia, 1854.

México. Secretaría de Guerra y Marina. Estado Mayor. *Ley de organización, 1899–1900.*

———. *Memoria de guerra y marina, presentado al Congreso de la unión por el secretario de guerra.* México, DF.

México. Secretaría de Guerra y Marina. Estado Mayor, and Bernardo Reyes. *Ley orgánico del Ejército Nacional, Nov. 1, 1900.* México, DF: Tipografía de El Partido Liberal, 1900.

Meyer, Michael C., and William H. Beezley, eds. *The Oxford History of Mexico.* Oxford: Oxford University Press, 2000.

Moisés, Rosalio, J. H. Kelley, and W. C. Holden. *A Yaqui Life: The Personal Chronicle of a Yaqui Indian.* Lincoln: University of Nebraska Press, 1971.

Mondragón, Manuel. *Proyecto de organización del ejército sobre base del servicio obligatorio.* México, DF: Tip. Mercantil, 1910.

Morgan, Zachary R. "The Revolt of the Lash, 1910." In *Naval Mutinies of the Twentieth Century: An International Perspective,* edited by Christopher M. Bell and Bruce A. Elleman, 35–54. Portland, OR: Frank Cass, 2003.

Morris, Charles. *The Story of Mexico: A Land of Conquest.* New York: Underwood, 1914.

Mosse, George L. *The Image of Man: The Creation of Modern Masculinity.* New York: Oxford University Press, 1996.

Mott, Frank Luther. *A History of American Magazines.* Cambridge: Cambridge University Press, 1939.

Nash, Linda. *Inescapable Ecologies: A History of Environment, Disease, and Knowledge.* Berkeley: University of California Press, 2006.

Nesvig, Martin. "The Lure of the Perverse: Moral Negotiation of Pederasty in Porfirian Mexico." *Mexican Studies* 16, no. 1 (Winter 2000):1–37.

Neufeld, Stephen. "A Performative Army: The Military and Imaginings of Nation in Porfirian Mexico, 1876–1911." MA thesis, University of British Columbia, 2003.

———. "Servants of the Nation: the Military in the Making of Modern Mexico, 1876–1911." PhD diss., University of Arizona, 2009.

Neufeld, Stephen, and Michael Matthews, eds. *Mexico in Verse: A History of Rhyme, Music, and Power.* Tucson: University of Arizona Press, 2015.

Niemeyer, E. V. *El General Bernardo Reyes*. Translated by Juan Antonio Ayala. 2nd ed. Monterrey: Universidad de Nuevo León, 1966.

Nunn, Frederick M. "Latin American Militarylore: An Introduction and a Case Study." *Americas* 35, no. 4 (1979): 424–74.

———. *The Time of the Generals: Latin American Professional Militarism in World Perspective*. Lincoln: University of Nebraska Press, 1992.

———. *Yesterday's Soldiers: European Military Professionalism in South America, 1890–1940*. Lincoln: University of Nebraska Press, 1983.

Oriel, J. D. *The Scars of Venus: A History of Venereology*. New York: Springer-Verlag, 1994.

Ortega, Leopoldo. *Breves consideraciones sobre algunos puntos de higiene militar*. México: Imp. de Ignacio Cumplido, 1882.

Ortiz Rubio, Pascal. *Los alojamientos militares en la República Mexicana*. México, DF: Dir. De Talleres Gráficos, 1921.

Overmyer-Velazquez, Mark. *Visions of the Emerald City: Modernity, Tradition, and the Formation of Porfirian Oaxaca, Mexico*. Durham, NC: Duke University Press, 2006.

Ozouf, Mona. *Festivals and the French Revolution*. Translated by Alan Sheridan. Cambridge, MA: Harvard University Press, 1988.

Parsons, Timothy H. *The British Imperial Century, 1815–1941: A World Historical Perspective*. Boulder, CO: Rowman and Littlefield, 1999.

Pavía, Lazaro. *El ejército y la política*. México, DF: n.p., 1909.

Paz, Eduardo. *A dónde debemos llegar: Estudio sociológico militar*. México, DF: Tipografía Mercantil, 1910.

Peard, Julyan. *Race, Place, and Medicine: The Idea of the Tropics in Nineteenth-Century Brazil*. Durham, NC: Duke University Press, 1999.

Pérez Montfort, Ricardo. *Estampas de nacionalismo popular mexicano: Diez ensayos sobre cultura popular y nacionalismo*. 2nd ed. México, DF: Centro de Estudios Superiores en Antropología Social, 2003.

Pérez Montfort, Ricardo, Alberto del Castillo Yurrita, and Pablo Piccato. *Hábitos, normas y escándalo: Prensa, criminalidad y drogas durante el Porfiriato tardío*. México, DF: Ciesas: Plaza y Valdes Editores, 1997.

Piccato, Pablo. *City of Suspects: Crime in Mexico City, 1900–1931*. Durham, NC: Duke University Press, 2001.

———. "'El Paso de Venus por el disco del Sol': Criminality and Alcoholism in the Late Porfiriato." *Mexican Studies/Estudios Mexicanos* 11, no. 2 (1995): 203–41.

———. *Tyranny of Opinion: Honor in the Construction of the Mexican Public Sphere*. Durham, NC: Duke University Press, 2010.

Pilcher, Jeffrey. *¡Que vivan los tamales!: Food and the Making of Mexican Identity*. Albuquerque: University of New Mexico Press, 1998.

Pion-Berlin, David. *Civil-Military Relations in Latin America: New Analytical Perspectives*. Chapel Hill: University of North Carolina Press, 2001.

Plasencia de la Parra, Enrique. *Personajes y escenarios de la rebelión delahuertista, 1923–1924*. México, DF: M. A. Porrúa Grupo Editorial, 1998.

Pohanka, Brian C., ed. *Nelson A. Miles: A Documentary Biography of His Military Career, 1861–1903*. Glendale, CA: Arthur C. Clark, 1985.

Poniatowska, Elena. *Las Soldaderas: Women of the Mexican Revolution*. El Paso: Cinco Puntos, 2006.

Porter, Susie S. *Working Women in Mexico City: Public Discourses and Material Conditions, 1879–1931.* Tucson: University of Arizona Press, 2003.

Prieto, Guillermo. *Lecciones de historia patria: Obras completas XXVIII.* México, DF: CONACULTA, 1999.

Quétel, Claude. *History of Syphilis.* Cambridge: Polity Press, 1990.

Rabinow, Paul, ed. *The Foucault Reader.* New York: Pantheon Books, 1984.

Ramos, Julio. *Divergent Modernities: Culture and Politics in Nineteenth-Century Latin America.* Durham, NC: Duke University Press, 2001.

Rath, Thomas. *Myths of Demilitarization in Postrevolutionary Mexico, 1920–1960.* Chapel Hill: University of North Carolina Press, 2012.

———. 'Once We Were Warriors, Now We Are Soldiers': Army, Nation and State in Mexico, 1920–1970." PhD diss., Columbia University, 2008.

Reed, H. T. "The Mexican Military Academy." *Journal of the Military Service Institute* 31 (July, September, November 1902): 811–18.

Reed, Nelson. *The Caste War of the Yucatán.* Stanford, CA: Stanford University Press, 2001.

Remington, Frederick. "General Miles's Review of the Mexican Army." *Harper's Weekly* 35, no. 756 (July 4, 1891): 495.

Richard, Carlos Macías. "El territorio de Quintana Roo: Tentativas de colonización y control militar en la selva Maya, 1888–1902." *Historia Mexicana* 49, no. 1 (July–September 1999): 5–54.

———. *Nuevas fronteras Mexicana: Milicia, burocracia y ocupación territorial en Quintana Roo.* Chetumal, Mexico: Universidad de Quintana Roo, 1997.

Robins, Nicholas A. *Native Insurgencies and the Genocidal Impulse in the Americas.* Bloomington: University of Indiana Press, 2005.

Robinson, Amy. "Mexican Banditry and Discourses of Class: The Case of Chucho el Roto." *Latin American Research Review* 44, no.1 (2009): 5–31.

Rocha, Sóstenes. *Estudios sobre la ciencia de la guerra.* México, DF: Imprenta y librería Pablo Dupont, 1878.

Rodríguez, Ángel. *Profilaxis de las afecciones venéreo-sifilíticas en el ejército.* México, DF: Imprenta Gobierno, 1893.

Rodriguez, Julia. *Civilizing Argentina: Science, Medicine, and the Modern State.* Chapel Hill: University of North Carolina Press, 2006.

Rodríguez, Linda Alexander, ed. *Rank and Privilege: The Military and Society in Latin America.* Wilmington, DE: Scholarly Resources, 1994.

Rodríguez O., Jaime E., ed. *The Divine Charter: Constitutionalism and Liberalism in Nineteenth-Century Mexico.* Lanham, MD: Rowman and Littlefield, 2005.

———. *Down from Colonialism: Mexico's Nineteenth-Century Crisis.* Los Angeles: Chicano Studies Research Center Publications, University of California, 1988.

Rohlfes, Laurence J. "Police and Penal Correction in Mexico City, 1876–1911: A Study of Order and Progress in Porfirian Mexico." PhD diss., Tulane University, 1983.

Rojas, Basilias. *Un gran rebelde: Manuel García Vigil.* Mexico: Editorial Luz, 1965.

Rugeley, Terry, ed. *Mayan Wars: Ethnographic Accounts from Nineteenth-Century Yucatán.* Norman: University of Oklahoma Press, 2001.

———. *Rebellion Now and Forever: Mayans, Hispanics, and Caste War Violence in Yucatán, 1800–1880.* Stanford, CA: Stanford University Press, 2009.

———. *Yucatán's Mayan Peasantry and the Origins of the Caste War, 1800–1887*. Austin: University of Texas Press, 1996.

Rugeley, Terry, and Ben Fallaw, eds. *Forced Marches: Soldiers and Military Caciques in Modern Mexico*. Tucson: University of Arizona Press, 2012.

Salas, Elizabeth. *Soldaderas in the Mexican Military: Myth and History*. Austin: University of Texas Press, 1990.

Salter, Mark. "The Global Visa Regime and the Political Technologies of the International Self: Borders, Bodies, Biopolitics." *Alternatives: Global, Local, Political* 31, no. 2 (April–June 2006): 167–89.

Sánchez Lamego, Miguel A. *Generales de ingenieros del Ejército Mexicano, 1821–1914*. México, DF: n.p., 1952.

Sánchez Rojas, Luis Ignacio. "La educación del ejército porfiriano, 1900–1910." *Tzintzun: Revista de Estudios Históricos* 54 (July–December 2011): 93–127.

Santa Cruz, Juan Luis Ossa. *Armies, Politics, Revolutions: Chile, 1808–1826*. Liverpool: Liverpool University Press, 2015.

Santoni, Pedro. "A Fear of the People: The Civic Militia in Mexico 1845." *Hispanic American Historical Review* 68, no. 2 (1988): 269–88.

———. *Mexicans at Arms: Puro Federalists and the Politics of War, 1845–1848*. Fort Worth: Texas Christian University Press, 1996.

Savage, Kirk. *Standing Soldiers, Kneeling Slaves: Race, War and Monument in 19th Century America*. Princeton, NJ: Princeton University Press, 1997.

Savarino Roggero, Franco. *Pueblos y nacionalismo, del régimen oligárquico a la sociedad de masas en Yucatán, 1894–1925*. México, DF: Instituto Nacional de Estudios Históricos de la Revolución Mexicana, 1997.

Schama, Simon. *Dead Certainties: Unwarranted Speculations*. New York: Vintage Books, 1991.

Schell, William. *Integral Outsiders: The American Colony in Mexico City, 1876–1911*. Wilmington, DE: Scholarly Resources, 2001.

Schiff, Warren. "German Military Penetration into Mexico during the Late Díaz Period." *Hispanic American Historical Review* 39, no. 4 (1959): 568–79.

Shilling, Chris. *The Body and Social Theory*. London: Sage, 1993.

Schivelbusch, Wolfgang. *Tastes of Paradise: A Social History of Spices, Stimulants, and Intoxicants*. Translated by David Jacobson. New York: Vintage Books, 1993.

Schwaller, John, ed. *The Church in Colonial Latin America*. Wilmington, DE: Scholarly Resources, 2000.

Scott, James C. *Domination and the Arts of Resistance: Hidden Transcripts*. New Haven, CT: Yale University Press, 1990.

———. *Weapons of the Weak: Everyday Forms of Peasant Resistance*. New Haven, CT: Yale University Press, 1985.

Seed, Patricia. *Ceremonies of Possession in Europe's Conquest of the New World, 1492–1640*. Cambridge: Cambridge University Press, 1995.

Serrano Ortega, José, coord. *El contingente de sangre*. México, DF: INAH, 1993.

Sharman, Julian. *A Cursory History of Swearing*. 1884; repr., New York: Burt Franklin, 1968.

Smith, Cornelius Cole. *Emilio Kosterlitzky, Eagle of Sonora and the Southwest Border*. Glendale, CA: A. H. Clark, 1970.

Smith, Phyllis. "Contentious Voices amid the Order: The Porfirian Press in Mexico City, 1876–1911." PhD diss., University of Arizona, 1996.

Snyder, R. Claire. *Citizen Soldiers and Manly Warriors: Military Service and Gender in the Civic Republican Tradition.* New York: Rowman and Littlefield, 1999.

Soto, Shirlene. *Emergence of the Modern Mexican Woman: Her Participation in Revolution and the Struggle for Equality, 1910–1940.* Denver: Arden Press, 1990.

Spicer, Edward H. "The Military History of the Yaquis from 1867–1910: Three Points of View." Paper presented at "Views on the Military History of the Indian-Spanish-American Southwest: 1598–1886," Fort Huachuca, AZ, June 12–21, 1975. http://huachuca.army.mil/pages/history/spicer.html.

Splete, Allen P., and Marilyn D. Splete, eds. *Frederic Remington: Selected Letters.* New York: Abbeville Press, 1988.

Stavig, Ward. *The World of Tupac Amaru: Conflict, Community, and Identity in Colonial Peru.* Lincoln: University of Nebraska Press, 1999.

Stealey, John E., III. *Porte Crayon's Mexico: David Hunter Strother's Diaries in the Early Porfirian Era, 1879–1885.* Kent, OH: Kent State University Press, 2006.

Stevens, Donald Fithian. *The Origins of Instability in Early Republican Mexico.* Durham, NC: Duke University Press, 1991.

Stevenson, Robert. *Music in Mexico: A Historical Survey.* New York: Thomas Y. Crowell, 1952.

Súarez Pichardo, Jorge. *Hechos ilustres de la clase de tropa del Ejército Mexicano.* México, DF: D. Hernández Mejía, 1909.

Sullivan, Paul. *Xuxub Must Die: The Lost Histories of a Murder in the Yucatan.* Pittsburgh: University of Pittsburgh Press, 2004.

Taibo, Paco Ignacio, II. *Yaquis: Historia de una guerra popular y de un genocidio en México.* México, DF: Planeta, 2013.

Taylor, Chloë. "Foucault and Familial Power." *Hypatia* 27, no. 1 (Winter 2012): 201–18.

Taylor, Diane. *Disappearing Acts: Spectacles of Gender and Nationalism in Argentina's Dirty War.* Durham, NC: Duke University Press, 1997.

Taylor, William. *Drinking, Homicide, and Rebellion in Colonial Mexican Villages.* Stanford, CA: Stanford University Press, 1979.

Tello, Aurelio. "El patrimonio musical de México: Una síntesis aproximativa." In *El patrimonio nacional de México,* edited by Enrico Florescano, 2:76–110. México, DF: Consejo Nacional Para la Cultura y las Artes, 1997.

Tenenbaum, Barbara A. *The Politics of Penury: Debt and Taxes in Mexico, 1821–1856.* Albuquerque: University of New Mexico Press, 1986.

Tenorio-Trillo, Mauricio. *I Speak of the City: Mexico City at the Turn of the Twentieth Century.* Chicago: University of Chicago Press, 2012.

———. *Mexico at the World's Fairs: Crafting a Modern Nation.* Berkeley: University of California Press, 1996.

———. "1910 Mexico City: Space and Nation in the City of the Centenario." *Journal of Latin American Studies* 28, no. 1 (February1996): 75–104.

Thompson, E. P. *Customary Practice: Studies in Traditional Popular Culture.* New York: New Press, 1993.

———. *Customs in Common: Studies in Traditional Popular Culture.* New York: New Press, 1993.

Thompson, Guy P. "Bulwarks of National Liberalism: The National Guard, Philharmonic Corps, and Patriotic Juntas in Mexico." *Journal of Latin American Studies* 22, no. 1 (1990): 31–68.

Torpey, John. *The Invention of the Passport: Surveillance, Citizenship, and the State.* Cambridge: Cambridge University Press, 2000.

Tovar, Antonio. *Código del duelo.* México, DF: n.p., 1891.

Toxqui Garay, María Áurea. "'El Recreo de los Amigos': Mexico City's Pulquerías during the Liberal Republic, 1856–1911." PhD diss., University of Arizona, 2008.

Troncoso, Francisco, and Ministerio de Guerra y Marina. *Las guerras con las tribus Yaqui.* México, DF: Tip. del Departamento de Estado Mayor, 1905.

Truett, Samuel. *Fugitive Landscapes: The Forgotten History of the US-Mexico Borderlands.* New Haven, CT: Yale University Press, 2006.

Universidad Veracruzana. *Memorias e informes de jefes políticos y autoridades del régimen Porfiriano, 1883–1911.* Estado de Veracruz Xalapa: Universidad Veracruzana, 1997.

Urquizo, Francisco Luis. *De la vida militar mexicana.* México, DF: Herrero Hermanos Sucesores, 1920.

——. *Fui soldado de levita de esos de caballería.* México, DF: SEP, 1967.

——. *Memorias de campaña.* México, DF: SEP, 1971.

——. *Tropa vieja.* 1921; repr., México, DF: SEDENA, 1984.

Vallarta Vélez, Luz del Carmen. *Los payobispenses: Identidad, población y cultura en la frontera México-Belice.* Chetumal, Mexico: Universidad de Quintana Roo, 2001.

Van Creveld, Martin L. *Men, Women and War.* London: Cassell Military, 2001.

Vanderwood, Paul J. *Disorder and Progress: Bandits, Police, and Mexican Development.* Revised and enlarged ed. Wilmington, DE: SR Books, 1992.

——. *Juan Soldado: Rapist, Murderer, Martyr, Saint.* Durham, NC: Duke University Press, 2004.

——. *The Power of God against the Guns of Government: Religious Upheaval in Mexico at the Turn of the Nineteenth Century.* Stanford, CA: Stanford University Press, 1998.

Vaughan, Mary Kay. *Cultural Politics in Revolution: Teachers, Peasants, and Schools in Mexico, 1930–1940.* Tucson: University of Arizona Press, 1997.

Vaughan, Mary Kay, Gabriela Cano, and Jocylyn Olcott, eds. *Sex in Revolution: Gender, Politics, and Power in Modern Mexico.* Durham, NC: Duke University Press, 2006.

Villa-Flores, Javier. *Dangerous Speech: A Social History of Blasphemy in Colonial Mexico.* Tucson: University of Arizona Press, 2006.

Vinson, Ben. *Bearing Arms for His Majesty: The Free-Colored Militia in Colonial Mexico.* Stanford, CA: Stanford University Press, 2003.

Viqueira Albán, Juan Pedro. *Propriety and Permissiveness in Bourbon Mexico.* Translated by Sonya Lipsett-Rivera and Sergio Rivera Ayala. Wilmington, DE: Scholarly Resources, 1999.

von Humboldt, Alexander. *Ensayo político sobre el reino de la Nueva España.* México, DF: Editorial Porrúa, 1966.

Warren, Richard A. *Vagrants and Citizens: Politics and the Masses in Mexico City.* Wilmington, DE: Scholarly Resources, 2001.

Weber, Eugen Joseph. *Peasants into Frenchmen: The Modernization of Rural France, 1870–1914*. Stanford, CA: Stanford University Press, 1976.

Wells, Allen, and G. M. Joseph. *Summer of Discontent, Seasons of Upheaval: Elite Politics and Rural Insurgency in Yucatan, 1876–1915*. Stanford, CA: Stanford University Press, 1996.

White, Hayden. "Introduction: Historical Fiction, Fictional History, and Historical Reality." *Rethinking History* 9, no. 2/3 (June/September 2005): 147–57.

Wickham-Crowley, Timothy, and Hendrik Kraay, eds. *I Die With My Country: Perspectives on the Paraguayan War, 1864–1870*. Lincoln: University of Nebraska Press, 2004.

Winter, Jay. *Sites of Memory, Sites of Mourning: The Great War in European Cultural History*. Cambridge: Cambridge University Press, 1995.

Wunderli, Richard. *Peasant Fires: The Drummer of Niklashausen*. Bloomington: University of Indiana Press, 1992.

Xavier-Guerra, François. *Le Mexique: De l'ancien regime a la Revolution*. Vol. 1. Paris: L'Harmattan, 1985.

Xavier-Guerra, François, and Mónica Quijada. *Imaginar la nación*. Cuadernos de Historia Latinoamericana, no. 2. Münster: Lit, 1994.

Young, Elliot. *Catarino Garza's Revolution on the Texas-Mexico Border*. Durham, NC: Duke University Press, 2004.

Young, Warren L. *Minorities and the Military: A Cross-National Study in World Perspective*. Westport, CT: Greenwood Press, 1982.

Index

Page numbers in italic text indicate illustrations.